The
KENNEDY
DETAIL

The
KENNEDY DETAIL

JFK'S SECRET SERVICE AGENTS BREAK THEIR SILENCE

GERALD BLAINE
with LISA McCUBBIN

G

GALLERY BOOKS
New York   London   Toronto   Sydney

Gallery Books
A Division of Simon & Schuster, Inc.
1230 Avenue of the Americas
New York, NY 10020

First Gallery Books hardcover edition November 2010

GALLERY BOOKS and colophon are trademarks of Simon & Schuster, Inc.

For information about special discounts for bulk purchases,
please contact Simon & Schuster Special Sales at
1-866-506-1949 or business@simonandschuster.com.

The Simon & Schuster Speakers Bureau can bring authors to your live event. For more
information or to book an event contact the Simon & Schuster Speakers Bureau
at 1-866-248-3049 or visit our website at www.simonspeakers.com.

Designed by Jaime Putorti

Manufactured in the United States of America

10 9 8 7 6 5 4 3 2

Library of Congress Cataloging-in-Publication Data

Blaine, Gerald.
    The Kennedy detail : JFK's secret service agents break their silence / Gerald Blaine
with Lisa McCubbin. — 1st Gallery Books hardcover ed.
      p.   cm.
    Includes index.
    1. Kennedy, John F. (John Fitzgerald), 1917–1963—Assassination.   2. United States.
Secret Service—Officials and employees—Biography.   I. McCubbin, Lisa.   II. Title.
    E842.9.B545 2010
    973.922092—dc22   2010038035

ISBN 978-1-4391-9296-2
ISBN 978-1-4391-9304-4 (ebook)

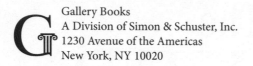

This book is dedicated to the agents who served on the Kennedy Secret Service White House Detail and their wives and families whose lives were dramatically, yet silently, impacted by the events described in this book, and to all Special Agents of the United States Secret Service dedicated to the mission of protecting our country's leaders.

CONTENTS

Prologue by Gerald Blaine   ix
Foreword by Clint Hill   xv
Introduction: When Time Stood Still   1

PART ONE: THE MEN

1   On the Detail   9
2   The President-Elect Detail   32
3   The Threats   57
4   The Advance   75
5   The Risks   93
6   The First Lady's Detail   103

PART TWO: THE JOB

7   The Summer of '63   119
8   The Reelection Campaign   135
9   Rising Tensions   152
10   Texas   157

PART THREE: THAT DAY

11   The Final Hours   181
12   Six Seconds in Dallas   197
13   Breakdown   220
14   The Unimaginable   243

15   Darkness Falls   251
16   No Time for Tears   264
17   Burial   283

PART FOUR: OUR LIVES

18   The End of Camelot   301
19   The Johnson Detail   315
20   The Pendulum Falls   326
21   The Verdict   338
22   Confronting Conspiracies   346
23   Clint Hill: Witness to History   365
24   Clint Hill: Don't Call Me Hero   379

Epilogue by Gerald Blaine   395
Acknowledgments   403
List of Abbreviations and Code Names   405
Index   409

PROLOGUE

By Gerald Blaine

While I am the author, this is not only my story. It is the story of all the United States Secret Service agents who served on the Kennedy White House Detail. I was not present when many of these events occurred, but have written the story using details provided by the agents who were involved. For that reason this book is written in the third-person narrative form.

The impact of John F. Kennedy's assassination caused memories to remain at the forefront of every Kennedy Detail agent's mind as they continued on with their careers and responsibilities. Some of the fifty-year-old memories have become blurry, while others were so painful they were buried long ago. Fortunately, most agents on the Kennedy Detail saved copies of their daily reports, expense accounts, investigations, and advance reports, many with scribbled notes regarding the Kennedy years. These helped jog recollections as this book was being written. In many cases agents went to the attic or basement to open boxes that had been sealed right after the assassination. Some of the deceased agents had written private memoirs of the Kennedy years that surviving family members provided. Where there were questions, archives and shift reports that are now public record were researched to fill in the blanks. Sometimes there were conflicts between archived reports and the agents' personal daily reports. These were researched and resolved.

It is important to note that while the Secret Service agents operated as a unit, the majority of their work was done individually. Most security advances were conducted by one individual unless the agent was fortunate enough to have an assistant. Posts were individually manned. Thus, interface with the president, first lady, and the children were typically one-on-one encounters. Many of the personal stories included in the book are taken from those private moments that were so special to the agents who served the Kennedy family.

What you are about to read is the true story of the events leading up to and following the assassination of President John F. Kennedy, from the perspective of the Secret Service agents who were there.

Since resigning from the Secret Service in 1964 I have made it a point to steer clear of political rallies. But when one of the candidates in the 2008 presidential election made a campaign stop near my home, I was curious. I wanted to see how the Secret Service had changed, how a potential United States president would be protected in today's society.

The speech was not scheduled to start until 7:00 P.M., but when my wife, Joyce, and I arrived at 4:00, the parking lot was nearly full. The baseball stadium could seat twenty-one thousand people and it looked like half that many were already standing in lines that wrapped around the open-air arena and down the length of the adjoining football field. The crowd appeared excited and full of anticipation, but peaceful. Still, I had learned more than forty-five years ago to be skeptical of crowds, with their unpredictable nature. I knew how quickly events could change the mood, and suddenly I wondered whether I really wanted to go through with this.

"Are you okay, Jerry?" Joyce asked. "It looks like the security process could take hours."

I wasn't sure whether Joyce was worried about my artificial hips holding up or that she could sense the anxiety that was slowly building inside me. She knew well my aversion to crowds.

"Well, we've come this far, let's just see how it goes," I said. "It looks like the forecasters might have gotten it right this time, though. Why don't you grab your umbrella?"

There were two lines—one for VIPs and one for the general public. Fortunately we had VIP passes that allowed us into the shorter of the two lines, but apparently we weren't all that special. Even as the line moved steadily and orderly, it was an hour and a half before we reached the security checkpoint.

There was an elaborate security setup much like what you'd go through at an airport. Sixteen officers from the Secret Service and the Transportation Security Administration supervised the parcel check station and the four magnetometers that would detect any concealed metal. As Joyce stepped up to the screening area, one of the officers said, "I'm sorry, ma'am, but we'll have to take your umbrella."

Apparently umbrellas are now considered weapons. Without saying a word, Joyce handed the man the umbrella and he threw it into a large bin with dozens of others. She put her purse on the table, where another Secret Service officer carefully checked its contents as she walked through the magnetometer.

When I stepped through, as usual the metal joints in my hips set off the alarm.

The officer asked me to step aside and proceeded to brush the detection wand along every inch of my body.

"I've got chrome where my hips used to be," I quipped. My eyes crinkled as I smiled at the officer.

"Yes, sir," the young man said—he couldn't have been more than twenty-five—as he proceeded to pat me down with his hands. Finally assured that I was truly just a white-haired, crippled old man with nothing to hide, the agent said, "Thank you, sir. Enjoy the event."

We found seats in the mid-level, to the left of the stage that was set up behind the pitcher's mound. Some kind of pop music—the kind you can't decipher the words to because the singer mumbles and the bass overpowers the voice—was blaring from speakers set up all over the stadium. It was an effort, I suppose, to put the crowd in an upbeat mood, but I would have preferred a mellow Frank Sinatra record. Three years of gunfire during the Korean War, and another year in Indochina, followed by five years of countless rounds of practice on the Secret Service pistol range with no ear protection had made me deaf in one ear, with 70 percent hearing loss in the other. Yet still that damn music was blaring into my head. I ripped the hearing aid out of my ear and stuffed it in my pocket in an effort to dim the confusing noise. I was ready to go home.

As people continued to fill the bleachers and temporary folding chairs, I remembered my reason for attending. I looked around to get a sense of the security. I easily spotted a couple dozen Secret Service agents scattered throughout the stadium—obvious by their demeanor and stance rather than any telltale uniform, but verifiable by the earphones coiling from their ears. I also spotted a few without earpieces who were mingled in the crowd. Two uniformed Secret Service countersniper teams were poised on either side of the upper deck of the stadium. I estimated there had to be close to sixty Secret Service personnel, supplemented by a few federal enforcement officers and what appeared to be the entire local police department.

The sheer magnitude of the security stunned me. During the 1960 presidential campaign in Philadelphia, I was one of six Secret Service agents who protected President Eisenhower and Vice President Nixon. Now, in 2008, more money must have been spent on protecting *candidates* than was in the entire annual Secret Service budget in 1963, when I was one of thirty-four men on President John F. Kennedy's detail.

The crowd erupted into cheers and hollers when the candidate, who had arrived by motorcade, walked onto the stage surrounded by a dozen stone-faced Secret Service agents who were scanning the crowd. When the candidate reached into the audience to shake hands with the zealous supporters in the front row, with the television cameras capturing every moment, I thought to myself, *This is the legacy of John F. Kennedy.*

That night I tossed and turned in bed, unable to fall asleep. My mind replayed the huge arena with the screaming crowd, the flashes going off in the stands, the politician basking in the glory, as the TV reporters captured it all. In the bleachers and on the stage I saw the young Secret Service agents. But in my mind, they weren't the ones I had seen earlier—they were Clint and Paul and Win. And then the memories came flooding back, like they always did, as if it were yesterday. I knew it was pointless to fight the phantoms, so I turned on my side, placed my arm around Joyce, and waited for sleep to rescue me from the past I couldn't forget.

• • •

My initial goal in writing the story of the Kennedy Detail was to set history straight, to leave a book for my grandchildren that they could read and know was the truth beyond any measure of a doubt. But what happened during the writing of the book, and took me completely by surprise, was the personal journey that occurred in the process.

Although I had remained close with several of the agents with whom I served on the White House Detail, and had been in contact with many others over the years, the subject of President Kennedy's assassination was rarely broached, rarely discussed. We would talk about how things had changed in presidential protection, how the training had evolved, and how technology had changed not only the protective measures, but also the types of threats. But never did we talk about our feelings, or how we had grieved. Those things were unmentionable—they were our deepest, darkest secrets. As I began to work on this project, I found myself feeling emotions that I had suppressed for decades. The feelings would be sparked by a letter or email or photograph received in the mail from one of the agents. But it was the phone conversations that really forced the memories to come flooding back. I would hear a familiar voice, a laugh, and it was as if we were back in 1963, and suddenly the uncontrollable feelings of guilt, anger, frustration, and overwhelming sadness would wash over me. At times I wasn't sure that I could continue. Not only was I reopening the wounds in my own heart: I knew I was inflicting pain on the others as well. But I had made a commitment to myself to write this book, and now it seemed that the agents were also counting on me. They'd been holding everything in as long as I had, and they wanted their stories told. I couldn't let them down.

One of the most difficult moments during the process was when I learned what had happened to Andy Berger. Andy had been such a happy-go-lucky guy, with a great sense of humor, but after the assassination his personality changed forever. The last time I spoke with Andy was in 1988. Andy had retired from the Secret Service and was living in North Carolina when he called to tell me that he'd received a call from an old friend—Frank Sinatra. Sinatra was going to be performing at the new Charlotte Coliseum and he had asked if Andy would handle security for him.

"I thought you'd get a kick out of that, Jer," he said.

I laughed and said, "Be sure and tell Frank I said hello."

When I began writing the book, I was saddened to hear from Andy's wife, Dolly, that Andy was in a full-time care facility, suffering from Alzheimer's disease. The previous years had been difficult on their close family as the disease slowly and steadily stole the memories of his lifetime.

As Andy's health deteriorated and his mind could no longer recall the names or recognize the faces of his own family members, the one thing that remained in his memory was a man named Kennedy and a tragic day in Dallas.

When Andy died in 2007 it was tough. I became more and more determined to finish what I had started, and I realized I was running out of time. None of us was getting any younger. So many of the Kennedy Detail agents were already gone. At some point I realized that even though I had reached out, I was still hiding—hiding behind the computer. I felt comfortable with computers and email—I had, after all, spent the better part of my life working for IBM—but so many of my counterparts were not "connected." For some reason, it was harder for me to pick up the phone than to send an email.

Finally, one day I gathered the courage to pick up the phone and start calling. It wasn't long before I noticed something remarkable was happening. What would begin as a phone call to one of the agents to verify or clarify some information for the book would turn into an hour-long conversation. A dialogue began—a dialogue that should have taken place forty-six years earlier.

It didn't happen the same with everybody—indeed a few of the agents are still unable to talk about the tragedy they witnessed nearly half a century ago. But for those I was able to reach, confronting the demons that have haunted us all for so long has been healing.

Clint Hill and I, especially, began talking more and more. We hadn't seen each other since the 1990 former agents' reunion in San Antonio. And never before had I dared broach the subject of the assassination with him, for I knew that Clint, more than any of us, had suffered tremendously. But as we acknowledged and shared our feelings of depression and grief, as we reminisced about good times and bad, gradually our former personalities began to shine through. The healing had finally begun.

FOREWORD

By Clint Hill

It has been nearly fifty years since President John F. Kennedy was assassinated before my eyes but the memories of that dreadful day in Dallas are as clear and painful as if it happened only yesterday. Nearly every day, it seems, something will be on the radio or on television or in the newspaper that will refer to JFK, and inevitably my mind rewinds to 1963. It has taken me decades to learn to cope with the guilt and sense of responsibility for the president's death, and I have made it a practice to keep my memories to myself. I don't talk to anybody about that day.

When Jerry Blaine called to tell me he wanted to write a book about the Kennedy Detail, I was not immediately enthusiastic about participating. Indeed, if it were anybody else, I would have simply hung up the phone. It is only because of my complete faith and trust that Jerry would tell our story with dignity and unwavering honesty that I agreed to be involved. I knew the ensuing discussions would inevitably reopen wounds that have never fully healed, but I also realized that, for the sake of history, it was important.

In 1961, when John F. Kennedy became president, there were about forty men on the White House Secret Service detail. Five of us were responsible for protecting Mrs. Kennedy and the children, Caroline and John, Jr. At that time, we had no earpieces for our large radios nor did we have computer databases of threat suspects. Our mission depended on teamwork and trust. We had no choice but to rely on each other, and there was never any doubt that we could rely on every single member of the team. We spent so much time together that we knew each other's idiosyncrasies, and could communicate with one glance or quick hand motion. Beyond the professional part of the job, there was a respect among all of us that was the closest thing to brotherhood I have ever experienced.

We came from a variety of backgrounds with various experiences. Some of the agents' service dated back to the Franklin D. Roosevelt administration. I became an agent during the Eisenhower administration. We were not aligned with any political party, group, individual, or ideology. The Secret Service credentials we carried read in part: "is commissioned to protect the President of the United States and others as authorized by statute" and "is commended to those with whom he may have official business as worthy of trust and confidence." We took those words very seriously. Our loyalty was to the Secret Service and to the words of our commission. We pledged to protect the occupant of the office of President of the United States, whoever that might be.

Both the president and Mrs. Kennedy were exceedingly kind to the agents on the detail. They knew all our names and inquired about our families. They really cared about us as people, and in turn, we grew to care about them.

Being on Mrs. Kennedy's detail was very different from being on the President's Detail. There was a lot more informality and flexibility, but often more responsibility because most of the time, it was just the two of us. She trusted me. She trusted that I would protect her, but she also knew without a doubt that the things she told me in confidence wouldn't go any further. She'd vent about problems with a staff member or something and use me as a sounding board—just like anybody does with a trusted friend. But Mrs. Kennedy also respected my job and the reason I was there. Despite our close relationship, she always referred to me as "Mr. Hill."

The motorcade in Dallas on November 22, 1963, began much the same as countless other motorcades I'd worked while assigned to presidential protection. President Kennedy loved to be among the people and all the agents knew full well how crowds reacted to him—people would literally jump out of the crowd, race toward the president's limousine, and throw themselves at the car. It was crazy. We had to assume that anybody charging toward the president, even if it was a young lady dressed in a skirt and high heels, could be a potential assassin. Motorcades were always high-adrenaline events for the agents.

The one big difference in Texas was that Mrs. Kennedy—I always called her "Mrs. Kennedy"—was traveling with her husband. She was intensely private and preferred to stay out of the limelight. In fact, that trip to Texas was her first political trip in the United States since her husband had been elected three years earlier. Sadly, it would be her last.

Nobody can say what they would or wouldn't do when a sudden cata-strophic event occurs. Your instincts and adrenaline take over completely. Much of our training as Secret Service agents was practicing just such an event so that our actions would be as automatic as possible. But as combat soldiers and critical response teams know, no matter how much training you've had, nothing prepares you for the emotions and nightmares that follow the horror of seeing a human being alive one instant, their head blown open the next.

As I said earlier, I don't like to talk about that day. I have shared with Jerry Blaine more than I've shared with anyone and what follows is an ac-curate portrayal of the events as I remember them and know to be true. I would be very pleased if the results of the Warren Commission and its in-vestigation would be accepted as the final word. However, I know that the researchers, writers, and filmmakers who continue to question those find-ings will never accept those as the truth. The information presented by the majority of these people is theory, not fact. They were not witnesses to the assassination; have little or no knowledge of protective procedures; did not know the dedicated agents on this assignment; and simply were not in our shoes that day in Dallas. It would be a great tragedy if history were al-lowed to repeat itself. We must learn from the real facts of what happened.

Thank you, Jerry, for telling the story, as related by the agents who ac-tually lived it. That dreadful day in Dallas is forever seared in each of our memories.

The
KENNEDY
DETAIL

When Time Stood Still

A man may die, nations may rise and fall, but an idea lives on.

—JOHN F. KENNEDY

NOVEMBER 22, 1963

It was one of those rare moments in history when time stood still and people the world over remember where they were and what they were doing.

That particular Friday afternoon, Secret Service agent Chuck Zboril was lying in bed in his Alexandria, Virginia, apartment desperately trying to fall asleep. He'd just come off the midnight shift at "Atoka," the Kennedys' quiet retreat in Middleburg, Virginia, and after two weeks working the day shift, his body wasn't cooperating with the new schedule. It was rare for a Kennedy Detail agent to get a full eight hours of sleep in any twenty-four-hour period anyway, but when you changed shifts every two weeks, it caused the sleep cycle to rebel. After three hours of tossing and turning, Chuck decided he might just as well get up.

It was 1:30 in the afternoon, and other than the sound of a couple of young kids riding their tricycles on the sidewalk, the Larchmont Village apartment complex was quiet. As he flipped his legs over the side of the bed, Chuck's stomach growled. His wife, Jean, was at work, but he was hoping she'd left him a sandwich or a plate of leftovers in the fridge. Dressed in his Jockey briefs and a T-shirt, he walked through the living

1

room, and out of habit, turned on the Motorola television as he headed into the kitchen. He had just opened the refrigerator door when he heard a distinctly familiar voice coming from the other room. Two words caught his attention: *Kennedy* and *shot.*

He slammed the refrigerator door and bolted into the living room. On the black-and-white screen, a somber-faced Walter Cronkite was reading from a news bulletin.

The first reports say that President Kennedy has been seriously wounded by this shooting.

Chuck sucked in a deep breath, reached for the telephone, and dialed the number to the White House. The line was busy. He hung up and tried Jean at work. Another busy signal.

"Come on, for Christ sake!" he yelled out loud as he slammed down the receiver in frustration. His mind was racing. He couldn't believe the report was true, but then again he couldn't recall ever getting a busy signal from the White House switchboard. *What the hell is going on?*

He strode back into the bedroom, put on a clean shirt and a pair of pants, and grabbed his gun and credentials off the nightstand. His mind raced with possible scenarios as he mentally went through the list of agents he knew had gone on the trip. Win Lawson had done the advance. Roy Kellerman and Emory Roberts were the Agents in Charge. Clint Hill would be there with Jackie. With five stops in Texas—San Antonio, Houston, Fort Worth, Dallas, and Austin—and motorcades in each city, the agents had been spread thin. And where was Blaine? Which shift was he working this week?

Jerry Blaine and his wife, Joyce, were two of Chuck and Jean's closest friends on the detail. Chuck had been honored when they'd asked him to be godfather to their son Scott, who was born the previous June. *Christ*, he thought. *Blaine's always with the president.* He had to find out if Joyce had heard the news.

The Blaines lived in the same apartment complex, in the next building over. Not trusting the phones, Chuck decided it would be best to tell Joyce in person anyway. He locked the door behind him and bounded down the stairs.

Joyce was accustomed to her husband being away—as a Secret Service agent on the Kennedy White House Detail, Jerry went where the president went, whether it was a weekend to Bing Crosby's house in Palm Springs, or an official visit to Berlin—and when he'd left for Fort Worth the day before, there was no reason to think this trip would be any different.

Joyce's closest friends were the wives of other White House Detail agents, many of whom lived nearby. With their husbands traveling all the time, and necessarily secretive about their jobs, the wives relied on each other for moral support, babysitting, and camaraderie. They had baby showers for each other and made casseroles when new babies were born, got together for coffee and playtime with their young children, and tried to find ways to get in a weekly game of bridge.

On this Friday afternoon, Joyce had just put five-month-old Scott and two-year-old Kelly down for their afternoon naps and intended to spend the next hour ironing, uninterrupted, while she watched *As the World Turns*. She'd just turned on the television when Ann Kivett showed up at the apartment unexpectedly, her toddler son perched on her hip.

"Come on in," Joyce said in a whisper. "I just put the kids down." Then, realizing the kitchen table was piled with laundry, she added, embarrassed, "Excuse the mess."

Ann and her husband, Jerry—a Secret Service agent on Vice President Lyndon Johnson's detail—lived in a neighboring apartment.

"Joyce," Ann said, "your phone must be off the hook. I've been trying to call you."

Joyce looked over at the telephone attached to the kitchen wall and sure enough, Kelly must have tugged on the cord and knocked the receiver off. Again.

"Oh, gosh," Joyce said as she walked over and replaced the receiver in its cradle. "What's up?"

"Are you interested in taking the kids over to Gifford's for ice cream later this afternoon? I'm going stir-crazy."

"You know I'm always in the mood for Gifford's," Joyce said with a laugh. With ten-cent cones for the kids, Gifford's Ice Cream & Candy was an affordable treat.

"I'll call Gwen Hill, too," Joyce added. "I'm sure she'd love to join us since Clint's gone as well."

Gwen Hill was another good friend whose husband, Clint, was Jackie Kennedy's Special Agent in Charge (SAIC). It was unusual for all three of their husbands to be on the same trip. In fact, now that Joyce thought about it, she couldn't remember a time the president, vice president, and Mrs. Kennedy had ever traveled together before.

Suddenly a signal interrupting the television program for a special news bulletin caused the women to turn their heads to the black-and-white TV on the other side of the room.

And that's when they heard the news.

"President Kennedy has been shot?" Joyce asked in disbelief. The bulletin lasted just thirty seconds and then the station returned to *As the World Turns*. Ann and Joyce stood in front of the television, waiting anxiously for more details.

Suddenly there was a loud banging at the door. Chuck had sprinted up the stairs and was breathing heavily.

"Joyce," he said as she opened the door. "Did you hear what's happened?"

"We just saw a news bulletin that shots were fired at the president's motorcade. Chuck, what's going on?"

"I don't know. I tried calling the White House and the lines were tied up."

The CBS station continued broadcasting the soap opera as if the break in programming hadn't occurred.

Then, another newsflash. Walter Cronkite appeared at a working desk and read from a piece of paper in his hands.

This is Walter Cronkite in our newsroom. There has been an attempt, as perhaps you know now, on the life of President Kennedy. He was wounded in an automobile driving from Dallas Airport into downtown Dallas along with Governor Connally of Texas. They've been taken to Parkland Hospital there, where their condition as yet is unknown.

Chuck and the two women stood in the small living room of the two-bedroom apartment, too stunned to speak. They each envisioned, in their own minds, the chaos that must be occurring in Dallas at that moment. The wives knew that during presidential motorcades their husbands would be riding on the back of the president or vice president's limousine, or on the running boards of the follow-up car to thwart and prevent such an attack. Something had gone terribly wrong.

"I have to call Gwen," Joyce said. She dialed Gwen Hill's number, and Gwen answered on the second ring.

"Gwen, it's Joyce. Do you have the television on?"

"Yes," said Gwen, breathless. "I was sitting here on the floor, under the hair dryer, when Walter Cronkite came on. The next thing I know my neighbor is at the door telling me she's so sorry, and asking what can she do? She heard Clint's been shot! But I can't get through to the White House."

"Oh my God, Gwen. Chuck Zboril is here. And Ann Kivett. Even Chuck can't get through to the White House. We'll let you know if we hear anything else and please, Gwen, don't worry. It seems like nobody knows what's going on."

"I know. I know," Gwen said, as she took a deep breath. If there was anything she'd learned from Clint, it was to remain calm in a crisis. "I'm going to try to keep the line free in case somebody calls from the White House."

"Okay, Gwen. It's going to be all right. Don't worry."

More than half an hour had passed since they'd heard the first bulletin, but it seemed like time stood still, like the world was holding its breath.

It was strange to see the image of the evening news anchor Walter Cronkite sitting at the news desk, in his shirtsleeves, without a suit coat, in the middle of the day. The normally stoic newsman appeared to be delivering the intermittent news reports, unrehearsed, as soon as they came over the wire.

After that shooting incident, of course, pandemonium broke out. Secret Service men, well trained in their job, immediately began fanning out into the crowd, looking for the assassin. They have spread a giant dragnet around the city of Dallas and they say they are searching for a white man, about thirty, of slender build, weighing about one hundred sixty-five pounds. They say he apparently shot the president with a thirty-thirty rifle.

Chuck Zboril knew immediately that what Walter Cronkite had just said about the agents couldn't have actually happened as it was reported. None of the men on the Kennedy Detail, not one, would have fanned out into the crowd. They wouldn't have gone looking for the assassin. The single mission of the White House Secret Service agents was to act as a human shield around their assigned person—whether it was the president, the vice president, Jacqueline Kennedy, or the Kennedy children. Zboril knew that every single one of the agents would have instinctively rushed toward President Kennedy, protecting him with their bodies the instant there was any sign of danger. The last thing they would have done was fan out into the crowd.

Chuck stood silent as the wives voiced their disbelief. Everything they were hearing was beyond comprehension.

Then, another announcement—reports that indeed a Secret Service agent had been shot.

Ann and Joyce both stiffened, and Chuck could see that they were assuming the worst—maybe Clint Hill had been shot.

"Listen," Chuck said as he put a hand on each of the women's shoulders. "We need to wait for the facts to come in. Don't rush to conclusions." His voice was even and calm—the trademark of every Secret Service agent. "I'm going to the White House to find out what's going on. I'll call as soon as I can."

He headed toward the door, and as he turned the handle, he glanced back into the living room, toward the television.

Walter Cronkite reached across his desk, grabbed a piece of paper, and put on his black reading glasses. His hand went to his eyes, wiping away a tear as he announced:

From Dallas, Texas, the flash apparently official: President Kennedy died at one P.M. Central Standard Time, two o'clock Eastern Standard Time, some thirty-eight minutes ago.

PART ONE

★

THE MEN

1

On the Detail

The pay is good and I can walk to work.
—JOHN F. KENNEDY

NOVEMBER 8, 1963
TWO WEEKS EARLIER

At the post outside the door to the Oval Office, Special Agent Jerry Blaine stood with his shoulders back, his ears tuned to pick up the slightest disruption, while subconsciously his elbow pressed loosely on the handle of the snubnose .38-caliber revolver strapped to his hip. The gun was hidden beneath the jacket of his navy blue suit so that, to the casual observer, Blaine looked like he could be a member of the president's staff. But if you looked closely you could see the vague outline of the revolver, where the hammer and gun handle had rubbed the fabric thin. Behind the closed door he could hear President Kennedy's muffled voice, his words rolling out rapid fire in the clipped Boston accent. Blaine surmised the conversation had something to do with the civil rights bill President Kennedy so desperately needed to pass, but he wasn't listening for specific information. As a United States Secret Service agent on the White House Detail, Jerry Blaine's sole mission was to protect the president, not worry about public policy. He was trained to be paranoid, to observe and anticipate danger around every corner, ready to react in a millisecond if the president pushed the emergency buzzer located under the big mahogany desk, or if somebody came running toward the door. Every agent who'd ever served on the White House Detail would agree that standing outside the Oval Office had to be one of the most challenging parts of the job.

It had nothing to do with the danger—it was all because of the floor. Everybody hated the damn tiles.

The floor of the long, narrow hallway outside the main door of the Oval Office was tiled in a black-and-white checkerboard pattern that glared like a puzzle before your eyes. The urge to count the tiles was overwhelming. For a White House Detail Secret Service agent, ironically, the hours spent on duty at the White House were often the most tedious—simply because it was boring. An attacker would have to break through multiple levels of security to get to the point where Jerry Blaine was standing. The chances of an assassination were negligible. In order to keep your mind alert between visitors, your only choice was to count the tiles. The problem was that every time you began counting the squares somebody would come walking down the hall, interrupting the count. As the hall emptied, you'd have to start all over again. This would go on for thirty minutes, until it came time for rotation, leaving the next agent with the same frustrating puzzle.

Seventy-seven, seventy-eight, seventy-nine, eighty. Blaine was well into his seventh count when Agent Chuck Zboril from the 4:00 to midnight shift came around the corner.

"Hey, Jer, today's your lucky day," Zboril said. "The chopper's on its way. I'll take over the count until the Boss leaves," he added with a grin.

It was nearly three o'clock in the afternoon and as part of the day shift, Jerry Blaine had arrived at the White House at 7:15 A.M., rotating the four White House security posts with a half-hour break at the end of each rotation. He'd already worked a full day, but the Boss—President Kennedy— was headed to New York City for the night, and the day shift had to get there before him to set up security.

It was an official trip with a speech at the Hilton Hotel, but an "off-the-record" visit after the speech, which meant no press, no motorcades, and minimal police presence. Not even the Secret Service agents were briefed ahead of time as to the president's entire agenda. To the Kennedy Detail agents, "off-the-record" meant expect the unexpected.

"Thanks, sport," Jerry said with a smile.

"Not a problem. I'm here to serve," Zboril quipped.

Twenty-seven-year-old Chuck Zboril was one of the newer agents on the Kennedy Detail, having transferred from the New York Field Office back in April. Standing just a little over six feet tall, Zboril carried himself in a ramrod-straight Marine Corps posture and wore his hair in a "butch" crew cut, so that he appeared taller. A native of Detroit, Chuck spoke with a midwestern accent and always had a pleasant smile on his face. He'd grown up working in the family sausage business, and with a desire to see something more of the world, had enlisted in the Marine Corps immediately upon graduation from high school. He returned to Michigan two years later, attended Michigan State University, and graduated in 1962 with a degree in law enforcement, hoping to join the Secret Service. Within months he was hired by the Secret Service New York Field Office.

When Chuck and his wife, Jean, moved into the Larchmont Village apartment complex where the Blaines and a few other agents lived, the two couples had hit it off immediately. Jean adored the Blaines' two young children and Chuck looked up to Jerry as his mentor on the detail.

"You'd better haul ass, Blaine," Zboril said as he took his place next to the door. "Sounds like your ride is here."

The distinctive whir of the military helicopter hovering over the South Lawn of the White House was one of those sounds that always seemed to stir emotions deep inside Agent Blaine. Eleven years earlier, when he was a young enlisted man in the U.S. Navy involved in special operations off the coast of North Korea, the sound of a military chopper coming closer signaled either an attempt to rescue a downed pilot or a sudden *it's time to get the hell out of here* evacuation. It was a sound that used to evoke tension and caused a sudden adrenaline rush. Now, as Jerry Blaine strode rapidly toward the Secret Service Office, barely glancing at the paintings of previous presidents that lined the walls, the sound of the chopper made him smile. He was, at thirty-one years old, one of just thirty-four men responsible for protecting the President of the United States of America— and the helicopter was his taxi ride. There could be no better job.

The Secret Service shift office was a ten-by-twelve-foot windowless room located next to the north entrance to the West Wing lobby. Furnished sparsely with a single desk and chair, a bookshelf, a metal filing cabinet, and a couch that could seat three—or four if absolutely necessary—the office was basically a place for the agents to store their belongings, type their reports, and hide out when off post. A large gun case stacked with riot guns and Thompson submachine guns stood along one wall next to a coatrack. The lone wall decoration was a plaque that said *Fame is Fleeting*. Nobody seemed to know who had hung the plaque—it had been there for as long as anybody could remember.

As Jerry approached the office he heard familiar voices. The rest of the agents on the day shift had already been relieved from their various posts around the White House and were gathering their things: Dave Grant, Ken Giannoules, Joe Paolella, and Walt Coughlin would be establishing security at the Hilton Hotel with Jerry. Their shift leader, Assistant to the Special Agent in Charge (ATSAIC) Art Godfrey, had flown to New York several days earlier to arrange all the logistics for the president's one-night visit—the "advance." Additionally, five agents from the midnight to 8:00 A.M. shift had come on duty early to make the trip to New York City. The tiny office was packed.

Stewart Stout, the leader of the midnight shift, was standing near the door as Blaine walked in.

The soft-spoken shift leader wore his hair in a short crew cut, and with his square face and stocky frame, he bore a strong resemblance to FBI director J. Edgar Hoover. Stout was so often mistaken for Hoover that he had learned to just shake his head when people inquired and give the pat reply: "No, I work for another organization."

"Hi, Stew," Blaine said. "You were called in a little early, weren't you?"

Stew smiled. "Thought you guys needed an escort."

Working double shifts had become so common since Kennedy became president that it was now almost routine. The three eight-hour shift rotation operated normally when the president was in the White House, but when he was traveling or attending an off-site function, one shift had to be on site before the president arrived at his destination, while another shift moved with him, providing a protective shield around the president at all times. With just eight agents on each shift, plus supervisors and drivers, there simply weren't enough bodies to allow for a normal eight-hour workday. Scheduled shift changes and timely rotations were impossible. It had become common for the Secret Service agents on the White House Detail to log an average of eighty hours of overtime each month. With the minimal extra pay received for overtime, the $4,980 annual salary the agents got paid to protect the leader of the free world worked out to about $1.80 per hour. Nobody was in this job for the money.

Blaine pulled his suit bag and black trench coat off the rack and grabbed his flight bag—a small airline carry-on compliments of Pan American Airways. Inside the flight bag were several blank daily report forms, the latest *Newsweek* magazine, travel vouchers, shoe polish and brush, his toiletry kit, extra ammunition, and a few bags of peanuts. He'd learned early on to always keep the bag packed and ready to go, and always replenished with snacks. Protecting the president on a trip—especially an "off-the-record" trip like this one—was a completely different ball game than standing post at the highly secured White House. There'd been plenty of times when a handful of peanuts had been Blaine's only nourishment for an entire day. The peanuts were critical.

"Okay, let's move out," Stout said.

Even if you didn't know that the ten men filing out of the tiny office were all armed and master marksmen, there was something about their demeanor that made them a formidable-looking group. They averaged six feet in height, were all clean-shaven, and all of them were dressed in the unofficial Secret Service uniform—a tan or black trench coat, a navy or charcoal gray suit, a crisp white dress shirt with a narrow, dark-hued tie, and wingtip shoes that were polished to a high sheen. They didn't get a clothing allowance, despite the fact that suits and shoes seemed to last only about three or four months, so they all bought their clothing at Louie's or Schwartz's, where they got generous discounts. Overzealous crowds combined with the rubbing of their sidearm wreaked havoc with their clothes. You could ruin a suit and a pair of shoes in one motorcade, easy.

Along with their hidden revolvers and a pair of handcuffs, every agent carried three necessary protective tools: a pair of Polaroid reflective lens sunglasses, their commission book, and a stack of flash cards. The sunglasses weren't used for fashion or intrigue, or even necessarily for sun protection. They were meant to hide the agents' eyes. You could have your head turned in one direction, yet be staring at a person who appeared suspicious without their knowledge. And that's where the flash cards came in. There were dozens of known threat suspects kept on file at the Secret Service's Protective Research Section (PRS), and every agent had index cards on each of the most serious suspects. The photo of the suspect was pasted on one side of the card, with a typed description and their last known whereabouts on the back. The agents knew these suspects like they knew their own children; they could scan a crowd of thousands and pick out their faces in a matter of seconds. They'd seize the suspect first, snap on a pair of handcuffs, and ask questions later. And finally, if their authority was ever questioned, one flash of the commission book with the agent's photo and the embossed gold Secret Service star on the front told anybody all they needed to know.

Beyond the similarities in the agents' appearances, if you really studied their faces you'd realize that deep within each of these men was a tenacity and steadfast allegiance that was unbreakable. They'd had to prove themselves to be members of this elite organization, and while they appeared cool on the outside, God have mercy on anyone who came between them and the President of the United States.

To get to the South Lawn, where the helicopter was waiting, the agents had to walk through the first-floor lobby. Not surprisingly, the lobby was filled with White House press corps members and correspondents who were curious about the president's departure. United Press International (UPI) reporters Helen Thomas and Merriman "Smitty" Smith were sitting on the massive leather couch chatting with NBC's Sander Vanocur and CBS's Bob Pierpoint, while Marianne Means from Hearst sat nearby, scribbling on her notepad. Several other reporters and photographers were scattered in small groups. When the Secret Service agents entered the lobby with their luggage in tow, the reporters' conversations came to an abrupt halt.

"Good afternoon, gentlemen," Merriman Smith called out in his gravelly voice. Fifty-year-old Merriman was the senior White House press correspondent. He'd been around for years.

"Afternoon, Smitty," the agents replied in unison, each giving a perfunctory nod to Smith.

The Kennedy Detail agents had a good rapport with the reporters and photographers; they often traveled together on the press plane, and on the longer flights even played lively games of poker. The reporters had been given the text of the short speech the president would be making in front of a Protestant group later that evening in New York City, but with no press pool today Blaine could tell that the savvy members of the press were curious as hell as to what was on the agenda after that.

"Where you headed after the speech?" Smitty asked.

The agents ignored the question, keeping their gazes focused straight ahead.

The reporters knew it was unlikely any of the agents would offer up any information, yet still a few of them responded to the obvious brush-off with audible groans and sour looks.

The Secret Service agents picked up their pace as they continued through the doors, down the hallway past White House Press Secretary Pierre Salinger's office and the Cabinet Room. Blaine chuckled to himself as he thought about the look of disappointment on Merriman's face, on all their faces. What they wouldn't give to know what the agents knew. Any one of the Kennedy Detail agents could regale them with dozens of stories that would knock their socks off, shoot them straight to the top of their profession. But being tight-lipped was a critical part of being a Secret Service agent, and Jerry Blaine, like every other White House Detail agent, had been selected for this elite position because he'd proven to be worthy of trust and confidence.

Worthy of Trust and Confidence. It was the motto of the United States Secret Service, emblazoned on their commission books—and drilled into their psyches. This one discipline was the single most critical component to their mission. It was engraved into their thought processes in the same way that their physical response to an attacker had been drilled in so deeply it had become instinctive. The first day Jerry reported for duty at the White House three and a half years earlier, Jim Rowley, the Special Agent in Charge of the Eisenhower Detail, had made it abundantly clear that being "worthy of trust and confidence" was a vital requirement of the job. The mantra was repeated by every supervisor down the line. Now, as one of the senior agents, Jerry passed the credo on to the new guys.

Protocol also accompanied the responsibility of being a White House Detail agent. When addressing the president it was always "Mr. President." If you were talking to another agent you would refer to the president as the "Boss," and in mixed company you'd call him "the president" or "President Kennedy." At home or with close friends it was okay to call him "JFK," a term the rest of the nation had picked up as an abbreviation, similar to how Eisenhower was known as "Ike." Finally, when you were on an open radio frequency, you used code names for everything: President Kennedy was "Lancer."

The helicopter was waiting just beyond the Rose Garden, its rotors whirring, the pilot poised to take off the minute the passengers were all aboard. The chopper would drop off the agents at Andrews Air Force Base, where they'd take a military plane to New York's Idlewild Airport, then return to the White House to pick up the president immediately thereafter. When the president was aboard the chopper, it became known as "Marine One." The body of the helicopter was the traditional military olive green, while the upper half was painted white, which signaled it as the presidential helicopter. As soon as the president boarded the specially designed Boeing 707 that would take him to New York along with the agents on the evening shift, the plane would become "Air Force One."

Beyond the noise of the helicopter's engine, Blaine heard someone calling his name.

"Blaine! Wait up!"

Jerry turned to see Jerry Behn, the Special Agent in Charge of the White House Detail, pacing rapidly toward him from the East Wing. It wasn't uncommon for outsiders to be confused by the similar and rhyming names of the two Kennedy Detail agents: Jerry Blaine and Jerry Behn. Indeed, SAIC Behn often joked about getting Agent Blaine's mail by mistake.

As the SAIC—the most senior Secret Service agent on the detail— Jerry Behn was at the president's side whenever Kennedy was away from the White House. From a distance, SAIC Behn could very well have been President Kennedy himself. The two men were exactly the same height— although Behn, who had played football at Michigan State, was a bit heavier—and both had thick, chestnut-colored hair that was always impeccably groomed. When they walked side by side they had the same gait such that, from behind, it was often difficult to tell who was who. Behn always traveled with the president on Marine One and Air Force One, and would be within an arm's length of Kennedy whenever he appeared in public. In motorcades, SAIC Behn sat in the front right passenger seat of the presidential limousine, directly in front of President Kennedy.

It was clear that JFK appreciated both Behn's professionalism and his laid-back style, not to mention his sense of humor. President Kennedy preferred to be around people who could make him laugh, and Jerry Behn fit the bill perfectly. Behn was professionally attentive to the president without being obvious about the unspoken reason for his presence, and in turn, President Kennedy trusted him completely. Kennedy's staff made sure that the SAIC was informed of all travel plans or changes of schedules well in advance. On certain occasions, such as a visit to the dentist or eye doctor, Jerry Behn traveled alone with the president in order to avoid unnecessary commotion. He knew how much Kennedy missed little slices of normal life, and he tried his best to accommodate him whenever possible.

Despite his closeness and constant proximity to the President of the United States, Jerry Behn never portrayed an ounce of arrogance or pretense, and was a constant picture of composure. Nothing rattled him. To the agents on the detail his standard greeting was an easygoing "What's up?" or "What's new?" Yet when it came to communicating orders or anything to do with protective business, Behn was precise and unmistakably clear.

As the SAIC approached, Agent Blaine dropped behind the other agents.

"Hey, Jer, I just wanted to give you heads-up for the schedule for the next two weeks," SAIC Behn said. "We're going to be busy."

Blaine pondered the words. When weren't they busy? The Secret Service was so overworked and understaffed, *busy* was a relative term.

In his typically relaxed yet serious tone, Behn said, "It seems that the campaign of '64 is upon us. The Boss is going to Florida next week. He'll be in Cape Canaveral on the sixteenth, then make appearances in Tampa and Miami on the eighteenth."

Appearances in Florida? In just over a week? Even though President Kennedy spent most winter weekends at the "southern White House" in Palm Beach, he hadn't made a public appearance in the state of Florida since he and Mrs. Kennedy greeted the returning "Bay of Pigs" prisoners the previous December. The Secret Service had identified numerous threats from Cuban sources, mostly in Florida, as a result of Kennedy's botched invasion of Cuba almost three years earlier. Surely Jerry Behn had briefed the president on the risks of a public appearance in Florida.

Blaine kept his thoughts to himself as Behn continued with the assignment. "You'll be in charge of the advance for Tampa—you'll need to leave on Monday, as soon as you get back from New York. In Tampa there's going to be a private reception and briefing at MacDill Air Force Base, a public speech at an open-air stadium, a speech at the National Guard armory, another speech to a union leadership group, and a fairly long motorcade through the city of Tampa. I'm guessing it's going to be close to thirty miles. Yeager will be assisting you."

"Okay. Got it," Blaine answered. Four stops were not unusual for the president's visit to a particular city, but *a thirty-mile motorcade*? Of the dozens of motorcades Blaine had advanced all over the world, he couldn't remember ever having a route that long. And he'd have just a week to co-ordinate the entire security planning. Thank God Behn was giving him Frank Yeager to help. Even with the two of them, though, time was going to be at a premium.

"That's not all," Behn added. "I'm gonna need you to leapfrog immediately from Tampa to Dallas because they're planning a sweep through Texas three days later, which will include motorcades in San Antonio, Houston, Fort Worth, Dallas, and Austin, followed by a stay at Johnson's ranch."

"The vice president is going on the trips, too?" Blaine asked.

"Just for the Texas portion."

Blaine nodded. Now he understood why the SAIC had wanted to give him some advance notice; this was indeed an ambitious schedule. JFK's push for a civil rights bill had shredded his popularity with Southern Democrats and clearly he would have to campaign heavily in the South to get reelected. But combine the civil rights tensions with the Cuba concerns, and Florida and Texas had to be two of the most volatile states right now. Indeed, just two weeks earlier, United Nations ambassador Adlai Stevenson had been in Dallas making a speech about UN Day when he was heckled, spat on, and assaulted with a placard by an angry right-wing mob as he exited the Dallas Memorial Auditorium. The South was not Kennedy country.

Compounding the underlying political tensions, the fact that the president and vice president would be traveling together meant additional manpower and security measures would be needed. It was rarely prudent for both the president and the vice president to attend public events at the same time, but now Kennedy's political advisors had planned not just one appearance, but a series of back-to-back events in Texas, including five motorcades.

Motorcades were the Secret Service's nemeses. There were an endless number of variables that had to be considered when planning a motorcade route, and you could never predict how a crowd would react. Blaine had seen firsthand, a number of times, how quickly a motorcade could go terribly wrong. He figured that's why Behn had assigned him the Tampa advance, where the motorcade would be exceptionally long. With the inherent risks in Florida, there could be nothing left to chance. Every detail would have to be planned to the minute.

The president's chief political advisors—and longtime friends—Ken O'Donnell and Dave Powers typically planned these sorts of trips. Their objectives were to raise money and get Kennedy in front of as many voters as possible. Security wasn't their problem. That challenge was left to the Secret Service. The SAIC could advise against certain scenarios or suggest a less risky alternative, but in the end the Secret Service was not authorized to override a presidential decision. It was a constant improvisation, a tug-of-war between politics and protection.

"O'Donnell is still working out the details," Behn continued. "Floyd Boring will brief you before you go. He'll cover the Tampa stop and Kellerman will cover Texas . . . I won't be making the trips."

Blaine couldn't hide the surprised look on his face. *Behn wasn't going on the trips?* Behn always traveled with the president. In the three years since Kennedy had been elected, Jerry Behn had not taken one day of vacation. And rarely did he get a full day off in any given week. Either his wife, Jean, or President Kennedy must have realized he needed a break before the 1964 campaign began in earnest. Of course, Floyd Boring and Roy Kellerman, the two Assistant Special Agents in Charge (ASAICs), were both well qualified to step in for Behn—there was no doubt about that. But the fact that Jerry Behn was taking some time off made Blaine realize that next year was going to be grueling. More importantly, Blaine wondered where the hell they were going to come up with enough agents to handle all these stops in Florida and Texas.

In the past two months alone, eleven of the most experienced agents on the Kennedy Detail had been replaced. It had been a purely personal choice by the agents—they'd requested, and been granted, transfers to field offices. With weekends and holidays in either Palm Beach or Hyannis Port, combined with travels to Europe and Latin America and the occasional visit to Palm Springs, President Kennedy traveled far more than any other president ever had. With the 1964 campaign just around the corner, nearly a third of the agents had decided they just couldn't do it any longer. Too many missed birthdays and anniversaries, too many holidays away from home. They'd had to choose between their families and the detail.

SAIC Behn was looking straight into Blaine's eyes. Blaine sensed the SAIC had the same concerns about adequate staffing. And almost as if he were reading Blaine's mind, Behn added, "As of today, it appears that Mrs. Kennedy will also be going on the Texas trip. So at least we'll have Clint Hill, and probably Paul Landis, helping us out."

Before Agent Blaine could respond, SAIC Behn looked toward the chopper and said, "You better go. Kellerman is taking over as SAIC for tonight in New York, so I probably won't see you until you get back from Texas."

"Okay. See you in a couple of weeks." Blaine gave a quick nod as he sorted out the implications of what the next two weeks would bring. He was about to turn around and head toward the helicopter when a small movement on the upper portico of the White House caught his eye. He squinted and realized it was John-John, President Kennedy's nearly three-year-old son, waving at the helicopter. His nanny, Maud Shaw, stood closely behind.

The sight of the tousle-haired boy standing at the edge of the balcony made Blaine smile. What a pistol. The agents who were assigned to John, Jr., and six-year-old Caroline on the "Kiddie Detail" often talked about John-John's fascination with the choppers and how he loved to watch them land and take off from his backyard. He'd learned that when a chopper arrived on the lawn, it meant one of two things: either Daddy was leaving, or Daddy was coming home.

Jerry Blaine clutched his flight bag tightly and jogged toward the chopper. As he approached, the pilot increased the speed of the rotors in preparation for takeoff. Blaine climbed aboard the helicopter and even before

he was seated, the master sergeant crew chief slammed the door behind him.

The sun was low on the horizon as the helicopter lifted above the
White House grounds and circled around the Washington Monument toward the Capitol, with the Lincoln and Jefferson memorials shining white
in the distance. Blaine never tired of the magnificent sight of the nation's
capital from the air. But as the helicopter sped toward Andrews Air Force
Base, he barely even noticed how the trees along the river had turned to
gold and bronze. The loud chop of the helicopter's rotors made conversation impossible, leaving Blaine to replay in his mind the conversation he'd
just had with SAIC Behn.

Besides the revelation that Behn wasn't coming on tonight's trip to New
York, nor going to Florida or Texas, Jerry Blaine was surprised to learn
that the first lady would be joining the president on a campaign trip. Jerry
Behn might just as well have announced that Fidel Castro was coming. If
Blaine hadn't heard all this information directly from the SAIC himself, he
would never have believed it. Apparently that's why Behn had made it a
point to tell him face-to-face.

Just three months earlier, in August, Jackie Kennedy had given birth
to the couple's third child—another son, whom they named Patrick Bouvier Kennedy. Tragically, the baby was born prematurely with a serious
lung ailment, and he died two days later. The unexpected loss was devastating for the president and Mrs. Kennedy, and heartbreaking for the
agents who were so close to the family. But along with the fact that Jackie
was still mourning the loss of her child, it was no secret that she despised
campaigning. Her decision to go on a purely political trip was completely
unexpected.

From the advance standpoint, Mrs. Kennedy's presence compounded
the security issues immensely. While President Kennedy had his detrac-
tors, everybody seemed to love the first lady. Anytime she appeared with
the president the crowds would double in size. People just wanted to get a
look at her. It was like traveling with a movie star.

The good news, as Behn had pointed out, was that because Jackie was
coming on the trip, her agents would be there as well. Clint Hill was the
Special Agent in Charge of the first lady's detail and happened to be one

of Blaine's closest friends. Both Hill and Paul Landis had been on the President's Detail prior to being assigned to the first lady, so they were both
experienced agents. Blaine couldn't remember working a motorcade with
Paul Landis in the past, but he and Clint had manned the Secret Service
follow-up car together all over the world. More importantly, because Hill
and Landis were by Mrs. Kennedy's side wherever she went, they knew exactly how her presence impacted crowds. Hill and Landis would be essential during the motorcades.

The five-minute flight to Andrews Air Force Base went by quickly and
as the helicopter landed, Blaine realized he didn't have time right now to
worry about the upcoming weeks—he had to focus on the current assignment. Protecting the president in New York City was never an easy
task.

The agents boarded the waiting Air Force twin-engine prop plane at Andrews and arrived at New York's Idlewild Airport right on schedule, just
a few minutes before six o'clock. Shift leader Art Godfrey, the advance
agent for the trip, was already waiting at the bottom of the ramp when
they arrived.

Godfrey, with his muscular build and steel gray hair that stood erect
in a precision crew cut, was a man of few words. The agents assumed his
no-nonsense attitude came from the years he served in World War II,
but that was something he rarely spoke about. Nobody on the detail even
knew that he'd been awarded both the Silver and Bronze Stars—two of
the military's highest honors—for heroic actions during the Anzio beach
landing in Italy. Godfrey wasn't the type of man to brag or embellish. He
simply did his job, constantly going above and beyond what was expected.
He was a true role model for the younger and senior agents alike.

As soon as the midnight shift leader, Stewart Stout, stepped onto the
tarmac, Godfrey tossed him a set of rental car keys.

"Your shift has the black station wagon," he said as he turned his head
toward the row of three cars parked about twenty yards away. When time
was tight, as it typically was on advance assignments, Godfrey didn't
bother with formalities. His tone and demeanor were clear indications
that the agents needed to react with a sense of urgency.

"Brooks Keller is the field agent who helped with the advance. He's waiting for you at the Carlyle Hotel with keys to a couple of rooms for your shift. The president's speech should be over at about ten-thirty and the current plan is for him to return to the Carlyle. But you know as well as I do, things could change."

The agents were all well aware of President Kennedy's spontaneity, especially on off-the-record visits. The agents on the off-shift had to be prepared to jump back into action at any given moment in case the president had a last-minute change to his plans or merely decided to make an unscheduled visit somewhere. The on-duty agents would be with him at all times, which left the off-duty agents responsible for establishing security at the intended destination. They could have anywhere from an hour's notice to just ten minutes.

As Stout and the five midnight shift agents strode toward their car, Godfrey turned to the agents on his shift—Grant, Blaine, Giannoules, Coughlin, and Paolella.

Godfrey tossed a set of keys to Dave Grant and said, "You've got the white wagon."

He looked at his watch and added, "The Boss is scheduled to arrive here in about forty minutes, so you guys get set up at the Hilton. Here are your assignments. Harry Gibbs from the New York office is at the Hilton to brief you."

He handed Dave Grant a carbon copy of the advance report, which clearly outlined where each agent was to be posted while President Kennedy was giving his speech.

The five agents threw their bags into the back of the station wagon and climbed into the car. As the senior agent on the shift, Dave Grant drove while Blaine sat next to him on the front bench seat. Paolella, Coughlin, and Giannoules squeezed into the back.

Grant turned the key in the ignition, and as the engine started, Jerry Blaine sat up straight in his seat and, in his best impression of President Kennedy, said, "To the Hilton, Agent Grant. I presume you know the way?"

Grant played along and said, "Yes, sir, Mr. President. And just to make it an off-the-record covert trip so nobody will notice us, I think I'll do it with my eyes closed."

Grant put the car in gear and put one hand over his eyes, as the agents in the back chuckled.

It was rush hour and the traffic was slow moving, but at least it was moving. Dave Grant had been to New York so many times in the past three years with President Kennedy that he knew these streets as well as he knew those in his hometown of Chicago. He expertly navigated the fifteen-mile route from Idlewild in Jamaica Bay, and thirty minutes later they were pulling into the Hilton garage.

Meanwhile, back at Idlewild Airport, ATSAIC Art Godfrey had been standing on the tarmac for about two hours. Now that the sun had gone down, the temperature had dropped considerably, sending a chill through his body. He hadn't thought to bring gloves with him, forgetting that New York was just that much colder than Washington this time of year, and he rubbed his hands together to keep warm.

Suddenly a loud screech sounded from the walkie-talkie in the pocket of his trench coat. He pulled it out and held it up to his ear. The handheld radio was tied directly to the Air Force One frequency. Roy Kellerman's voice came through the receiver.

"Dangle, do you read me?"

Code names were always used over the radio. The senior Secret Service agents all had code names that began with the letter D, and Godfrey's was Dangle.

"This is Dangle. Over."

"Five minutes your location. Over."

"All set. Over and out."

A minute later he heard a car door slam and looked over to see Officer Sandy Garelick getting out of the unmarked police car that would escort President Kennedy's car to the Hilton.

"Five minutes to arrival," Officer Garelick said matter-of-factly. Sandy was on top of things as usual.

"Yep," Godfrey replied as he held up the heavy military green walkie-talkie. "They've got some radio system on Air Force One. It still amazes me that they can call me on this state-of-the art equipment—the same state-of-the-art we used in the war," he said with a smirk on his face, as he shoved the World War II–model walkie-talkie back into his trench coat pocket.

Sandy Garelick was a senior police officer who headed up the New York City Bureau of Special Services and Investigations (BOSSI) squad and was the point man for setting up additional security for the president's frequent visits to the city. He had handpicked his squad and the team was great to work with. Professionally they were among the best in the country. Garelick, however, had a strong personality that could present a real challenge for the Secret Service advance agents. Garelick didn't seem to realize that the borders of the United States extended beyond New York City, and he wanted to know what the president would be doing every minute he was in BOSSI territory. Garelick thrived on the attention the publicized presidential visits brought to his unit and proudly utilized the thirty thousand New York Police Department officers to ensure the president's security. The conflicts came during off-the-record visits like this one when President Kennedy wanted to slip into the city as quietly as possible, with no fanfare. There had been enough clashes in the past three years that you could almost see President Kennedy cringe the minute he saw Sandy Garelick.

Somehow ATSAIC Art Godfrey had found a way to compromise with Garelick, though, and thus he was almost always given the advance assignments to New York. None of the other agents knew for sure if Godfrey really got along with Garelick, or if he was just smart enough to realize that an advance assignment in New York meant an extended stay at the Carlyle Hotel.

Exactly four minutes later Air Force One—the stunning silver and blue Boeing 707—landed and taxied to the secured arrival area. A portable staircase was moved into place and Art Godfrey took his place at the bottom, to be the first on the ground to greet the president.

Bill Greer, the president's Secret Service driver, came down the steps first, followed by ATSAIC Emory Roberts—Art Godfrey's counterpart for the evening shift—and the rest of the 4:00 to midnight shift agents. Agent Chuck Zboril was the last man out the door, before President Kennedy appeared with Assistant Special Agent in Charge Roy Kellerman a step behind.

At six feet, four inches, Kellerman was a full three inches taller than President Kennedy, with a large-boned, trim, muscular frame. Of all the White House Detail Secret Service agents, Kellerman had the most intimidating appearance. He had black hair that had grayed at the temples, a handsome, chiseled face, and a naturally tanned complexion that looked like he had spent much of his life outdoors. Kellerman was all business—he would never tell a joke, but easily laughed along with others at a good one—and it was clear that President Kennedy trusted him completely.

President Kennedy walked quickly down the steps, holding on to the rail for support. His back always stiffened on the airplane, even on these short flights, and the agents kept a close eye on him as he navigated the stairs. There was always a concern that his back would seize up and he'd fall down the stairs.

"Good evening, Art," President Kennedy said as he stepped onto the ground. "How are you? Been enjoying the Carlyle?" he asked with a smile. He knew the agents loved the Carlyle Hotel as much as he did. None of them could ever afford to stay there on their own, and he got a kick out of their delight with the grandeur of the opulent hotel.

"I'm fine. Thank you, Mr. President. And yes, the Carlyle is as superb as always," Godfrey said. "They're looking forward to your visit."

Officer Sandy Garelick strode toward the president and reached out his hand.

"Welcome back to New York, Mr. President," he said.

The president nodded courteously. "Sandy."

ASAIC Kellerman knew the president's aversion to BOSSI, who he felt was incapable of the understated protection he preferred, so he quickly led Kennedy to the black hardtop Lincoln Town Car where Bill Greer had already taken his place in the driver's seat and had the engine running. Kellerman held the back door open for the president and waited while Kennedy got situated, before taking his normal place in the front passenger seat.

The 4:00 to midnight agents filed into the leased black Ford sedan that would serve as the Secret Service follow-up car. Garelick and Godfrey would be in the unmarked police car leading the small procession through the New York City streets. The idea was to have no fanfare and hopefully draw as little attention as possible to the president. ASAIC Kellerman checked to make sure the follow-up car was ready to go and pushed the button on his radio.

"Lancer departing," he said. Even though the president was in the middle car, driver Greer would control the pace of the motorcade. It was up to the cars ahead and behind to adjust their speeds accordingly.

Art Godfrey in the lead car and ATSAIC Emory Roberts in the Secret Service follow-up car received the transmission, and the three cars began moving at a uniform pace. The object was for the driver of the president's car to remain between five and ten feet behind the lead car—just close enough to impede another car from coming between them, but far enough away that if he needed to make a fast break, he could step on the gas and swerve left or right. The Secret Service follow-up car was to remain a consistent five feet behind the president's car, no matter what. Maintaining this formation in traffic was sort of like flying a Blue Angels maneuver.

Chuck Zboril sat on the front bench seat between driver Sam Kinney and ATSAIC Roberts. Shoulder-to-shoulder in the backseat were Agents Bill Payne, Bob Burke, and Bill Duncan. On the floor of the backseat of the car lay an open gun case that contained a fully loaded .223-caliber AR-15 rifle.

Rush hour had waned, but it was a Friday night in New York City. Without motorcycle escorts or police cars stationed along the route, the three-car procession would have to stop at every red light along the way, which made Kennedy a sitting target for anybody who had caught wind that he was in town. It was unlikely on an off-the-record, but you had to assume the worst at all times.

The cars pulled onto the highway and instantly the procession was surrounded by fast-moving traffic. Bill Greer was maintaining a close distance behind Sandy Garelick when all of a sudden Garelick's brake lights went on, forcing Greer and follow-up driver Sam Kinney to do the same. A small piece of the roadway was under construction and the only warning was a row of construction barrels blocking the lane. Three lanes of traffic had to merge to two, and the follow-up car was about to be cut off by a car in the next lane over. Agents Bill Payne and Emory Roberts quickly rolled down the windows on the right side of the follow-up car. The agents were motioning and yelling for the car to slow down and let them pass, but the other driver wasn't about to give way.

Agent Burke, sitting in the middle of the backseat, picked up the rifle from the floor and pointed it so the barrel was visible to the driver through the open window. The man turned white as a sheet and slammed on his brakes, which caused a chain reaction of braking cars behind him. It was just the opening the follow-up car needed to get through and stay behind the president's car.

The screeching of brakes caused the president to turn around to see what was going on behind him and when he saw Bob Burke holding the rifle, he turned abruptly around. Burke knew the president would have a few harsh words for him for overreacting as soon as they got to the hotel, but in the front seat Emory Roberts remained calm and said simply, "Let's hope that's the last bit of excitement we have tonight."

Roberts knew that part of the president's reason for insisting on minimal BOSSI coverage was an attempt to reduce inconvenience to New York City drivers. However, this little incident would surely give Sandy Garelick one more reason to insist on a stronger police presence the next time the president came to town.

Meanwhile, the day shift agents had had just twenty minutes to check the security setup. Agent Harry Gibbs walked the agents quickly around the lobby and ballroom where the president was to speak, noting the restrooms and emergency evacuation routes. Gibbs introduced the agents to several New York City police detectives who would be posted around the hotel during the banquet. The detectives were all wearing a specific lapel pin that verified each's identity.

By the time the president arrived, all the guests were seated in the ballroom, and the agents were at their assigned posts. The crowd erupted into a standing ovation when the president took the stage, while the Secret Service agents constantly scanned the room for any sign of sudden movement or the lone guest who just didn't seem to fit.

As the guests dined on the lavish meal, Jerry Blaine stood at his post, listening for anything unusual above the clanking of silverware, and tried not to focus on the smell of the roast chicken that permeated the room. An audible growl sounded from his stomach and he realized he hadn't eaten since his thirty-minute break around eleven that morning. There'd been no time for a dinner break and right now there was nothing he wanted more than a hot cup of coffee and a hamburger. The burgers at the Carlyle's Bemelmans Bar were as famous as the fanciful murals that decorated the walls of the renowned New York landmark, and at this point Blaine was so hungry, he could nearly taste one.

President John F. Kennedy was in his element when he was in front of an adoring crowd, and tonight he was practically glowing with charm. His well-crafted speech evoked laughter and thoughtfulness, without sounding preachy, and by the time he had finished you could bet that at least 90 percent of the people in the room would be casting their vote to have him reelected a year from now.

As it turned out, Art Godfrey's hunch that President Kennedy might want to make an unplanned stop before heading back to the Carlyle turned out to be right. The president's brother Senator Ted Kennedy was in town, staying at their sister Jean's house on Fifth Avenue, and the president wanted to pay a quick visit.

Art Godfrey relayed the change of plans to Blaine, Grant, and the rest of the day shift.

"I'm gonna need you guys to stay on post at the Carlyle until the Boss gets back from his sister's place." He looked at his watch. It was already after 10:00 P.M.

"The midnight shift will relieve you if the Boss isn't back before twelve." The agents nodded. They knew the drill. Dinner would have to wait.

"I'll get the car," Dave Grant said.

Blaine reached into his coat pocket and pulled out the bag of peanuts he'd stuck there earlier. As he ripped open the small palm-sized bag, he looked at the other agents on his shift and said, "Hors d'oeuvres, anyone?"

At 11:15 the midnight shift relieved Blaine and the rest of the day shift at their posts around the Carlyle Hotel. President Kennedy still had not returned to the hotel, but finally the day shift was off duty. At this point fatigue was stronger than their hunger, and they decided they'd all better call it a night.

Rooms at the Carlyle were at a premium, and it was common for the agents to share.

Grant had collected the keys from reception and said, "We've got three rooms. Two rooms with doubles and one with a king. Somebody's gonna have to sleep alone."

"Let's flip," Blaine said as he reached into his pocket for a coin.

Coughlin won the toss, and the room alone with the king-size bed. Grant and Blaine would share one room, Giannoules and Paolella the other.

By the end of a hectic day like this, when their senses had been on high alert for hours, the agents were wound up so tight, it was impossible to fall asleep right away. As soon as the door to their room was shut, Blaine and Grant started recapping the day's events. They couldn't discuss specifics of their protective duties with anybody outside the detail—not even wives or other family members—so to unwind and vent they had only each other.

"I'm beat," Dave said as he threw his trench coat over the chair in the corner of the room. "Me, too," Jerry said as he pulled off his white dress shirt. Wrinkled and soiled around the collar, it looked nothing like the freshly ironed shirt Joyce had laid out for him that morning. "It's been a long day."

Joyce had dropped him off at the White House that morning at 7:15. Dressed in a bathrobe with her hair in curlers, she'd kissed him good-bye and driven off quickly because the baby was crying in the backseat. She wasn't going to be happy when he told her about the upcoming schedule. She'd been making more and more comments lately about how difficult it was to juggle the household and the two young kids with Jerry gone all the time.

Grant sat down on one of the beds and began untying his shoes.

"Hey, Jer, what was Behn talking to you about before we left the White House?"

Blaine had almost forgotten. He'd been waiting all day to talk to Dave about it.

"I'm going to Tampa to do an advance as soon as we get back, and from there I'm leapfrogging to Dallas to help with another advance."

Grant lifted up his head and looked at Blaine with wide eyes.

"Dallas?"

Blaine laughed. "I thought that might get your attention."

A couple of months earlier, Dave had been introduced to Gloria Brown while she was visiting her sister, Gwen, and brother-in-law Agent Clint Hill at their rented cottage near Hyannis. Dave and Gloria had hit it off immediately. Unfortunately, Gloria was based in Dallas, where she was a flight attendant for Braniff Airways, so the relationship thus far had developed only by telephone. Grant had racked up some significant long-distance phone bills, and everybody on the detail knew he was smitten.

"Go on," Dave said. "I'm listening."

"Well, I've been on the road most of the past six months since Scott was born, and I was just thinking that if you could take my place for the Dallas advance, then I could fly back to D.C. with the president in between Tampa and the Texas trip, and spend a couple of nights at home. I feel like my kids are growing up without me, you know?"

Blaine paused.

"Of course I'll have to run it by Godfrey first. That is, if you don't mind taking over the advance in Dallas."

"Mind? Are you kidding? If you can arrange for me to do the advance in Dallas, Jer, you would have my undying gratitude."

"I'll remember that," Blaine replied as he walked into the large marble bathroom. He turned back toward Dave and smiled. "You owe me one."

By the time Blaine and Dave turned the lights out it was well past midnight. Blaine couldn't seem to turn off his mind. He had just about drifted off to sleep when he heard a flurry of activity outside. He got up and looked out the window, which had a clear view of East Seventy-sixth Street.

President Kennedy was just stepping out of the Lincoln Town Car, with the acting SAIC Roy Kellerman at his side.

Blaine looked at the clock: 12:40 A.M.

Where does he get his energy? Blaine wondered.

As he crawled back into bed, Blaine's thoughts turned toward the day he met John F. Kennedy. Had it really been just three years ago? It seemed like a lifetime had passed, and yet it had gone by in a flash.

2

The President-Elect Detail

Do not pray for easy lives. Pray to be stronger men.
—JOHN F. KENNEDY

THREE YEARS EARLIER

On November 8, 1960, Americans from Boston to California gathered in their living rooms to watch the nation's first televised election results. In its last weeks the contest between Nixon and Kennedy had turned into a nail-biter.

Richard M. Nixon, the Republican nominee and sitting vice president, had been the odds-on favorite for most of the campaign. It was expected that Nixon would easily ride the coattails of President Dwight D. "Ike" Eisenhower—who had a 60 percent approval rating—right into the Oval Office. Nixon promised that the "peace and prosperity" the nation had enjoyed as a result of Eisenhower's policies would continue under his leadership. His younger opponent, he claimed, lacked experience.

On the Democratic ticket, forty-three-year-old John F. Kennedy suggested the country needed to go in a new direction. It was time for change. He sought to align himself with the reform traditions of Franklin Roosevelt and Harry Truman, and promised innovative legislation. Kennedy realized the civil rights movement was not going away—indeed, it seemed to be gaining momentum—and when Martin Luther King, Jr., was arrested in Georgia for leading civil rights protests before the election, Kennedy called King's wife to offer help in securing her husband's release. It was a risky move with such a divisive issue so close to Election Day. But Kennedy's backing of King guaranteed him huge support in the black community.

In the end, Kennedy won the electoral vote by a decisive 303 to 219, largely due to his popularity in urban and industrial states. But the popular vote showed how close the race truly was. Out of 68 million votes cast, Kennedy had beat Nixon by just 118,000 votes—a difference of less than two-tenths of 1 percent.

Clearly Americans were divided as to how the country should move forward in a rapidly changing world environment. Along with the burgeoning civil rights movement, tensions were rising in the Cold War between the United States and the Soviet Union. Cuba's new leader, Fidel Castro, had aligned himself with Soviet premier Nikita Khrushchev, which heightened fears that communism could spread through the Western Hemisphere. Recent polls indicated that more than half of Americans believed war with the Soviet Union was inevitable. The newly elected President Kennedy faced some unprecedented challenges.

At that time, fifty-five-year-old James J. Rowley was the Special Agent in Charge of the White House Detail. Not only did he have to manage outgoing President Eisenhower's Secret Service detail, but as soon as Kennedy was elected, Rowley had to have men in place to protect the president-elect as well. Rowley had served three presidents over the course of his twenty-one years on the White House Detail, and he understood better than anyone the importance of a smooth transition period between the time a president was elected and the time he took office.

When Rowley began his White House Secret Service career with President Franklin Delano Roosevelt, just fifteen agents were responsible for protecting the president. Though many Americans never realized it, Roosevelt was immobile and confined to a wheelchair. For public speaking engagements, Secret Service agents had to stand him up in front of the microphone and strap him securely to the podium. The media was sworn to secrecy. As World War II progressed, FDR became weaker and weaker. In spite of this, he traveled a great deal by train, and even flew to the Ukraine to attend the Yalta Conference in February 1945, where he met with Winston Churchill and Joseph Stalin to negotiate the boundaries of the postwar world. The Secret Service served as caretakers, moving the president from location to location.

When Roosevelt died of a sudden stroke in April 1945, Rowley and Agent Floyd Boring happened to be on duty. They both witnessed the difficulties of a sudden, unplanned transition from a deceased president to a sitting vice president, in this case Harry S. Truman. Suddenly the presidency was filled by a man who was extremely active and started every day with a brisk walk on the streets of Washington, D.C. Truman was fearless. He talked fast, moved fast, and traveled far more than Roosevelt had. The Secret Service had to adapt to this new president, with no increase in personnel.

Issues had piled up as Roosevelt's health diminished and Roosevelt had failed to keep Vice President Truman informed. Two months after succeeding Roosevelt, Truman was notified that the atomic bomb—something about which he had no knowledge—had been successfully tested. Truman's decision to detonate the weapon over Hiroshima and Nagasaki was the most difficult decision a president had ever faced. The bomb succeeded in ending World War II, but killed tens of thousands in an instant.

The fifteen-man Secret Service detail traveled with Truman around Europe in the aftermath of the war, as the new president attempted to renegotiate some of the deals FDR had made with Britain and the Soviet Union. In 1946, Harry Truman made Jim Rowley the SAIC of the Truman White House Detail.

Four years later, an assassination attempt on President Truman showed Jim Rowley just how important it was to find exceptional men to protect the president, and to make sure they received top-notch training.

President and Mrs. Truman had been living in Blair House—the guesthouse that was normally used for visiting heads of state—while the White House was being renovated to include a nuclear fallout bomb shelter. Located just across Pennsylvania Avenue from the White House, Blair House at the time was a two-story brick town house that stood just about ten feet from the sidewalk. A five-foot-high decorative wrought-iron fence was the only thing separating it from the heavily trafficked street. Three uniformed White House police officers guarded the exterior of the house; the small staff of Secret Service agents rotated shifts and positions throughout the interior when the president was in residence.

On November 1, 1950, Agent Stewart Stout was standing post in the front hallway just inside the front door while President Truman was taking his daily afternoon nap upstairs.

It was a warm, sunny day and shortly after two o'clock in the afternoon, thirty-five-year-old agent Floyd Boring had stepped outside. Floyd was a great kidder and storyteller and was chatting with White House police officer Joseph Davidson, who had just rotated into position at the west-end booth. Officer Donald Birdzell was standing at the front door while Officer Leslie Coffelt took over the post at the east-end booth. People were walking along the sidewalks on both sides of the street. Suddenly Floyd Boring heard a metal click, which he immediately recognized as someone dry-firing a weapon. He turned toward the front door and saw Officer Birdzell running into the street as a slight man in a suit was slapping an automatic handgun against his hand. As Boring and Davidson drew their weapons the assailant's gun went off; the shot hit Birdzell in the kneecap just as he was pulling out his own firearm. Officer Davidson started firing double action as fast as he could while Boring, who was an excellent marksman, cocked the hammer back on his snubnose revolver and took aim at the moving target. Boring shot off a round, which went through the assailant's hat and skimmed the top of his head. Momentarily dazed, the shooter turned back toward Birdzell, who was struggling to get on his feet, and shot him again before whipping around to fire on Davidson and Boring. Boring had slipped behind a tree to take cover, and as horrified pedestrians scattered in all directions, Boring aimed again and steadily squeezed the trigger. This round likely found its mark as the gunman staggered, as he sat on the stairs to load another clip, then toppled over—out of action.

At the same time the attack on Birdzell began, a second gunman had approached from the east. He jammed his 9mm Luger into the guard booth and shot Officer Leslie Coffelt at point-blank range with a number of rounds. As Coffelt sank to the floor, the gunman turned his weapon on a plainclothes White House police officer by the name of Downs, who was just returning to Blair House after buying groceries for the Trumans. The shots hit Officer Downs in the hip, shoulder, and neck, sending him to the ground. Then the attacker took aim at Officer Birdzell, who was kneeling, wounded, in the street. But the attacker's weapon was now empty, so as he stopped to put another clip of bullets into his weapon, he didn't notice the mortally wounded Officer Coffelt steadying his revolver. Just before he drew his last breath, Coffelt managed to squeeze off a round that entered one ear of his assailant and went out the other, killing the man instantly.

The dramatic gun battle lasted just forty seconds.

Inside Blair House, the moment Agent Stout heard the first shots he ran to the gun cabinet and grabbed a Thompson .45-caliber submachine gun. Stout pushed in the magazine and started up the staircase to the second floor, where President Truman was in his bedroom. A house servant was yelling at Stout to go outside to help, but Stout knew he was the last line of defense for the president. He reached the second floor, pulled the activation bolt, and pointed it at the main door. If an assailant attempted to enter, he'd be dead in a second.

It turned out the two men were Puerto Rican nationalists and the poorly planned assassination attempt was an effort to further their cause of Puerto Rico's independence. President Truman was unscathed by the gun battle, but when SAIC James Rowley reiterated the need for more agents on the Secret Service detail, Truman finally agreed to push Congress for funding. Shortly thereafter, the number of agents went from fifteen to thirty-four.

Agent Floyd Boring became a living legend from that day on, and although he and Stewart Stout rarely mentioned the Blair House shooting, their presence on the Secret Service detail was a constant reminder that assassins rarely give advance warning.

Jim Rowley remained as the Special Agent in Charge through Truman's seven and a half years and Eisenhower's two full terms. In those fifteen years, Jim Rowley had seen the types of threats change, and he'd become ever more concerned that the Secret Service just didn't have enough resources or agents to protect the president with confidence.

With the news of John F. Kennedy's election, every agent on the Eisenhower Detail was wondering what would happen next. On January 20, when JFK became president, suddenly Ike would be on his own. A few of the agents were already working on helping him learn how to drive a car again and other things in civilian life that he hadn't done in a very long time, but they had no idea what to expect when it came to protecting the new, much younger Kennedy.

The agents were comfortable with President Eisenhower and had learned how to deal with his personality to protect him effectively. They knew his idiosyncrasies well enough to know that he tended to get angry over a muffed golf shot and that incompetence at any level made him testy. Most of the agents were decorated veterans of World War II or the Korean War, and they idolized the commander in chief. For God's sake, the man had organized the defeat of Nazi Germany. Indeed, he treated the agents as if they were soldiers standing post, and that seemed natural to them. By the end of his second term, he'd lost all interest in learning the names of the newer agents and if he needed one's attention, he'd simply call out, "Agent!" That was Eisenhower's way.

There hadn't been any attempts on President Eisenhower's life during his two terms in office, but there were always threats, and Ike understood that the role the Secret Service played was not just for his personal protection, but was for the protection of the Office of the President. The world seemed to be hanging by a thread, delicately balanced between the forces of freedom and communism. If the President of the United States were killed, the future of democracy could easily be in peril. Dwight D. Eisenhower had spent his entire life fighting for the values of the United States Constitution, and he wasn't about to take any unnecessary risks.

With Ike, everything ran with military precision. Every agent knew his responsibility and Eisenhower operated in sync with them. He had trust and confidence in his agents, and had not a narcissistic bone in his body. He was in the twilight of his presidency, with no desire or need to mingle with the American people. For the Secret Service, Eisenhower was the perfect president to protect.

Kennedy, on the other hand, was an unknown.

The day after the election, President Eisenhower had flown to Augusta, Georgia, to begin his transition into retirement. He'd campaigned hard for Nixon the past few weeks, and now he was ready to put politics behind him.

Agent Jerry Blaine was standing in the rough near the seventeenth hole of the azalea-lined Augusta National Golf Club monitoring the surroundings for anybody or anything unusual. Twenty-eight-year-old Blaine watched as the president lined up for his shot. He'd watched Ike hit enough golf balls to know that they didn't always land on the fairway. Ike tended to hook left.

Along with Blaine, three other agents were spread around the course, posing as fellow golfers, dressed in golf shirts, slacks, and the ever-present Polaroid sunglasses. The four Secret Service agents moved ahead of President Eisenhower from hole to hole, hauling their government-provided golf bags, each of which contained a couple of banged-up clubs and a loaded Thompson submachine gun.

Jerry Blaine had been on President Eisenhower's Secret Service detail just seven months, but he felt as if he'd been preparing for this job his entire life. Blaine's childhood was not unlike those of many who grew up in the wake of the Great Depression. His mother had gotten pregnant and married quickly, but with the dismal economy her new husband couldn't find work, and shortly before Jerry was born, his father simply disappeared. For the first few years of his life, Jerry was passed from one relative to another as his mother struggled to make ends meet. Eventually his mother married a devoted man named Howard Blaine, who adopted Jerry and raised him as his own. Finally he was in a stable household in a rural suburb of Denver, but the knowledge that his real father had left before his birth was stored deep in the back of his mind. Jerry Blaine always felt like he had something to prove.

The world was at war during Jerry's formative years and he, like most children of that era, spent Saturday afternoons at the local movie theater, where you could have an afternoon of entertainment for ten cents. Prior to the feature attraction, there was always the latest film of the Allies' progress in World War II. By the time Blaine graduated from high school at age eighteen, he knew there was only one path for him to follow. He joined the U.S. Navy and was promptly sent off to Korea.

He spent three years at the edge of enemy territory, participating in a war that seemed to make no sense at all. By the end of the Korean War, more than 54,000 Americans had died, more than 100,000 had come home wounded, and still there was no resolution to the conflict. By this time Americans were sick of war—World War II, in which millions had died, was still fresh in the nation's memory—and Korea became "the Forgotten War." The Korean War veterans returned to the United States without the cheering crowds or a sense of accomplishment. However, this was not a complaining generation and they set about rebuilding the future for themselves and their country.

Blaine returned home, married his high school sweetheart, Joyce Hazlett, and thanks to the GI Bill, was able to enroll immediately at the University of Colorado. He earned a degree in business management, but it was his courses in history and criminology that really sparked his interest. As his June 1959 graduation neared, Blaine had realized the last thing he wanted was a desk job.

By sheer coincidence, Blaine ran into Paul Rundle, an old high school acquaintance, a few months before graduation. Rundle had just been accepted into the U.S. Secret Service and suggested Jerry apply. It was a long shot, for sure. There were no open positions at the time, but Jerry went through the background check and took the rigorous physical, personality, and intelligence tests anyway. After hearing Rundle's enthusiasm and description of the work, Blaine couldn't imagine doing anything else. He turned down several corporate job offers—much to Joyce's chagrin—and ended up tending greens on a golf course after graduation, hoping a Secret Service slot might somehow open up.

Unbeknownst to Blaine, the chief of the Secret Service, U. E. Baughman, had petitioned Congress for more funding and, in the summer of 1959, the Secret Service created thirty new field positions nationwide. It was to be the largest number of new hires since the Secret Service was formed in 1865. More than forty thousand men had applied around the country, but Blaine's scores and qualifications put him in the top thirty. On September 1, 1959, he became a Special Agent with the U.S. Secret Service in the Denver Field Office.

He started off doing field investigation work and rotating on a shift protecting President Dwight D. Eisenhower's mother-in-law, Mrs. Doud, who lived in Denver. As part of his training, Blaine was sent to Treasury Law Enforcement Training School in Washington, D.C., where he met SAIC Jim Rowley and the supervisors of Eisenhower's Secret Service detail. Blaine didn't realize it at the time, but he was being evaluated as a potential addition to the elite presidential protective team. Immediately after returning to the Denver office, Blaine was transferred to the White House

Detail without going through the normal thirty-day evaluation period. He'd be joining his old pal Paul Rundle, who had been promoted to Ike's detail several months earlier, along with two other agents from the Denver Field Office—Clint Hill and Dave Grant.

Dave Grant was on the Eisenhower grandchildren's detail, but Rundle, Hill, and Blaine were put on the same shift and now spent more hours with each other than they did with their wives or children. It was a strange existence being responsible for protecting the President of the United States, traveling with him all over the world, yet unable to talk to anyone outside the detail about the things you overheard or witnessed. Nobody else could possibly understand. The thirty-four men protecting the president were a close-knit group, members of an elite club that was unlike any other organization in the world.

The sun was shining brightly on the Augusta National golf course that crisp November afternoon in 1960. Agents Paul Rundle and Bill Skiles were posted on the fairway just ahead of Ike, while SAIC Jim Rowley stood about four yards behind the president, just out of swinging range. Jerry Blaine and Clint Hill were posted on either side of the fairway, closer to the green.

President Eisenhower swung at the ball and sent it sailing down the fairway. Agent Blaine watched as the ball bounced and rolled to a stop just short of the green. Standing under a huge magnolia tree on the opposite side of the fairway, Clint Hill looked at Blaine and gave the thumbs-up sign. It was an unusually good shot for Ike. Blaine laughed at the look of mock surprise on Hill's face.

Standing nearly six feet tall, with a muscular build, Clint Hill was an imposing figure. He'd played football, basketball, and baseball in college and was still competitive when it came to sports. He had thick black hair and dark eyebrows that framed his soft blue eyes. He looked as if he might have been of Italian descent, but Hill didn't know his heritage. Born in Larimore, North Dakota, in 1932, in the throes of the Great Depression, Clint had been dropped off at the North Dakota Children's Home seventeen days after his birth. Fortunately, his stay in the orphanage was brief. Three months later, Clint was adopted by Chris and Jennie Hill, a young couple from Washburn, who also had a four-year-old adopted daughter. Chris Hill had a stable job as the county auditor and Jennie was a devoted mother and housewife. Jennie was, however, severely hearing impaired and Clint grew up learning to be his mother's ears, always feeling protective of her.

During World War II, the Hills had many close family friends who were killed or wounded. Being of Norwegian descent, they were especially interested in what was happening in northern Europe. They received papers in both English and Norwegian, and listening to the nightly news on the radio was a must. The family was not wealthy and when relatives came to visit, Clint was often relegated to sleeping on the front porch of their two-bedroom house. He knew he was lucky to have been adopted into such a loving home, but there was something missing. Clint always felt as if he never really knew who he was.

Clint attended Concordia College in Minnesota and thought he might become a teacher. After graduation he enlisted in the U.S. Army, though, and was selected to attend Army Intelligence School; upon graduation he was made a Special Agent in the Counter Intelligence Corps. He realized he loved the challenge of investigative work. When he heard that there was a rare opening in the Denver Secret Service office in 1958, friends urged him to apply. He'd passed the tests and background checks with ease, and was hired almost immediately. It turned out that Paul Rundle had just been transferred to the White House Detail, which created the opening in Denver. Less than a year later, Clint was targeted as an ideal candidate for the White House Detail as well. He'd come a long way from the doorstep of the orphanage where he'd been dropped off on a cold January morning twenty-seven years earlier.

When the round of golf was over, SAIC Rowley motioned for Paul Rundle to join him at the president's side. Rundle jogged over to Rowley.

"Paul, I need you to stay with the president. I've got to take care of a few things in the office. Tell Skiles, Blaine, and Hill to meet me at the command post in thirty minutes."

SAIC Rowley was sitting behind a small desk piled with papers and brown envelopes and was talking on the phone as Agents Blaine, Skiles, and Hill appeared at the doorway. Rowley waved them to come in and sit down. As soon as he finished the call, he got right down to the business at hand.

"I have some personnel shuffling to do," Rowley began. He moved his eyes from one agent to the next.

The three agents stood there, each wondering what their personal fate would be. No one was ready to go back to a field office.

"Jerry and Bill," he said to Blaine and Skiles, "you'll be on the president-elect detail. Mr. Kennedy is going to spend the next month and the holidays at his father's estate in Palm Beach, Florida. Sign a GTR for a flight to West Palm Beach this evening."

All agents carried a stack of Government Transportation Requisition (GTR) slips with them at all times. They were for times like this when you had to get somewhere in a hurry.

"Boring will meet you at the airport," Rowley continued in his cool, even tone. "And by the way, better make some arrangements to get some warm-weather clothing; you're liable to be there until inauguration."

Rowley turned his gaze to Clint Hill.

"Clint, Defense Secretary Thomas Gates is flying back to Washington this afternoon. You're to fly back with him and head straight to Chief Baughman's office. Baughman will talk to you personally about your assignment."

Clint Hill nodded. *Why would Baughman, the chief of the Secret Service, want to speak with him directly?*

The SAIC turned his gaze back to Blaine and Skiles.

"Anybody have any questions?"

Blaine and Skiles had just been told they'd be spending Thanksgiving and Christmas in Florida, away from their families, while Hill was left wondering exactly what was in store for him. But it wasn't in any of their natures to question an assignment.

"No, sir," they replied in unison.

"Okay. Ike has been very pleased with the jobs you've all done. He wanted me to pass that along to those of you who are leaving his detail. Good luck in your new assignments."

• • •

For the life of him, Agent Clint Hill could not figure out why on earth he was being summoned to speak with the chief of the Secret Service. It couldn't be good. He thought for sure he was being sent back to a field office, or maybe even fired. He'd received nothing but praise from his supervisors since he'd joined the White House Detail, but he couldn't help but imagine the worst.

When Clint showed up at Chief Baughman's office in the Treasury Building, next to the White House, he was surprised to see both Deputy Chief Russell "Buck" Daniels and Assistant Chief Edgar Wildy waiting for him as well. He'd never been called into a meeting with the three top men in the Secret Service all present at once. This most certainly was not a good sign.

"Good afternoon, Clint," Baughman said as he stood up and greeted Agent Hill. "Come on in and sit down."

As it turned out, Jim Rowley had recommended Clint for the First Lady's Detail. Because Mrs. Kennedy was just thirty-one years old, Rowley wanted to have someone fairly close to her age on her detail, someone with whom she'd feel comfortable. Clint was well liked by all the agents, and at twenty-eight years old, he seemed to be an ideal candidate for the job. But Baughman wanted to check out Clint for himself. The three men grilled Agent Hill on his entire life story and looked him up one side and down the other. Clint tried to relax, but he felt as if he were on trial. Baughman and his deputies liked the fact that Clint had a young child— Clint's son was nearly the same age as the Kennedys' daughter, Caroline. In the end, he passed the once-over with no problem, and was assigned to be the number-two man on Jacqueline Kennedy's detail, under the supervision of Agent Jim Jeffries, effective immediately.

As Clint drove home that night, over Memorial Bridge toward Arlington, Virginia, where he lived in a small duplex with his wife, Gwen, and their son, Chris, he was filled with mixed feelings. He was relieved he wasn't being sent to a field office, but he also felt like he'd just been demoted to the second team. He loved the excitement of being on the President's Detail, the challenge of the advance work, the travel opportunities. What the heck was he going to do with the first lady? Visions of endless tea parties filled his mind, and as he pulled up in front of his house, he wondered how Gwen would take the news that he was going to be protecting the elegant Jacqueline Kennedy.

In order to come up with enough people to staff round-the-clock protection for President-elect Kennedy, Chief Baughman had needed to pull in agents from field offices to serve temporarily on the detail until the transition of power took place on January 20. Arrangements had been made for the agents' extended stay in West Palm Beach at a motel called Woody's, not far from Ambassador Joseph Kennedy's estate. Woody's Motel looked like it had been around for decades and was in need of some updating, but it advertised air-conditioned rooms and fit the Secret Service per diem allowance for lodging. The U-shaped building surrounded a small, rectangular swimming pool that the agents soon found out created an echo throughout the rooms whenever anybody went for a swim. The thinly walled rooms were basic but clean, and by the time all the agents had flown in from around the country, they'd pretty much taken over the whole motel.

Emory Roberts and Floyd Boring had been assigned as the two Assistant Special Agents in Charge of the president-elect detail. Boring had gone to Hyannis Port and had briefed Kennedy and his family, while Emory Roberts had been sent to Palm Beach. ASAIC Roberts was waiting to brief Skiles and Blaine when they arrived at the Kennedy estate the next morning. After brief pleasantries, Emory got down to business.

"Mr. Kennedy is in Hyannis Port, Cape Cod, but he's headed down here tomorrow with Floyd," Emory said as he walked with the agents down the palm-tree-lined driveway. "As you know, Mrs. Kennedy is pregnant and due in about a month, so she's staying at their Georgetown residence to be close to her doctors. Presumably she'll be down here after she has the baby.

"As you can see, this is a large piece of property that's not only vulnerable in the front, but also out to the ocean in back, along with a vacant lot next door that's used by neighbors to access the beach. We've got to establish security before Mr. Kennedy arrives. I'll give you a quick tour and then we'll get to work."

The two-story Spanish-style stucco house was large, but unpretentious.

It sat in the middle of the grounds, surrounded by lush tropical vegetation, which camouflaged a full-size tennis court. The back of the house opened up to a wide lawn that contained a saltwater swimming pool and a breathtaking view of the turquoise ocean. There were high walls on both sides of the property, and a retaining wall stood as a bank against the seven-foot drop from the lawn to the beach. A decorative wrought-iron gate allowed access to a short set of stairs down to the sand.

Blaine stood at the edge of the pool and looked out to the sea, where a couple of sailboats danced in the distance.

"Not a bad place to hide out while you're waiting for a job," he said to Skiles and Emory Roberts.

"Think of it as your home away from home," Emory said. "From what I understand, the Kennedys plan to split their weekends between here and Hyannis Port, depending on the season."

Emory started walking back toward the house and said, "Okay. Let's get to work."

The house was located on North Ocean Boulevard, the main road that paralleled the beach. Monterey Road intersected with North Ocean Boulevard directly in front of the Kennedys' walled-in property. The agents were concerned that if a car or truck got up to a high enough speed, it could potentially crash through the wall. The only way to prevent this was to turn the street into a one-way street headed away from the compound. Fortunately the Palm Beach Police Department agreed and the two-way street was made one-way only. The PBPD would also maintain a constant patrol and keep a patrol car posted out front when the president-elect was in residence.

Connected to the front wall was a garage that was also used for storage. The agents decided they could establish a post on top of the roof that would provide a view of the street in front.

The biggest problem was that the back of the house was completely exposed to the ocean. The beach seemed to go on for miles and people were able to walk directly behind the house. Anybody could cruise by in a boat, and if someone had a rifle with a scope, it wouldn't be difficult to shoot the president as he lounged by the pool. The retaining wall served as a divider between the back lawn and the beach area, but it was meant to prevent erosion. It hadn't been designed with security in mind.

It was decided that there'd need to be a Coast Guard boat patrolling the waters behind the compound twenty-four hours a day, even when the president wasn't in residence. That would be the first perimeter of defense. Then there would be two posts at each corner of the back of the property for the Secret Service agents to observe the beach area leading to the compound.

By the time President-elect Kennedy was due to arrive, the agents felt comfortable with the security measures they'd set up.

Mr. Kennedy flew into West Palm Beach airport on *Caroline*, the private plane named after his firstborn daughter that he'd used during the campaign. He'd just spent the past two days with Floyd Boring and another agent, Forrest Guthrie, and was slowly getting accustomed to the idea that from now on, he would get very little privacy. The Secret Service would be with him at all times, and would need to know in advance wherever he was going.

When Blaine, Skiles, and Roberts arrived at the small airport to meet Kennedy, they were surprised to see a crowd gathered outside the terminal, waiting on the tarmac like a local welcoming committee. A few held signs that said, "Congratulations, President Kennedy!" and many held cameras in their hands. The media had been covering Kennedy's every move and clearly somebody had announced the date and time of the president-elect's arrival into Palm Beach.

As Kennedy stepped out of the plane, the crowd started cheering and clapping. Deeply tanned and dressed in khaki slacks and a lightweight cardigan sweater, he looked much more suited to the casual style of Palm Beach than did the Secret Service agents, who were wearing their usual uniform of dark suits, ties, wingtips, and fedora hats.

"Congratulations, Mr. President!" one woman called.

Kennedy smiled, waved, and walked directly toward the group of people, with Floyd Boring right behind him.

Blaine, Skiles, and Roberts moved into position around Kennedy, creating an envelope of security. They hadn't even had time to introduce themselves, but their training made it instinctive for them to get as close as possible to their protectee in such an insecure situation. They scanned the crowd, moving alongside the president-elect as he shook hands and greeted the people.

Blaine and Skiles made eye contact with each other briefly at one point; they were both thinking the same thing. *Eisenhower never would have done this.* The schedule called for Kennedy to get off the plane and proceed directly to the waiting cars.

"Let's get into the car, Mr. Kennedy," Floyd Boring said calmly, a couple of times. Obviously Floyd hadn't expected Kennedy to jump into the crowd like that, either.

Either Kennedy didn't hear him over the noise of the crowd, or he was choosing to ignore Boring's strong suggestion.

It was easy to see why Kennedy garnered such attention. Unlike Ike, who might glance at a crowd like that and give a courteous nod and a brief wave, John F. Kennedy seemed as if he truly wanted to meet the people and greet each one of them directly. He was strikingly handsome and at six foot one, he seemed to tower over most of the people there. He had an easygoing, charming way about him that could be classified only as charisma. You couldn't help but be drawn to him.

After about five minutes, Kennedy finally succumbed to Floyd's increasingly insistent tone and waved good-bye to the well-wishers. The entourage piled into the three Lincoln Town Cars that were parked nearby.

As soon as Kennedy and the agents arrived at the compound, the president-elect told Boring that he needed to be introduced to everybody.

"I imagine we're all going to be spending a lot of time together," Kennedy said to ASAIC Boring, "and as everybody knows my name, I think it's only fair that I know theirs as well."

Not only did Kennedy want to know the agents' names, but as he met each one, he inquired about their backgrounds and whether they were married, or had children. From that point on, JFK addressed each of the agents by their first names, and rarely made a mistake.

The next day, a few new agents arrived to supplement the president-elect detail. SAIC Jim Rowley was still shuffling people in an effort to make sure both Eisenhower and Kennedy were properly and adequately protected. Agent Harry Gibbs had been in Gettysburg, Pennsylvania, with the Eisenhower grandchildren and was sent to Palm Beach on short notice. As soon as he arrived at the compound, ATSAIC Roberts told him to stand post at the left corner of the backyard, on the seawall.

It was a typical warm and sunny afternoon on Florida's east coast and

President-elect Kennedy had brought a stack of briefing files outside to read. Dressed in shorts and a T-shirt, Kennedy sat at a table next to the swimming pool and became engrossed in the documents. Every so often, he would look over in Harry Gibbs's direction. Harry's attention was focused on the sea and beach area, but in his peripheral vision, he noticed Kennedy looking at him. At one point Kennedy waved, so Agent Gibbs waved back. Having come directly from the cooler climate of Pennsylvania, with no time to change, Gibbs was dressed in his traditional attire of a charcoal gray wool suit, tie, and a gray fedora. Beads of sweat were dripping down his face and he hadn't realized that he kept lifting his hat to wipe his brow so the sweat didn't seep into his eyes.

Harry wiped his sleeve across his face again and suddenly Kennedy got up out of his chair and started walking toward Harry.

Harry stepped off the retaining wall as Kennedy approached.

"What's your name?" Kennedy asked. "I don't think I've met you."

"Agent Gibbs, Mr. President-elect, sir. My name is Harry Gibbs."

"Nice to meet you, Harry," said the president. "Now, what are you doing out here in this blazing heat wearing that winter suit?" Kennedy asked.

Harry didn't quite know how to respond. What should he have been wearing?

"I've just flown in from Washington," Harry replied. "It's a lot cooler there and I didn't have time to change."

"Well, why don't you move over there," Kennedy said, pointing to a shaded area next to the pool. "At least you'd be in the shade."

"Thank you, sir, but I'm not allowed to leave my post."

Kennedy paused in thought for a moment.

"How many agents are on post right now, Harry?"

"There are four, sir."

"Okay, I'll be back," Kennedy said. He turned and walked determinedly toward the house. Gibbs couldn't imagine what was going on.

Ten minutes later, Kennedy came outside, carrying an armload of short-sleeved shirts.

He put them down on the lawn in a neat pile and said, "Pass these out to the agents with my compliments. I think you'll do a better job of protecting me if you're not uncomfortable."

Harry Gibbs was dumbfounded. "Thank you, sir. I certainly will. That's very thoughtful of you, Mr. Kennedy."

President-elect Kennedy had planned to return to Washington, D.C., the first of December to be with his wife for the birth of their second child, but on November 25, he got a call that she'd gone into early labor.

Agents Boring, Roberts, Skiles, and Blaine grabbed their overnight bags and joined Mr. Kennedy on the *Caroline* for the flight up to Washington. Mrs. Kennedy had delivered a healthy baby boy and Mr. Kennedy was absolutely giddy with joy.

The fact that there were now going to be young children in the White House meant that several agents would need to be assigned to protect them. There wasn't so much a concern that somebody would kill the president's children—the Secret Service worried more about kidnapping.

Agent Ed Tucker was one of the agents first assigned to the children's detail, which quickly became known as the "Kiddie Detail." He was standing watch outside the door to Mrs. Kennedy's hospital room when one of the nurses came out of the room with a strange look on her face.

"Um, excuse me," she said to Tucker. "Mrs. Kennedy said she wants to talk to 'Mr. Tucker, the agent out in the hall.' Is that you?"

"Yes. Is she all right?"

The nurse laughed. "You may not believe it, but she wants to borrow some money."

Agent Tucker walked into the room, where Jacqueline Kennedy was sitting up in bed, under the white hospital sheets. Her baby son was sleeping in a hospital bassinet next to her.

"Yes, Mrs. Kennedy. You wanted to see me?"

She glanced up with her dark eyes and smiled.

"Hello, Mr. Tucker," she said in a soft, demure voice. She looked down as if she were slightly embarrassed.

"Would you happen to have a twenty-dollar bill on you? My hairdresser is coming over to do my hair and I don't have any money on me."

Ed Tucker smiled as he pulled out his wallet. He didn't normally carry much cash, but it just so happened he'd gone to the bank the day before. He pulled a twenty-dollar bill from his billfold and handed it to her.

"No problem, Mrs. Kennedy," he said.

"Oh, thank you, Mr. Tucker," she said. "My secretary, Mrs. Gallagher, will reimburse you. I do appreciate it."

Tucker and the rest of the agents would soon learn that neither the president-elect nor Mrs. Kennedy ever carried money and it was always a good idea to keep a twenty in your wallet, just in case.

Shortly after Mrs. Kennedy was released from the hospital, she and the two children—baby John, Jr., and three-year-old Caroline—flew to Palm Beach, along with the five agents assigned to their protection.

Agent Bob Foster had just been transferred to the Kiddie Detail to work with Ed Tucker, and another agent, Lynn Meredith. After spending a few days around the Kennedy family, Foster was chatting off-duty with some agents and said, "Mr. Kennedy sure seems like a nice guy—I wish I had voted for him."

A couple of days later, Kennedy approached Foster as he was standing near Caroline. "Hi, I'm Jack Kennedy," he said as he reached out his hand. "And you are?"

Foster smiled and held out his hand. "Agent Bob Foster, sir."

As the men shook hands, Kennedy got a quizzical look on his face and replied, "Oh, yes. Mr. Foster. I hear you didn't vote for me."

Bob's smile disappeared and he felt like his heart had dropped into his stomach. He knew his time on the White House Detail was over. He'd probably be sent on the next flight to Alaska.

President Kennedy broke into a big grin, said nothing else, and walked away.

Foster remained on edge for the next few days until he realized that Kennedy wasn't bothered at all by the fact that Foster hadn't voted for him. Quite the opposite: he seemed to get a kick out of it.

During December a steady stream of candidates for the president's cabinet flew into Palm Beach. John F. Kennedy's father, Ambassador Joseph Kennedy, spent a good deal of time at the compound, as well as people the agents would soon come into contact with on a daily basis. Pierre Salinger would become the press secretary, Evelyn Lincoln would be Kennedy's personal secretary, and his close friends Ken O'Donnell, Dave Powers, and Larry O'Brien—later to be dubbed "the Irish Mafia"—would be his top political advisors. There was always a large group of people around the compound and the agents had to do a quick study of who was who and what role they would play in the new administration.

John F. Kennedy was the first Catholic to be elected president and he made it a point to attend Mass each Sunday, no matter where he happened to be. On Sunday, December 11, the Secret Service escorted him to St. Edward Church, which was a short distance from the family's oceanfront home.

Jerry Behn, who had been named as the Special Agent in Charge of President Kennedy's detail, sat in the pew directly behind Kennedy, while two other agents sat a couple of rows back, along the aisles. Agent Blaine was posted at the entrance of the church, observing people as they came in.

People were dressed in their Sunday finest—the men in suits and ties, the women in fancy dresses and high heels. When a disheveled elderly man walked through the front door, Blaine watched him carefully. He just didn't seem to fit.

The man stood at the back of the church and looked around. When he saw President-elect Kennedy sitting in a pew about six rows back from the front, the man's eyes became transfixed, and he began walking in that direction.

Blaine followed him down the aisle until he was certain the man was headed for Kennedy's pew, then grabbed the man by the elbow and pulled back as gently as he could, so that anybody who was watching might think he was a church usher.

Once he had a hold on the man's arm, Blaine tightened his grip, turned the man around, and headed back toward the entrance. Blaine let go as he stared into the man's eyes, without saying a word. A few minutes passed, and finally the man turned and walked out of the church. Blaine watched as the man got into his car and before he drove off, Blaine took note of the car's description and license plate. Later, Blaine reported his suspicions to SAIC Behn, who notified the Palm Beach Police Department to keep an eye out for the car.

Meanwhile, the name of a seventy-three-year-old man from New Hampshire had reappeared as a threat case in the Secret Service Protective Research Section (PRS). He'd been in the files for years for writing threatening notes to previous presidents, and the election of John F. Kennedy had set him off again. A nationwide Teletype alert was sent out with details of the man's description and his ramshackle Buick sedan.

Four days later, seventy-three-year-old Richard Pavlick was arrested when the Palm Beach police spotted him in his car, not far from the Kennedy compound. Inside the car were sticks of dynamite, spools of wire, and a homemade detonation device.

After questioning, Pavlick admitted that he had planned to assassinate the president. He believed Kennedy's father had bought the election and JFK had won unfairly. Pavlick thought he'd be doing the nation a favor if he killed John F. Kennedy before he was inaugurated. So he'd driven by the house earlier that previous Sunday morning, turned up the one-way street, and parked on a side street where he could watch for the president to come out the front gate. He had wired the dynamite and was about ready to turn onto the one-way street going in the opposite direction. His plan was to crash into the president's limousine and detonate the charge. But the gate had opened and out came Mrs. Kennedy. This wasn't what he'd expected. He didn't want to hurt her; he was only after the president. It was then that he decided he'd kill the president-elect when he came out of church. But when Agent Jerry Blaine stopped him, he got nervous and drove off, trying to figure out another plan.

Richard Pavlick fit the typical threat profile case. His name had been on the PRS listing for a number of years and his aggressiveness transferred from president to president, which is a normal pattern for a chronic threat case. It was unusual, however, that Pavlick had focused on Kennedy before he'd taken office.

After eight years without an assassination attempt on President Eisenhower, the Pavlick incident was a grim reminder that the White House Secret Service detail could never let down their guard.

For the agents on the Kiddie Detail, the dangers were of a different sort. Agent Ed Tucker was in charge of Caroline Kennedy, but when he came down with the flu, Agent Lynn Meredith stepped in for a few days while Tucker recuperated at Woody's Motel. One day Lynn took Caroline, her cousin Christopher Lawford, and another friend to a Palm Beach park to play at the playground. When his shift was over, Lynn stopped by Ed's room at the motel.

"How'd it go?" Ed asked.

With a grim look on his face, Lynn slowly removed his sidearm from its holster.

"Hold it, Lynn. Things can't be that bad!"

Lynn chuckled as he flipped out the cylinder of his .38 service revolver and dumped the cartridges into his palm. Out of the six cartridges, two of the casings were empty.

"Oh my God, Lynn. What happened today?" Ed was imagining the worst. A kidnapping attempt? An attack on Caroline?

Not exactly. The three children had become bored with the slides and swings so they started exploring. During their adventure, they decided to turn over a couple of logs. When Christopher flipped up one of the logs, a big ugly snake coiled up.

The kids started screaming and backing away. Lynn recognized the snake as a poisonous eastern diamondback rattlesnake. Without hesitating, he drew his gun and shot the snake, twice.

"I'm probably going to be fired," Lynn said. "But it's better than trying to explain how Caroline got bitten by a rattlesnake."

As it turned out, Maud Shaw, the children's nanny, convinced Caroline that the incident would be her and Caroline's little secret. There was no need to share it with Mommy or Daddy.

Christmas and New Year's came and went in Palm Beach with the Kennedys' extended family joining them for big celebrations, while the agents tried not to focus on how much they missed their own families. Mrs. Kennedy would sit by the pool every afternoon, working on her tan for the strapless gowns she planned to wear for the inaugural balls, and it was all the agents could do not to stare as they rotated posts. Over the course of those weeks in Palm Beach, though, the Kennedys and the agents on their detail slowly became comfortable with the new routine. It was a transition on both sides.

By the time President and Mrs. Kennedy returned to Washington, D.C., preparations for the inauguration were well under way. The inauguration is one of the few events where every government official is in attendance and gathered in one small geographic area. For the Secret Service, inaugurations are security nightmares.

The inauguration swearing-in stand construction was secured from the moment work started. The work area was sealed off except for the workers who were subject to background checks and screenings. It had been learned that the Russians had been experimenting with imbedding explosives, microphones, and radioactive materials in plywood and other building supplies, so after construction was completed the stand was examined inch by inch with metal and Geiger detection devices, as well as checks for traces of biological or chemical compounds. Fencing was constructed around the stand with D.C. police securing the area twenty-four hours a day.

The day before the inauguration, security posts were established at strategic locations around the stand and on the Capitol grounds to ensure the areas were secure prior to the arrival of the general public. At that point the Secret Service conducted a follow-up inspection of the swearing-in structure and took control of the security in that area. It was an elevated structure designed for maximum visibility for the estimated two hundred thousand people who were expected to attend the event. The presidential seal was placed in the middle and buntings adorned the railings. There was a roof and a number of rows of seats for top-level dignitaries. There were heaters in the event the weather turned frigid and, if the forecasters were right, they were going to be used. The open area around the stage was fenced off and would be secured until the inauguration, with Capital and Park police manning the security posts.

The inaugural parade route had been thoroughly inspected. The tunnels underneath Pennsylvania Avenue were searched for explosive devices and then the manhole covers were sealed to prevent entry. Building owners were instructed to keep windows closed.

Nearly every one of the two hundred Secret Service agents from field offices around the country had been called in to help with security.

The night before the inauguration, Agent Jerry Blaine was assigned to assist ASAIC Floyd Boring with the security advance at the upscale Paul Young's Restaurant, on Connecticut Avenue, where Jack Kennedy's father, Ambassador Joseph Kennedy, was hosting a black-tie private party for the entertainers and celebrities who had attended or performed at the pre-inauguration gala that night.

It was a star-studded event the likes of which Jerry Blaine had never imagined he'd ever see. The men were dressed in tuxedos, the ladies in floor-length ball gowns. And the guest list read like a who's who of Hollywood: Frank Sinatra, Ella Fitzgerald, Bob Hope, Bette Davis, Janet Leigh, Tony Curtis, Kim Novak, Sidney Poitier, Peter Lawford, Milton Berle, Nat King Cole, and many others. As the advance agent, Blaine was able to wander the room rather than standing post. He was awestruck to see so many movie stars in one place. He and the other agents tried to remain cool, but every so often they'd find themselves shooting a glance at the lovely Juliet Prowse or Angie Dickinson.

Blaine had been on his feet for twelve hours, and it wasn't until 1:00 A.M. that he finally found a way to break away briefly. He was dying to call Joyce and tell her about all the celebrities who were there. She'd get a kick out of it. He found a pay phone outside the restroom and dialed his home number.

After a few rings, Joyce answered in a groggy voice.

"Hello?"

"Joyce!" Jerry said excitedly. "You can't believe this party. I think every movie star in Hollywood is here."

On the other end, Joyce could hear clinking glasses, animated voices, and dance music that was clearly being played by a live band.

"I've stood right next to Frank Sinatra, Janet Leigh, Tony Curtis . . ." Jerry rattled.

Suddenly the line went dead.

It took Jerry a moment to wonder what had happened, and then it dawned on him. He had broken the unwritten code that agents lived by. Joyce was eight months pregnant, she'd spent Christmas and New Year's alone, and at one o'clock in the morning the last thing she wanted to hear was how much fun Jerry was having. That was the last time he'd call home from a lively presidential event.

Jackie Kennedy left the party around two, but President-elect Kennedy stayed until four o'clock in the morning.

A cold front had been forecast for the Washington, D.C., metropolitan area and as the party raged into the wee hours, the weather took a turn for the worse. By the time the agents left the restaurant, several inches of snow were already on the ground, the temperature had gone from cold to bone-chilling, and a steady mixture of icy sleet and snow was pummeling down.

Agent Blaine managed to navigate the icy roads back to his apartment in Alexandria. He was afraid of the reaction he'd get from Joyce when he got home, but she didn't say a word. She even fixed him a hot plate of eggs and bacon while he changed out of his tuxedo and took a quick shower. There was no time to sleep. He had to be back at the Capitol well before the inauguration at noon.

By sunrise, eight inches of snow blanketed Washington and the surrounding area, and while the snow had stopped falling, the wind had picked up and the temperature had dropped into the teens. When you walked outside, the sudden blast of icy wind was instantly numbing to any exposed flesh. The only saving grace was that the sun had come out and there was a crisp blue sky hanging over the city.

Several of the agents had been unable to make it back to their homes, and Bob Lilley was one of them. Agent Lilley had worked into the wee hours of the morning and realized there was no way he could drive home to Maryland and make it back in time for his scheduled post at the front door of the Kennedys' townhome in Georgetown by 6:45 A.M. He ended up staying in the small command post that had been set up on the lower floor of the Kennedys' home and managed to shave in the laundry room before he had to be on duty.

When President-elect Kennedy stepped outside, dressed in a tuxedo with tails and top hat, he noticed Lilley standing next to the front door, shivering, his fedora coated with a film of ice. Lilley had no gloves, no scarf, a hole had broken through the bottom of his shoe, and after being in the sleet the night before, he was soaking wet from head to toe.

Kennedy took one look at him and went back inside. He came out a few minutes later with gloves and a scarf.

"Put these on and come inside for a while to get yourself warmed up," JFK said as he handed Lilley the garments.

"Sir, I can't leave my post out here," Lilley said, trying to keep his teeth from chattering. "But I'll gladly accept your offer of the gloves and scarf."

With that, Kennedy hopped into the waiting limousine and headed off to his inauguration.

At noon, on January 20, 1961, John F. Kennedy took the oath of office and was sworn in as the thirty-fifth President of the United States.

3

The Threats

*The path we have chosen for the present is full of
hazards, as all paths are. The cost of freedom is always
high, but Americans have always paid it. And one path
we shall never choose, and that is the path of surrender,
or submission.*

—JOHN F. KENNEDY

SATURDAY, NOVEMBER 9, 1963

Agent Jerry Blaine and his shift departed New York City at 1:25 in the afternoon, and by the time the chopper from Andrews Air Force Base delivered them to the White House, it was nearly 4:00 P.M. It was shift-change
day, so Blaine and his shift would now be working midnights.

The president was taken by helicopter directly from Andrews to
the family's new retreat in Atoka, Virginia, near Middleburg, where
Mrs. Kennedy and the children were spending the weekend. Mrs. Kennedy
had designed the house, which sat on a large piece of property on Rattlesnake Mountain overlooking the Blue Ridge Mountains, and it had only
just been completed in October. Mrs. Kennedy had dubbed the place
"Wexford" after the county in Ireland where the Kennedys were from, but
the Secret Service just called it "Atoka."

Blaine had to report to Atoka in a few hours, but he still needed to pick up his advance information for Tampa. He decided to stop in at the White House before going home.

With the president and the family away, the White House was quiet. Jerry checked his mail slot in the Secret Service office. Sure enough, Eve Dempsher, the Secret Service secretary, had typed everything up and had a package of information waiting for him. Inside the envelope were his hotel and flight arrangements, confirmation for the leased cars from Ford, the president's scheduled itinerary in Tampa, along with press tags and identification pins for plainclothes officers and other security personnel.

Eve, a longtime civil servant, was the mother hen of the detail agents, and they referred to her as Miss Moneypenny, of James Bond lore. Eve was simply remarkable. Responsible for keeping track of forty agents, she made sure their reports were accurate and on time, and made flight arrangements and hotel reservations for every trip. It was as if she were a master juggler, and no matter how many extra balls you added, she found a way to keep them in the air, always with a smile on her face, though perhaps a little scolding, too. The agents adored her and relied on her completely, but she was also an ally to the Secret Service wives. She had empathy for the wives and was always thoughtful to contact them if there were ever any emergencies, delays, or unexpected departures. Eve knew that because of the secretive nature of their jobs, the agents couldn't share much information with their wives, and she understood how difficult it was for the wives to be at home with crying babies and handling household emergencies while their husbands were staying in elegant hotels and rubbing elbows with world leaders and movie stars.

Blaine looked at his watch. Before he left for Tampa on Monday, he had to check for updated threat suspects at the Protective Research Section. If he went to PRS now, he would have tomorrow free to catch a few hours of sleep and spend some time with Joyce and the kids before the midnight shift at Atoka. He put the envelope in his flight bag and headed across the street to the PRS office.

Agent Blaine loved doing advances. To him it was the most exciting and challenging part of being on the White House Detail. He'd much rather be coordinating security in a new city or foreign country than standing post on a dark night in Hyannis Port or Palm Beach, looking out at the black ocean.

In reality, the advance work was 95 percent of the effort in guaranteeing the president's safety on a trip. The political team put together the president's itinerary and it was the Secret Service's job to figure out how to move the president safely from one place to the next, how to secure every venue and every route. You had to think like an assassin.

The first stop before any advance was always the PRS. Located in the Executive Office Building, next door to the White House, the PRS offices were the nerve center for tracking threat cases. Any time there was a threat made against the president's life—whether it was a written letter, a phone call, details gathered from an informant, field investigation, or an unstable person trying to get inside the Northwest Gate of the White House—an investigative report was initiated and a case file number issued. A PRS agent would type the report on carbon paper so there would be multiple copies, noting the threat maker's name, last known address, a synopsis of the threats made, a description of the person, and their medical history, if known.

Cases were analyzed and categorized according to the seriousness of the threat. They ranged from "extremely dangerous" to the innocuous "gate crasher." There were always people who would show up at the Northwest Gate demanding to see the president about one thing or another. If they didn't have credentials, obviously they weren't let in, but sometimes the people were mentally unstable and would try to climb over the White House gate.

Whenever somebody made a threat against the president, they would be categorized as a permanent risk. There'd be an evaluation, the individual would be monitored, and the case file would remain in the Protective Research file for as long as the person was still alive. It wasn't uncommon that a person who made a threat against one president would continue making threats against each subsequent president. This could go on for thirty or forty years, so some of the case files were quite thick.

The records room of the PRS office contained rows and rows of gray metal four-drawer file cabinets that held thousands of threat suspect files, organized by case number. There were smaller file cabinets where index cards of each suspect were organized both geographically and alphabetically. The cards were cross-referenced to the case files. Thus if you knew either the name of a suspect or their last known location, you could go to the small index drawers, locate the card, which would have the case number on it, then go to the large filing cabinets to get the master file.

The most serious threat suspects were the ones on the flash cards every agent carried with them at all times. It was the nature of threat makers to wander as vagabonds or itinerants, moving from town to town or state to state. You never knew when or where one of them might show up.

Agent Blaine had called PRS from New York City earlier that morning and requested any Florida files be pulled. When Blaine entered the records room, Cecil Taylor, the Special Agent on duty, had some index cards and manila file folders laid out on the table for him.

"Hi, Jer," Cecil said. "I searched the Geo file and came up with two active cases in the southeast region. I've also pulled out a possible new threat that has just come to our attention."

Blaine picked up one of the files.

The subject was a man named Wayne Gainey. The picture showed a nice-looking, clean-shaven young man with a crew cut. He could have been a bagger working at the supermarket, or an elementary school teacher. Threat subjects could be men or women, young or old, peaceful or sinister. They could be your neighbor next door and you'd never know it.

Blaine flipped over the card to read the profile:

Subject made a statement of a plan to assassinate the President in October 1963.

Subject stated he will use a gun, and if he can't get close he will find another way.

White Male—Age 20—5'9"—155 Lbs.—Hazel Eyes—Brown Hair Light complexion—slender build

Blaine sat down in the chair and began reading the file. The investigating field agent in Tampa, Arnie Peppers, had been conducting regular follow-up visits with the young man's parents and the attending psychiatrist. Blaine knew Arnie Peppers well; his investigations were always thorough.

Blaine put the papers back in the file and picked up the other one Cecil had laid out for him. The second file was much thicker. John William

Warrington. White male; age fifty-three; five feet, nine and a half inches; medium build; blue eyes; thin, graying hair; slightly stooped. The man had a long history of letter writing and making verbal threats.

The most recent entry in the file showed that Warrington had written a number of threatening letters addressed to President Kennedy postmarked October 15, 16, and 17 in Tampa. He'd also sent an extortion letter to a local bank president, which had gotten him arrested on October 18 in Tampa. He was currently being held in the Tampa city jail.

Special Agent Arnie Peppers had handled Warrington's case as well. Apparently Warrington had been diagnosed as paranoid schizophrenic. He had been in and out of mental hospitals and veterans' hospitals for the past fifteen years. He'd told Peppers he was going to use the extortion money to assassinate the president. Seemed he didn't like JFK's association with Martin Luther King, Jr.

"Is this all you have in the files for the Southeast?" Blaine asked.

"That's all in the Geographic file," Cecil said. "A new one was submitted for a guy in Chicago, who is currently under evaluation."

Cecil handed Jerry the one-page fact sheet on the new case.

"His name is Vallee. Thomas Arthur Vallee. The Chicago office investigated this case about two weeks ago. Some landlady found a peculiar collage made from newspaper clippings taped to the wall of one of her tenants' rooms. She called a friend of hers at the Chicago PD, and as soon as the officer saw the collage, he called the Chicago Secret Service office."

Blaine knew that Ed Tucker—one of the agents who had been assigned to the Kiddie Detail when JFK was elected—had transferred back to the Chicago field office.

"So presumably Ed Tucker and Tom Strong handled it?" Blaine asked.

"Yes. Tucker and Strong went to the apartment complex, and since Vallee was at work, the landlady let them into the apartment. The guy had cut out newspaper and magazine articles about the president and local politicians, and had covered a whole wall with them. What was disturbing to the agents were the threatening comments he'd scribbled all over the weird collage . . . and this was two days before the president was due to visit Chicago for the Army–Air Force football game."

Blaine scanned the sheet as Cecil continued.

"The next day Tucker received a telephone call from the landlady notifying him that Vallee was planning to take the next day off—November first—the day the president was going to be in town."

"So you've got an illegal search and a hunch," Blaine said.

"Right. So, Tucker contacted the Chicago PD and explained the situation," Cecil continued.

"Do a stop and chances are you have a reason to detain until the president leaves town," Blaine said. The Secret Service couldn't wait for probable cause. They might end up with a dead president.

"An all-points bulletin was immediately sent out, and Vallee was picked up almost immediately for a minor traffic violation."

Blaine nodded with a smile. "The Chicago way."

Cecil laughed. "Yeah, so get this. The cops see an illegal knife lying on the front passenger seat, so they search the car. The guy had an M1 rifle and close to a thousand rounds in the trunk. So they locked him up during the time Kennedy would be in town. Subsequent investigation showed he is a member of some group called the John Birch Society—a right-wing conservative organization—and has had mental problems. But then the president canceled the trip . . ."

"Right. Because of the coup in Vietnam when the Diem brothers were assassinated," Blaine said. He shook his head. He'd been on post at the White House when President Kennedy walked into the Cabinet Room with Attorney General Robert Kennedy, Secretary of State Dean Rusk, National Security Advisor McGeorge Bundy, CIA director John McCone, and every ranking member of the Joint Chiefs of Staff. The last time Blaine had seen that many national security members together was during the Cuban Missile Crisis. They'd worked late into the night and reconvened the next morning.

"That was a long day. Not a good time for the boss to go to a football game in Chicago. So where's Vallee now?"

"He's currently under observation and evaluation in Chicago until an assessment can be made as to his potential for danger. They'll notify us if he leaves Chicago."

"Okay, let me get a copy of the Gainey and Warrington files. And can you make up some extra copies of the photographs, too?"

"Sure thing," Cecil said as he picked up the files.

Blaine walked over to the bulletin board where the PRS kept a list of current threat makers or gate crashers from around the country who were of immediate concern. Most of the cases were familiar names from the flash cards he already had. Gainey and Warrington had been added to the list and were the only cases in the Florida area.

Blaine turned to Taylor, who was mimeographing and preparing more flash cards.

"Are there any active files for Texas?" Blaine asked.

"No. Roy Kellerman just gave me a heads-up about the president's upcoming trip, so I did a thorough check. There weren't any active threats in Texas. This is all we have on the current nationwide active list."

Taylor pointed to the bulletin board as Blaine reviewed the names on the list, which had been updated to include the names of Gainey and Warrington.

1. Stanley Berman—professional gate crasher
2. Carl Brookman—on record with FBI subversive activities in the Nazi Party and possible association with the Communist Party. Possesses firearm.
3. William Robert Bennett—disabled veteran
4. John Francis Donovan—letter and telegram writer. Considered a nuisance.
5. Johnnie Mae Hackworth—letter writer, religious fanatic who made threats against the president; arrested in 1955 and 1960.
6. Josef Molt Mroz—picketer and "Polish Freedom Fighter"
7. Barney Grant Powell—threatened Truman, extreme temper, violent man with assault background; carries firearms.
8. Peppi Duran Flores—threatened Vice President Lyndon Johnson. Says he is a communist and pro-Castro.
9. Wayne L. Gainey—claimed the KKK authorized him to kill the president in 1963. Teenager.
10. John William Warrington—mental; wrote five letters threatening JFK for his association with Martin Luther King, Jr.; says he will be lying in ambush in Florida.

"Here you go, Jer," Cecil said as he handed Blaine the copies. "We'll let you know if anything new pops up. Obviously Arnie Peppers has a good handle on things down there."

"Yeah, he's great. Thanks, Cecil. Appreciate your help," Blaine said as he put all the copies into a folder.

Blaine was relieved to know that Arnie Peppers was still in the Tampa area. His biggest concern was the anti- and pro-Castro groups, but he knew that Peppers and another Florida field agent, Ernie Aragon, had established a source network in Miami and Tampa that was so well tuned, they heard about any new faces in the Cuban community the minute they stepped foot into Florida. Arnie would be a huge help on this advance.

By the time Jerry walked into his second-floor apartment in Alexandria it was seven o'clock. He had just a few minutes to drop off his dirty clothes and pack some clean ones before he had to leave for Atoka to work the midnight shift.

He put his bags down and yelled out, "Daddy's home!"

Joyce came running in from the children's bedroom.

"Shhh," she whispered. "I've just got the kids down to sleep."

She put her arms around his neck and kissed him. "I thought you were going to be home much earlier."

"Yeah, I know," he said. He was disappointed he didn't get to see the kids awake, especially in light of how his plans had changed.

"I had to stop at PRS. I've got to go to Tampa, Florida, on Monday."

Joyce's face sunk.

"But when you left for New York, you said you'd be in town all this week."

"Yeah, I know. It came as a surprise to me, too. I've got an advance, so I'll be gone a week, and then I'm supposed to jump to Dallas straight from there. I may not be back until the twenty-third."

"And then it's Thanksgiving," she said. She knew how it went. Thanksgiving in Hyannis Port. Christmas and New Year's in Palm Beach. It had been the same for the past three years. And if Kennedy won a second term, Kelly would be eight years old, and baby Scott would be five before they'd have a Christmas with their daddy. Joyce knew Jerry loved his job. And she knew he loved her and the kids. It was just that sometimes, she wondered which came first.

MONDAY, NOVEMBER 11, 1963

Blaine had never worked with Frank Yeager on an advance before, but he'd heard that Yeager was conscientious and thorough. Yeager had grown up in Vero Beach, Florida, and with his blond crew cut, rugged features, and muscular build, he could easily pass for a Florida surfer. What would be most helpful, though, was his knowledge of the geography and social climate of the state.

Most advances were handled by a single agent, but whenever there was a motorcade with multiple stops, two agents would be assigned. You had to have been on the White House Detail for at least six months before you could conduct an advance on your own. Suddenly, with all the turnover in the last two months, less than half the agents on the Kennedy Detail were qualified to do an advance. Between the three-city trip to Florida and the two-day, five-city stop in Texas, almost every experienced Secret Service agent would be conducting advances. That left the newer agents to take over the shift duty for the president's protection.

After working the midnight shift at Atoka, Dave Grant dropped Blaine off at the airport in the shift car at 9:00 on Monday morning. Frank Yeager was waiting for him at the National Airlines counter. Blaine signed the GTR, and the two boarded the plane minutes before the doors closed.

Having had next to no sleep in the past twenty-four hours, Blaine was asleep before takeoff.

By the time Yeager and Blaine checked into their rooms at the International Inn in Tampa, it was the middle of the afternoon, and they were anxious to get things moving. They had just six and a half days to coordinate the entire security plan for the president's visit.

"Frank, why don't we drop our bags in the rooms, then grab a quick bite to eat."

"Yeah, I guess we were both sound asleep when the stewardesses came around with lunch. I'm starving," Yeager said.

Sitting in the small café of the hotel, Yeager and Blaine talked about the Redskins and who had the best college team—Colorado or Florida. Anybody who overheard their conversation would never guess that they were Secret Service agents. They couldn't talk business in public places.

Blaine and Yeager paid in cash for their checks, and put the receipts in their pockets. "Okay. Let's go on up to my room and get to work," Blaine said.

As they approached Blaine's room, the two agents heard voices inside. Blaine turned the key and opened the door.

Bill Elder from the White House Communications Agency was standing near the desk watching as a technician from the Bell Telephone Company installed the White House telephone.

"Oh, hi, Jerry. Hi, Frank," Elder said as he turned toward the door. "We're just about all set up here."

The U.S. Army Signal Corps had a unit assigned to the White House called the White House Communications Agency, and every time the president went on an out-of-town trip, a member of the WHCA would travel to the location with the advance agents to establish a local switchboard that would connect all the telephones to be used during the president's visit.

There were two switchboards at the White House—a civilian one with the telephone number 456-1414, which was operated by a group of wonderful and capable women, and the WHCA switchboard with a confidential number. When the president traveled within Washington, a direct hot telephone line was established from WHCA to the location of the president. For trips outside Washington the WHCA installed lines at each venue as well as in the advance agent's hotel room that would connect directly to the local switchboard. The temporary switchboard allowed a direct linkage to the White House and to any phone in the world, with a secure frequency. WHCA also set up the radio frequencies to be used during motorcades.

Also linked to this organization was an Army warrant officer who carried the "football"—the briefcase containing all the codes and responses in the event of a nuclear attack on the United States. The WHCA members were excellent in their work and essential to keeping the president immediately in touch with the rest of the world. The Secret Service would not have been able to work effectively without them.

"Jerry, here is a card with the phone locations," Elder said as he handed Blaine an index card with typed numbers and locations on it. "The base station will be set up at MacDill and I'll be working on the radio network later. We'll be using the 'Charlie' net radio and I'll be setting up the press filing locations at Lopez Stadium, the Hesterly Armory, and MacDill. If you need me I'm in room four-twenty."

Frank Yeager was already seated at the small table in Blaine's room and was getting his notepad and pencil out as Elder left the room. Blaine grabbed his briefcase and placed it on the table.

"Let's take a look at what we've got and then maybe we can take a drive around town to get our bearings," Blaine said.

Blaine reached into his jacket pocket and pulled out the neatly folded, typewritten schedule Eve Dempsher had left in his mail slot.

"Here's the plan Belm got from O'Donnell. Hopefully it won't change much before the actual visit." It wasn't uncommon for the political aides to change venues or add programs to the itinerary right up until the day before the president's arrival.

Suddenly there was a knock on the door. Blaine got up, walked over, and opened the door.

He was surprised to see Arnie Peppers, the Tampa resident agent, standing there.

"Well, if it isn't Arnie Peppers," Blaine said with a smile. "How'd you know we'd be here?" Blaine asked as he gestured for Peppers to come into the room.

"Well, I knew Ford hadn't delivered your car yet, so I figured you couldn't have gone far."

"Your timing is impeccable. We were just going over the schedule."

"Let's have a look at that," Arnie said as he pulled out a chair and sat down.

Peppers scanned the itinerary and read it out loud. "Arrival at 10:45 A.M. MacDill Air Force Base. Meeting with the base commander, then lunch and a short speech to the military personnel and their dependents. Depart by helicopter 2:15 P.M. to Al Lopez Stadium. Arrival at 2:25 P.M. Chopper departs for Miami after dropping off the president at Lopez Field. A motorcade run with stops at Fort Hesterly Armory, International Inn, and back to MacDill for departure."

Peppers looked up at Blaine and Yeager.

"Looks like a darn ambitious schedule," Peppers said. "How long is he gonna be here? Three days?"

Blaine and Yeager laughed.

"Less than six hours on the ground," Blaine said. "We have a four-thirty departure for Miami."

"Well," said Pepper. "Guess we better get to work."

The first item Blaine and Yeager wanted a status on was the threat suspects from PRS. Peppers had both files with him.

"The Gainey kid is under the care of a psychiatrist. His parents have been very cooperative. I'll make sure he's in his parents' custody during the visit. I'm not worried about Gainey, but for assurance I'll have an agent keep the house under surveillance."

Peppers picked up the photo of John Warrington and shook his head.

"Warrington's a sad old nutcase. We've been dealing with him for years. He's in the Tampa city jail as we speak. He will damn sure be behind bars next week when the president's here, but I'll double-check. Don't worry. We've got enough on him that it won't be a problem to keep him locked up."

"Great," Blaine said. "Chicago has a case on a guy by the name of Thomas Vallee. He's a mental. They've got him undergoing an evaluation to determine how bad he is. Other than that, your friends Gainey and Warrington are the only threat cases PRS had for Florida. Actually the entire Southeast."

"Kind of surprising, actually," Yeager said. "We know the boss isn't too popular down here."

Blaine nodded. "Yeah. Frank and I are a little concerned about the Cuban issue."

"What's your take?" Blaine asked. "Anything going on?"

Peppers leaned over and reached into his briefcase.

"I'll give you the short story," he said as he placed a two-inch-thick file folder onto the table.

For the next half hour Peppers went over a flowchart he'd prepared of the Cuban community, augmenting the diagram with a colorful summary of each group. He had an impressive network of sources and informants.

"One group has already filed for a demonstration permit, but we don't expect them to be violent," Peppers said. "The Cuban community is quite diverse, and not very unified. They have pro-Castro spies interspersed within the anti-Castro groups and vice versa. It's a tangled web, to say the least."

"For good reasons," Yeager said.

Yeager and Blaine knew that Tampa was a hotbed for politically active Cuban exiles who had fled to southern Florida following the overthrow of Cuban dictator Fulgencio Batista by Fidel Castro's guerrilla fighters in 1959. Initial enthusiasm for Castro had turned sour when he announced that he was a communist and allied with the U.S.S.R. In April 1961, just three months into his presidency, President Kennedy decided to follow through with an invasion of Cuba using a plan that had been developed by the CIA during the Eisenhower administration that was meant to make the invasion look like a homegrown Cuban uprising. The plan called for two air strikes against Cuban air bases, followed by a shore invasion by 1,300 Cuban exiles who had been trained in Guatemala by U.S. forces.

The original site for the exiles' shore landing was on the Miami side of Cuba—just ninety miles from the U.S. border—where the landing party could quickly move into the hills and thick vegetation. But President Kennedy had changed the site to the Bay of Pigs, farther away, to make it appear that the United States was not involved.

The initial attack using B-26 World War II bombers painted to look like Cuban air force planes failed to destroy Cuba's air force arsenal, and Castro realized the United States was behind the attack. Kennedy immediately canceled the second air strike so the administration could distance itself from the incident. When the 1,300 ill-equipped exiles landed ashore, they were met by twenty thousand Cuban troops supported by heavy Russian tanks, and none of the promised U.S. air support. The U.S. supply ships were bombed and sunk by the Cuban air force, leaving the exiles trapped on the beach. Nearly one hundred of the exiles were killed and the rest were captured.

The embarrassing failure of the Bay of Pigs invasion made Kennedy appear weak, inexperienced, and indecisive. The Soviet premier, Nikita Khrushchev, tried to capitalize on the youthful American president's failings, and four months later Khrushchev began building the wall that would divide communist East Berlin from West Berlin. A year later Khrushchev and Castro began installing nuclear missiles on Cuba—an action that resulted in the Cuban Missile Crisis and nearly ignited a nuclear war.

In December 1962, Kennedy paid a $53 million ransom of medical supplies and baby food to Fidel Castro for the release of the surviving Bay of Pigs prisoners, who had been held captive for twenty months. When the prisoners returned to the United States, President and Mrs. Kennedy welcomed them home with a big ceremony at the Orange Bowl in Miami. But still, many Cubans living in Florida resented Kennedy's failure to oust Castro from their homeland.

Blaine had been on duty when the whole Bay of Pigs fiasco began and had made the trip to the Orange Bowl, where he'd seen the malnourished exiles, many with missing limbs. It was understandable that now, less than a year later, the Cuban Americans were still divided on Kennedy.

"We're just going to have to play it by ear," Peppers continued. "The groups are well-known for their unpredictability, so I don't think we can be too careful."

"How is your rapport with the police force?" Blaine asked.

"Excellent," Arnie replied. "I've got you all set up to meet with Chief J. P. Mullins tomorrow morning. He's eager to help out with whatever resources you need. And the same goes for our office."

"Terrific," Blaine said. It was a huge help having someone like Arnie Peppers in the field. "Actually, there is just one more thing."

"Sure, what is it?" Arnie asked.

"If you've got any connection with the man upstairs, we'd love to have it be pouring with rain next Monday."

Peppers laughed. He understood Blaine's concern. No matter how many police you had on the streets, no matter how many threat suspects were behind bars, and no matter how many demonstrators might be lining the route, the biggest vulnerability in a motorcade was the open-top car.

"I'll see what I can do. But remember, this is Florida, the Sunshine State. I wouldn't count on it."

After meeting with Peppers, Blaine and Yeager went over the itinerary. They had to split up the responsibilities if they were ever going to get everything done.

"As a matter of fact, before we finish up for the day, let's take a drive to all the sites. I want to have a feel for the area before my meeting with Chief Mullins," Blaine said.

Even though Agent Peppers had provided some great background information, Blaine was deeply concerned about the length of the motor-cade. Just looking at the map, he could tell it was going to be unusually long. And as Peppers said, this was the Sunshine State. Chances were, the president was going to be riding through the city, waving to the crowds in an open-top car. Blaine just didn't have a good feeling about it.

Two-year-old John Kennedy, Jr., was marching up and down the hallway outside the Oval Office, wearing a white cardigan sweater with blue trim, matching blue shorts, and an oversize army helmet. He'd just flown back from Atoka in the helicopter with his father and sister, Caroline, and he was giddy with excitement. Helicopters were his first love, but anything having to do with soldiers, guns, or the military came a close second. Agent Bob Foster could hardly keep from laughing at the serious look on John-John's face as he high-stepped back and forth, back and forth, his arms rigid at his sides.

At the retreat yesterday, Mrs. Kennedy had been trying to explain to John-John what Veterans Day was all about and how he was going to get to see real soldiers with their swords when Daddy took him to the cer-emony. She'd explained that Daddy was the commander in chief, and all the soldiers would be saluting him, so perhaps John should salute him, too. He'd practiced several times before anybody realized he was using his left hand. Once he got the hang of raising his right hand to his forehead, though, his arm had grown tired, and the salute was rather droopy.

"Mr. Foster will help you practice again tomorrow, John," Mrs. Kennedy had said. "You'll look just like the other soldiers when you salute the com-mander in chief."

Agent Bob Foster looked at his watch. "Okay, John-John," he said gently. "Let's leave the helmet here. It's time to go."

John tilted the heavy helmet back on his head and looked up at Foster with wide eyes. "To see the soldiers?"

Foster laughed. "That's right, we're going to the Tomb of the Unknown Soldier, and there will be plenty of soldiers there."

The president's annual Veterans Day wreath-laying ceremony was a fairly short event that President Kennedy had thought would be just about the right length for John-John's attention span. He knew his son would enjoy seeing the pageantry of the uniformed military officers, with their swords and guns.

The sun was nearly overhead as Bill Greer maneuvered the president's limousine gently around the sharp curve in the road and eased onto Memorial Bridge. As the car crossed the Potomac River, the rolling hills of Arlington National Cemetery lay just ahead, on the other side of the bridge. A few trees still clung to their brown leaves, but most of them had gone bare. Crisp yellow and burnt orange leaves lay scattered among the endless rows of tombstones.

Several thousand people had gathered for the ceremony and as the president began walking toward the Tomb of the Unknowns, flanked by Commandant of the Marine Corps General David Shoup and Administrator of Veterans Affairs the Honorable John Gleason, with Bob Foster and John-John hand in hand behind them, the loud shot of a cannon echoed through the air.

John-John instinctively put his hands to his ears. Another shot rang out, and then another.

In the distance, the announcer at the podium said, "Ladies and gentlemen, your attention please. The president has entered the cemetery and is receiving a twenty-one-gun salute at the present time."

The loud blasts of the howitzer cannon could be heard rippling throughout the nation's capital.

The president walked silently toward the Tomb of the Unknown Soldier and placed the presidential wreath against it. The uniformed military color guard saluted in unison, and standing on the sidelines, Bob Foster leaned over to John-John and whispered, "Okay. Time to salute Daddy."

His hand was still a bit curved, more like he was shading his eyes from the sun, but John-John had remembered to use his right hand. Unfortunately, his father didn't get to see it, but Foster would have John-John reenact the scene for him when they got back to the White House. The president would get a real kick out of it.

Jerry Blaine had sketched out what appeared to be the most direct route for the motorcade in Tampa, but as he and Yeager drove it, they realized some changes would need to be made. There were a lot of potential security problems that weren't evident from looking at the map, such as one-way streets, drawbridges, and overpasses. These were all items they'd have to discuss with Chief Mullins and his staff at the meeting the next day.

As in most cities, the biggest problem was traveling through the downtown area and all the exposures that presented. Because of the number of venues, Blaine had calculated the distance of the motorcade would be somewhere around twenty-eight miles. He doubted Chief Mullins had enough personnel to handle everything they were going to request.

It was after nine o'clock by the time Blaine and Yeager returned to the hotel.

"I'm beat," Blaine said. "I think I'll head up to my room, give Joyce a quick call, and hit the sack. How about we meet in the lobby tomorrow morning at seven o'clock?"

"Perfect," Yeager said. "I'll see you in the morning."

As Blaine got off the elevator and headed down the hall to his room, he realized how tired he truly was. Going from the day shift to one night of midnights, then back to a day schedule, had finally caught up with him. He knew as soon as his head hit the pillow he'd be out cold.

When he called Joyce, she could tell he was exhausted, so they didn't talk long. He was brushing his teeth in the bathroom when the phone rang.

Joyce must've forgotten to tell him something.

"Hello?"

"Hey, Jerry. It's Bert."

Bert DeFreese was the agent conducting the advance for the Miami stop.

"Hi, Bert. How's Miami?"

"Well, the weather's great, but this advance is going to be tricky. Sometimes I wonder if Ken O'Donnell and Dave Powers think we're magicians."

Blaine laughed. "What's going on?"

"The way they've got this schedule set up, the only way I can get the boss from the Miami airport to his speaking engagement on time is by chopper. Unfortunately, there aren't a lot of open areas for a helicopter to land in downtown Miami."

"I see your problem," Blaine said. "What does the police department say?"

"Well, I've got a meeting with them tomorrow to try to figure out some way to make it work. But, hey, this isn't the reason I called.

"We just got a tip from the Miami Police Department," DeFreese continued. "An informant notified them of a recorded conversation he had a couple of days ago with a man from Georgia named Joseph Milteer. Apparently Milteer is a racist, right-wing political activist and he told the informant that a plot is in the works to kill the president. He said the president could easily be shot from an office building with a high-powered rifle. I'm getting a copy of the transcript of the call and Agent Robert Jamison down here in the Miami field office is following up."

"Geez," said Blaine. "Thanks for the heads-up. Keep me posted as soon as you have anything new."

"Sure thing," DeFreese said.

Blaine hung up the phone. He wrote some notes in his steno pad about what DeFreese had just told him. He'd call Floyd Boring in the morning and give him an update. Unless the president changed his mind about the motorcade, or agreed to ride in a closed-top car—something Blaine knew just wasn't going to happen—the only way to have a chance at protecting the president against a shooter from a tall building would be to have agents posted on the back of the car. Even then, if somebody had the advantage of looking down on the motorcade and was a good enough marksman to hit the president with the first shot, there was little an agent could do. No matter how quickly you reacted, no man was faster than a speeding bullet.

4

The Advance

*A nation which has forgotten the quality of courage which
in the past has been brought to public life is not as likely
to insist upon or regard that quality in its chosen leaders
today—and in fact we have forgotten.*
—JOHN F. KENNEDY

TUESDAY, NOVEMBER 12, 1963

At his home in Arlington, Virginia, Kennedy Detail Agent Winston G. "Win" Lawson rose early, packed his suitcase, and ate a quick breakfast. He'd organized his briefcase last night, but he checked it again to ensure he had everything he needed for the advance in Dallas. He sorted through the maps and press corps identification tags, and made sure he had an adequate supply of the multicolored lapel pins that would immediately identify authorized people to the Kennedy Detail agents.

Eve Dempsher had typed out a list of contacts in Dallas, and he'd mimeographed it. He stuck one copy in the briefcase and the other in his suitcase.

The last item in the briefcase was the White House Advance Manual. The manual was basically the bible for the Kennedy Detail advance agents. It provided detailed information on protocol, spotting and securing the presidential plane during a visit, checklists, emergency medical plans, media provisions, setting up arrivals and departures, motorcycle and motorcade configurations, securing venues, banquet measures, and pre-liminary and final advance report outlines. Every agent was issued a numbered manual after they'd assisted on an advance. The manual had been newly updated and even though Win knew every aspect by memory—he'd done countless advances in his two and a half years on the detail—he always carried it for reference.

Win and his wife, Barbara, had a five-year-old son named Jeff, and they'd just adopted a five-month-old baby girl named Andrea a month earlier. With the two kids in the backseat, Barbara drove Win to the White House and dropped him off at the Southwest Gate. Before he got out of the car, he gave Barbara a hug, a comforting smile, and a kiss.

"I'll give you a call when I arrive," he said.

"Okay. Good luck. I'll miss you," Barbara said. She wasn't looking forward to him being gone, but she knew this trip was going to be just as hard on him. He'd really bonded with their new daughter and had been helpful with the feedings and diaper changes since they'd brought her home.

Win opened the back door, leaned in, kissed the baby on the forehead, and reached over to give Jeff a squeeze.

"Be good for your mommy while I'm gone, sport," he said.

"I will, Daddy," Jeff said as he opened his eyes wide. "I'm a big help with the baby."

Win laughed. "That you are, son. I'll be back soon."

The day before, Win Lawson had checked PRS for threat suspects in Texas, specifically in the Dallas area, and had been pleasantly surprised to find that there weren't any. Still, things could have changed overnight, so he made sure he had time to stop in one more time before his flight.

Because there were so many Kennedy Detail agents and political advance men heading to Texas for advances at the same time, Eve Dempsher had arranged an Air Force charter flight for all the advance teams. The plane would drop off Win Lawson in Dallas, Bill Duncan and Ned Hall in Fort Worth, Dennis Halterman in San Antonio, Bill Payne and Bob Burke in Austin, and finally, Ron Pontius in Houston.

The White House staff had assigned Jack Puterbaugh as the political advance man for President Kennedy's trip, and on the flight to Dallas, Puterbaugh entertained Win with some background on Texas politics. The noise of the prop plane limited conversation but Jack spoke loudly enough to make sure he was heard.

"Texas politics is similar to working with nitroglycerin," Jack explained to Win. "They're all Democrats, but they range from extreme liberal to extreme right wing. When you shake them up they become volatile. The current split is so traumatic that many Democrats are threatening to switch to the Republican Party."

Win had seen the political shift all through the South, but it was strange hearing it from a Democratic political advance man.

"Governor Connally is the leader of the conservative wing of Democrats and Senator Ralph Yarborough heads up the liberals and there is constant bickering. I'm probably going to get involved in some fence mending since Lyndon is going to be in Dallas and there's no love lost between him and Yarborough. Yarborough feels the liberals were responsible for JFK winning Texas in the last election, and he wants to control the program in Dallas, but I know Connally won't allow that. Should be interesting."

Win was happy that Puterbaugh was going to be in Dallas to handle the squabbles. His job would be hard enough without having to charm warring politicians.

Jerry Blaine awoke to the bright early morning sun streaming through the hotel window. After an invigorating shower, he dressed quickly. As he looked in the mirror to make sure his tie was straight, he realized the feeling of unease that had crept over him last night had completely disappeared. Sure, the three-stop, twenty-eight-mile motorcade was probably going to go down on record as the longest ever for President Kennedy, but Blaine realized he was excited to take on the challenge.

The key to effective protection during the president's visit depended almost entirely on how Blaine handled today's meeting with Chief Mullins and his staff. The Secret Service wasn't equipped to handle security for the huge crowds a presidential visit inevitably attracted; they needed the cooperation of the local police force. The local taxpayers paid the budgets of the police, fire, medical, and public services, and the president's visit would be an imposition on resources. Blaine couldn't demand support; he had to humbly request it. Having the right attitude from the beginning was essential to getting the resources he needed and would impact any future visit the president might pay to the city.

A big part of being a good White House Detail agent was the ability to motivate. You had to be able to establish immediate rapport with local law enforcement, public works officials, venue sponsors, and elected city and congressional representatives. The support of the local police was essential. They knew their jurisdiction inside and out. In one meeting with the chief of police you could find out where there were high areas of crime, what ethnic conflicts existed, and whether there were underlying issues that could present a potential danger. Local law enforcement understood chokepoints, knew which areas might present a problem of ambush, and knew the options if the Secret Service suddenly had to evacuate the president from any given point.

After a quick breakfast in which Yeager introduced Blaine to grits— a Southern staple that Blaine had never ventured into—the agents headed to the Tampa Police Department headquarters.

Chief J. P. Mullins had a reputation as an effective administrator and was well respected by his staff. He spoke softly but with an air of authority that you could tell came from years of duty on the streets. When Agents Blaine and Yeager walked into his office, he greeted them warmly.

After brief pleasantries, and a bit of banter about the best toppings for grits, Chief Mullins escorted Blaine and Yeager into the conference room, where three officers were seated around the table. The men stood up as the chief entered, and he introduced them as his three captains who would be coordinating the various aspects of security.

Blaine got down to business, but he was careful to keep his tone relaxed.

"We understand that while President Kennedy's visit to Tampa is an exciting event for your city, it will also be rather disruptive. We really appreciate any assistance you can provide."

"By all means," Mullins said. "Just let us know what you need."

Blaine began with a brief rundown of the president's scheduled agenda and led gently into the motorcade, which would require a huge amount of resources in terms of planning hours, road blockages, and manpower.

"Let me spend a few minutes talking about the motorcade setup," Blaine said. "There will be a lead car, which, if you're open to it, Chief Mullins, is typically driven by the chief of police."

Blaine looked at Mullins to gauge his reaction.

"Why, certainly," Mullins said as he tried to contain a smile. Blaine hadn't had a chief yet who'd declined the offer to lead a presidential motorcade through his city. It was an honor for the chief, of course, but what was most important to the Secret Service was that the driver directly in front of the president's car knew the city inside and out. If there were an emergency that required a sudden evacuation, the chief would be able to navigate the roads ahead of the president's driver and get him quickly to a safe location.

"Does the president use an armored car?" Mullins asked.

It was a common misconception that the president's limousine was bulletproof. In fact, the car had been designed mostly for political show and exposure. The Secret Service working agents had very little input into the car's features.

Designated "SS100X," the 1961 midnight blue Lincoln Continental was modified by the Ford Motor Company and Hess & Eisenhardt, a custom automobile company. The stock four-door convertible was lengthened three and a half feet and had various configurations of removable tops. There was a hard top, a canvas roof panel, and a transparent plastic bubble top, all of which were stackable and could be stored in the trunk. None of the tops was bulletproof.

The car originally came with a privacy window between the driver and the rear of the limousine, but when the bubble top was installed, the air-conditioning couldn't cool the backseat, which made it very uncomfortable. So the privacy window was removed and a metal roll bar was installed. Both the privacy window and the bar created a barrier between the Special Agent in Charge who sat in the front passenger seat and the president, making it impossible for the agent to react quickly if there were an emergency.

Attached to the back of the driver's bench were two auxiliary jump seats, used primarily to reward political friends who could ride with the president during motorcades. Handgrips were cut out of the stainless steel roll bar so the president could stand and wave at the crowd while the car was moving. Alternatively, he had a hydraulic seat that allowed him to raise himself an additional ten inches, to be seen better by the crowd. And God forbid the president ever traveled in an open-top car at night: interior floodlights would illuminate him to the crowd. None of these political exposure features had the stamp of approval of the Secret Service.

In an attempt to add security features, two platform steps and hand bars were installed on the back of the car, which gave the agents ready access to the president, and so they could shield his back. Often the agents would be holding on with one hand and pushing away overzealous crowds with the other. There were also two retractable steps on both sides of the limousine, but neither Kennedy nor the Secret Service found them useful, since when they were extended they could injure the agents as they were running alongside and fending off the crowd. The whole point of the car was for political benefit—not protection, as most people might have imagined.

SS100X cost the Ford Motor Company two hundred thousand dollars to build, but the Secret Service didn't have that kind of money in the budget. So Ford leased the car to the Secret Service for five hundred dollars a year. The Secret Service couldn't afford to look a gift horse in the mouth.

"No," Blaine answered simply. "The car is not armored."

He went on to mention that not only would this be the longest motorcade ever traveled by President Kennedy; it would also be a record number of stops in one city. As Blaine looked around the room, he could almost see the chief and his staff puff up with pride.

"Agent Yeager and I drove to each of the venues last night, but you guys know this city far better than we do, so we could really use your help in determining the safest and most effective motorcade route."

"No problem," Mullins said. "We have a lot of experience handling parades. And between the police department and the sheriff's office, we have about twenty bikes that can be used as escorts."

Blaine bristled internally at the mention of the word *parade*. That was exactly what he didn't want this to be. And the idea of twenty motorcycle escorts brought back a sudden flood of memories. While every police department operated somewhat differently, Blaine had seen one common thread through police departments all over the world: their motorcycle escorts were a tremendous source of pride. There was no better opportunity to bring them out in full force than when their city was being visited by a popular American president. But Blaine had seen over and over again how well-meaning police motorcyclists had inadvertently put the president's life in danger.

Just six months earlier, Blaine had accompanied President Kennedy on a highly publicized tour of Europe that included stops in Ireland, Germany, and Italy. Two of the craziest and most dangerous motorcades occurred in Italy.

Overseas trips brought many challenges to the Secret Service, in large part because every country's law enforcement agencies felt as if they could adequately protect the American president on their own. This required a lot of trade-off and compromise on the part of the advance agents. Art Godfrey—the agent who had learned to master the challenges with Sandy Garelick in New York City—had been given the advance assignment in Italy since he had fought there in World War II, and thus had some idea of the Italian mind-set. Of course, the last time he'd been on Italian soil his mission was to kill as many Italian soldiers as possible, but still the hope was that he could get further with negotiations than someone who'd never been to the country before. To Godfrey's amazement the Italians agreed to nearly everything he proposed. They'd negotiated to have the two presidents ride in Kennedy's limousine for the Rome motorcade, and in President Antonio Segni's car in Naples. The Italians demanded that their security personnel be used throughout the visit—including a large motorcycle escort—so Godfrey consented, only under the condition that Kennedy's Secret Service detail drove directly behind the presidential limousine with no impediments.

Air Force One landed in Rome and there was much pomp and circumstance for President Kennedy's arrival. Honorary guards in silver helmets and plumes were in formation, and it seemed as if every man, woman, and child in the city had taken the day off to line the motorcade route from the airport to the Italian president's residence. President Kennedy's SS100X limousine had been shipped directly from Berlin and was lined up in the motorcade with the rest of the vehicles, as Art Godfrey had agreed.

Presidents Kennedy and Segni climbed into the backseat of the limousine while SAIC Jerry Behn was crammed in the front seat between driver Bill Greer and Segni's head of security.

Driver agent Hank Rybka drove the follow-up car, with Chief Rowley in the front passenger seat. Agent Roy Kellerman sat in the jump seats with JFK's political aides Ken O'Donnell and Dave Powers. Agents Win Lawson and Paul Burns were posted on the running boards, while Agents Dave Grant and Jerry Blaine were alongside the presidential car. Grant and Blaine would jog next to the car unless the motorcade sped up to the point that they couldn't keep up; then they'd fall back onto the running boards of the follow-up car.

Immediately after the procession began, an Italian security car pulled in front of the Kennedy Detail follow-up car and stopped. Twenty-six motorcycles ridden by Italian police seemed to come out of nowhere from both sides of the parade route. The motorcycles surrounded the presidents' car, forcing Grant and Blaine to fall back to the follow-up car, which was now boxed in by two other Italian security cars.

Sitting in the lead car, ahead of the presidential limousine, Art Godfrey realized he had been double-crossed.

The Italian security car driver acted as if his car had stalled, but clearly it was a prearranged maneuver to allow the motorcycle squad prominent placement, thus thwarting the previously negotiated motorcade lineup.

Blaine had never heard Jim Rowley swear before, but a loud litany of profanities poured out of the usually unflappable chief's mouth. Rowley's face had turned beet red. He was furious. Finally Hank Rybka put the car in reverse, veered around the stalled Italian security car, and sped up to join the motorcade. But he couldn't get between the presidential limousine and the throng of motorcycles.

When the procession arrived at Segni's residence, Art Godfrey confronted the Italian head of security. He wasn't about to let the Italians think their stunt had gone unnoticed. If Godfrey had had his M1 with him, the guy would have been running for the hills.

Two days later, there was another motorcade through Naples, where the president would be leaving Italy. The crowds in Naples were estimated to be over a million strong.

Before the motorcade started, Chief Rowley huddled with Grant and Blaine.

"By God, if those bastards pull that stunt again, I want you two to jump on the trunk of the presidents' car and ride there. Do not let the crowd overrun the car."

As President Kennedy and President Segni walked toward the latter's parade limousine, which Godfrey had consented to use on the trip through Naples, Chief Rowley was on the verge of exploding. Once again twenty-six motorcycles were poised to take their positions in the motorcade. Rowley had no objection to the fifteen motorcycles lined up in a spearhead formation directly behind the lead car, but off to the side, eleven more motorcycles were primed to move into the motorcade as soon as it got moving. The Italian follow-up car and the Secret Service follow-up car were parked directly behind the presidential limousine, but sure enough there was another Italian security car just like the one that had stalled out in Rome, waiting in the wings. Rowley had no doubt the eleven motorcycles had instructions to fall in between the presidential limousine and the follow-up cars.

"Grant, you and Blaine hit the trunk and stay there!" Chief Rowley shouted over the roar of the motorcycles.

Already headed that way, Dave Grant and Jerry Blaine received darting glances from the Italian motorcycle riders as they leapt aboard the trunk of the departing presidential limousine.

President Kennedy turned around and smiled with a wink to Grant and Blaine as the motorcade set out for Naples and the airport.

On the highway the coordinated motorcade was an impressive sight. The motorcycles were doing a good job of crowd control, and Grant and Blaine were feeling a little foolish sitting on the trunk.

President Segni had given Grant and Blaine some questionable looks throughout the procession, but finally he leaned over to President Kennedy and said, "Shall we tell them to get off the back of the car?"

President Kennedy said simply, "No, I want them there."

When the motorcade hit the narrow streets of Naples, the size of the crowds multiplied. People were jammed alongside the streets, leaving little room for the procession to pass. Within the first few blocks of the downtown area, motorcycles started falling over as the crowd surged forward. The bikes forced the follow-up cars to come to a sudden stop and, as if on cue, the people swarmed around the presidential car, fervent to shake President Kennedy's hand.

Grant and Blaine were scanning the crowd for weapons, but when the people started pressing on the car, they had to focus their attention on pushing the screaming fans away from the president. There were no handrails like they had on President Kennedy's limousine, and they found themselves throwing people off the car while trying to stay aboard the rounded trunk. People were weaving in between the motorcycles and one by one the riders became engulfed by the crowd. At one point Blaine felt his sleeve rip and his watch fall to the ground as he shoved people away. The agents felt as if they were fighting for their own lives.

By the time the presidential car arrived at the airport, just one motorcycle officer was still aboard his bike. The others had been overtaken by the swarming crowd. Grant and Blaine looked as if they'd been in a massive brawl, with their ripped clothes and bruised arms.

When Rowley and the follow-up car finally caught up, Rowley looked over to Grant and Blaine and with a huge grin on his face, gave them two thumbs-up.

Meanwhile, Godfrey was fuming. He couldn't wait to get out of the country. He turned to Rowley and said, "The Italians haven't changed since the last time I was here. The only difference is, now we can't shoot at 'em."

The Naples memory was still fresh in Jerry Blaine's mind as he directed his attention back to Chief Mullins and the Tampa officers.

"We appreciate that you have a number of good bike riders," Blaine said, "but with a motorcade this long, we're going to need them for intersection control. The Secret Service relies on the agents to respond to a person rushing the president's car. What we've seen happen so many times is that if the motorcycle misses the opportunity to force back an individual charging toward the car, the officer has to dump his bike and respond. That of course is a hazard for the motorcade and precious time is lost as well. We don't mind a spearhead formation or outriders, but we have a standard placement of motorcycles so they don't interfere with the path from the follow-up car to the limousine."

Blaine looked from one officer to the next, hoping he hadn't offended them. Fortunately, they were all nodding in understanding.

Blaine continued: "We can cover all that in our next meeting. For now, what I'd really like help with is the motorcade route."

Chief Mullins didn't hesitate. "Absolutely. Why don't you and Mr. Yeager take a drive with Captain Bowen, who's going to be coordinating everything you need for the route in terms of manpower and traffic diversions."

"Sounds great," Blaine said. "You've been a big help. Just one more thing . . . Would it be possible for you to set up a meeting on Thursday so I can brief all the agencies who will be assisting?"

"Consider it done," Mullins said.

WEDNESDAY, NOVEMBER 13, 1963

After checking into the Sheraton Dallas hotel the night before, Win Lawson had taken a walk around the downtown area. There had been some disturbing incidents in Dallas recently, and Lawson wanted to get a feel for the city's attitude. Just three weeks earlier, United Nations ambassador Adlai Stevenson was heckled as he gave a speech at the Adolphus Hotel on UN Day, and then was assaulted and spat on as he walked from the Dallas Memorial Auditorium to his waiting limousine. Tensions had been running high throughout the Southern states, as the divide between liberals and conservatives seemed to be growing wider all the time, mainly due to civil rights. President Kennedy had won 70 percent of the black vote in 1960, but by the summer of 1963, the lack of a civil rights bill had black leaders frustrated, and demonstrations were turning violent. At the end of August, more than two hundred thousand people—80 percent of whom were African-Americans—had marched on Washington, and when JFK met with Martin Luther King, Jr., in the White House, he promised to push Congress for a bill before the end of the year. But he knew as well as anybody that unless he gathered support, a civil rights bill could mean political suicide. He had to bolster support in key Southern states, and the two with the largest number of electoral votes were Florida and Texas.

In Dallas, it seemed to Win Lawson that the city had slowly but quietly been integrating blacks and whites. Schools and public places were mostly integrated, and even the upscale Neiman Marcus department store had hired a black hair stylist. But Forrest Sorrels, the Special Agent in Charge of the Dallas Field Office, had briefed him on some underlying issues that could potentially wreak havoc with the president's visit.

ATSAIC Art Godfrey had approved the switch between Jerry Blaine and Dave Grant so that now Grant would be assisting Win Lawson on the advance.

But, because the agents were spread so thin, Lawson would be handling the Dallas advance on his own until Dave Grant arrived on the nineteenth to give him some last-minute help. With the president scheduled to arrive on Friday, November 22, Lawson knew he'd have to have the advance plans well in place before Grant arrived.

Usually one of the first items to get settled was the motorcade route, but there was still a major piece of the president's visit to Dallas that was yet to be determined. After Air Force One landed at Love Field there would be a motorcade through downtown Dallas, ending up at a luncheon for 2,600 people, where President Kennedy would be the honored guest and speaker. What hadn't been decided yet was where the luncheon would be held. Behn wanted Lawson to check out both options and report back.

The first stop of the advance was to the Dallas Secret Service office. Win Lawson and Jack Puterbaugh had set up a meeting with SAIC Sorrels. Sorrels was Texan through and through. He had been in the Secret Service since the 1930s and knew every person of importance in Dallas.

"Good morning, Forrest," Win Lawson said with a genuine smile. He reached out to shake hands with Sorrels, who was wearing a western hat that mostly covered his thinning gray hair. "How have you been?"

Sorrels answered in his soft, steady Texas twang. "Well, you know how it is, Win, out here in the field. They keep giving us more and more cases to handle with the same amount of staff, so we're at the point where every agent is investigating about a hundred and fifty cases at a time."

"Yeah, I'd heard you guys were really strapped," Lawson replied. "I know Chief Rowley has been trying to get Congress to approve a budget increase, but it's politics as usual in Washington. You'd think when it came to protecting the president, they'd open up their purse strings a little."

Sorrels laughed. "Damn politicians. While they're bickering, we just keep doin' what we're doin'."

Jack Puterbaugh and Win Lawson briefed Sorrels and another agent on the tentative schedule.

"Well, obviously the first thing we need to do is get a decision on where they're going to have lunch," Sorrels said. "You've got the Women's Building at the fairgrounds and the Trade Mart, which is just off Stemmons Freeway, not far from here. I've got us appointments with some folks from the local host committee and they're gonna take us through both facilities today. There are drawbacks to both places, but I'll let you see for yourself."

Lawson was pleased that Sorrels had already done some of the legwork. Moreover, he was impressed that Sorrels would be working directly with him on the advance. In many field offices, the job was shuffled off to an assistant.

"Oh, and the chief of the police department, Jesse Curry, has called me a couple times already," Sorrels added. "He's eager to meet with us as soon as we know the plan."

"Okay, let's get moving, then," Lawson said as he picked up his briefcase and started heading for the door.

The Trade Mart was only five years old and was a modern structure with soaring ceilings. As he walked through the building, Win Lawson made notes as to what he saw were security issues. There were dozens of entrances into the building, plus a variety of ways to access the room that would hold the luncheon. The room was a sort of atrium that had catwalks and balconies on the second and third floors overlooking it. It would take a lot of manpower to secure every entrance and exit as well as the balconies.

As the group drove up to the Women's Building at Fair Park, Win Lawson could see immediately that it had a completely different feel. First of all, it was enormous.

"This is where they have exhibits during the state fair," Sorrels explained. "All kinds of handiwork and things like that. They tell me it's got forty-five thousand square feet and I'm guessing you could seat five thousand people in here."

"Yeah, but it's not exactly the kind of place to bring the President of the United States," Jack Puterbaugh noted. The building was old with low ceilings. All the piping and air-conditioning equipment that had been installed after the building was built was exposed. It was just plain ugly.

Lawson and Sorrels agreed.

"The security, however, would be a cinch," Lawson noted. There were just two end openings to the building and there was actually an area where you could drive a car into the facility.

Meanwhile, in Tampa, Agents Blaine and Yeager had split up the duties of meeting with representatives from the four different venues where President Kennedy would stop. Blaine drove the motorcade route suggested by the police and made notes of what he saw as potential problem areas where they'd need extra security. He and Yeager had agreed to meet back at the hotel at 6:00 to regroup.

"Hey, Jer, Arnie gave me the name of a good Cuban restaurant not too far from here. Are you up for some local culture?"

"Sure, that sounds super," Blaine said. "I just realized I didn't have lunch."

The restaurant turned out to be a popular hangout that served truly authentic Cuban fare. When Blaine and Yeager walked in, they heard nothing but Spanish being spoken. As a scantily dressed young lady with jet-black hair, hoop earrings, and a short skirt led them to their table, Blaine and Yeager noticed the other patrons glancing at them as they walked by. The two tall, blond-headed men in their gray suits looked completely out of place in the laid-back restaurant, where every other man was wearing a traditional Cuban-style white short-sleeved shirt and the ladies were in strappy sundresses.

Blaine didn't recognize anything on the menu, so Yeager ordered for them. *Lechon asado*, roast suckling pig, for himself and *vaca frita*, shredded skirt steak marinated in garlic and lime juice, for Blaine.

"And bring plenty of rice and beans," Yeager added.

The service was quick, the food was delicious, and laughter and conversation filled the air. As the agents ate, they surveyed the lively clientele, but didn't overhear or see anything remotely hostile.

"Hey, Jer," Frank said, "I keep meaning to ask you—Win Lawson told me to be sure and have you tell me about your Easter golfing experience with the Boss. He wouldn't tell me a thing, just kept laughing and said, 'You gotta hear it from Blaine.' "

Jerry broke into a grin and shook his head. It was Win's favorite story.

"Well, it was Easter weekend 1961 and we were down in Palm Beach. President Kennedy decided to go golfing with his father and a couple of friends. It was the first time he'd played since becoming president. And there was a big deal made of it because he wouldn't allow the press to come along. During the campaign, the Kennedy camp had routinely questioned the amount of golf Ike was playing when he should have been paying attention to more urgent issues, so President Kennedy didn't want any publicity.

"So," Jerry continued, "Win Lawson was with us on a three-week temporary assignment—before he became permanent—and since I was the senior agent, I had to instruct Win on how to conduct the surveillance on the golf course. As we're walking down the fairway, I'm telling him, 'You go out about two hundred to two hundred twenty-five yards, fade back into the rough, and keep an eye on the adjacent fairway to make sure there are no questionable people in the area.'

"Now, I had watched Ike play plenty of rounds of golf, and for some reason I guess I assumed that Kennedy would have the same tendency to hook left. So I told Win to take the left-hand side and I would cover the right."

Yeager shook his head and chuckled.

"I had told Win to watch carefully when each of the golfers teed off, just in case you needed to take cover if the ball headed your way," Blaine continued. "So, by protocol, the president teed off first. I watched him make contact with the ball and then I glanced over at Win to make sure he was in place, and I see him staring in my direction with his mouth wide open. The next thing I know, a golf ball in full flight hits me on the left side of my head. I immediately fell to my knees. The ground was spinning, but I was determined not to lose consciousness."

Yeager was trying so hard not to laugh, but suddenly he couldn't help himself. He could just picture it.

Jerry ignored Yeager's laughter and continued. "So I feel the side of my head and there's blood running down my face. By this time Win is standing over me asking if I'm okay. 'What happened?' I asked him."

Yeager was cracking up. "So how did Win explain it?"

"He said it made a thwacking noise and bounced right straight in the air. The president took a mulligan."

Blaine started laughing. "So I went to the hospital and had X-rays taken and everything was fine. Apparently my mother was right when she said I was thickheaded."

"Oh my God, Jer. That's a great story."

"But wait," Jerry said with a smile. "There's more. So, the press got hold of this and there were some reports in the newspaper. As it turned out, Kennedy was scheduled to make a speech in front of the American Newspaper Publishers Association a couple of weeks later. He opened the speech by saying something like 'I realize that your staff and photographers may be complaining that they don't enjoy the same green privileges at the local golf courses that they once did. It is true that my predecessor did not object as I do to pictures of one's golfing skill in action. But neither, on the other hand, did he ever bean a Secret Service man.' "

Yeager was in hysterics. "Just like him. I'm sure they loved it."

"Oh yeah, and for weeks afterward, the president would seek me out on post at the White House. He'd have a senator friend or somebody with him and he'd come up to me and say, 'Jerry, tell him how far out you were standing when I beaned you.'

" 'Mr. President,' I'd say, 'I was out three hundred yards and I assumed I was out of your range. You can really hit a golf ball.' He loved it. I swear every time he saw me, he'd ask me the same question. 'How far out were you standing when I beaned you?' "

Blaine and Yeager finished their meal, returned to the hotel, and made plans for the next day. They had the scheduled meeting with Chief Mullins and the various agencies that would be supplying security and emergency services. They also needed to get an update on Joseph Milteer—and the alleged plot to kill the president.

In Washington, Jerry Behn was sitting in his office when Win Lawson called from Dallas.

"Behn," Jerry Behn answered into the receiver.

"Hello, Jerry. It's Win. I wanted to give you an update on the two venues in Dallas."

Win explained the pros and cons of each facility, adding that there were some catering issues with the Women's Building, but he'd concluded that they could successfully secure either location.

"It'll just be a matter as to how we route the motorcade," Lawson said.

"Okay, thanks, Win," Behn said. "From what you're telling me, I'm guessing the White House is going to go with the Trade Mart, just because of the aesthetics. But hopefully I'll have a decision from O'Donnell by tomorrow."

Win Lawson was probably the most conscientious and thorough advance agent you could ask for. He'd proven that with the advance to Berlin, in June.

President Kennedy's tour through Ireland, Italy, and Germany had been a logistical nightmare for the Secret Service, and prior to the trip, the biggest concern was Berlin, where the wall that divided the city into East and West had become a symbol of the division between democracy and communism. SAIC Behn had assigned the Berlin advance to Win Lawson in part because he thought Win's precise, straightforward, and detail-oriented personality would mesh well with the German security people. Soviet premier Khrushchev had ordered the construction of the Berlin Wall in 1961 to stop the flood of people leaving communist-controlled East Germany for the West, and President Kennedy was deeply disturbed by the photographs and stories he'd seen of people being killed as they tried to climb over the wall to freedom. A primary reason for his trip to Europe was to see the situation for himself.

When Kennedy arrived in Berlin, it was clear that Win Lawson had done a brilliant job of working with the West German police to ensure the president's safety. As SAIC Behn stood alongside President Kennedy atop a viewing platform that provided a look over the wall and into East Berlin, the sight of East German security guards just yards away with automatic weapons was unnerving, but never did he feel that the president was in imminent danger. The emotional impact of seeing how the people of Berlin were isolated from their friends and relatives on the other side of the strictly guarded concrete block wall was unforgettable. When a million

people packed into Berlin's Rudolph Wilde Platz on June 26, 1963, to hear
the American president speak, the roar of the massive crowd was deaf-
ening. Many had tears in their eyes as President Kennedy proudly proclaimed that he'd stand alongside them in the fight for freedom, with one
short German phrase: *Ich bin ein Berliner*—I am a Berliner. It turned out
to be one of President Kennedy's finest hours, and it wouldn't have happened without Win Lawson.

Lawson wasn't a risk taker, and Behn knew if there were any concerns
in Dallas, Lawson wouldn't hesitate to tell him.

With his mind at ease about the venue issues, Behn turned to his bigger problem: where the heck was he going to come up with enough agents
to provide adequate protection for the president on these trips to Florida
and Texas?

With his most experienced agents out on advances, he'd have to call
in some extra help from PRS and some of the field offices. Using temporary help on such high-profile trips wasn't by any means ideal, but he just
didn't have enough bodies.

5

The Risks

If anyone is crazy enough to want to kill a president of the United States, he can do it. All he must be prepared to do is give his life for the president's.
—JOHN F. KENNEDY

THURSDAY, NOVEMBER 14, 1963

In Tampa, Jerry Blaine and Frank Yeager still had a huge amount of coordinating to do before the president arrived on Monday. They had to meet with the sponsors of each event, listen to the proposed plans, and respond with their approvals or rejections. At every venue Yeager and Blaine had to figure out exactly where the president would enter the facility, where the organizers intended his table or podium to be, where the restrooms were located, and whether there would be receiving lines before or after the event. Press arrangements had to be coordinated. Where would the press be set up? How many press passes were needed? Both Yeager and Blaine had done dozens of advances, so they'd developed certain routines, but still, the number of details that needed to be coordinated was staggering.

The agents collected the lists of all the people who would be in proximity to the president and sent the lists to Washington, where PRS and the Federal Bureau of Investigation would conduct background checks. After the lists had been checked and rechecked, the cleared names came back from headquarters to the Jacksonville Field Office via Teletype. The event sponsors would handle the identification checks at the door, with an agent nearby in case there were any conflicts.

After hearing about the tangled web of Cuban immigrants and their unaligned allegiance, Blaine was deeply concerned that the president's visit provided an opportunity for someone—or some group—to make a statement. It was only a year earlier that friction between Cuba and the United States had nearly sent the world into a nuclear war. The tension of those thirteen days in October 1962 was still as clear in Jerry Blaine's mind as if it had happened last week.

On October 15, 1962, Blaine and a new agent on the detail, Bob Burke, had flown to Springfield, Illinois, to do the advance for the president's planned visit there four days later. President Kennedy would be visiting the tomb of President Abraham Lincoln and giving a speech at the Illinois State Fairgrounds before flying on to Chicago for another event.

On the morning of October 16, McGeorge Bundy, President Kennedy's national security advisor, took the elevator to the president's quarters. Less than three hours later, every top-ranking military and security advisor had arrived at the White House and was filing into the Cabinet Room.

An American U-2 spy plane had photographed nuclear missile sites being built on the island of Cuba by Soviet soldiers, and the missiles were pointing directly at the United States. President Kennedy knew that the Soviets had installed defensive weaponry on the island, and had believed Premier Nikita Khrushchev's repeated promises that those were the only missiles in Cuba's arsenal. Kennedy had warned Khrushchev that if the Soviets ever introduced offensive weapons, "the gravest issues would arise." The photographs provided conclusive evidence that Khrushchev had been lying, and now Kennedy had no choice but to respond. The question was, how? And to what extent?

In order not to arouse suspicions with the media or the public, President Kennedy tried to maintain his schedule as much as possible, while the Executive Committee—"ExComm"—of the National Security Council worked on a strategy to deal with what would become known as the Cuban Missile Crisis.

When President Kennedy arrived in Springfield, Illinois, on October 19, Blaine could see that he was clearly preoccupied. The president moved into the crowd that had come to greet him at the airport, but the usually affable and gregarious Kennedy looked as if he were merely going through the motions. It was the same when he visited Lincoln's tomb and made his speech. The audience wouldn't have noticed anything perceptibly wrong, but Blaine had no doubt something was deeply troubling the president. He'd never seen Kennedy like this before.

The president flew on to Chicago, but during the flight, word came from the White House that the situation required his immediate return to the capital. As soon as he landed in Chicago, the president feigned a head cold and Air Force One headed to Washington, D.C.

The following day, Blaine was on duty with the 4:00 to midnight shift when President Kennedy and his advisors agreed that the United States would order a blockade or "quarantine" by U.S. Navy ships around Cuba to prevent the introduction of more missiles. Kennedy would demand that the Soviets withdraw the missiles already there and, at that point, the next move was Khrushchev's.

The standoff had worldwide implications. In 1961, Khrushchev and the East Germans had built a wall around West Berlin as a stopgap measure to halt the exodus of East Germans from Soviet-controlled areas, and Kennedy had promised the one and a half million West Berliners that the United States would protect them from Soviet takeover. Kennedy saw the installation of missiles in Cuba as a preparatory move to a showdown in Berlin, and clearly, Khrushchev was testing JFK's resolve. It was time to let the American people know about the Soviet missiles in Cuba.

On October 22, 1962, television photographers and reporters packed into the Oval Office with their bulky black cameras and radio transmitters. Agents Jerry Blaine and Dennis Halterman stood by as President Kennedy, sitting behind his big mahogany desk, somberly addressed the American people on live television and radio.

When the president signed off and stood up from his chair, the room was dead quiet.

President Kennedy walked out of the office with a hollow look in his eyes and proceeded to the elevator that would take him to the Situation Room, in the basement of the West Wing. Agent Halterman stayed on post outside the Oval Office door while Blaine followed the president into the elevator.

President Kennedy looked weary and as if he'd aged a decade in the past week. He was deep in thought. Blaine stood in silence, wondering what the consequences of the president's announcement would be.

Inside the Situation Room, where the red phone with a direct line to Moscow sat conspicuously beneath the projected map of Cuba, the ExComm members stood as President Kennedy walked into the room. Blaine closed the door and waited outside, where all he could hear was the sound of muffled voices.

The briefing was short, and when the president walked out a few minutes later, Blaine again followed him into the elevator.

As soon as the doors closed, President Kennedy turned to Blaine and said, "You know, Jerry, we're in a bit of a pickle."

Blaine didn't know what to say. The world was on the verge of nuclear war. What could you say to the man who held the balance in his hands?

"Yes, sir," Blaine replied. "I know."

"Now, you know that if anything happens, you're coming with me."

"Yes, Mr. President. Of course." If it appeared that the Soviets were going to fire the nuclear missiles, Blaine and the rest of the Kennedy Detail agents would move swiftly with the president to a safe and undisclosed location. That was understood. Blaine didn't understand what Kennedy was getting at.

Kennedy looked directly into Blaine's eyes. There was intensity, yet concern, in the president's gaze. Blaine had never communicated with the president on a matter of state with such dire implications.

"Have you thought about what your family will do?" President Kennedy asked. "You need to be prepared."

The elevator stopped, and in the moment before the doors slid open, Blaine realized what President Kennedy was trying to tell him.

"Thank you, sir. I understand."

At home that night, Jerry slept fitfully as he wrestled over the very real possibility that he would be in a safe bunker with the president while Joyce and one-year-old Kelly could be exposed to a nuclear attack. He wanted desperately to talk to Joyce about it, but he couldn't. To divulge something of this magnitude would be breaking the Secret Service code.

In the days that followed, Blaine and the other agents noticed the president seeking their thoughts on the standoff. He'd come out of the Cabinet Room strategy sessions with his top advisors, turn to whichever agent happened to be on post outside the door, and ask something like, "What would you do in this situation?" It was as if he hoped somebody would come back with a solution his advisors had overlooked.

The agents would usually answer along the lines of, "You have no alternative but to see it through, Mr. President."

On October 24, Russian ships carrying missiles to Cuba turned back, and four days after that, Khrushchev agreed to withdraw the missiles and dismantle the missile sites. In exchange, Kennedy agreed not to invade Cuba.

Moments after he and Khrushchev came to an agreement, President Kennedy walked out of the Cabinet Room, where Jerry was on post outside the door.

"I think we could all use a trip to Palm Springs. What do you think, Jerry?"

In typical fashion, the president had broken the tension with levity. He'd thwarted nuclear war, at least for the time being, and a weekend in Palm Springs sounded like a damn fine idea.

The memories of the Cuban Missile Crisis and the subsequent release of the Bay of Pigs prisoners were constantly in the back of Agent Blaine's mind as he went through the advance checklist for Tampa. Blaine and Yeager had just three more days to make sure all the details were in place.

At the four different stops, President Kennedy would be speaking in front of more than twenty-five thousand people. There was no way every person could be background-checked or searched for weapons upon entering the facility. And then there was the motorcade, for which more than one hundred thousand people were expected to line the streets of downtown Tampa. If the threat revealed by Joseph Milteer to the informant was authentic, and there was a plan to kill the president, Tampa would be the ideal place.

In Dallas, Agent Win Lawson and the Dallas Special Agent in Charge Forrest Sorrels spent the morning at Love Field, meeting with the director and assistant director of aviation. There would be three aircraft arriving— Air Force One, the vice president's plane, and the press plane—and Win had to figure out where the aircraft should best be "spotted." A spot would be painted on the tarmac for each of the planes so the pilots would know exactly where to park. Then Win would determine where to put up fencing and other barriers for the public to stand behind, as well as a viewing platform for the press.

The arrival of Air Force One was always an impressive sight and the local media loved to cover it live. The public arrivals, however, created tense moments for the Secret Service agents. Ideally the president would get off the plane and walk directly to the waiting limousine with the agents providing an envelope of security around him. But President Kennedy found it difficult to ignore a screaming crowd, especially when the television cameras were rolling. The agents never knew exactly what the president would do, but they'd learned to expect him to dive into the crowd and shake as many hands as possible.

With the airport arrangements under way, the next item of priority was to figure out the motorcade route. Sorrels had mapped out several options, so as soon as the meetings with the airport directors concluded, they decided to drive one of the routes. The Trade Mart had been selected for the luncheon, so the final leg of the routing was clear. There was no option off Main Street other than the right turn on Houston Street for a short block, followed by a sharp left on Elm Street. The entrance to Stemmons Freeway was just a few hundred yards or so beyond that, with a right-lane merge after the underpass. The decision that had to be made was how the motorcade would get from Love Field to Main Street, where the majority of the crowds would be waiting.

The timing of events was planned to the minute, so the path the motorcade took was somewhat dependent on the time available. The arrival at Love Field was scheduled for 11:40 A.M. and the president was due to arrive at the luncheon at 12:30. You had to allow a few minutes for a receiving line at the bottom of the stairwell off the airplane, followed by a few minutes in which the president would invariably greet the crowd. That left thirty minutes for the motorcade procession.

Sorrels took the wheel so Lawson could take notes and pay attention to any security concerns like overpasses or bridges. They pulled out of Love Field and Win started timing.

"Stay around thirty miles an hour out here by the airport," Win said, "but as we start getting into more populated areas, we'll have to slow it way down."

As they neared the downtown area, Sorrels checked the odometer and slowed down to about fifteen miles per hour.

"That's good," Win said.

"Now we're about to turn onto Main Street," Sorrels said. "Once we get onto Main, there's only one practical way to get to the freeway."

There was little traffic at this time of day, and Win noticed that even the sidewalks seemed sparsely used for a city this size. There were a few businessmen dressed in suits who appeared to be heading back to their offices, and a handful of ladies dressed in cotton dresses and cardigan sweaters carrying shopping bags from Neiman Marcus and the Florsheim shoe store, but other than that, the downtown area was fairly quiet.

Win knew that the ambiance would change dramatically on the day of the motorcade. He tried to imagine the sidewalks jam-packed with people yelling and clapping. As the car passed by Walgreens drugstore, Win noticed a small balcony on the second floor of a building on the other side of the street. No doubt there would be people standing out there for a glimpse of the president and Mrs. Kennedy. He made a note to make sure officers were posted nearby to keep it under observation.

Win turned his head up and as his eyes scanned the tall buildings lining both sides of the street, he realized that many of the windows were open. It was indeed a warm day for this time of year.

"This is like a canyon," Win said. "We have to assume the car will be open. Unless it's raining, I know the president will want the top off. With all the open windows, it creates quite an exposure. Somebody could easily lob something onto the motorcade or take a pot shot. Will we have plenty of law enforcement personnel posted along here?"

"We'll have to talk to Chief Curry about it tomorrow," Sorrels said. "Obviously there's no way to check every building, but I imagine he's gonna do whatever he can. After what happened with Ambassador Stevenson you can bet Curry will have his men out in full force. He sure as hell doesn't want an embarrassing incident like that when the president is here."

Win was taking notes as they continued down the twelve-block stretch.

Even with police officers monitoring the crowd, he knew how easily things could change.

"Yeah, well, we'll have to make sure they clearly understand their roles. I don't expect it being a problem, but then again I didn't expect it to be a problem in Ireland, either," Win said with a chuckle.

Sorrels turned his head and saw Win smiling and shaking his head.

"What happened?" Sorrels asked.

"It was crazy," Win said. "The advance team had given the Irish law enforcement specific instructions about how to observe the crowd, and the importance of keeping their backs to the president's limousine when his car rolled by. But I don't think anybody expected the massive crowds that turned out for the motorcade. The pubs were empty, let me tell you, and every man, woman, and child in the city of Dublin had come to welcome their Irish son."

Sorrels laughed as he slowed the car to a stop at the red light at the corner of Main and Field.

"We didn't have the bubble top, just the Secret Service open-top follow-up car, so the president was riding in that. Jerry Blaine and I were standing on the running boards on either side of the president—which he didn't like because we blocked the view of him from the crowds—but he realized that if we weren't there, somebody was gonna jump right in the car with him.

"Well, all of a sudden, the motorcycle escort got squeezed up in front of the car and suddenly a huge mass of people surged toward us. I got shoved backward and ended up right in the president's lap!"

Sorrels was cracking up. "Oh God, what did Kennedy say?"

"Well, I don't remember him saying anything. What I do remember is that I looked up and saw half a dozen Irish cops mixed in with the crowd and reaching their hands toward the president trying to shake his hand!"

The light turned green and Sorrels continued down Main Street. "Well, I can assure you we won't have that problem here in Dallas," Sorrels said. "Chief Curry and his men understand how serious this is. They'll do a good job."

Win knew the scenario was unlikely in Dallas, but even still, as he looked up again at all the open windows, he was concerned about the exposure. Fortunately they'd have SS100X in Dallas, which had the rear steps and handholds so two agents could be perched directly behind the president and could react quickly. He'd be sure to tell Roy Kellerman, the Special Agent in Charge for the Texas trip, that when the motorcade was driving through downtown, agents would need to be on the back of the car.

A few blocks farther down, Main Street intersected with Houston.

"Okay now, up here this is Dealey Plaza. We've got to turn right onto Houston here to get to the Stemmons entry ramp," Sorrels said as he steered the car onto Houston Street.

Win looked down at the map. The way Sorrels was going they'd have to make a sharp left turn at the next block. "Why can't we go straight here and then hop over to the entrance on Stemmons?"

"You'll see," Sorrels said. "It's a traffic hazard."

He drove the short block—it was really a half block—on Houston and then at the next light, took the sharp left onto Elm Street in front of the Texas School Book Depository building.

The road curved, dipped down a hill, with the grassy, parklike Dealey Plaza on both the left and right. About fifty yards later was the right-hand merge onto Stemmons Freeway, just beyond the triple underpass.

"Look here," Sorrels said as he pointed to the left-hand side of the car. "There's a cement curb over here, designed to keep the traffic from cutting from Main Street to Elm Street onto the freeway. There's no other way—unless you jump the curb—to get onto Stemmons going to the Trade Mart."

Now it made sense to Lawson. Sorrels was right. If the motorcade procession was to go down Main Street, this was the only option to get to the Trade Mart.

Sorrels merged onto Stemmons Freeway and sped up to keep up with the fast-moving traffic. Win Lawson checked his watch to see how the timing was working out. So far, it seemed just about right.

"Now, one more issue here," Sorrels said as he checked his mirrors and turned to look over his right shoulder. "You've got to cross these five lanes of traffic to get over to the right lane so you can exit for the Trade Mart."

Sorrels waited for a break in traffic and then moved over one lane, then another, and another, while Win Lawson took more notes.

"We'll have to make sure this portion of the freeway is blocked off for five or ten minutes before the motorcade gets here, then," Lawson said. He was glad he'd driven the route with Sorrels to see all the obstacles that needed to be worked out with Chief Curry during their meeting the next day.

As they pulled up to the Trade Mart, Lawson looked down at his watch and saw that it had taken exactly five minutes to get here from Dealey Plaza. The entire route had clocked at thirty-eight minutes. Perfect timing.

6

The First Lady's Detail

*I am the man who accompanied Jacqueline Kennedy to
Paris, and I have enjoyed it.*
—JOHN F. KENNEDY

Her husband had been Jacqueline Kennedy's Secret Service agent for
three years, and still Gwen Hill had never met the first lady.

"I just don't understand it, Clint," she said as she watched her husband
pack his suitcase for another weekend in Atoka. He had the suitcase laid
out on the bed and was pulling socks and undershirts from the dresser
drawer. "Why couldn't you have just waved us over and introduced us?"

Agent Clint Hill had gotten tickets for Gwen and their two sons, Corey
and Chris, to see the Scottish Black Watch military brigade performance
on the White House lawn two days earlier. Gwen had gone to the beauty
shop to have her hair frosted, and had taken special care with her outfit
and makeup, with the assumption that she'd be meeting the first lady and
maybe the president, too.

"I told you, I was working," Clint said. "My job is to protect her. It just
seemed inappropriate to introduce you while I was on duty."

"Well, I think I'm the only Secret Service wife who hasn't met her,"
Gwen said. She was holding two-year-old Corey on one hip and shifted
him to the other side. "Doesn't that seem ironic?"

103

Clint closed the hard Samsonite suitcase and locked the clips next to the handle. He pulled the suitcase off the bed and walked over to Gwen. Several half-filled moving boxes were scattered around the room, and Clint pushed one to the side with his foot as he walked by. Now that their two boys were seven and two years old, Clint and Gwen had realized they needed more room, and a quieter location. Gwen had found a larger apartment in Alexandria for just a few dollars more a month. They could move in on December 1, although Clint still didn't know when his schedule would allow him to take a day off to move everything to the new place.

"I guess I didn't realize how important it was to you," he said as he set the suitcase on the floor. "The next time there's an opportunity, I promise I'll make sure you get to meet her."

At almost six feet tall, Clint was a good eight inches taller than his wife. He leaned over to give her a quick kiss and pulled her petite frame in close for a hug.

"Okay," she said. She could never stay angry with him for long. "Promise?" she asked.

"Promise," he said.

When Clint had come home from the meeting with Secret Service chief Baughman right after Kennedy's election and told Gwen he'd been "demoted" to the First Lady's Detail, she'd felt sorry for him. But as the months and years went on, the pity had eventually disappeared and—while she wouldn't admit it—had turned to jealousy.

It was one thing when your husband was on the President's Detail and traveling all the time. It was a whole different issue when your husband spent every weekend and holiday and nearly every day in between with the most idolized woman in the world. It had gotten to the point that when Gwen met someone new and they asked what her husband did for a living, she answered, "He works for the government—Treasury Department." She didn't want to have to explain that her husband was Jackie Kennedy's Special Agent in Charge, but the closest she'd come to the first lady was watching her recent tour of the White House on television.

As for Clint Hill, it hadn't taken long for him to get over the feeling that he was "second team." From the moment he met Mrs. Kennedy, there had been a kind of quiet understanding between the two of them. Hill quickly realized that while being on Mrs. Kennedy's detail wasn't perhaps as rigorous or high profile as the President's Detail, the job certainly had its own challenges. He also realized he was now responsible for what was most important to the president—his wife and children.

Jackie was eight months pregnant when Hill was first assigned as the number two man on her detail in November 1960, and while her husband went to Palm Beach to plan his administration, she stayed at their home in Georgetown with daughter Caroline, to be close to her doctors. Barely two weeks after Agent Hill met Mrs. Kennedy, she went into early labor. It took President-elect Kennedy several hours to get back to Washington, leaving Clint Hill to pace outside the delivery room when John, Jr., was born on November 25, 1960. It was to be the first of many bonding experiences between the first lady and her trusted agent, Mr. Hill.

Clint had a quick yet subtle sense of humor that made Mrs. Kennedy laugh, and his gentle and confident manner made her feel comfortable and secure. Unlike her husband, Jacqueline Bouvier Kennedy didn't need to be in the limelight. She had a great appreciation for the arts, a deep love for animals, and was intent on making sure her children grew up as unspoiled as possible, despite the fact that they had been born into one of the wealthiest families in America. Not to mention that they were the children of the President of the United States of America. Jackie had just a few close friends outside the family, and as she spent more time with Clint Hill than anyone else, she grew to rely on him for friendship as well as protection.

As Mrs. Kennedy settled into her role as first lady she realized she had certain obligations, as well as opportunities, to make a difference in the world. She'd always been fascinated by India and Pakistan, and when she proposed an ambassadorial trip to her husband, he was all for it. President Kennedy called on their good friend John Kenneth Galbraith—who happened to be the ambassador to India—to help with the arrangements.

In early February 1962, Clint Hill called Jerry Blaine. Even though their wives had become close friends and spent a lot of time together, because of the president's and the first lady's separate travel schedules, Blaine and Hill rarely had time to catch up outside of work.

"Hey, Jer. It's Clint."

"Clint, how are you? Where've you been?"

"Oh, you know, just living the good life at Glen Ora," Clint said.

Blaine laughed. Glen Ora had been the Kennedys' weekend retreat in Middleburg, Virginia, before Atoka was built. There was very little going on there other than Mrs. Kennedy's daily horseback ride or a leisurely walk through the woods, and while Jackie loved the place, the Kennedy Detail agents thought of it as a professional rest stop to be used as a reprieve after working weeks on end without a break. Clint wound up spending considerable time there simply because Mrs. Kennedy did.

"Yeah, I heard Paolella has turned into quite the equestrian," Blaine said with a chuckle.

Agent Joe Paolella had come back from a weekend on duty in Glen Ora and told the story of how he nearly paralyzed the first lady.

"Oh, geez," Clint said. "What a disaster that was. Mrs. Kennedy wanted to go for a ride, so we'd gotten the saddle on the horse and next thing I know, she turns to Joe and says in her sweet little voice, 'Agent Paolella, could you give me a hand?' "

On the other end of the phone Blaine was cracking up. Clint's impression of Mrs. Kennedy's voice was hilariously accurate.

"So she turns toward the horse and puts her foot in the air for Joe to cup his hands and give her a lift to the saddle," Clint continued. "Well, you know Paolella. He's got the big muscles, which he likes to show off, so what does he do? He grabs her by the waist and lifts her up over the saddle and then he lets her go. Literally throws her over the horse."

Blaine had heard the story, but to hear Clint tell it was priceless. He was doubled over with laughter.

"So I see Mrs. Kennedy fall to the ground on the other side of the horse and rush over to make sure she hasn't broken her neck. Thank God she was fine, but I was about to rip into Paolella when Mrs. Kennedy looks up at me and says, 'Mr. Hill, perhaps we need to give Mr. Paolella instructions on how to give a lady a hand into the saddle.' "

"Oh God, Clint," Blaine said through his laughter, "when Joe told me the story I said, 'Well, that wasn't the brightest way to get out of Glen Ora duty,' but who knows, after that he may never have to go back again."

On the other end of the phone Clint was shaking his head. "Yeah, well, I was just happy there weren't any photographers around. I could just see the headlines: 'Secret Service Agents Nearly Kill the First Lady.' "

Blaine was doubled over. It was only funny because it was so true.

"Anyway, Jerry, the reason I called . . ."

"Yeah?"

"I was wondering, are you up for some curry and chicken tandoori?"

"What? Sure," Blaine replied. "Name the place."

"How about New Delhi? Mrs. Kennedy's planning a visit to India and Pakistan, so Jerry Behn told me to pick my team. I need advance people. Are you interested?"

"Sounds great. When do we leave?"

"I'm just now working out the details with the White House and State Department," Clint said. "Ambassador Galbraith has got a crazy, ambitious schedule laid out, so I'm trying to rein it in a bit, but we're looking at sometime in the next two weeks. She's taking her sister Lee and the visit for now is off the record. Probably won't be announced until after we've departed."

"Count me in," Blaine said.

The Islamists and Hindus of India had been in constant conflict during the British rule of India, and when India won her independence after World War II, the clash between the two ideological and religious groups escalated into massive violence that cost the lives of millions on both sides. The end result of the conflict was to partition the Muslims into Pakistan while leaving India largely Hindu. Both countries were vying for the attention of the United States, but it was their historically dynamic and grandiose cultures that enthralled Mrs. Kennedy.

The first lady's four-day trip would cover New Delhi, Agra, Jaipur, Udaipur, and Benares in India, along with a few stops in Pakistan. Every city would need to be advanced by the Secret Service, but since the First Lady's Detail consisted only of two agents—Clint Hill and Special Agent in Charge Jim Jeffries—a bunch of agents needed to be pulled from the president's and vice president's details, as well as a number of field agents. Mrs. Kennedy's jaunt to Southeast Asia with her sister, Lee Radziwill, was no minor undertaking.

On February 16, 1962, fourteen Secret Service agents—including Clint Hill, Jerry Blaine, Dave Grant, Bill Skiles, Paul Rundle, and Ron Pontius—set off for India on Pan American Airways. Two days later—after stops in London, Frankfurt, Munich, Istanbul, Beirut, and Tehran—they arrived in New Delhi.

Shortly after checking into the Ashoka Hotel, the Secret Service team received word that Mrs. Kennedy would have to delay her visit for a few days. Additionally, in the two days they'd been traveling, several more stops in Pakistan had been added to the agenda. The only sensible option was for the agents to stay in India, work the advances, and wait for Mrs. Kennedy's arrival. The "few days" ended up being six weeks. Somebody in Washington calculated that it was cheaper to leave the agents in India for the six weeks rather than have them make the same trip twice. The Indian government was so eager to please that they invited the agents to stay as their guests and offered to pick up the cost of the hotel rooms. This left the fourteen agents with some things they weren't used to: a bit of extra pocket money from their unused per diem allowance, and free time.

Not ones to remain idle, the Secret Service detail called upon their Indian government security hosts for suggestions of challenging adventures or travel agendas to fill up their newfound time. The agents had split up into seven two-man advance teams and the teams inevitably turned competitive as they tried to outdo each other with creative and diverse activities. The teams would take off on their separate adventures and each weekend meet back in New Delhi, where the Marines posted at the U.S. embassy would throw a party for the agents. The parties were great opportunities to unwind and embellish on their various escapades.

While working on the advance plans for Agra, Jerry Blaine and Forrest Guthrie were in a car with a chatty Indian driver when an enormous black cloud appeared out of nowhere. The driver slammed on the brakes and screamed to the agents to roll up their windows. An instant later, the inside of the car was pitch-black as the car was immersed in a swarm of locusts. Conversation was impossible over the roar of the buzzing wings and the sound of the large insects slamming into the car. Fifteen minutes later, the daylight began to reappear through the slimy brown juice that had coated the windows. When it was all over, the driver got outside, wiped the windows, and continued with the tour, leaving Blaine and Guthrie to wonder whether this was a normal, everyday occurrence.

This was nothing compared to the adventure story Agent Paul Rundle came back with that week. Rundle, an avid hunter, had learned from a Marine at the U.S. embassy that a hunt was on for a man-eating Bengal tiger that had been terrorizing villages, and he offered to help. Rundle and the Marine joined up with the Indian scout who was responsible for controlling the hunt, and were loath to discover that the guides were planning to use the remains of a human as bait, figuring the tiger would return to finish off the carcass. Instead, the two Americans suggested they kill a nilgai—a wild, grass-eating animal similar to an antelope, only much larger, sometimes reaching 1,500 pounds—and use that as bait. The Indian guide agreed, and they were successful in bagging a large nilgai on the first day. Now they had to set up a blind on the ground where they could wait out the tiger, which hunted at night.

For three nights, Agent Paul Rundle and the Marine waited in the blind with the Indian hunter, often thinking that a tall tree might be a better hiding spot. This was, after all, a man-eating tiger. Numerous smaller game came to sniff the dead nilgai, but the waiting hunters shooed them away. After three nights with no sign of the tiger, Rundle and the Marine returned to the embassy, exhausted and disappointed that they'd been unsuccessful.

The Marines had challenged the Secret Service agents to a softball game—which would become a weekly competition—and despite an error by Paul Rundle, who was suffering from lack of sleep, the Kennedy Detail agents squeaked out a one-run victory. The good fortune was that the Marine hunting companion, who was similarly exhausted, dropped a fly ball, which allowed the winning run. The agents also had a ringer in that Agent Larry Short was their pitcher. Unbeknownst to the Marines, Short had pitched AAA softball prior to joining the Secret Service.

Undaunted, Paul Rundle the next week set out to hunt ducks. There were numerous ducks and geese, which had flown south from the Russian grain fields. The ducks were larger than the American variety and because of concern over rumors of nuclear testing fallout, the locals wanted nothing to do with the potentially radioactive ducks. However, this did not deter Rundle. He set out with his Marine friend and they ended up at a lake encircled by a tramway system and noisy traffic. With no dog for a retriever, they knew that if they got one, finding the damn thing when it dropped—they'd need to bring it back to the embassy as proof of their success—was going to be an even bigger challenge. After a short while a flock of ducks flew over the lake and Paul shot a couple of them. Before he had time to blink, two boys in their underwear came running from behind and dove into the lake to retrieve the downed birds. Only in India.

The sights in India ranged from magnificent to indescribably wretched. At one end of the spectrum was extreme wealth, epitomized by the Taj Mahal, while at the other end was mind-numbing poverty, the likes of which the agents could never have even imagined. In some places, maimed children begged for food and lived in squalor while lepers roamed the streets threatening to grab you and share their disease if you didn't give them a few rupees. Cows, monkeys, and other animals protected by the Hindu religion roamed freely on the highways, stalling traffic while the travelers seemed to take it all in stride. But perhaps the most stifling and unfamiliar sensation was the heavy, putrid haze that constantly filled the air—the result of elephant dung being burned for cooking fuel combined with the ash and smoke of the bodies being burned on funeral pyres during the traditional Hindu outdoor cremations. The oppressive smog seemed to level off around the sixth floor of the Ashoka Hotel. Fortunately, Clint Hill had arranged for all the agents' rooms to be above that level.

Gordon Parks from the White House Communications Agency accompanied the agents on the trip, and his first task was to set up a radio connection to the White House in one of the hotel rooms. The agents tried to use the radio to call home, but the connection was so bad and so little was interpreted during the conversations that it seemed a worthless exercise. Finally, they all agreed to tell their wives and families that the radio broke down.

In the meantime, while the two-man teams of agents were finding unique ways to fill the time, Clint Hill, as the advance coordinator, was given the task of working with Ambassador Kenneth Galbraith. Galbraith was a brilliant economist who had been appointed by President Kennedy as the U.S. ambassador to India, and at six feet seven inches tall, he was an imposing character. He was thrilled that Jackie was coming to India and had an overwhelming desire to show her as much as possible. Every afternoon, Clint would meet Galbraith at the ambassador's residence, and over a cup or two of tea, Galbraith would lay out his latest plan. One day he was adding Hyderabad, the next a jaunt to Bangalore. Clint could only stare in amazement at the ever-expanding itinerary. If the ambassador got his way, it would be another six weeks before the agents and Mrs. Kennedy would return back home.

Because of the thirteen-hour time difference, Clint would have to wait until midnight to call Washington with the latest updates. President Kennedy was reviewing the plans and was not at all in favor of Jackie extending the trip. With such sensitive negotiations going on behind the scenes, Clint didn't want to use the embassy phone or radio since his communication would undoubtedly be passed back to the ambassador, and thus he had no choice but to use the shortwave radio phone in the hotel room. But just as when the agents called home, the transmission was terrible. Clint had to deal with echoes, delays, and often, total fade-out. By the time he delivered the latest plan and received the response, it was usually three in the morning before he got to bed. The next afternoon he would have to renegotiate the schedule with the ambassador.

When the Indian government heard that Jackie was following her trip to India with an equivalent trip through Pakistan, they rescinded their generous offer to pay for the agents' hotel rooms. This created a big problem for a few of the guys who had already spent the per diem money on souvenirs and gifts. They were left with a meager budget for the rest of the trip.

Paul Rundle and Dave Grant were sent ahead to Pakistan to handle the advance in Lahore, and once again found themselves with a couple of extra days. There was no big-game hunting there, but somehow the Japanese government learned of the two American Secret Service agents' presence, and Rundle and Grant were enlisted to work the follow-up car for the crown prince of Japan and his wife during their short visit to the city. Between the tiger hunt and his stint working for the Japanese, Rundle definitely won the prize for the most adventuresome schedule, while the rest of the agents shook their heads wondering what would have been the ramifications if there'd been an assassination attempt on the crown prince, or an unfortunate incident with the tiger.

There is a belief in India that certain noble people are closer to God, and if you can touch them, perhaps their holiness will rub off on you. Some of the agents had experienced the consequences of this when President Eisenhower had traveled to India and the police had had to break out truncheons to beat off the surging crowds as they attempted to touch the American president. Because of Jacqueline Kennedy's extreme popularity, the agents were genuinely concerned with keeping the first lady's visit as private as possible. She was extremely uncomfortable with crowds, and they knew she would be mortified if she witnessed anybody being beaten—especially if it was due to her presence.

By the time Special Agent in Charge Jim Jeffries arrived with the first lady and her sister, Clint and the advance agents had a good feeling for the Indian culture and had tried to plan for every foreseeable crisis. It was suggested that a suitcase be filled with Kraft macaroni and cheese dinners, processed cheese, and saltine crackers just in case the Indian cuisine didn't agree with Mrs. Kennedy, and to give her the option of eating something familiar prior to the official dinners. One thing the Secret Service never anticipated, however, wound up becoming a problem for the White House Social Office and the State Department Office of the Chief of Protocol.

It's customary for visiting dignitaries to present their hosts with gifts—something from the visitor's home country. The gifts that had been selected by somebody in Protocol for Jackie Kennedy to hand out to her Indian hosts turned out to be a variety of picture frames covered in cowhide. Since cows are considered sacred in India, the frames were completely inappropriate—and could have potentially caused an international embarrassment. The U.S. embassy staff in New Delhi had to scurry around and find some other suitable gifts. The first lady wound up handing out sterling silver picture frames to her royal hosts that were *made in India.*

Clint Hill had given the advance agents detailed instructions as to what Mrs. Kennedy and her sister wanted to do on the trip, along with specific directives as to what should be avoided. Unfortunately, Ambassador Galbraith and the Indian government officials had their own ideas, which made for strained relations during the four-day visit.

At the Taj Mahal, in Agra, one of the hosts convinced Jackie and Lee to take impromptu rides on an elephant and a camel, which had not been on the planned agenda. Mrs. Kennedy and her sister were laughing with delight as they bounced along, seated in a regal throne on top of the elephant, but the camel was a different story. As the Indian press photographers started snapping away at the image of the first lady and her sister seated sideways on the camel saddle, Agents Blaine and Guthrie suddenly realized the shots would be extremely embarrassing as the two sisters were both wearing dresses. The agents signaled, as discreetly as they could, for them to cross their legs.

Whether it was because of the camel ride or some other behind-the-scenes problem, halfway through the trip Mrs. Kennedy's SAIC Jim Jeffries was called back to Washington for reassignment, and Clint Hill, who was in Karachi, Pakistan, at the time, suddenly became the Special Agent in Charge of the First Lady's Detail.

In Pakistan, things were even more intriguing. One of the stops was Peshawar—a city adjacent to Afghanistan and the Khyber Pass that was home to various Pashtun tribes that operated under a warlord system. However, the rough, sinister-looking leaders with their long gray beards and unkempt hair took the agents under their protection and went out of their way to be good hosts. As was their custom, the Pashtuns insisted on slaughtering a goat to honor Mrs. Kennedy's visit. It was a sight the agents knew would horrify the animal-loving first lady, and while it took a bit of wrangling, the agents negotiated to have the sacrificial slaughter occur as Mrs. Kennedy was departing. Clint Hill tried to distract the first lady so she wouldn't notice the bleating cry of the poor goat as they sped away from the village.

One of the main reasons for traveling to Pakistan was for Jackie to visit Pakistan's president, Ayub Khan, in Lahore. Khan had traveled to Washington the year before and he and Mrs. Kennedy had discovered their shared passion for horses. Jackie's trip coincided with the International Horse Show in Lahore, and after attending the show together, Khan presented her with a magnificent dark chestnut-colored stallion named Sardar as a gift. She was thrilled with the thoughtful present, and it was left to the two governments to figure out how to get the animal back to the United States. Sardar spent several weeks in quarantine while Jerry Blaine and several of the other agents returned to Washington with a nasty intestinal bug that lingered for weeks.

Mrs. Kennedy had thoroughly enjoyed the trip, and one day upon their return, she was reminiscing with Clint about all the magnificent things they'd seen. When Clint didn't offer an appropriately enthusiastic response to one of Mrs. Kennedy's questions, she looked at him and asked, "Doesn't anything ever impress you, Mr. Hill?"

• • •

Eventually Sardar from Pakistan ended up at Glen Ora, joining a menagerie that resided there or at the White House. There were the ponies: Macaroni, Caroline's favorite, and Tex, a gift from Vice President Johnson. The dogs: Charlie, the family's beloved Welsh terrier; Shannon, a cocker spaniel; Wolf, an Irish wolfhound; Pushinka, the puppy of Soviet space dog Strelka; and Clipper, a German shepherd that flunked obedience training class. There was also a variety of birds, a cat, and a rabbit. It was like the United Nations for animals.

At Glen Ora, whenever Jackie wanted to go anywhere, she just called Mr. Hill and they took off in the station wagon that was kept at the farm. One day they were on the way back to the house, driving down a dirt road, when the car came upon a turtle crossing the road. The turtle's shell camouflaged into the brown dirt, and Clint saw it a moment too late. He cringed when he heard a crunch and a crack.

Mrs. Kennedy turned to him in horror, and exclaimed, "Mr. Hill! What have you done?"

Hill apologized profusely, but he could tell she was really upset. She never mentioned it again, but from then on, Agent Hill kept a close eye out for living creatures along the road.

With the reassignment of Jeffries, Agent Paul Landis was chosen to move from the President's Detail to the First Lady's Detail to assist Hill. Code-named "Debut" because he was "the young one" at just twenty-six years old and unmarried, Landis was slim and had a boyish look that women found irresistible. Originally from Ohio, his calm, even voice and gentle exterior disguised a quick sense of humor that often took people by surprise—a trait that endeared him immediately to Mrs. Kennedy and the children.

But even though Paul Landis blended seamlessly into his new role on the First Lady's Detail, there was no mistaking the fact that Mrs. Kennedy relied on Clint Hill more than anybody. She trusted him to be her protector as well as her confidant, and the two had developed a close bond that came from spending great amounts of time with each other. One of the secrets Clint kept for Mrs. Kennedy was her enjoyment of a cigarette every now and then. Clint was a habitual smoker and always had a package of cigarettes in his pocket, along with a Zippo lighter. They'd be out somewhere—just the two of them—and Mrs. Kennedy would get a sly smile on her face and ask, "Mr. Hill, might I have one of your cigarettes?"

Clint would pull out a cigarette, stick it in his mouth, light it up, and then hand it to her. If, God forbid, anyone came into the area, Mrs. Kennedy would quickly hand the cigarette back to Clint as if he were the one smoking. She never had her own cigarettes, and never smoked in public. She didn't smoke all that often—it was just one of their little secrets.

As Clint Hill drove to the White House that Friday morning in November, he realized that Gwen had a point. It wasn't right that of all the Secret Service wives, she was one of the few who hadn't met the president and first lady. Perhaps subconsciously he'd been keeping Gwen and Mrs. Kennedy apart. As soon as he got back from Texas, he'd find a way to introduce them.

PART TWO

★

THE JOB

7

The Summer of '63

To state the facts frankly is not to despair the future nor indict the past. The prudent heir takes careful inventory of his legacies and gives a faithful accounting to those whom he owes an obligation of trust.
—JOHN F. KENNEDY

For every agent on the Kennedy Detail, it was almost as if they were leading separate lives. They had their wives and children at home in Washington, but because the president and Mrs. Kennedy spent so much time away from the White House, so too did the agents. The two worlds did not, and could not, mix. Because they were sworn to be worthy of trust and confidence, much of what the agents experienced with the Kennedys could not be shared with their own wives or families. The only people who would even understand were the other agents on the Kennedy Detail. For they alone knew that behind the glamour, behind the public façade, the Kennedys were a family that had its triumphs and tragedies, just like any other.

When the agents did attempt to share a funny story or event that was not of a secretive or personal nature, often—as Jerry Blaine had learned during the party with the movie stars at the inauguration—the stories backfired. The wives were home with babies and toddlers, cutting coupons to try to make ends meet, while their husbands seemed to be living a far more heady existence. Indeed, one of the president's trips to Palm Springs, California, ended up being tabloid fodder.

President Kennedy's sister Pat was married to actor Peter Lawford, who was a member of the infamous Hollywood "Rat Pack." The Rat Pack was basically a group of entertainer friends—Frank Sinatra, Sammy Davis, Jr., Dean Martin, Joey Bishop, and Kennedy's brother-in-law Peter Lawford— who would often show up onstage at each other's Las Vegas gigs, thereby giving the audience an impromptu and usually hilarious performance. Their 1960 movie *Ocean's 11*, with Angie Dickinson, brought them all together on the big screen.

President Kennedy enjoyed hanging out with the Hollywood set, which was so different from the Washington political crowd, and Palm Springs was exactly the distraction he needed after the Cuban Missile Crisis in December 1962.

Floyd Boring, Jerry Blaine, and a young agent from Stew Stout's shift named Andy Berger were assigned the advance for the president's trip. Andy Berger was a twenty-six-year-old agent who had been plucked from the New York Field Office earlier that year. He was a New Yorker through and through, and while he and his wife, Dolly, had had a tough time adjusting to life in Washington, he loved being on the Kennedy Detail. It had been a tense few weeks in Washington and the agents were looking forward to the week in sunny Palm Springs.

Shortly before they left Washington, Ken O'Donnell—the president's aide—informed Floyd Boring that the president would be staying at Bing Crosby's home and that the agents would be in charge of securing the property.

Unbeknownst to the Secret Service advance team was the fact that the president's brother-in-law Peter Lawford had been helping with behind-the-scenes arrangements, and had committed to Frank Sinatra that the president could stay at Sinatra's home. In the weeks prior to the president's visit, Sinatra had a state-of-the-art security system installed, along with a helipad on his desert property.

The three-man Secret Service advance team flew to Palm Springs, settled into their hotel, and visited the Crosby residence the next day. Mrs. Crosby gave the agents a tour of the house and they immediately began establishing posts for the coverage for the area. No sooner had the three agents started the survey than Peter Lawford showed up at the house. He had a look of deep concern on his face and wanted to see what he could do about changing the president's quarters from the Crosbys' to the Sinatra residence.

Politically the White House had concerns about rumors of Frank Sinatra's possible connections with organized crime, but rather than risk any fallout, they'd let the Secret Service agents be the designated hit men. Nobody in Washington had bothered to tell Sinatra or Lawford about the change in plans. Floyd Boring explained the situation to Lawford, who was nervous about breaking the news to his buddy Sinatra. Boring offered up Blaine and Berger to go with Mr. Lawford to visit Mr. Sinatra.

When Peter Lawford, Jerry Blaine, and Andy Berger showed up at the Sinatra residence, the agents could detect a heavy cloud descending over President Kennedy's brother-in-law as they waited for someone to answer the door. As the more senior of the two agents, Blaine had offered to be the bearer of the bad news. But when Sinatra opened the door, Blaine suddenly felt awkward. He was a huge Sinatra fan, and this was not going to earn him any points with the crooner.

"Come on in," Sinatra said cheerfully.

Blaine was trying to be cool and confident. He knew he had to say something right away.

"Good morning, Mr. Sinatra," Blaine started. He could feel Lawford urging him to speak.

"Uh . . . Mr. Sinatra, I'm afraid I must inform you that Mr. Bing Crosby's home has been selected for the president's visit this weekend."

Sinatra looked at Lawford with raised eyebrows.

Poor Peter Lawford looked dejected and humiliated. "Sorry, Frank," he said. "We got overruled. I just found out myself."

Sinatra was very astute and ultimately understood that the agents were operating on orders that must have originated fairly close to the president. He knew what it was all about.

Andy Berger stepped up to the plate. "It's not his fault, Mr. Sinatra. This was purely a security decision made by the Secret Service."

The minute Andy Berger spoke up, Frank immediately detected his New York accent and asked Andy where he was from. Suddenly the mood switched and Andy and Frank began talking about their New York–New Jersey connection. Before long, Frank Sinatra invited them in for a soft drink, and they ended up laughing and talking for about a half hour.

Sinatra was gracious and said he understood. Miraculously, it seemed, the problem had disappeared.

By the time the president arrived, everything had smoothed over—nobody wanted to make a big deal over the issue in his presence. Blaine and Berger sensed a rift between Sinatra and Lawford, but when the story was relayed back to the Secret Service supervisors, everybody agreed that had it not been for Andy Berger's New York roots, the situation could have ended up much worse.

Except for the president's occasional and solo visits to Palm Springs, most winter weekends and holidays were spent with Mrs. Kennedy and the children at the Palm Beach house—the "southern White House." Then, from Memorial Day through Thanksgiving, weekends were nearly always at the "summer White House"—the Kennedy compound at Hyannis Port on Cape Cod.

Hyannis Port was where the president felt most at home. It was a place where he could truly relax and simply enjoy being with his family in privacy. When the first family was at the Cape, they seldom ventured from the family compound—unless it was for a trip to Mildred's Chowder House. Usually somebody would be sent out to bring back a huge pot of the creamy white New England chowder that the president loved. Early on, he'd sent some out to the agents, and one taste was all it took. From then on, every Saturday each one of the shifts made their way in the shift car to Mildred's without fail. It was that good.

In Hyannis the shifts would be assigned to beach cottages with sufficient room to house the shift, plus a driver or an agent from the children's or first lady's detail. This allowed the agents to reduce their expenses and the agents would throw money into the pot to buy groceries. There were a couple of guys who enjoyed cooking and tried to outdo each other, which was fine for the rest of the agents, who were happy to be the tasters.

The days at the Kennedy compound were filled with touch football games with cousins, aunts, and uncles; building sand castles on the beach; and always, always there was sailing. Because the compound was considered secure, there was no need to call in additional shifts for overtime duties, so the Kennedy Detail agents also got a bit of a breather. These were also the times in which the agents and President Kennedy got to know each other on a personal basis.

Just as Agent Berger had connected immediately with Frank Sinatra, so too had he with President Kennedy. From the moment the gregarious young man from the Bronx and President Kennedy met, there was an instant bond. Like Kennedy, Andy was Catholic, but the two also shared a similar sense of humor and zest for life. In many ways Andy was like a younger version of Jack Kennedy—handsome, charming, fiercely competitive, and a consummate practical joker.

One weekend in Hyannis Port, Andy was standing on the beach with a couple of other agents watching as the president and a few friends sailed on a small boat. After they came ashore, President Kennedy urged Berger and the other agents to take the boat out.

"Go on. The water's calm and the boat's easy to handle," Kennedy said.

None of the agents had ever sailed a boat before. Like Berger, the rest of them were city kids. It didn't take long for the boat to capsize, dumping all three of them into the water. As they struggled to right the boat, they looked to the shore, where President Kennedy was standing there laughing so hard, he had tears streaming down his face. As soon as they realized they'd been set up, and how ridiculous they must have looked, all the agents could do was laugh right along with him.

One trait all the White House Detail agents had in common was competitiveness. It ran from card games to tennis, to basketball, football, softball, and everything in between. During the first summer at Hyannis Port, shift leader Art Godfrey and Agent Dave Grant came up with the idea to pit the shifts against each other in some friendly competitions. They found a shop in Hyannis that made up customized sweatshirts and handed them out to the shift agents. From that day on the three shifts were known as "Godfrey's Guerillas," "Stout's Scouts," and "Roberts' Raiders."

Softball games became regular occurrences, which sometimes cut into the sleep of those who happened to be on the midnight shift. The matches were often wildly competitive and ended up with quite a few Kennedy family spectators. Every so often, a few members of the Kennedy clan would even step in to round out a team.

It was in this relaxed environment where temporary agents were often brought in from field offices to be evaluated for potential placement on the permanent White House Secret Service detail. Extra sweatshirts were always on hand to pass out to the temporary agents so they could feel part of the team. How well they handled the competitions and fit in with the others turned out to be an excellent way of evaluating the temporary agents' characters. In order for the White House Detail to operate effectively, they had to work together as a team. There could be no whining, no complaining. The rotations in Hyannis Port and at the White House were the easy parts of the job. If you couldn't cut it here, you had no business traveling with the president when you'd work fourteen- or sixteen-hour days without breaks or meals.

Even though President Kennedy owned a small house behind his father's expansive beachfront home, in the summer of 1963 he decided to lease a larger house nearby that would provide more space and privacy for the family. The rambling, gray-shingled house sat on a secluded piece of beachfront property on Squaw Island—a geographical misnomer because it was not an island at all—only about a mile from the compound. Mrs. Kennedy and her children would stay for the entire summer, with the president joining them nearly every weekend.

One agent who served a temporary assignment in the summer of 1963 was twenty-two-year-old Radford "Rad" Jones. Jones was the youngest man ever hired as an agent, but after finishing first in his class at Treasury Law Enforcement Training School and obtaining the top score in every shooting qualification course, his age seemed irrelevant. Still, he had to fulfill the character assessment. He was assigned menial duties and was left for long hours on boring posts, such as the one every agent disliked—staring out into the black Atlantic Ocean on a rainy night. Not once did Rad complain. You could tell he was thrilled to be given the opportunity of serving the President of the United States and had the attitude to go along with his intellect and shooting skills.

One Friday afternoon, Rad was at one of the oceanfront posts when President Kennedy and his Secret Service detail arrived for the weekend. The president liked to hit golf balls from the backyard of the home, and as soon as he'd gone in and changed into a short-sleeved shirt and Bermuda shorts, he came walking out of the house with his seven iron. Trotting alongside the president was a small mongrel puppy that was just one of the many dogs the family had accumulated.

President Kennedy set the golf ball on the ground, and to Rad's horror, the dog immediately grabbed the ball in his mouth and raced directly toward Rad. The dog dropped the ball at the agent's feet and then sat at attention, wagging his tail.

The week prior, the agents had been playing with the dog when they weren't on duty and had taught him to retrieve a thrown ball. The president did not look happy as he strode toward Rad. The young agent was mortified and figured his dream of serving on the White House Detail had just ended.

Rad explained what had happened and apologized profusely. President Kennedy could see that the poor young agent was truly regretful—and of course, it had been an innocent gesture. He smiled and said, "Just ask the guys not to do this anymore."

"Yes, sir, Mr. President. Don't worry. It won't happen again," Rad promised. Rad made sure that a sign was put up in the command trailer, and from then on, the poor puppy seemed to wander around aimlessly searching for the balls that had all suddenly disappeared.

When Mrs. Kennedy found out she was expecting again in early 1963, Clint Hill was one of the first people she told. She was so excited. There was nothing that gave Mrs. Kennedy more joy than her children. She had had a miscarriage and a stillborn daughter before Caroline was born and with John, Jr., having arrived early, her doctors recommended she slow down her active schedule. As much as she had wanted to accompany her husband on the trip to Ireland, Italy, and Germany in late June of 1963, the first lady realized the best thing was for her to settle into a routine on Cape Cod for the summer and the last few months of the pregnancy.

Because Agent Hill would be with Mrs. Kennedy in Hyannis Port, he knew he'd rarely get a day to see his own family. He'd completely missed the previous two summers with his boys, so he decided he might as well rent a house on the Cape for the summer, too. The tiny two-bedroom cottage he could afford was on a busy street, far from the beach, but at least he was able to see Gwen and the boys most evenings and take them to the beach on the occasional day off.

One day Mrs. Kennedy was sitting outside watching John and Caroline play in the water when she turned to Hill and said, "Mr. Hill, I understand your family is staying here in Hyannis Port. Why don't you bring your boys over to play with John and Caroline?"

Hill raised his eyebrows as he tried to comprehend what she was suggesting.

"Oh, Mrs. Kennedy, that's not a good idea."

"Why not? They're nearly the same ages. I'm sure they'd get along fine."

"It's not that. It's just that I'm here to do a job and if my kids were here, well, it would be like bringing my kids to work. It just isn't a good idea."

Hill had a hard time convincing her that it just wouldn't be proper. His kids playing with the children of the person he was protecting? His boys playing with the children of the President of the United States? In the end, she seemed to understand and the subject was never brought up again.

The pace was slow during the weekdays as John-John and Caroline played with their cousins or friends, with the Kiddie Detail shuttling them back and forth between Squaw Island and the Kennedy compound. The permanent Kiddie Detail now consisted of Agents Tom Wells, Bob Foster, and Lynn Meredith. Caroline would be holding Agent Tom Wells's hand as they walked to the ice cream shop as if he were just another one of her uncles, while Bob Foster would spend hours answering two-and-a-half-year-old John-John's endless questions about helicopters and airplanes. On Friday afternoons there would be a flurry of activity as the president and his Secret Service detail arrived. For John-John, it was the highlight of the week. The agents would have to hold him tight to keep him from running toward the big helicopter as it landed on the front lawn of his grandpa's house. He could hardly contain his excitement. He just loved helicopters.

Caroline, like her mother, loved horses and took horseback riding lessons at a farm that was quite some distance from the family compound. On Wednesday, August 7, 1963, Mrs. Kennedy had decided to go along to watch the lesson, even though she was very pregnant at the time. So Paul Landis had driven the first lady and Caroline to the farm and another agent followed. While Mrs. Kennedy was watching Caroline, suddenly she turned to Agent Landis and said in an urgent tone, "Mr. Landis, I think we should head back to the compound *right now*. We can leave Caroline here. We better hurry."

The two-lane country road had dips in it like a roller coaster where your stomach goes up and down. Paul Landis radioed the command post at Squaw Island requesting the helicopter be ready when they arrived as he raced along the bumpy road at eighty miles per hour.

Next to him in the front seat, Mrs. Kennedy kept repeating, "Mr. Landis, please go a little faster. Please go a little faster!"

"Call Clint and tell him we're headed to Otis," Landis said into the radio as he navigated around a pothole. They got back to the compound just as the helicopter was arriving.

Clint Hill happened to have the day off. He was sleeping at the cottage he'd rented when the phone rang. It was the agent at the command post.

"Clint, Paul Landis just radioed. Mrs. Kennedy has gone into labor. He and Mrs. Kennedy are taking the helicopter to Otis Air Force Base to the hospital."

"Oh God," Clint said. "I'll meet them there." Mrs. Kennedy's due date wasn't for another five or six weeks. This was not good news.

At the White House, SAIC Jerry Behn walked determinedly toward Agent Jerry Blaine, who was on post, and said, "Get ready. The Boss is departing." Blaine could sense the urgency in Behn's voice, and he knew that there were no scheduled departures that day. Something was terribly wrong.

Ten minutes later SAIC Behn and the day shift agents boarded the helicopter with the president for the short ride to Andrews Air Force Base. Unfortunately, when they arrived they discovered that Air Force One was on a check flight and not immediately available. The president, anxious to get to the Cape as soon as possible, was understandably irritated. Two Air Force seven-passenger JetStars were quickly arranged and at 12:30 P.M. the president and his agents were airborne for Otis Air Force Base. The hour-long journey to Cape Cod was silent and somber.

Once again Clint Hill paced outside the door, as Mrs. Kennedy underwent an emergency Cesarean section. The baby arrived before the president could get there. Five and a half weeks premature, and weighing less than five pounds, the baby boy was born at 12:32 P.M. He was alive, but there were serious complications.

Clint saw Mrs. Kennedy and the tiny baby briefly, before the child was whisked away by the doctors.

Oh, God, please don't let anything happen to this child, Clint thought as he sat with Mrs. Kennedy. If the baby didn't make it, it would tear her apart.

He wasn't sure he could handle it, either.

The president arrived, saw his newborn son, and went directly to Jackie's hospital room. The baby, whom they named Patrick Bouvier Kennedy, had been born with a serious lung ailment and needed to be flown immediately to Boston Children's Hospital. Jerry Blaine was immediately sent in one of the JetStars to Boston to prepare security for the president's impending arrival.

Clint Hill stayed with Mrs. Kennedy while the president and his agents flew to Boston.

For the next two days, Clint, Paul Landis, and the children's agents waited and hoped and prayed with Mrs. Kennedy while the president and his Secret Service agents sat vigil in Boston.

The two days seemed like an eternity. The power of the office seemed to have deserted President Kennedy as he became engulfed with emotion. When the news came that Patrick had died, the anguish flowed from the president and Mrs. Kennedy down to each and every agent, all of whom felt as if they too had lost a child.

The private funeral Mass was held the following day in Boston, which meant that Jackie Kennedy, still recuperating from the C-section, couldn't attend the funeral of her son. As Cardinal Cushing delivered the Mass, the Secret Service agents struggled to contain their emotions at the sight of President Kennedy bowed over in grief, softly weeping.

Later, at the Kennedy family plot in nearby Brookline Cemetery, the scene was so heart-wrenching, nothing could stop the tears. The agents who prided themselves on hiding their emotions wept openly as they watched President Kennedy's shoulders heave up and down with deep, heavy sobs as the tiny white coffin was placed in the ground. They couldn't imagine a deeper pain.

In the following weeks, it was as if a dark cloud hung over the White

House. The president sunk himself into the problems of the nation—problems that needed his attention if he were to be reelected—while Mrs. Kennedy fell into a deep depression.

The Kennedys' family and closest friends rallied to offer support. The last few weekends of the summer were spent at the Squaw Island house, surrounded by the Kennedy clan, and then, in September, Jackie decided she wanted to be at Hammersmith Farm, the forty-eight-acre estate in Newport, Rhode Island, that belonged to her stepfather, Hugh Auchincloss. Jackie had spent childhood summers at the twenty-eight-room Victorian mansion that overlooked Narragansett Bay, which had also been the site of her and Jack's wedding reception. As they'd done with the homes in Hyannis Port and Palm Beach, the Secret Service had ongoing security at Hammersmith Farm so that when the president and his family were there, it was very familiar and considered a relatively secure location. The family could relax while the Secret Service agents rotated posts on schedule, ever vigilant and as unobtrusive as possible.

The weekend of September 21, 1963, the president, Mrs. Kennedy, and their children were joined at Hammersmith by some of their closest friends, Paul "Red" Fay and his wife, Anita. The Fays were the sort of friends with whom Jack and Jackie had a long history and with whom they could completely relax.

During World War II, Red Fay and Jack Kennedy were assigned to the same squadron on separate PT boats in the South Pacific. In the early hours of August 2, 1943, a two-thousand-ton Japanese destroyer rammed Kennedy's PT 109, causing a deadly explosion that tore the boat in half. Two men were killed, but the twenty-six-year-old Kennedy and ten others survived. With an injured back, Kennedy towed a badly burned comrade more than three miles through dark, shark-infested waters to a deserted island, and the men were rescued a few days later. Around the same time, Red Fay's boat was hit by an air strike, and while there was no explosion, Fay and his crew managed to get the badly damaged boat back to shore before it sunk. Kennedy and Fay wound up together, sharing a Quonset hut in the Solomon Islands, and their friendship was cemented. After Kennedy became president, he appointed Fay to be the undersecretary of the Navy.

On that Sunday afternoon in September 1963, the Kennedys and the

Fays cruised Narragansett Bay aboard the *Honey Fitz*, the ninety-two-foot presidential yacht, while Art Godfrey and Jerry Blaine followed in a speedboat. The president and Secretary Fay, both fun-loving Irishmen, were having a grand time reminiscing and after a few rounds of afternoon cocktails, the mood was relaxed and laughter filled the air.

Being out on the ocean seemed to have brightened Mrs. Kennedy's spirits, too.

One of the White House photographers, Robert Knudsen, was taking films of the group on the cruise, and both the children and the adults were hamming it up. Mrs. Kennedy truly seemed to be enjoying the outing.

By the time the *Honey Fitz* returned to the pier at Hammersmith Farm, it was late afternoon. Godfrey and Blaine were waiting on the dock, with Agents Paul Landis and Roy Kellerman standing by to follow the presidential party back to the house, when Mrs. Kennedy came walking briskly toward them. Her hair was windblown from the cruise and she'd gotten just a hint of color on her cheeks and nose from the afternoon on the water. She was practically beaming.

"Mr. Kellerman? Would you please do us a favor?"

"Sure. What do you need, Mrs. Kennedy?" Roy Kellerman asked.

"We're making a film about the president's murder and we'd like you and the other agents to drive up to the front of the house, then jump out and run toward the door."

"You want us to drive up now?" Kellerman asked.

"No, just as soon as Mr. Knudsen is ready," she said, her soft voice filled with enthusiasm.

It was a strange request, but it was nice to see her smiling for a change.

She turned around and practically skipped back toward the rest of the group.

Jerry Blaine thought he must have misheard what Mrs. Kennedy had asked. He gave Art Godfrey a quizzical look.

Godfrey laughed. "She sure seems to be enjoying herself," he said.

"Art, get your shift ready," Kellerman called to Godfrey. "When we get to the house, we're being featured in a film classic."

The cars had been parked at the end of the long pier, and as the agents piled into the black sedan that served as the follow-up car, Blaine looked over to see Paul Landis shaking his head, chuckling.

"Clint was telling me she loves making movies," Blaine said with a laugh as he started the engine. "I think deep down she really wants to be a director."

The short drive on the dirt road from the pier up to the house was one of the few places President Kennedy could actually drive his own car, and he thoroughly enjoyed these short bursts of freedom. The president got into the driver's seat of the white Lincoln convertible as Jackie and their guests piled in, with the kids giggling as they climbed aboard the top of the backseat for the bumpy ride back to the mansion.

The agents dutifully put on their sunglasses, primed for the scene, and followed the convertible for the short drive.

President Kennedy pulled up to the front of the house and the kids who were riding on the back where the top folded down slid off the trunk and raced to the front door, laughing and yelling. Everybody was having a wonderful time. The president and his guests picked up the gear they had taken to the boat and went inside while Mrs. Kennedy stayed outside with Knudsen.

Knudsen had apparently been briefed on the plan and called out directions to the agents in the follow-up car.

"Okay, drive the car up from the command post and pull up to the front of the house, and make a mad dash for the door," Knudsen directed as Mrs. Kennedy nodded in agreement.

"Look desperate, like you heard shots and are concerned that the president might be hurt and you need to respond fast," she added.

Blaine backed up the car to the designated starting point, a ways down the dirt road. Then, as he drove toward the house, he turned, pressed his foot down hard on the gas, and slammed on the brakes, bringing the car to a screeching halt right in front of the house. The photographer focused on the agents as they jumped out of the car and ran up the porch stairs to the front door.

Mrs. Kennedy clapped her hands and looked at Knudsen.

"That was great! Did you get it?"

"Got it," he said. "Great action sequence."

"Thank you, gentlemen," Mrs. Kennedy said as she and Knudsen walked into the house to finish the film.

Godfrey turned to Kellerman. "I don't believe we have a starring role, but at least she got authentic character actors."

"Wonder what that was all about?" Blaine asked.

"She said something about the president being murdered," Roy said.

"By who?"

"She didn't say," Roy said as he walked back to the car to drive it back to the command post.

"All in a day's work," Godfrey said with a chuckle. The agents laughed as they separated to their assigned posts around the property.

They all agreed that it was certainly refreshing to see her in good spirits, having a bit of fun with the president. It had been a rough couple of months, but it appeared that perhaps she was coming out of her depression. Several weeks earlier President Kennedy had suggested that a trip to Europe with Jackie's sister might help to revive her spirits, and Jackie had agreed. Clint Hill was in charge of handling arrangements for an unforgettable trip to Greece and Morocco.

Clint was worried that the trip would backfire if the media found out about it, so all the details were kept closely guarded. The last time Jackie and her sister, Lee, had gone to the Mediterranean they had created quite a stir. They'd rented a villa on the Amalfi Coast and the Italian press went crazy trying to get photos of Jackie in her bathing suit. Clint Hill and Paul Rundle were constantly on the lookout for boats zooming into the shore. It had become such a dangerous situation that the agents convinced Jackie that it would be best if she would just pose for a couple of photos and be done with it. Rundle and two Italians stepped into the photo with Jackie, Caroline, and Lee's son, and after it was plastered in newspapers and magazines all over the world, the media finally left them alone.

Fortunately, the Greek shipping tycoon Aristotle Onassis understood the need for privacy following Patrick's death and offered to host Mrs. Kennedy on his 325-foot yacht *Christina* for a two-week cruise around the Mediterranean. Agents Clint Hill and Paul Landis accompanied Mrs. Kennedy, Lee, and Franklin D. Roosevelt, Jr., and his wife on the yacht as it sailed from Athens to Istanbul.

Clint Hill was somewhat impressed by the magnificent yacht, but Landis was overwhelmed. He never imagined that such a lifestyle existed. "Oh my gosh, Clint, it's fantastic. Unreal. It has everything . . . a swimming pool that turns into a dance floor, sailboats, a Chris-Craft cruiser, runabouts, anything you want to do."

The yacht even had a seaplane that was used to collect the mail. The seaplane was lowered into the water and the pilot would fly to Athens to get the mail every day. Then when he returned, he'd fly over the yacht, circle and roll the plane, and buzz the bow of the boat. Everybody would come out to watch. It was a daily event. Then the pilot would land in the water and the crane would bring the plane back up to the yacht.

Landis found it hard to believe that people lived this way, but in the end he realized that they were real people . . . they just lived differently.

Clint did a lot of the advance work. He'd talk to the captain to find out where they were heading and make the security arrangements. But Onassis was very sneaky. He kept trying to ditch the agents. One day Clint went ahead in the runabout and was waiting in a limousine onshore where Paul Landis was supposed to meet him with Mrs. Kennedy and the rest of the group. Onassis was driving the Chris-Craft toward shore with all the passengers, when all of a sudden, with a twinkle in his eye, he took a detour.

Paul panicked. "Where are we going? What are we going to do?" But when Clint saw the Chris-Craft heading off he jumped into the limo and started racing along the shoreline trying to keep up with the speedboat. He had no idea what was going on, not a clue where Onassis was taking Mrs. Kennedy. Finally, when Onassis pulled up to a dock, much farther down the coast than was planned, there was Clint. He opened the limo door and got out as if he'd been waiting there the whole time.

Landis was impressed and chuckled to Hill later, "It blew Ari away. I don't think he'll be trying to ditch us anymore."

The trip turned out to be exactly what Mrs. Kennedy had needed, and by the time she returned in late October, she seemed ready to move forward with her life.

It appeared to the agents that the president and Mrs. Kennedy's commitment to each other had deepened after the loss of their child. They'd always been close, but Patrick's death had brought them closer, and the agents believed perhaps this was something good that had come from such tragedy.

Even though the Mediterranean cruise had lifted Mrs. Kennedy's spirits, it had still surprised Clint when Mrs. Kennedy had told him she was going to go on the campaign trip to Texas with the president. In the three years she'd been first lady, she hadn't been on one domestic political trip. It had been only three months since she'd lost the baby, but it truly seemed that she wanted to do her part to make sure Jack got reelected. Or maybe she was just looking for a way to keep her mind busy and be with her husband at the same time. Whatever the reason, Clint hoped more than anything that the trip to Texas would be a turning point for the woman he'd come to admire and respect, and who had suffered so deeply.

8

The Reelection Campaign

We choose to go to the moon in this decade, and do the other things—not because they are easy, but because they are hard.

—JOHN F. KENNEDY

MONDAY, NOVEMBER 18, 1963

In Tampa, in his room on the fourth floor at the International Inn, Agent Frank Yeager woke up early, walked to the window, and pulled the black-out curtain open. The sudden bright light of the morning sun caused him to blink his eyes, and after a quick adjustment he saw nothing but blue sky overhead. Not a single cloud in sight.

He walked over to the dresser and flipped on the radio, hoping perhaps a passing shower might be in the forecast later in the afternoon. The weather was just being announced. *It's going to be another beautiful day in the Tampa Bay area. Warm and plenty of sunshine. A perfect day to come out and catch a glimpse of President Kennedy in the parade through our great city.*

With no chance of rain, Yeager knew the president would want the top off the presidential limousine for sure.

The president's bubble-top limousine and the Secret Service follow-up car, which the agents called "Halfback," had been transported on a C-130 Air Force cargo plane the night before. Driver agents Sam Kinney, Hank

Rybka, and George Hickey had flown from Washington to MacDill Air Force Base with the cars and had made sure they were securely stored overnight. Because of the tight time schedule the president would be choppered from MacDill to Lopez Stadium, so Kinney and Rybka needed to drive the cars to Lopez, where the motorcade would start. Yeager would meet them there, make sure everything was set, and then drive back with Rybka to MacDill to handle the president's arrival. The logistics had to be timed to the minute.

The Secret Service driver agents were trained strictly as drivers, but were classified as agents. The drivers operated through their own command chain, headed up by Special Agent in Charge Morgan Gies, and were typically recruited from the White House police force—the uniformed police, which was a completely separate organization from the Secret Service, and which recruited its people from the District of Columbia police force. Thus the driver agents had police training and were proficient with weapons and protection, but they worked out of the White House garage and were trained separately from the shift agents. Their training focused on the unique skills required to drive the president's car and the follow-up car, and the security aspects involved with maintaining and transporting the cars wherever they were needed. The driver agents were not updated on threat subjects, nor did they travel with the shift agents.

Down the hall from Yeager, Jerry Blaine was in his hotel room on the telephone with Bert DeFreese, the Kennedy Detail agent doing the advance in Miami.

"The guy I told you about—Joseph Milteer," DeFreese began. "He's currently in Georgia and doesn't appear to be a problem. Apparently Milteer started some right-wing political group, but there's no evidence that he or anybody from the group is a serious threat."

"Was he just mouthing off or what?" Blaine asked.

"That seems to be his history. Get this: he told the informant that Kennedy had fifteen look-alikes the Secret Service used."

Blaine couldn't help but chuckle. "Fifteen look-alikes? Where do these people come up with this stuff? Looking after one Kennedy is hard enough—what the hell would we do with fifteen?"

"Rowley would probably receive thirty requests for transfer," Bert quipped back. "Nobody seems to be worried about this guy. Like I said, he's got a history of blowin' smoke, but we've still got him under investigation."

"Okay. Great," said Blaine. "That's one less thing I have to worry about. Also, we've got the logistics for Marine One worked out for you."

Because there wasn't enough time in the schedule for the president to have a motorcade in Miami, DeFreese needed the president's helicopter on standby to transport President Kennedy from the Miami airport to the downtown venue for his last appearance in Florida. The problem was that Marine One was also being used in Tampa. Blaine had had to figure out the timing to get the president's helicopter from Tampa to Miami in time.

"We'll use Marine One to take the president from MacDill to Lopez Stadium here in Tampa," Blaine explained. "After that he'll be traveling by motorcade to the various stops here in Tampa. So, as soon as he's dropped off at Lopez—which should be around one-thirty P.M.—we'll send Marine One down to you in Miami. It should get there before four P.M."

"Sounds good," Bert said. "What's your weather like?"

"Sunny and clear," Blaine replied. "The president will love it. What's the weather like down there?"

"Same," Bert replied.

"Hey, Bert, I gotta hustle. Good luck in Miami," Blaine said.

He hung up the phone and went over his checklist one last time to make sure there were no details he'd forgotten. Everything looked good.

He pulled out the notes from yesterday's closeout meeting with the Tampa law enforcement. Chief Mullins had brought in a dozen command officers from the greater Tampa region to assist in implementing the plan, and Blaine felt that the meeting had gone well. The support of the local law enforcement was critical to every presidential visit.

Blaine had verified with the officers that the two PRS subjects, Gainey and Warrington, should not be of concern: arrangements had been made with the twenty-year-old Gainey's parents to keep him at home and an agent would be assigned surveillance on the house; Warrington was incarcerated in the local jail. As a safeguard, Blaine had passed around copies of their photos and backgrounds to the officers in the rare event one of them might escape.

Blaine had reiterated that a presidential visit had the potential to incite an unstable person to violence, and had asked the officers at the meeting to think about whether they'd come across anybody who needed to be watched. These were questions the advance agents always posed, just to make sure the local law enforcement was thinking in the same mind-set as the Secret Service.

"Have any of you encountered any new subjects or people of concern?" he'd asked. "I'm talking about a sociopath personality, an unpredictable criminal, a political rabble-rouser . . . anybody who might potentially present a problem to the president. It's critical that you let me know if you or any of your personnel have come across anybody that fits this profile."

The officers had shaken their heads in unison. No new subjects to report.

At the end of the meeting Chief Mullins had confirmed that the various police and fire agencies were committing around 650 security people for the president's visit. It was a huge amount of personnel, and Blaine couldn't have been more pleased, but with four venues, twenty-eight miles of motorcade, and an estimated 125,000 people to whom the president would be exposed, even 650 police officers would be stretched thin.

Despite the positive outcome of his negotiations with Chief Mullins and the lack of any new subjects or threat suspects, Blaine was still edgy about the substantial Cuban population. The Secret Service had dealt with a rash of situations with Cuban nationals, even before the Bay of Pigs and the Cuban Missile Crisis. Blaine remembered the first one as if it had happened last week.

In April 1961, less than three months into Kennedy's presidency, and two weeks prior to the Bay of Pigs invasion, newspapers around the United States reported that the Secret Service had uncovered a plot by pro-Castro Cubans to kidnap the president's then three-year-old daughter, Caroline. The story had come as a complete surprise to the Secret Service. They had no knowledge of such a plot but of course jumped on the information and conducted a rapid but thorough investigation.

It turned out that the story originated when an alleged pro-Castro Cuban employed at a Miami garment plant was overheard saying something along the lines of "We ought to abduct Caroline Kennedy to force the United States to stop interfering with Cuba's government." Somebody reported the incident, and as the story was passed from one government agency to the next, it grew and transformed every step along the way. By the time it ended up at the U.S. State Department, the Cuban employee's remarks had turned into a plot in which four Cubans in four different cars were planning to not only abduct Caroline Kennedy in Palm Beach, but also slaughter the entire Kennedy family. When the Secret Service investigated the garment worker, they found that he was in fact *anti*-Castro, and that a personal enemy trying to get the man in hot water had most likely started the story. The entire report had no validity whatsoever.

The Secret Service field office in Florida spent much of their time following up on plenty of similar leads that turned out to be unfounded. There had been a myriad of alleged Cuban plots to assassinate the president, but thus far not one case had turned out to be a real threat. In one instance, the Secret Service intercepted an interesting letter, postmarked in Havana, that was sent to a Cuban immigrant named Bernardo Morales in Miami. The letter referred to a plan to kill President Kennedy, but the investigation found that Morales—the recipient—was again an anti-Castro supporter who was being framed by the other side, in an effort to get Morales thrown in jail. Nine times out of ten, the leads turned out to be hoaxes, but the Secret Service couldn't take any chances. They investigated everything that came to their attention.

Even with the tremendous cooperation of the Tampa law enforcement and the lack of any currently known Cuban threat, Blaine was still concerned about the president's unprecedented exposure in the twenty-eight-mile motorcade. He'd wrestled with various ideas but had come up with only one solution that would put his mind at ease. He was going to strongly recommend that two Secret Service agents be posted on the back of the president's limousine for the duration of the motorcade. Typically a couple of agents would jog alongside the president's car when the pace was slow and then drop back to the follow-up car running boards when the pace was faster. The president didn't like them hovering directly behind him unless it was absolutely necessary. But Blaine kept thinking back to the trips to Italy and Ireland, and how quickly things had gotten out of hand. At least if the agents were on the rear steps of the president's limousine, they could respond quickly. The whole idea of having the Secret Service agents close to the president was for them to be able to shield him with their own bodies. The farther away they were from him, the longer it took to react. Blaine had discussed it with Frank Yeager, and Yeager agreed that in light of the historically tenuous situation in Florida and the length of the motorcade, it was a sensible recommendation. The only question was whether President Kennedy would agree that the unusually close coverage was necessary.

Blaine put his steno pad and the White House Advance Manual into his briefcase, and looked at his watch: 7:30 A.M. Four hours until showtime. He picked up the receiver of the phone that had been installed in his room and waited for the White House switchboard operator.

"White House."

"It's Blaine. Connect me to Palm Beach."

President Kennedy had arrived in Florida with Ken O'Donnell and Dave Powers on Friday evening, November 15. Saturday morning, the president had a spectacular visit to Cape Canaveral in which he saw a test launch of a Polaris missile by the submarine USS *Andrew Jackson* and was briefed on the progress of the space program that he believed was so important to proving America's scientific and military superiority over the Soviet Union.

The race to space had begun in 1957 when the Soviets launched Sputnik, the first artificial satellite, and early in his presidency Kennedy had convinced Congress to fund an American space program with the goal of landing a man on the moon and returning him safely to earth before the end of the decade. After astronaut John Glenn successfully orbited the earth in February 1962, Kennedy's vision seemed within reach, and an entire industry was inspired as scientists, engineers, test pilots, medical researchers, and businesspeople embraced the challenge to beat the Soviets to the moon. Fifteen months later, the knowledge of this new frontier had grown exponentially and in May 1963, three more astronauts—Scott Carpenter, Walter Schirra, Jr., and L. Gordon Cooper—completed another successful orbit.

At Cape Canaveral, Dr. Wernher von Braun, the brilliant director of the NASA Space Flight Center, told President Kennedy he was confident America would see a man set foot on the moon and return safely home by

Special Agent Jerry Blaine, 1959. (PERSONAL COLLECTION OF GERALD BLAINE)

Jerry and Joyce Blaine with their two children, Kelly and Scott, taken shortly before the assassination. (PERSONAL COLLECTION OF GERALD BLAINE)

Agents Jerry Blaine, Floyd Boring, and Ron Pontius scan the crowd as JFK enjoys the Army-Navy football game in Philadelphia, flanked by the "Irish Mafia": Dave Powers, Larry O'Brien, and Ken O'Donnell. (PHOTOGRAPH BY CECIL STOUGHTON, WHITE HOUSE, JOHN F. KENNEDY PRESIDENTIAL LIBRARY AND MUSEUM, BOSTON)

President Kennedy swarmed by fans in Rome. Left to right: SA Bill Payne, SA Win Lawson, JFK, SA Jerry Blaine. (PHOTOGRAPH BY CECIL STOUGHTON, WHITE HOUSE, JOHN F. KENNEDY PRESIDENTIAL LIBRARY AND MUSEUM, BOSTON)

Motorcade turns to chaos in San Jose, Costa Rica, March 1963. (PHOTOGRAPH BY CECIL STOUGHTON, WHITE HOUSE, JOHN F, KENNEDY PRESIDENTIAL LIBRARY AND MUSEUM, BOSTON)

Floyd Boring and JFK; ASAIC Boring had been in the Secret Service since Franklin Delano Roosevelt was president and was highly respected by all the agents, as well as by JFK. (PHOTOGRAPH BY CECIL STOUGHTON, WHITE HOUSE, JOHN F. KENNEDY PRESIDENTIAL LIBRARY AND MUSEUM, BOSTON)

(Below) JFK cherished his weekends at the "Summer White House" in Hyannis Port. John, Caroline, and two cousins escort him to the waiting helicopter, as Agents Sam Sulliman, Jerry Behn, and Tom Wells follow. (PHOTOGRAPH BY CECIL STOUGHTON, WHITE HOUSE, JOHN F. KENNEDY PRESIDENTIAL LIBRARY AND MUSEUM, BOSTON)

SAIC Jerry Behn was always by President Kennedy's side. He took his first vacation in four years the week JFK was assassinated. (PHOTOGRAPH BY CECIL STOUGHTON, WHITE HOUSE, JOHN F. KENNEDY PRESIDENTIAL LIBRARY AND MUSEUM, BOSTON)

ATSAIC Emory Roberts, SA Bob Faison with President and Mrs. Kennedy and Vice President Lyndon Johnson. (PHOTOGRAPH BY CECIL STOUGHTON, WHITE HOUSE, JOHN F. KENNEDY PRESIDENTIAL LIBRARY AND MUSEUM, BOSTON)

Agent Ron Pontius in Berlin, June 1963. (PERSONAL COLLECTION OF GERALD BLAINE)

SA Bob Foster keeps a close vigil on John Kennedy, Jr., on the dock at Hyannis Port. John always provided good entertainment. (PHOTOGRAPH BY CECIL STOUGHTON, WHITE HOUSE, JOHN F. KENNEDY PRESIDENTIAL LIBRARY AND MUSEUM, BOSTON)

Special Agents Ham Brown, Bob Faison, Ron Pontius, and ATSAIC Art Godfrey. (PHOTOGRAPH BY CECIL STOUGHTON, WHITE HOUSE, JOHN F. KENNEDY PRESIDENTIAL LIBRARY AND MUSEUM, BOSTON)

Secret Service Chief James J. Rowley (OFFICIAL WHITE HOUSE PHOTO/PHOTOGRAPHER UNKNOWN)

John Kennedy, Jr., loved to greet his father at Andrews Air Force Base. Here he holds SA Tom Wells' hand as Air Force One arrives.
(PHOTOGRAPH BY CECIL STOUGHTON, WHITE HOUSE, JOHN F. KENNEDY PRESIDENTIAL LIBRARY AND MUSEUM, BOSTON)

Special Agents Dennis Halterman and Jerry Blaine stand at the door to the Oval Office as President Kennedy announces that the United States and Russia are on the brink of war during the Cuban Missile Crisis.
(PHOTOGRAPH BY CECIL STOUGHTON, WHITE HOUSE, JOHN F. KENNEDY PRESIDENTIAL LIBRARY AND MUSEUM, BOSTON)

Montana citizens swamp President Kennedy and the Secret Service the month before the assassination as the president tested citizens' acceptance of his policies prior to traveling to the South. (PHOTOGRAPH BY CECIL STOUGHTON, WHITE HOUSE, JOHN F. KENNEDY PRESIDENTIAL LIBRARY AND MUSEUM, BOSTON)

Thousands fill the Orange Bowl as President and Mrs. Kennedy welcome the returning Bay of Pigs prisoners, December 1962. SA Ron Pontius checks his watch in the background. (PHOTOGRAPH BY CECIL STOUGHTON, WHITE HOUSE, JOHN F. KENNEDY PRESIDENTIAL LIBRARY AND MUSEUM, BOSTON)

President and Mrs. Kennedy shake hands with the wounded Bay of Pigs
prisoners at the Orange Bowl, December 1962. (PHOTOGRAPH BY CECIL
STOUGHTON, WHITE HOUSE, JOHN F. KENNEDY PRESIDENTIAL LIBRARY AND MUSEUM, BOSTON)

Agent Tom Wells and John, Jr., watch President Kennedy and his guests aboard
the *Honey Fitz* from the Secret Service chase boat. (PHOTOGRAPH BY CECIL
STOUGHTON, WHITE HOUSE, JOHN F. KENNEDY PRESIDENTIAL LIBRARY AND MUSEUM, BOSTON)

Robert F. Kennedy, left, Marilyn Monroe, and President John F. Kennedy in 1962. Historian Arthur Schlesinger is on the far right. Singer Harry Belafonte can be seen facing the camera in the rear. (PHOTOGRAPH BY CECIL STOUGHTON, COLLECTION OF KEYA MORGAN, LINCOLNIMAGES.COM: HTTP://LINCOLNIMAGES.COM)

SA Paul Landis jogs alongside Caroline riding Macaroni on the White House grounds. Signed by Jacqueline Kennedy and Caroline. (PHOTOGRAPH BY CECIL STOUGHTON, WHITE HOUSE, JOHN F. KENNEDY PRESIDENTIAL LIBRARY AND MUSEUM, BOSTON)

SA Paul Landis comforts
John after a fall. (PHOTOGRAPH
BY CECIL STOUGHTON, WHITE
HOUSE, JOHN F. KENNEDY
PRESIDENTIAL LIBRARY AND
MUSEUM, BOSTON)

SA Tom Wells helps John, Jr., pilot a boat at
Hyannis Port. (PHOTOGRAPH BY CECIL STOUGHTON,
WHITE HOUSE, JOHN F. KENNEDY PRESIDENTIAL
LIBRARY AND MUSEUM, BOSTON)

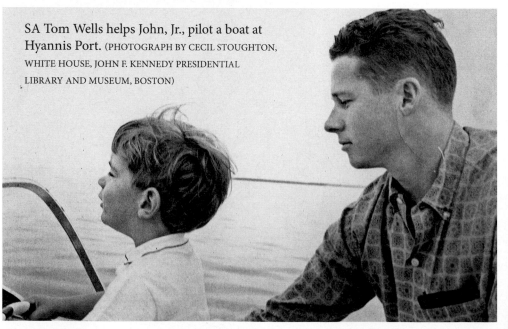

The happiest days were when the family was together. Seen here in the summer of 1963 in Hyannis Port surrounded by their beloved dogs.
(PHOTOGRAPH BY CECIL STOUGHTON, WHITE HOUSE, JOHN F. KENNEDY PRESIDENTIAL LIBRARY AND MUSEUM, BOSTON)

Driver Agent Bill Greer with the Kennedy family in Palm Beach.
(PHOTOGRAPH BY CECIL STOUGHTON, WHITE HOUSE, JOHN F. KENNEDY PRESIDENTIAL LIBRARY AND MUSEUM, BOSTON)

Jacqueline, John, and Caroline ride Sardar and Macaroni at their Virginia farm. (PHOTOGRAPH BY CECIL STOUGHTON, WHITE HOUSE, JOHN F. KENNEDY PRESIDENTIAL LIBRARY AND MUSEUM, BOSTON)

President Kennedy Berlin motorcade. Millions watched the procession led by the Berlin "White Mice" motorcycle team. (PHOTOGRAPH BY CECIL STOUGHTON, WHITE HOUSE, JOHN F. KENNEDY PRESIDENTIAL LIBRARY AND MUSEUM, BOSTON)

An estimated one million Berliners gather to hear President Kennedy speak on June 26, 1963. The crowd erupts when he proclaims *"Ich bin ein Berliner!"* (PHOTOGRAPH BY ROBERT KNUDSEN, WHITE HOUSE, JOHN F. KENNEDY PRESIDENTIAL LIBRARY AND MUSEUM, BOSTON)

Agents Jerry Blaine, Sam Sulliman, Paul Burns, Chief Jim Rowley, and ASAIC Roy Kellerman in Berlin, June 1963. (PHOTOGRAPH BY CECIL STOUGHTON, WHITE HOUSE, JOHN F. KENNEDY PRESIDENTIAL LIBRARY AND MUSEUM, BOSTON)

(Left) In County Cork, Ireland, the people clamor to touch their American Irish son, as Secret Service agents push them away. (PHOTOGRAPH BY ROBERT KNUDSEN, WHITE HOUSE, JOHN F. KENNEDY PRESIDENTIAL LIBRARY AND MUSEUM, BOSTON)

(Right) Irish police are unable to contain the crowds that spill into the street when President Kennedy visits Ireland in June 1963. (PHOTOGRAPH BY ROBERT KNUDSEN, WHITE HOUSE, JOHN F. KENNEDY PRESIDENTIAL LIBRARY AND MUSEUM, BOSTON)

President Kennedy with Secretary of State Dean Rusk, Presidential Assistant Dick Goodwin (dark hair, smiling), and an assortment of the press corps. SA Win Lawson is in the hat (at left), Agent Ernie Olssen stands near the helicopter. (PHOTOGRAPH BY CECIL STOUGHTON, WHITE HOUSE, JOHN F. KENNEDY PRESIDENTIAL LIBRARY AND MUSEUM, BOSTON)

Jacqueline Kennedy and her sister, Lee, pose with the First Governor of Rajasthan and members of his family during the first lady's historic trip to India and Pakistan in 1962. (PHOTOGRAPH BY CECIL STOUGHTON, WHITE HOUSE, JOHN F. KENNEDY PRESIDENTIAL LIBRARY AND MUSEUM, BOSTON)

```
GAINEY, WAYNE L.          CO-2-33,815
Route 2, Box 101          Nov. 8, 1963
Westville, Fla.

Subject made a statement of a plan to
assassinate the President in October,1963,
subject stated he will use a gun, and if
he couldn't get closer, he would find
another way. Subject is described as:
white, male, 20, 155, 5'9", hazel eyes,
brown hair, light complexion, slender
build.
```

(Left) Threat suspect Wayne Gainey, as posted on the front of the agents "flash cards" provided by PRS. (OFFICIAL SECRET SERVICE PHOTO)

(Right) Description of threat suspect Wayne Gainey on the back of the flash card. (OFFICIAL SECRET SERVICE PHOTO)

President Kennedy, Mrs. Kennedy, Caroline, and John look on as the Scottish Black Watch perform on the South Grounds of the White House. Five days later the Black Watch marched in JFK's funeral procession, at the request of Mrs. Kennedy. (PHOTOGRAPH BY CECIL STOUGHTON, WHITE HOUSE, JOHN F. KENNEDY PRESIDENTIAL LIBRARY AND MUSEUM, BOSTON)

Agent Jerry Blaine and a German security agent ride on the back steps of SS100X in Berlin as the White Mice motorcycle team escorts the motorcade. (PHOTOGRAPH BY CECIL STOUGHTON, WHITE HOUSE, JOHN F. KENNEDY PRESIDENTIAL LIBRARY AND MUSEUM, BOSTON)

1969. The president was overjoyed, and when he returned to the Kennedy estate in Palm Beach with Dave Powers and Ken O'Donnell, it was all he talked about for the rest of the weekend.

Shift leader Emory Roberts had accompanied Kennedy to Cape Canaveral and he too had been impressed. Now Emory was in the Secret Service command post at the Palm Beach estate, going over the plans for the long day ahead. At forty-nine years old and as one of the most senior agents on the White House Detail, Emory Roberts wasn't the type to get stressed, but the president's back-to-back trips to Florida and Texas had left him with a skeleton shift for today's visits to Tampa and Miami. On top of all the agents who were out on advances in Texas, another of Emory's experienced agents—Jack Ready—had just been informed of a tragic death in his family and had requested a short leave. Roberts was trying to figure out how to man the follow-up car for today's motorcade.

Emory had been in the Secret Service for twenty years, and on the White House Detail since Harry Truman was president. Unlike the younger agents, who had nearly all adopted the more modern crew cut, Roberts had a full head of black hair, which he parted down the middle and kept in place with plenty of Brylcreem. He had a wide face and sincere brown eyes that drooped slightly at the outside corners, making him appear as if he were always worried about something. Indeed he became known as the "Mother Hen" of the detail because he would go out of his way to take new agents under his wing, briefing them about procedures, administrative tasks, or peculiarities of the individuals the agents were protecting. He had a quick mind and could make snap decisions at the height of chaos, barking clear and concise orders about what needed to be done.

Emory Roberts had just one major fault: his snores sounded like a freight train. Whenever the agents had to share rooms—as they often did at the Carlyle Hotel in New York—losing the toss meant you had to share with Emory. Fortunately, for the president's frequent trips to Palm Beach, the agents stayed at Woody's Motel, where the rates were cheap and the agents got their own rooms. Of course the ambiance and service weren't even in the same solar system as the Carlyle, but at least nobody had to endure Emory's snores.

Emory had slept well the night before and had shown up at the command post early. With a cup of coffee in his hand, he was going over the itinerary yet again when the phone rang.

He set down the cup and picked up the receiver.

"Roberts."

"Emory. Hi, it's Blaine."

"Hey, Jer, what's up? Everything okay in Tampa?"

"Well, there's something I wanted to run by you and Floyd."

"Go ahead," Emory said.

"It's about the motorcade. Yeager and I have been discussing it, and we feel strongly that two agents need to be assigned to the back of the Boss's car for the entire route."

"Really? What's going on there?"

"Four stops, a chopper ride, thirty miles of motorcade, and a lot of people. There have been some petitions for demonstrations by a couple of Cuban groups, which makes me a little concerned as well."

"Okay, I get the picture. Sounds like taking some extra precaution would be reasonable," Emory replied.

"I also know you're pretty shorthanded. Who do you have on your shift right now?" Blaine asked.

"Well, Jack Ready had to go back to Washington because of a death in the family—he'll be back for the Texas trip—but now Zboril and Lawton are my only experienced guys. I just got Tim McIntyre from the Spokane office posted permanently on my shift, but he's only been with us a week. So I've got Bob Kollar, and George Hickey rounding out the team," Emory said.

Blaine was stunned by what Emory was telling him. George Hickey was a driver agent and Kollar was fairly new to the White House Detail. As far as Blaine knew, neither of them had ever worked the follow-up car. And Tim McIntyre was brand-new. Blaine had never even met him. It was worse than Blaine had thought. "That is all the more reason," Blaine said. "If we stick Zboril and Lawton on the back of the president's car, they won't wear themselves out running back and forth to the follow-up."

"You have a point there," Emory agreed. "I'll pass along the recommendation to Floyd. See ya in a few hours."

Emory had seen agents come and go, and he knew that if Blaine was making such a strong recommendation, there was good reason. Emory had seen firsthand how an angry mob could easily turn into a life-threatening situation. During Eisenhower's administration, Emory had been part of the small Secret Service detail sent to protect Vice President Nixon and his wife, Pat, on a trip to several Latin American countries in 1958. Nixon had ridden in an open-top limousine throughout most of the trip, but the Secret Service had convinced him to use a closed-top car for his last stop in Caracas, Venezuela, due to the high level of anti-American sentiment there. It turned out to be a lifesaving decision. In Caracas, an angry mob of pro-communist supporters surrounded Nixon's car when it stopped in traffic. When the violent crowd started pelting rocks and bashing the car with clubs, Emory Roberts and the other agents rushed from the follow-up car to stand between the attackers and the vice president's car. With the help of the Venezuelan police escort, the motorcade was eventually able to make its way to safety at the U.S. embassy. For his quick thinking and selfless action during the crisis, Agent Emory Roberts was awarded the Civilian Service Medal, the highest honor that can be bestowed on a civilian.

Like the story of Floyd Boring thwarting the assassination attempt on President Truman, the Nixon incident wasn't something Emory Roberts ever discussed or bragged about, but every agent on the detail knew the story and had the utmost respect for the shift leader.

As Emory Roberts had been talking with Jerry Blaine on the phone, the experience of the angry mob flashed back into his mind.

Emory had mentioned it rather casually to Jerry, but in reality he was concerned about the lack of experienced agents he had available. Since his team was now working the 8:00 to 4:00 day shift, they would be covering not only today's Tampa motorcade, but also three of the five motorcades in Texas later in the week. It was just the luck of the draw and the way the shift rotation worked. With the president traveling to so many cities in such a short time span, though, most of the experienced agents were off doing advances, leaving gaping holes in the shifts responsible for protecting the president.

Emory was pondering Blaine's recommendation when Floyd Boring barged into the command post. With SAIC Jerry Behn on vacation, Floyd Boring was the acting Special Agent in Charge for the Florida trip.

"Emory, what in the Sam Hill is going on?" Floyd asked.

Emory Roberts looked at his supervisor, perplexed. What was he talking about?

Floyd pointed to a contractor's van that was parked on the street outside the compound.

"Oh, that," Emory said as he realized Floyd's concern. "Remember the termite problem that was discovered a while ago?"

"Uh . . . yes," Floyd said hesitantly. He vaguely remembered something about it. When it came to protecting the president, termites weren't exactly on his priority list.

"Well, they found out that the termites had eaten into the floor beams in the kitchen and the whole floor was ready to collapse. The president's mother wanted the floor repaired before Christmas when the whole family will be here. Headquarters sent in Norton and Wunderlich from technical services to inspect the repairs for any electronic bugs or God knows what else. They'll conduct a sweep of the whole house after the Boss leaves."

"Okay," Floyd said. "But Jesus, somebody needs to let me know about this stuff." Now that he understood it was nothing to worry about, he relaxed. "Guess the place is older than it looks," he quipped. "Or the termites are hungrier than they are in Hyannis."

"I just hope the house doesn't collapse while the Boss is here," Emory said with a laugh.

Floyd grimaced at the thought. "God forbid. Speaking of the Boss, is he up yet?"

"I haven't seen him, but I did just get a call from Blaine. He said everything's ready to go in Tampa."

"That's good," Floyd replied.

"But there was something he wanted me to run by you," Emory said. "You know the motorcade is close to thirty miles long. Blaine feels strongly that we need to assign agents to the back of the president's limousine."

"For the whole route?" Floyd asked.

"Yes. That's what he's recommending."

"I have no objections, but I don't know what the president is going to say about it. What's the reasoning?" Floyd asked, furrowing his brow.

"Blaine's main concern is the distance and the expected size of the crowds, along with possible Cuban community demonstrations," Emory replied.

Floyd took a sip of his coffee and looked out the door of the small of-fice, toward the ocean. Through the palm trees he could just make out the U.S. Coast Guard boat patrolling the strip of turquoise water in the distance. "Well, you know as well as I do that unless there's an imminent or obvious threat, the president doesn't like us hovering so close. Let's see how it goes," Floyd said as he looked up at the clock on the wall of the command post. "We need to get organized if we're going to get the Boss out of here at eleven-fifteen."

The West Palm Beach airport was filled with tourists and locals who wanted to get a glimpse of JFK as he departed for Tampa. Beyond the fenced-off area for spectators, the stunning silver and blue Boeing 707 sparkled in the midday sunlight.

As had become his routine, President Kennedy strode to the barriers to shake hands while Floyd Boring stayed within an arm's length of him, scanning the enthusiastic crowd. Boring couldn't help but notice that the president was in a particularly good mood. The trip to Cape Canaveral had really boosted his spirits.

On board Air Force One the president spent some time with the press pool to answer questions about the Tampa and Miami stops, and on his way back to his cabin he stopped next to his driver Bill Greer and Floyd Boring. Greer was next to the window, with Boring on the aisle.

President Kennedy placed his hand on Floyd's shoulder and with a big grin asked, "Are you ready for a long day, Floyd?"

"Yes, Mr. President." Floyd had been thinking about Blaine's request and how to approach it diplomatically with the president.

"Good, I have a feeling it's going to be a great day," Kennedy said.

Floyd took a deep breath. "Mr. President, we have a very long motor-cade, so we're going to have to stick to a tight time schedule." He knew he had to choose his words carefully to get the point across.

Floyd continued: "Two people have made threats against your life and even though we have them in custody, you might want to keep your stops during the motorcade to a minimum."

The president took his hand off Floyd's shoulder and said, "Floyd, this is a political trip. If I don't mingle with the people, I couldn't get elected dog catcher."

With that the president turned and walked away. The discussion was over. Floyd turned his head and with raised eyebrows looked at Emory Roberts, who was sitting directly across the aisle. Emory shrugged his shoulders. The Boss had spoken.

At 11:15 A.M. Air Force One landed at MacDill Air Force Base. Two years earlier, the United States Strike Command had been established at MacDill as a unified command with integrated personnel from all branches of the military, and the president was eager to get a firsthand look at the operations. "Hail to the Chief" was played upon the president's arrival, while a receiving line of Strike Command generals were waiting to greet him. After a briefing with the commanders, the president spoke at a luncheon for military base personnel and their families. Even though he was the commander in chief, Kennedy realized he still had to earn the votes of his military personnel.

At 1:20 P.M. Marine One, carrying the president, and the secondary chopper, carrying the shift agents and the press pool, left MacDill and headed to Al Lopez Stadium.

Red, white, and blue banners and large American flags decorated the stage that had been set up at one end of the open-air stadium. A band played as the twenty thousand spectators waited eagerly for the president's arrival. When the helicopter came into view, the crowd roared and the band could barely be heard. The excitement in the air was electric. As the president, his staff, and the agents walked toward the stadium entrance the two helicopters departed for Miami. They'd be waiting when the president arrived there a few hours later on Air Force One—fueled up and ready to transport the president to his evening political appearance.

As President Kennedy was delivering his speech to the enormous outdoor audience, Blaine talked briefly with Floyd.

"Did Emory give you my message?" Blaine asked.

"Yeah. I don't know how it's going to go over with the Boss, but let's try it and see how it goes."

After the speech, President Kennedy entered SS100X with Florida's Senator George Smathers and Congressman Sam Gibbons. At the wheel, Driver Bill Greer noticed that the president was smiling, relaxed, and visibly excited about how well the trip was going so far.

Sam Kinney was driving the follow-up car and as the agents took their places, Emory Roberts pulled Chuck Zboril and Don Lawton aside.

"I want you two to get on the back of the Boss's car and stay there. This is gonna be a long motorcade, and we're not sure what to expect."

When Jerry Blaine saw Agents Zboril and Lawton climb onto the footholds on the back of SS100X, he breathed a sigh of relief. Good. Apparently his recommendation had been passed along.

Once Blaine was assured everyone was in their places, he hopped into the passenger seat of the lead car with Chief Mullins at the wheel. Blaine carried the large walkie-talkie that would allow him to communicate with SS100X and the Secret Service follow-up car.

A crackling came over the speaker of the walkie-talkie and then Floyd Boring's voice. "Lancer departing."

The code name for the president was the signal for the motorcade to begin.

The lead car and the following procession turned west on Tampa Bay Boulevard, heading toward downtown Tampa. Chief Mullins maintained a steady pace as the motorcade proceeded. The police motorcycles performed magnificently on intersection control while the motorcycles doing the outriding maintained their assigned positions at the back of the presidential limousine and toward the curb.

The crowds lining the downtown streets were heavy, but sporadic. The standard operating procedure was for the agents to drop back to the follow-up car when the crowds thinned, but Lawton and Zboril stayed on the steps. As the car turned onto Dale Mabry Avenue, the crowds became noticeably larger and more enthusiastic. Suddenly Blaine noticed a group of about twenty Cubans holding up signs just ahead. He was about to radio to Emory Roberts to watch out, but then he saw the signs were all pro-Kennedy and were simply showing support. Zboril and Lawton jumped off the back steps of the car and moved to the side of SS100X to jog alongside. When the masses of people spilled into the streets and started surging toward the car, the best place for the agents to be was between the crowds and the president. They were joined by Bob Kollar and Tim McIntyre, who covered the front fenders of the presidential limousine, while George Hickey remained on Halfback's running board. When the car sped up, Kollar and McIntyre would drop back to the follow-up car, while Lawton and Zboril would jump back on board the rear steps of SS100X as they'd been instructed. There were a lot of spots where the spectators were sparse and since it was both uncomfortable and less protective to squat, Zboril and Lawton mostly stood erect on the back of the car, behind President Kennedy.

JFK was enjoying the crowds and was standing up and holding on to the wide roll bar that had hand slots for just that purpose. He suddenly bent down because of the motorcycle noise, so he could speak into Floyd's ear. "Floyd, have the Ivy League charlatans drop back to the follow-up car."

Floyd had known this was coming. He was actually surprised the president had let Lawton and Zboril stay back there for so long. The whole purpose of the motorcade was political and Floyd knew that Kennedy did not want to be shielded from the public.

Floyd grabbed the radio mike and said, "Halfback, Lancer requests the Ivy League charlatans drop back to your location."

The message came through loud and clear on Blaine's walkie-talkie. It was Floyd's voice, for sure, but Blaine knew that was not Floyd's vocabulary. Blaine understood the president's message—he wanted the agents off the back of the car—but the "Ivy League charlatan" phrase threw him for a loop.

What the heck is a charlatan? He had never heard the word before, so he jotted it on his notepad as a reminder to look it up in the dictionary when he got home.

In the three years he'd been with JFK, he'd never heard the president call the agents off the back of the car in the middle of a motorcade. Apparently politics was trumping the Secret Service.

Emory Roberts, sitting in the front passenger seat of the follow-up car, tried to motion Zboril and Lawton back, but since he was directly behind them, he couldn't catch their attention. He finally gave a short whistle, to which they both turned around, and then motioned for them to drop back.

At the same moment, Bill Greer suddenly sped up, and Zboril and Lawton both realized that to jump would have been dangerous. Zboril was hanging on with one hand and used his other hand to signal back to Emory that they were going too fast.

Emory pushed the button on his radio. "This is Halfback. We're going too fast. They can't drop back."

Floyd turned around to look at the president, who was standing up, waving to the crowd. Behind Kennedy, Zboril and Lawton were scanning the crowd while simultaneously trying to figure out just what Emory and Floyd wanted them to do. Floyd motioned to them to stay low.

In the lead car, Jerry Blaine heard the transmission over the radio and told Chief Mullins to slow the pace of the motorcade. Zboril and Lawton immediately jumped off the rear steps and seconds later hopped aboard the running boards of the follow-up car. Looking in his rearview mirror, Bill Greer saw that they were off, and stepped on the gas, leading the whole motorcade ahead at the faster pace.

When the motorcade arrived at the National Guard armory, President Kennedy reiterated to Floyd Boring that he did not want the agents standing on the rear of the car.

"It's excessive, Floyd," he said. "And it's giving the wrong impression to the people. Tell them to stay on the follow-up car. We've got an election coming up. The whole point is for me to be accessible to the people." The president didn't seem angry, but his message came through loud and clear.

For the last two legs of the motorcade, as they stood on the running boards of the follow-up car, Zboril and Lawton were at a heightened state of alertness. They were much too far from the president in this situation and it was unsettling. Their collective adrenaline pumped as they scanned the crowd and the open windows of the tall buildings above.

Five hours after he'd arrived in Tampa, President Kennedy boarded Air Force One, along with Agents Floyd Boring and Jerry Blaine, and headed to his second stop of the day—Miami.

Frank Yeager stayed in Tampa, cleaned up details, and caught a commercial flight to Austin, Texas, while the shift agents who'd worked the venues and the motorcade flew on to Miami in the press plane.

On the flight to Miami, President Kennedy stopped by where Blaine and Boring were seated.

The president was exuberant. He placed a hand on Blaine's shoulder and said, "Great job in Tampa, Jerry."

The Miami stop was a whirlwind. With no motorcade scheduled there, Marine One was waiting at the Miami airport to whisk the president off to his speech downtown, but a local group had organized a rally and four thousand cheering people greeted JFK at the airport. He couldn't ignore the crowd, so he spoke for a few minutes and then dove in to shake hands. There was the quick chopper ride to Haulover Beach Park, the speech at the Americana Hotel to the Inter-American Press Association, and then back to the Miami airport.

It was shortly after 9:00 P.M. when Air Force One left Miami and headed back to Washington. The president was exhausted and retired to his cabin, while Jerry Blaine sat with Floyd Boring.

Blaine was embarrassed and troubled. He was concerned that perhaps he'd overreached and in so doing had potentially compromised an essential protective tool. The Cuban demonstrators had turned out to be peaceful and not problematic at all. Indeed Blaine couldn't recall anything negative from the crowds at all. It had been as if Kennedy were visiting his home state of Boston. Still, he felt that he'd made the right decision to have Zboril and Lawton on the back of the car.

Blaine turned to Floyd and said, "Floyd, I hope I didn't stir up a problem with my request, but I thought it was essential we have the agents close by."

"I don't believe he was aggravated, Jerry," Floyd said. "He's more concerned with politics right now than security. I think he was worried about what the voters would think."

"I wouldn't have pressed the issue if I hadn't truly believed there were potential problems," Blaine said.

"Believe me, Jerry, I know that. But the fact of the matter is, he is the Boss and those are the parameters we have to work with. He knows our focus is to protect him. But he's also not naïve. Trust me, the president knows that being a target comes with the job. He understands that every time he steps into a crowd, it's a risk. But you don't get to be President of the United States without taking some risks."

Blaine nodded. It reassured him to know that Floyd wasn't upset.

"So forget it, Jer. You did the right thing. You heard him. He told you, you did a fine job in Tampa. Now let's try to get some rest. You think to-day was a long day, you should see the schedule we've got for Texas."

With the president safely on his way back to Washington, D.C., the rest of the advance teams from Florida were scattered on various flights headed for Texas. Walt Coughlin to San Antonio. Bert DeFreese to Houston. Frank Yeager to Austin. And Dave Grant, happy as could be, was on his way to Dallas.

9

Rising Tensions

*The very word "secrecy" is repugnant in a free and open
society; and we are as a people inherently and historically
opposed to secret societies, to secret oaths, and to secret
proceedings.*

—JOHN F. KENNEDY

TUESDAY, NOVEMBER 19, 1963

Win Lawson was up at dawn, going over the schedule he'd lined up for
the day. Thank goodness Dave Grant had arrived the night before. There
was still so much to do before the president and Mrs. Kennedy arrived on
Friday.

First thing on the agenda this morning was a meeting at the Dallas Secret Service office to type reports, make phone calls, and get Dave Grant
caught up on where Forrest Sorrels and Lawson were in the preparations.
When Lawson and Grant arrived at the downtown office, Sorrels greeted
them with a newspaper in each hand.

"Looks like somebody sent out a press release yesterday. The motorcade route is front-page news."

The publishing of motorcade routes was a constant battle between the
Secret Service and the president's political advisors. From the Secret Service standpoint, informing the public about the president's movements
in advance was like inviting the fox into the henhouse, while the politi-

152

cal folks looked at it as a necessity. From their view, the whole point of the motorcade was for JFK to be seen by as many people as possible.

Lawson and Grant scanned the articles. Shaking his head, Lawson said, "Well, O'Donnell and Powers will be happy about this. Where do you think the heaviest crowds will be?" Lawson asked Sorrels.

"Oh, definitely Main Street," Sorrels answered. "With all the tall office buildings there, I betcha we'll have people hanging out of windows and packing the sidewalks from one end to the other. That's where we need the most police protection."

Lawson put the newspaper down on a nearby table and said, "Okay, let's get moving. We have a lot of work to do."

"Dave," Lawson said, "Forrest and I will be handling the president's arrival and, of course, be in the lead car of the motorcade, so I need you to take charge of everything at the Trade Mart."

Dave nodded. It was standard operating procedure for the lead advance agent to handle the arrival and travel in the lead car.

Lawson continued: "We'll have to arrange transportation to the Trade Mart for the afternoon shift—which I think is Stu Stout's guys this week. You'll get them set in place while also handling the luncheon guests, making sure everybody is seated before twelve-thirty, when the boss arrives. It's going to be a tight schedule, as usual."

"I've set up meetings with the police department and the hosts at the Trade Mart for later this morning," Forrest Sorrels said, "so as soon as we wrap up a few things here, let's take Dave on over there."

The Trade Mart was a boxy, contemporary facility that had lots of large windows that let in plenty of natural light, making it feel spacious and bright. The ambiance was one of the reasons it had been chosen to host the luncheon for President and Mrs. Kennedy, but from a security standpoint it presented a multitude of challenges. Finalizing the intricate plans took up the rest of the day.

The agents made a security survey of the building, taking note of the numerous exits and entrances that would need to be manned. Police would be stationed in corridors, balconies, the freight area, stairways, foyer, kitchen, and near the luncheon guests around the head table. They discussed the roping off and policing of the parking lot and adjacent roof, how to screen the luncheon guests, the Trade Mart employees, and catering staff, and where the checkpoints would be. The building would be secured the night before the president's arrival, with police security beginning at 7:00 A.M. the day of the event. Firemen would be placed strategically with portable equipment near the president, among the guests, in the kitchen, and would be available to assist the crowd in an emergency.

Finally, at seven o'clock that evening, Win Lawson felt he had at least enough information to submit the Preliminary Survey Report.

"Okay, Dave," he said. "Great job today. I'm so glad to have your help. Now go charm that lady friend of yours and I'll see you bright and early tomorrow morning."

"Thanks, Win," Dave said. "See you tomorrow."

After dropping Grant off at the hotel, Sorrels and Lawson returned to the Secret Service office, where Lawson typed up the Preliminary Survey Report, in triplicate. The finished report was put in a sealed envelope, and now it needed to get to Washington, D.C.

Sorrels took the report to the airport and hand-delivered it to the pilot of the next commercial flight to Washington that night, while Lawson called the White House Detail and requested that an agent pick up the document as soon as it arrived.

Agent Jerry Blaine had arrived back in Washington just in time to join his shift for midnight duty at the White House. When Joyce picked him up at 8:00 A.M. he tried desperately to seem interested in her detailed descriptions of what she and the kids had done while he'd been gone, but he was so tired the words just seemed to drift into the air without entering his brain.

After the third time Jerry had responded "Oh, really?" Joyce looked over and realized he was already nodding off.

What do they do to these guys? she thought. All the wives remarked that their husbands came home the same way. There was no need to ask them about the trip because the answer was always the same: "Busy." But still, would it kill them to at least appear interested in the problems you'd had to deal with while they were gone? It seemed that all they wanted to do when they got home was sleep.

"I figured you would want to get some rest this morning, honey," Joyce said cheerfully as she pulled into a parking space outside their apartment building, "but I've arranged a babysitter for this evening so we could go out to dinner. Won't that be nice?"

"That sounds great, Joyce," he said, struggling to fight off yawning. "Just as long as I'm back at the White House by eleven-fifteen tonight."

WEDNESDAY, NOVEMBER 20, 1963

As Win Lawson and Dave Grant scrambled to cover every conceivable detail to ensure the president's visit to Dallas was as safe as possible, the tensions in the city seemed to be rising every day. The reality was that Dallas was a bastion of conservatives, and many anticipated trouble of some sort from them. The daily newspapers' editorials had become more and more inflammatory over President Kennedy's liberal programs, creating an angry undercurrent among some in the city. And in the past few days, an anonymous, derogatory flyer indicating that President Kennedy was a traitor was being circulated. The flyer was so hostile that Win Lawson wondered if it was a violation of federal law. He'd asked SAIC Sorrels to check with the FBI.

A small minority of people had provoked incidents in the past few years that had given Dallas a bad reputation, and Chief Curry was not about to let anything like that happen during the president's visit. He'd made it clear that no amount of disrespect or violence would be tolerated. Two days earlier, the Dallas City Council passed an ordinance that limited the public's right to demonstrate. The new hard-line approach had some people worrying about the police overreacting to demonstrators. The ordinance made it illegal "for any person, singly or in concert with others, to interfere or attempt to interfere with or intimidate another from freely entering premises where a private or public assembly is held; prohibiting any person, singly or in concert with others, from interfering with a public or private assembly by use of insulting, threatening or obscene language or intimidation."

From a political perspective, Jack Puterbaugh was worried that if police were overzealous it could lead to some unfavorable publicity for the president, so he'd asked Win Lawson to get a guarantee from Chief Curry that peaceful protests would be handled lightly.

Chief Curry wasn't concerned about the peaceful protesters, but he was rightfully concerned that President Kennedy's visit might incite some right-wing extremists to violence. That's how taut the city's politics had become. In order to make sure his message came across loud and clear, he made both a written and filmed statement for release to local newsrooms today.

Sitting in his office with photos of previous Dallas chiefs of police behind him, the balding, fifty-year-old former football player read from a prepared transcript:

> *Because of the unfortunate incident which occurred here during the visit of Ambassador Stevenson, people everywhere in the world will be hypercritical of our behavior. Nothing must occur that is disrespectful or degrading to the President of the United States. He is entitled to the highest respect of all of our citizens.*

The cameras cut to a close-up as Curry continued his stern message, his eyes surrounded by clear plastic horn-rimmed glasses, looking straight into the living rooms of people throughout Dallas.

> *And the law enforcement agencies in this area are going to do everything within their power to ensure that no untoward accident or incident occurs. We will take immediate action if any suspicious conduct is observed and we also urge all good citizens to be alert for such conduct. Citizens themselves may take action if it becomes obvious that someone is planning to commit an act that is harmful or degrading to the President of the United States.*

10

Texas

We stand today on the edge of a new frontier—the frontier
of the 1960s—a frontier of unknown opportunities and
perils—a frontier of unfulfilled hopes and threats.
—JOHN F. KENNEDY

THURSDAY, NOVEMBER 21, 1963

It was a gloomy morning in Washington, with gray skies and a constant drizzle, but John-John was as excited as could be. He'd stood mesmerized at the upstairs window while three Marine helicopters descended into his backyard. It was an impressive sight for anyone to see, but for a boy who was four days away from his third birthday, it just didn't get any better than this. And while John knew the choppers meant his daddy was going away, he was delighted because he was getting to ride with him on the short flight to Andrews Air Force Base.

Agent Bob Foster had been notified that the president wanted to bring John-John on the helicopter to Andrews, and when the elevator doors from the family's private residence slid open, he was right there as President Kennedy and John, Jr., walked out hand in hand.

"We're going in the helicopter, Mr. Foster!" John squealed. Foster and the president looked at each other and laughed. The boy's excitement was contagious.

Reporters from the White House press pool piled into one helicopter, while another was filled with various members of the president's staff and Secret Service agents Emory Roberts, Don Lawton, and Jack Ready, who had just returned from an emotional family funeral. Mrs. Kennedy, Bob Foster, and John-John joined Agents Roy Kellerman, Bill Greer, and Clint Hill in the last one, which, as soon as President Kennedy boarded, became Marine One. At 10:50 A.M. the three choppers lifted off, one by one.

John-John often got to accompany his daddy to Andrews before he left for a trip, but this time was different. This time his mother was leaving, too.

Ten minutes later they arrived at Andrews, where the magnificent blue, silver, and white airplane that proudly proclaimed UNITED STATES OF AMERICA on its side already had its right engines running, ready to transport the presidential party to San Antonio. As the passengers filed out of the helicopters, the president and Mrs. Kennedy hugged their son good-bye.

"It's just a few days, darling," Mrs. Kennedy said with empathy. "And when we come back, it will be your birthday."

Tears welled up in John-John's eyes. "I want to come," he whimpered.

"You can't, John," the president said gently with one last squeeze of the boy's shoulders. John-John began crying again in earnest, and Agent Foster could see how difficult this was for both the parents and the child.

President Kennedy looked at Agent Foster and said, "Take care of John for me, won't you, Mr. Foster?"

"Yes, Mr. President," Foster answered as he slipped into the seat next to the sobbing John-John and put an arm around the boy's shoulders. *That's strange*, Foster thought. John-John often cried when his father left, yet while they'd been through this same scene plenty of times in the past, the president had never before made such a remark.

On the flight to San Antonio, President Kennedy talked about the trip with his trusted aides Ken O'Donnell, Larry O'Brien, and Dave Powers, and what they hoped to accomplish. The threesome had come to be known as Kennedy's "Irish Mafia," a moniker JFK found amusing. Indeed, they were his most loyal and devoted friends.

Mrs. Kennedy listened to the itinerary with interest. It was going to be a fast-paced schedule. They'd arrive at San Antonio International Airport, where Vice President Johnson and Governor Connally and their wives would greet them, then proceed by motorcade through downtown San Antonio, on to Brooks Air Force Base, where the president would dedicate a new Aerospace Medical Center. From there the motorcade would continue to Kelly Field, where pilot Colonel James Swindal would have transferred the presidential plane and readied it for the immediate flight to Houston.

The press plane, the vice president's plane, and Air Force One would fly in succession to Houston, a forty-five-minute journey. Arriving just before 5:00 P.M., the whole group would repeat the procession with another motorcade from the Houston airport to the Rice Hotel, downtown, where the president and Mrs. Kennedy would make a brief appearance before the League of United Latin American Citizens—LULAC—followed by another motorcade to Sam Houston Coliseum, where they'd attend a banquet in honor of Congressman Albert Thomas. After the banquet, the whole entourage would reboard the three aircraft and fly on to Fort Worth. They'd be lucky if they got to sleep by midnight. Friday would be another exhausting repeat, with stops in Fort Worth, Dallas, and Austin.

There was good reason for the president to visit Texas, though. A recent poll indicated that Barry Goldwater, the Republican favorite for president in 1964, would win the state by four points. In 1960 Kennedy and Johnson had barely won Texas, even though it was LBJ's home state, and now three years later, the political picture seemed even more fragile. The president's popularity had been slipping, especially in the South, where his support for a strong civil rights program would clearly cost him votes. Kennedy needed to be assured of Texas's twenty-five electoral votes in order to enter the 1964 campaign with confidence. No Democrat had ever won the presidency without winning the Lone Star State. Powers and O'Donnell knew Kennedy's greatest asset was his charisma and that the more people they could get him face-to-face with, the more votes they were guaranteed. The president came across well on television, yes, but when it came time to vote, people would remember a handshake and a moment of eye contact. It's how he came out of relative obscurity to win the Democratic nomination and eventually the presidency in 1960. The fact that Jackie had decided to come along was a huge bonus. Everybody loved Jackie. If all went as planned, the couple would be seen by half the state of Texas during the two-day, five-city trip. Dave Powers had high expectations for an enthusiastic reception and had even brought along his own 8mm movie camera to capture the events. Hopefully there would be some good footage that could be used for the campaign.

When the president and his aides turned to discussing matters of national consequence, Mrs. Kennedy moved to sit with her secretary, Pam Turnure. President Kennedy had urged her to give a short speech in Spanish to LULAC, and she needed to practice if she was going to do it without note cards.

In the aft compartment of the airplane, the president and first lady's Special Agents in Charge—Roy Kellerman and Clint Hill—alternately dozed and read magazines. They knew that as soon as the wheels touched down in San Antonio, the quiet hum that surrounded them now would be replaced by screams, cheers, motorcycle engines, and half a million unscreened people, any one of whom could be a lunatic who'd woken up that day and decided to kill the president or harm the first lady. It would be many hours before they'd relax again. They'd learned from experience to take these moments as they came.

Secret Service agents had been spread to the various cities in advance, arranging the seemingly endless logistics and details with the local police force for every venue and every motorcade, in every city.

In San Antonio, Kennedy Detail Agent Dennis Halterman had done the majority of the advance, with Walt Coughlin coming in to assist on the 19th, after finishing up the Miami advance. Driver agents Sam Kinney, George Hickey, and Hank Rybka had flown in on a C-130 to deliver SS100X and "Halfback," the Secret Service follow-up car, from Tampa. The cars had been stored securely overnight and were now parked near the point where Air Force One would be spotted.

For San Antonio, the president's visit was a big deal. Public schools had declared the day a holiday and the police chief provided the *Express-News*, San Antonio's daily newspaper, with the route of the motorcade to ensure and entice huge crowds that would make San Antonio proud.

Meanwhile, in Houston, Agent Ron Pontius had been doing the same things as Halterman in San Antonio, Bill Duncan in Fort Worth, Lawson in Dallas, and Bill Payne in Austin. Bert DeFreese, who had conducted the advance in Miami, had flown directly to Houston to assist Pontius as soon as President Kennedy left Miami the night of November 18.

Because the president was visiting so many cities in such a short amount of time, there was no way to transport the presidential limousine SS100X and the Secret Service follow-up car to every location. The cars would not be used in Houston, so Pontius had arranged for Lincoln Town Car convertibles, provided by the Ford Motor Company, to transport the presidential party and the Secret Service agents in the motorcade that would meander through downtown Houston.

Agent Ron Pontius was tall, with movie-star good looks and a sharp wit, which came from being raised in a large Catholic family. He and President Kennedy would banter back and forth with quick quips that seemed as if they'd known each other for years. Something about the Catholic background gave them an immediate bond.

Originally from Chicago, Pontius had a brother on the Chicago police force, and was the go-to man whenever anybody had questions about that city's uniquely seditious environment. President Kennedy was wonderful about taking the time to meet agents' families and on one trip to Chicago, Pontius had set up a brief meeting in which Kennedy had charmed Ron's mother. From then on, whenever President Kennedy saw Pontius on post, he'd ask how Ron's dear mother was doing.

On this morning in Houston, Pontius and DeFreese were going over the last-minute items before the presidential party arrived.

"We're going to be really tight on time," Pontius said, shaking his head. "We're going to have to make sure the president doesn't stop and talk to every little kid or nun he sees along the way. We just don't have time in the schedule."

"It was the same in Tampa and Miami," DeFreese said. "We had to have the Marine helicopters flown ahead to Miami, and still we were sweating it out."

"I wonder if this is going to be the trend from now on," Pontius speculated. "I hate having to use leased cars. What's the point of having a specially designed limousine if we can't use it? I sure would feel a lot better if we had the bubble top here with the crowds they're estimating. At least we could have the agents on the back of the car."

"What? Didn't you hear? In Tampa the Boss told Floyd that he didn't want agents on the back of the car. Floyd told me in Miami."

Pontius looked at DeFreese in amazement. "Really? I've never heard the president say anything about agents on the back of the car. What happened?"

"I'm not sure," DeFreese answered with a shrug. "Blaine had the agents posted on the back of the car and in the middle of the Tampa ride, the Boss said something to Floyd like, 'Keep the Ivy League charlatans off the back of the car.' He didn't want the agents crowding him, and from what I understood, the directive was to be followed through here in Texas, too."

"Geez," Pontius said. "I need to call the White House to make sure they got my preliminary report. Maybe I can get hold of Jerry Behn and find out the reason behind this."

Pontius picked up the receiver of the White House phone that had been installed in his hotel room.

"Get me Jerry Behn's office."

There were a couple of clicks as the call was transferred from the switchboard.

"Behn here," the Special Agent in Charge answered.

"Jerry, it's Ron. I was just wondering if the preliminary report made it on time."

"Yeah, it sure did. I gave it to Roy before he left." In Jerry Behn's absence, Roy Kellerman was the acting SAIC for the Texas trip. Kellerman was responsible for overseeing the advance reports to ensure every detail was in place and he would be by President Kennedy's side throughout the trip.

"Okay. Great. Jerry, one more thing. Bert just told me about the order not to have the agents on the back of the bubble top. What's the story?"

"That's right. The order came from the Boss himself. He wanted the agents off the back of the car in order for the people to get an unobstructed view. He doesn't want to appear like he's not accessible."

"What was the Ivy League remark?" Ron asked.

"Oh, I think that was just his attempt to soften the order with some humor. Kind of like how he's always kidding around with me about going to Michigan State. I think that's all that was."

"Well, I guess we don't have to worry about agents on the back of the car here in Houston, because we're using leased Lincoln convertibles."

"Yes, I'm aware of that. But still, tell the agents not to be too overzealous in crowding the president. He's heading into the reelection campaign and he wants to be accessible to the people. Nobody likes it, but that's the message from the Boss."

"Okay. Got it."

"Everything else all set there?" Behn asked.

"All set."

"Great. Stay loose, Ron," Behn said as he hung up the phone.

Bert DeFreese had been listening intently to the conversation. "I thought Behn was on vacation," he said with a quizzical look on his face.

Pontius chuckled. "Yeah, me too. I don't think Behn knows what a vacation is. I talked to him briefly yesterday, too, and he said he was going back into the office Saturday since he had some work to catch up on."

"You can't say the man isn't dedicated to his job," DeFreese added.

"That's for sure," Ron agreed as he picked up his clipboard. "Let's get a move on. It's gonna be a busy day."

The final stop of the day would be in Fort Worth, where the president would stay at the Hotel Texas overnight to be ready for a breakfast appearance on Friday morning. The midnight shift would be there awaiting his arrival, in place to guard the hotel while the president slept.

Working midnights was now Art Godfrey's shift—Jerry Blaine, Ken Giannoules, Jerry O'Rourke, Paul Burns, and Bob Faison. They had flown direct from Washington to Fort Worth on a U.S. Navy prop plane, arriving into Fort Worth around 2:30 P.M.

Like the other two Kennedy Detail shifts, Godfrey's team had had some turnover in the past couple of months. Giannoules, Burns, and Blaine were the more experienced agents, while Bob Faison had been on the White House Detail only since September and Jerry O'Rourke since October. O'Rourke had come in from the Denver Field Office, while Bob Faison had spent the past fourteen months at the Washington, D.C., Field

Office, helping with President Kennedy's weekly departures and arrivals at Andrews Air Force Base. Both agents fit in perfectly with the rest of the team, but Bob Faison had made history. Faison was the first African-American permanently assigned to the White House Secret Service detail.

Both O'Rourke and Faison had served temporary assignments on the Kennedy Detail prior to becoming permanent White House Detail agents, and whether or not they knew it at the time, the other agents had been evaluating their every move. Field agents were often brought in for two-week stints when extra protection was needed or to fill in when the permanent agents were on advance assignments, but these temporary assignments were also ideal for assessing White House Detail candidates. The protection of the president required the agents to work as a team, a team that was so finely tuned and in sync that they could practically read each other's minds. There could be no hidden agendas, no petty bickering, no complaints; they all had to come with the same mind-set. Inviting new agents to the team was essentially a blackball system, designed to ensure cohesiveness and compatibility, and both O'Rourke and Faison had proved they fit the mold.

Bill Duncan, the advance agent in Fort Worth, had arranged transportation directly to the Hotel Texas. The shift agents were given a sheet of paper showing post assignments along with other critical information such as the lapel pins to be worn by plainclothes detectives and official party members. Ordinarily, profile pictures and intelligence sheets on any new threat cases would be handed out upon arrival, but none had been identified for the Dallas–Fort Worth stops. Win Lawson, acting SAIC Roy Kellerman, and Forrest Sorrels had all double-checked.

The drive to the hotel took only a few minutes, but by the time the agents walked into the lobby, they were eager to get settled into their rooms. Some craved sleep while others had planned to spend the few free hours shopping or meeting a local friend before they had to be on duty at 10:00 P.M.

They were a formidable-looking group. All of them were about six feet tall, dressed impeccably in dark suits, white shirts, and well-shined wing-tip shoes, and as they approached the front desk, it would appear to the casual onlooker that these six men were fearless.

A short, pale-skinned young man dressed in the hotel's standard uniform stood behind the desk looking down as if he were incredibly busy, despite the fact that nobody was checking in at the time. Art Godfrey walked up, rested his arm on the counter, and asked, "Do you have some rooms ready under the name of Godfrey or the midnight shift of the Secret Service?"

With so many dignitaries in town, Godfrey had been informed that his shift would have to share three rooms. The clerk looked up at Godfrey, made a futile attempt at a smile, and proceeded to rifle through a box of envelopes. Sure enough, there were three envelopes with room keys already prepared.

"Thank you," Godfrey said as he picked up the envelopes. The clerk, who seemed to have barely noticed the agents as they'd walked in the lobby, suddenly got a pained look in his eyes as he glanced from one agent to the next. Bob Faison stood near the elevator talking with Jerry O'Rourke.

"Wait . . . I'm sorry, Mr. Godfrey," he said as he raised his hand in protest, "but you will have to tell the *Negro* that he will have to stay somewhere else."

The agents stood there, not knowing what to say. Surely he must be joking. They'd never run into anything like this before.

Paul Burns stepped up to the counter and looked the young clerk dead straight in the eyes. "Do you know who we are?"

The young man flinched ever so slightly. "Uh . . . I assume you are with the Secret Service."

"That's right," Burns affirmed. "Can we talk to the manager?"

The clerk returned a few minutes later with the manager of the hotel. He reiterated what the clerk had said.

"That's right, gentlemen. It is hotel policy that we do not accommodate members of the Negro race."

Burns leaned over the counter and glared at the manager.

"Well, sir, we are the Secret Service agents here to guard the President of the United States. If our agents aren't good enough to sleep in your damn beds, then we won't sleep here . . . and neither will the president. We'll find somewhere else for him to stay."

The manager read the seriousness of the threat and excused himself to make a quick telephone call. Burns turned toward Bob Faison, who, fortunately, seemed unaware of what was being discussed.

When the manager came back, looking more than a little flustered, he said sheepishly, "It's fine. All of you are welcome to stay."

Burns wasn't satisfied. Staring at the manager, Burns squinted his eyes with intensity and said, "You better advise your staff and every single employee of your new policy so that we don't need to address this issue again. Is that clear?"

The manager, visibly shaken, nodded and said, "Yes, sir. You have my word. There will be no problems."

The agents settled into their respective rooms. Burns and O'Rourke chose to use the free hours for sleep while Art Godfrey and Jerry Blaine headed to a local shop famous for making Western hats. Dallas agent Mike Howard had sent a message that the store would give the agents a sizable discount. "Just give them your White House cards," he'd said. Every agent had a set of embossed business cards that displayed their name, U.S. Secret Service, White House Detail, and their telephone number. The cards often got them preferential treatment.

Blaine and Godfrey each purchased ten-gallon hats, and when they gave the clerk one of their cards, his demeanor suddenly changed, as if he were in the presence of President John F. Kennedy himself. He gave the agents the discount and, in return, Blaine and Godfrey had no doubt the shop would use the fact that the president's Secret Service agents had shopped there—and bought "good guy" white hats—in the next week's advertisements.

Bob Faison had promised his son a pair of cowboy boots, so he went in search of a similar deal, while Ken Giannoules went to see the movie *Mr. Roberts*, with the all-star cast of Henry Fonda, James Cagney, and Jack Lemmon.

In San Antonio, Agent Dennis Halterman scanned the overwhelming crowd that had come to San Antonio International Airport to welcome President and Mrs. Kennedy. There had to be five thousand people there, and at least a thousand were standing on a second-floor balcony waiting eagerly for the sight of Air Force One on the runway. Police were posted along the roped-off area and on the roof, but still, the sight of all those people looking down on the scene made Halterman uneasy. And this was just the beginning. Halterman had heard that the city had come out in droves, with an estimated 125,000 people lining the motorcade route.

The vice president's plane and the press plane had landed several minutes apart, and as Vice President Johnson, his wife, Lady Bird, and Texas governor John Connally and his wife moved toward their designated places in a receiving line, the motorcade vehicles were lined up.

It was a set procession that was outlined in the White House Advance Manual so that every motorcade would be arranged in the exact same formation, creating no surprises for the president or the Secret Service agents protecting him. The one unusual addition in Texas was that the vice president and his security detail would be traveling with the motorcade as well.

When Air Force One landed and President and Mrs. Kennedy came walking down the stairs, the thousands of onlookers went absolutely wild. As usual, the press commented on what Jackie was wearing—a high-collared, short-sleeved white suit with a narrow black belt, matching black beret-style hat, and elbow-length white gloves. The president, they noted, looked tanned and full of vigor.

Flags and banners thrashed in the air and people cheered and whistled. Meanwhile, the Secret Service agents on Emory Roberts's 8:00 to 4:00 shift took their preassigned positions and then moved in to form a protective shield around President Kennedy as soon as he came down the stairs. Clint Hill stayed close to Mrs. Kennedy, who seemed overwhelmed by the enormous number of people who had come to meet them. It had been quite some time since she'd traveled with the president on a public visit—most of her trips were off the record—and she wasn't used to the mania. Meanwhile, Mrs. Kennedy's other agent, Paul Landis, accompanied Stewart Stout's shift to the Air Force Base to be in place for the arrival there.

President Kennedy walked briskly toward the crowd, where women screamed and reached out their hands, hoping they'd be one of the lucky ones the president would touch. Jackie followed her husband's lead and reached her white-gloved hands out to the people who seemed to be just as excited to see her as the president. When the motorcade finally got under way, the agents assigned to the follow-up car jogged alongside the president's limousine. When Bill Greer picked up the speed, they dropped back to the follow-up car and jumped aboard the running boards, hanging on to the car with one hand as they continually scanned the eyes and hands of the crowd.

As the motorcade made its way out of the airport and toward downtown San Antonio, people continued to line the roadways, often spilling out into the streets. When the procession would slow—both for safety of the people in the streets, and to give them a better look at the dignitaries in the convertibles—once again the agents would leap off the follow-up car and jog alongside the president's limousine. They'd been given the instructions not to climb onto the back of the car, but Clint Hill, who was protecting Jackie, wasn't about to be that far away from her. The procession continued on for the fifteen miles to Brooks Air Force Base, with the agents jogging along, dropping back, and jogging again when the crowds came in too close. It was a particularly humid day and the agents were sweltering in their suits.

Nine thousand more people greeted the president at Brooks and after a short speech, everybody was back in the cars, headed for Kelly Field and the flight to Houston. On Air Force One, the president was thrilled with the reception he'd received, as were his political advisors, Ken O'Donnell and Dave Powers. O'Donnell and Powers had ridden in the jump seats of the Secret Service follow-up car and Powers had gotten some great movies of the huge crowds waving and screaming. The first stop had been successful beyond any of their expectations.

Meanwhile, spread among the three airplanes, the Secret Service agents were happy to have a brief chance to sit down. They had probably jogged the equivalent of eight miles. With no food on the planes, they grabbed Cokes or water and tried not to focus on the blisters that were forming on their feet. In less than an hour they'd be starting the same routine all over again, in Houston.

In Dallas, Win Lawson, Forrest Sorrels, and Dave Grant were in the conference room in Chief Curry's office at Dallas police headquarters wrapping up final details with Curry, his deputy chiefs, and other command officers for the president's arrival the next day. Lawson diagrammed the motorcade on the blackboard—placing particular emphasis on the use of motorcycles.

"The presidential motorcade follows a set pattern that we've determined, through plenty of experience—both good and bad—that allows us to keep the motorcade moving and intact, while deterring people from reaching the president's car," Win explained.

Sorrels and Grant handed out samples of all the identification that would be used, from the plastic pin-on badges to the colored lapel clips, with the exception of Secret Service and White House staff pins. For these they passed around photos to be used by the command officers to show the police officers under their direction. You didn't want any loose Secret Service pins floating around.

Next the Trade Mart went through the final check. Lawson and Grant explained the procedure for the identification of guests and officers at the luncheon. Because the Trade Mart had so many entrances, exits, and balconies, to properly secure it required seventy plainclothes officers. The Dallas Police Department was so strapped that Chief Curry had to borrow fifty men assigned to the Department of Public Safety and fifteen men from the sheriff's office to fulfill the security requirements, but he'd come through with the numbers.

The meeting was adjourned only after every detail of the president's visit had been discussed and Win Lawson was confident that every commander had confirmed that his area of responsibility was sufficiently covered.

The sun was low in the sky and a strong wind was blowing across the flat, open plain when Air Force One touched down in Houston. As in San Antonio, the press plane and Lyndon Johnson's plane were already on the ground.

Ten thousand cheering people greeted Mrs. Kennedy and the president at Houston International Airport—far more than had been expected. President Kennedy knew that Houston and the surrounding Harris County had gone for Nixon in the 1960 election, so when he looked out the window and saw the size of the crowd, he was elated.

Houston advance agent Ron Pontius was the man on the ground, directing the shift agents to their assigned places. Now that it was nearly five o'clock, the 4:00 to midnight shift would take over protective duties and the motorcade under the direction of Stewart Stout. The agents fully expected that the president would dive into the screaming mayhem to shake as many hands as possible.

And that is exactly what happened.

The president's car for the Houston stop was a standard white Lincoln convertible, so Mrs. Kennedy climbed into the backseat between the president and Governor Connally. Bill Greer drove, with Agent Roy Kellerman in the right front passenger seat.

The Secret Service follow-up car created a challenge for the Secret Service agents, since it too was a leased convertible. With no running boards, the agents would have to straddle the sides of the open-top car when the motorcade was moving at higher speeds, then jump off and jog alongside the president's car when the procession slowed down. It was not ideal, but with the tight time schedule between stops, there had been no way to transport SS100X and the Secret Service follow-up car to every stop. And while the President's Detail shifts had rotated, Clint Hill once again, as Mrs. Kennedy's Special Agent in Charge, worked the motorcade and Paul Landis was transported ahead to the next venue.

On the way from the airport to the Rice Hotel, the crowds were thick at times, often ten to twelve people deep. Traffic was backed up for miles throughout the city. At certain strategic points along the route, anti-Kennedy groups held up banners and posters that reminded the president, despite the huge numbers of smiling spectators, that this was Republican country.

WATCH KENNEDY STAMP OUT YOUR BUSINESS and BAN THE BROTHERS were two of the milder signs, while KENNEDY KHRUSHCHEV AND KING showed that Kennedy's recent negotiations with the Soviet premier and Martin Luther King, Jr., the civil rights leader, were not popular in this Texas oil town.

The small numbers of protesters were far outnumbered by the enthusiastic yells and cheers of supporters who had come to catch a glimpse of America's royal couple.

At the Rice Hotel, the president and Mrs. Kennedy were shown to a suite that had been redecorated especially for their arrival. They wouldn't spend the night but would simply use the room to change clothes and have a private meal together before the evening functions began. Even though dinner would be served at the Albert Thomas function, the Kennedys would be seated at the head table, with social duties, and experience had taught them it was always better to eat a meal prior to these kinds of events.

Meanwhile, the Secret Service agents were posted around the hotel, observing every passerby and hotel worker, with no time for food or drinks.

When the president and Mrs. Kennedy were ready to head downstairs to the Grand Ballroom, Clint Hill and Roy Kellerman were waiting outside the door of the suite.

Jackie Kennedy looked breathtaking. She had changed into a long-sleeved, black, cut-velvet dress and had a three-strand string of pearls around her neck. Her hair, which had been windblown after the two long motorcades, was now perfectly coiffed.

The president had been informed that the Albert Thomas banquet was not black tie, so he'd merely changed into a different suit, with a clean shirt and new tie. As the president and his wife walked down the hall toward the elevator, he guided her with his arm on her elbow. Clint Hill, walking a few paces behind them, thought to himself how nice it was that she'd come on this trip. It was good for her to take an interest in her husband's campaign, and clearly they were enjoying the time together.

A mariachi band was playing as the president and Mrs. Kennedy entered the LULAC event. The crowd seemed stunned that the president had actually shown up for their fund-raiser. President Kennedy made a brief speech about the Alliance for Progress, his ongoing effort to forge relationships between the United States and Latin American countries, and then welcomed his most popular asset to the podium.

"In order that my words will be even clearer to you, I am going to ask my wife to say a few words to you also."

The room erupted into cheers as Mrs. Kennedy walked to the podium. She didn't enjoy speaking in public, but you'd never know it. She smiled graciously and, without any note cards, proceeded to address the crowd in fluent Spanish. Her command of the language was classical, but the mostly Mexican-American crowd loved it.

"Olé!" they shouted. "Olé! Viva Jackie! Viva President Kennedy!"

Meanwhile, the Secret Service agents scrambled to escort President and Mrs. Kennedy and Vice President and Mrs. Johnson to the cars waiting outside. The motorcade wound through the city to Sam Houston Coliseum.

At the coliseum, Jack Valenti—a Houston advertising executive and the organizer of Congressman Thomas's banquet—was irate. Valenti didn't have the proper identifying pass and ATSAIC Emory Roberts wasn't letting him in. It wasn't until several Houston police officers identified Valenti that Roberts finally allowed him to enter.

Thirty-five hundred people were seated at long dining tables facing a large stage at one end of the coliseum. Against the backdrop of the stage, a large American flag hung on one side of the podium with the Texas flag proudly displayed on the other. There were more receiving lines and speeches. Despite the grueling day he'd had, the president appeared at the podium looking energetic and enthusiastic.

At one point as he addressed the crowd, reading from his notes he said, "Next month, when the United States of America fires the largest booster in the history of the world into space, for the first time giving us the lead—fires the largest payroll . . . payload into space, giving us the lead." Realizing the gaff he'd just made, saying "payroll" instead of "payload," he paused, looked down at his notes, and quickly recovered with his signature humor. Trying not to smile, he added, "It will be the largest payroll, too."

The audience burst into laughter and he laughed right along with them. They'd caught an unexpected glimpse into the president's sharp wit, and it made him all the more appealing. It was the best line of the night.

Finally, at 9:30 P.M., the presidential party excused themselves and piled into the now-familiar cars for their fifth motorcade of the day.

The advance agent Ron Pontius had been with the president and Mrs. Kennedy since they landed in Houston, and he could see the weariness in Mrs. Kennedy's eyes.

Pontius had conducted advances for Jackie's trip to London, Athens, and Rome in June 1961 and had barely made it home for the birth of his third child. His wife, Barbara, had sworn that he better not miss it, since he had missed the last one. By sheer will, she managed to delay labor until he arrived home. Ron Pontius knew Mrs. Kennedy, he knew the look of an exhausted and exasperated woman, and as the motorcade wound up back at Houston International Airport, Pontius had no doubt that Mrs. Kennedy was feeling a little of both.

By the time Air Force One was "wheels up," Pontius and his assistant advance agent Bert DeFreese were also physically and mentally drained. The tensions surrounding the president's visit to the hostile Houston atmosphere had taken their toll, but fortunately everything had worked out fine. As tough as it had been on them, though, they realized that the shift agents had had the most grueling jobs that day. They'd been in those shoes plenty of times, too. It had been a team effort and everybody deserved to feel great about how successful the trip had been.

In Dallas, after the final meeting with law enforcement, Lawson and Sorrels had met driver agents George Hickey and Sam Kinney at Love Field, where they were arriving from San Antonio on the special Air Force C-130 with the president's car and the Secret Service follow-up car. Kinney and Hickey unloaded the vehicles and then drove them to the basement of the airport terminal, where they were secured by a police guard overnight. Hickey and Kinney would relieve the guard early the next morning.

After a quick dinner at the Sheraton Hotel with Jack Puterbaugh and Arthur Bales from the White House Communications Agency, Win Lawson returned to the Trade Mart to check on the arrangements for the luncheon. Police were guarding the entrances as instructed, while the previously approved Trade Mart staff was setting the tables and arranging the stage for the head table and the podium where President Kennedy would speak.

Meanwhile, Air Force One, the press plane, and LBJ's plane were on their way to the final stop of the day—Carswell Air Force Base, on the outskirts of Fort Worth.

For everybody except the Secret Service agents, the day's work was done. The mood on Air Force One was jubilant, but everybody was exhausted. Aboard the press plane, cocktails were being consumed at a fast and furious rate. There was no food aboard, but drinks were plentiful, and the atmosphere turned into a party. The Secret Service agents still had responsibilities once they landed in Fort Worth, so for them, Cokes and coffee were the drinks of choice. They weren't allowed to drink while on duty and none of them would ever risk losing their jobs for the small pleasure of a beer, even after such a grueling day. Winding down for them would have to wait.

More than drinks, they craved food. The agents hadn't eaten all day and were starving. Emory Roberts's shift—the 8:00 to 4:00 shift—had reported to the White House at 7:15 A.M., so when the planes landed around 11:00 P.M., with the one-hour time difference they'd been on duty for sixteen hours straight, with at least another hour to go to handle the arrival at Carswell. Clint Hill and Paul Landis, as the only two agents protecting the first lady on the trip, had also been working the entire day without a break.

UPI reporter Merriman Smith had traveled with the Kennedy Detail agents for the past three years and was conscious that they'd worked all day without eating a thing, and without a complaint. He'd found out that the Fort Worth Press Club was staying open late for the White House reporters and had mentioned it to a few of the Secret Service agents.

"There's always a buffet at these things," he'd said. "And better yet, it's free. You guys are welcome to join us. There won't be anything else open this late."

The three airplanes landed in quick succession at Carswell Air Force Base, with Air Force One the last to arrive, at 11:07 P.M. Because a visit by a sitting president was such a rare occurrence, the base had opened its gates to the public and waiting there to greet President and Mrs. Kennedy were no less than six thousand people. The rain-drenched crowd screamed with hysteria as the all-American couple disembarked from the plane. Roberts's men—Jack Ready, Tim McIntyre, Don Lawton, and PRS agent Glen Bennett—scanned the crowd as the incessant flashing of the press photographers' huge flashbulbs blinded their tired eyes.

When the Kennedys finally climbed into the car and the motorcade departed, the day shift was finally off duty.

Stewart Stout's 4:00 to midnight shift handled the motorcade from

Carswell into Fort Worth—again in leased convertibles because the official presidential vehicles had been sent on to Dallas—but since it was raining, the convertible tops were closed. It was a small blessing because from the agents' perspective, the only thing worse than a motorcade in open-top cars was a motorcade in open-top cars *at night*. And while the shift agents had rotated, Clint Hill and Roy Kellerman, as the Special Agents in Charge of the president's and first lady's details, had been on duty nonstop the entire day, working arrivals, departures, motorcades, and every venue appearance.

At the Hotel Texas, the midnight shift went on duty at 10:00 P.M. Ken Giannoules and Jerry O'Rourke secured the lobby while Paul Burns and Bob Faison were stationed outside the presidential suite on the eighth floor. ATSAIC Art Godfrey and Agent Jerry Blaine were standing post at the hotel entrance and had watched as more and more people jammed the streets outside the hotel, hoping to catch a glimpse of President and Mrs. Kennedy. By the time the presidential motorcade arrived at 11:45 P.M. there had to be four thousand people surrounding the old hotel's entrance.

The schedule called for the Kennedys to go straight into the hotel—for heaven's sake, it was nearly midnight—but the president couldn't ignore the thousands who had waited in the rainy night to welcome him to Fort Worth. Without a word to the agents, President Kennedy bolted toward the crowd and began shaking hands, with Jackie following dutifully behind.

Once again the agents scrambled to cover them.

The Hotel Texas, a historic redbrick hotel, had been elegant in its day but had long since lost its luster. The halls were dark and musty, and while window air conditioners had been installed, the hotel was at the time in desperate need of updating. In an attempt to spruce up the presidential suite for President and Mrs. Kennedy, local Fort Worth supporters had gone to great lengths to add luxurious furniture and expensive works of art they felt suited Jackie's taste. By the time the president and Jackie retired to their suite, it was after midnight, though, and in reality, the only thing they truly cared about was falling into a comfortable bed.

Clint Hill and Roy Kellerman bid them good night and when the door closed, the midnight shift was now in charge of their protection, leaving the day and evening shifts finally off duty. In about eight hours they'd start the whole routine all over again.

The supervising agents—Kellerman, Stout, and Roberts—retired immediately to their rooms. They were all in their mid to late forties and had learned that as they aged, more sleep was required to feel alert the next day.

But when your senses are on high alert and your adrenaline is pumping so hard for so long, often sleep does not come easily. The winding-down process is different for everybody, but for many of the shift agents, the shared camaraderie of the day's events was a way to work out tension so they could finally fall asleep. They were young—most of them in their mid-twenties to early thirties—and fortunately their bodies were resilient. There had been plenty of days, days on end even, in which they'd worked eighteen or twenty hours, had four hours of sleep, and had woken up revitalized and able to do their jobs with ease. Somehow your body got used to it.

Special Agent Dave Grant had driven over from Dallas to brief the agents who'd be working the Trade Mart, because he would have little chance to give instructions after they arrived in Dallas the next day. While standing in the lobby with some of the other agents, a couple of reporters reminded them of the invitation to the press club. Afternoon shift agent Sam Sulliman declined, as did Tim McIntyre, the newest agent on the day shift. They just wanted sleep. But for the other eight agents who'd been on duty all day without a meal, the idea of a free buffet was something they just couldn't pass up.

Unfortunately, by the time Dave Grant, Clint Hill, Andy Berger, Dick Johnsen, Paul Landis, Ernie Olsson, Don Lawton, Jack Ready, and PRS agent Glen Bennett got to the club, all the food was gone. Nothing else was open at this time of night.

"Sorry about that," Merriman Smith said to the dejected-looking agents. "I bet the barman can scrounge up some peanuts or pretzels if you want to stay for a drink."

It was better than nothing. A beer or a scotch and soda would at least wash down the peanuts and hopefully help them relax enough so that sleep would come easily. Every Kennedy Detail agent knew there was absolutely no drinking while on duty, but there were no off-duty alcohol policies that were emphasized by management. The agents' characters and ability to perform were constantly being monitored and none of them would take the risk of overindulging in alcohol. Like anybody with a stressful job, a beer or two at the end of a long day was simply a way to unwind. On the White House Detail the reality was that there was no start or stop time for the agents.

The agents stuck to themselves and shared a few laughs about the day's hectic events while Dave filled them in on what to expect the next day in Dallas. Everybody had a beer or two, or a mixed drink, but with no food around, they all decided to leave. A few of the White House press corps had heard about an after-hours place a few blocks away called the Cellar, which was a beatnik type of coffee shop where scantily clad waitresses doubled as singers. The Cellar didn't serve alcohol, but perhaps they could get a sandwich.

Agent Dick Johnsen had already gone back to the hotel and Agents Andy Berger and Ernie Olsson were on the 4:00 to midnight shift and didn't have any responsibilities until noon on November 22. Glen Bennett, Jack Ready, and Clint Hill were assigned to the follow-up car in Dallas, and while Paul Landis hadn't been given his exact assignment, he assumed he'd be at the Trade Mart. As the number-two man on Jackie's detail, he'd been assigned to the various venues in San Antonio and Houston, and he had no reason to believe tomorrow would be any different.

Unfortunately, the Cellar didn't have much in the way of food, either, so after a couple of glasses of fruit juice, the group returned to the hotel. Paul Landis had struck up a conversation with an attractive female reporter and a Fort Worth police officer, and wound up not leaving until about 5:00 A.M. By this time the warm feeling he'd had from the scotch and soda several hours earlier had worn off, and when he got to his room, he fell dead asleep.

For the agents standing watch on the midnight shift it was a very unusual night. Everybody seemed to be wound up after the hectic and eventful day. Members of the press and the presidential staff were coming and going all night. At least the activity helped fight the fatigue of the agents standing post in the musty hotel.

There were four posts set up at the hotel, and the posts were rotated every half hour to keep the agents fresh. The rotation also allowed for each man to have a half-hour break to get a cup of coffee or some fresh air. The midnight shift agents had been told about the quirky coffee shop called the Cellar just a few blocks away, and as that was the only place open for coffee at this time of night, several of them walked down there during their breaks to check it out. The fresh night air felt good after standing in the stuffy old hotel, and though a cup of coffee would have been a great pick-me-up, as soon as they saw the sixty-cent-per-cup price tag, they turned right back around. Who in their right mind would pay sixty cents for a cup of coffee?

In Dallas, Win Lawson had double-checked the security of the Trade Mart one more time and made sure the bomb dogs had completed a sniff-down. By the time he finally got back to the Sheraton Dallas, it was 11:30 P.M. Sleep was slow in coming as he kept going over everything in his mind. This was always a problem when you were the lead advance agent on a presidential visit. If there were ever an incident, you sure didn't want it to happen on your watch.

PART THREE

THAT DAY

11

The Final Hours

Tolerance implies no lack of commitment to one's own beliefs. Rather it condemns the oppression or persecution of others.

—JOHN F. KENNEDY

FRIDAY, NOVEMBER 22, 1963

The rain had continued on and off throughout the night, but as dawn broke in Fort Worth, patches of white in the gray sky seemed to tease that the sun might actually break through. Despite the inclement weather, thousands of people had gathered in the parking lot outside the Hotel Texas, where the president was scheduled to make a few remarks before the Chamber of Commerce breakfast.

Standing watch outside the Presidential Suite, Agent Jerry Blaine heard the president moving around in the room, preparing himself for the long day ahead. He looked at his watch: 7:30 A.M. His shift was scheduled to depart at 9:30 for Austin, where the President would speak at a fund-raising dinner. He would later spend the night at LBJ's ranch. Blaine knew that as soon as he himself arrived at his hotel room in Austin, he'd crash. The last time he'd slept was a short nap before he and Joyce had gone out for dinner prior to his midnight shift duty two days before. If he'd stopped to calculate it, he would've realized he'd been awake for more than forty hours straight.

When Blaine had offered to let Agent Dave Grant take over the Dallas advance, he had failed to realize that the switch would put him on the midnight shift. Now, as he focused all his attention on keeping his eyes open and resisting the urge to lean back on the wall, he questioned whether it had been a good idea after all.

The sound of the elevator door opening down the hall snapped his mind back to attention as he turned instinctively to the sound. The president's political advisor Dave Powers stepped out of the elevator carrying a stack of newspapers and turned toward Art Godfrey, who was standing at the command post just outside the elevator doors.

"Morning, Art," he said with a chipper voice.

"Good morning, Dave."

"We've got another busy day ahead, I'm afraid," he said.

"That's for sure," Art replied. *Busy day?* That was an understatement.

There'd be two speeches here at the Hotel Texas, followed by the short flight to Dallas on Air Force One; the ten-mile motorcade from Dallas's Love Field to the Trade Mart; lunch at the Trade Mart with a couple of thousand guests; a flight to Bergstrom Air Force Base outside Austin, where the head coach of the University of Texas Longhorns would present the president with an autographed football; another motorcade through Austin; a series of receptions; a dinner speech at the Austin fund-raising banquet; a final motorcade; and a helicopter ride to the LBJ Ranch. If today was to be anything like yesterday, President Kennedy would be exposed to half a million people. Half a million voters, in Dave Powers's eyes, but to the Secret Service they were half a million unscreened strangers, any one of whom might be a potential assassin.

Powers walked briskly down the hall and as he approached the suite, Blaine knocked on the door to announce his arrival to the president.

"Good morning, Jerry," Powers said with a big grin on his face. "You guys are doing a great job. Everything went like clockwork yesterday."

"Thanks, Dave," Blaine said as he tried to suppress a yawn. Blaine appreciated the compliment, but he wondered if Powers had any clue what went into making the president safe on these whirlwind trips.

The day shift would be handling the morning activities in Fort Worth and would fly with the president to Dallas to cover the motorcade to the Trade Mart. Meanwhile, shift leader Stewart Stout and the afternoon shift would start their day six hours earlier than normal in order to secure the Trade Mart and be in position when President Kennedy and the motorcade arrived at 12:30 for the luncheon, while Blaine, Godfrey, and the midnight shift would already be in Austin, in place for the president's arrival. All the Kennedy Detail agents would be working double shifts. There were just too many locations, and too few agents to go around. It was indeed going to be another busy day.

As Dave Powers entered the suite, Jerry heard President Kennedy talking to Ken O'Donnell, who'd come in a few minutes earlier, about the impressive size of the crowd that had already gathered below his window. Yesterday's appearances in Houston and San Antonio had been a huge success and to see so many supporters brave the rain here in Fort Worth was a very positive sign.

"Morning, Dave," the president said in his unmistakable New England accent. "You were right—they loved Jackie!"

Dave had convinced President Kennedy that Jackie would be a tremendous asset on the campaign trail, and obviously the president was pleased she'd come to Texas. The door closed and all Blaine could hear were muffled voices.

A few minutes later, ATSAIC Emory Roberts stepped out of the elevator and greeted Godfrey. It was time for shift change. Punctual as usual, Emory looked well rested. Blaine had walked by Emory's room as he rotated posts and had heard the distinctive snores. Right now Blaine was so tired, he figured even Emory's snoring couldn't keep him awake.

"Good morning, Jerry," Emory said perkily as he walked down the hall.

"Morning, Emory," Jerry answered. "Dave and Ken are in with the Boss and he seems to be in a good mood."

"That's good news," Emory said. "It's gonna be another long day."

Blaine knew Emory was concerned about staffing the motorcade, but of course he wouldn't say anything. The president's order to "keep the Ivy League charlatans off the back of the car" in Tampa, four days earlier, had been circulated throughout the detail and Emory, despite his strong disagreement, had no choice but to comply. For Jerry, the comment still stung because it had been at his urging that the two agents were positioned on the back of the presidential limousine. Tens of thousands of people were expected along the motorcade route today and you just never knew how a crowd would react, or how one person charging the motorcade could change a peaceful parade into instant chaos. President Kennedy had seen it happen in Naples, in Berlin, in Dublin. None of the agents understood why he was willing to be so reckless. Especially in Texas. This was not Kennedy country. It wasn't like he'd be riding through the streets of Boston. What was he thinking?

Emory Roberts looked at his watch and said, "Kellerman should be here any minute. We'll escort the Boss outside for the speech he's giving in the parking lot before breakfast."

"Okay, Emory. We'll see you in Austin," Blaine said as he walked toward the elevator. He'd have just enough time for a quick shower before he needed to meet the rest of the midnight shift in the lobby for the ride to the airport.

It was shortly before 9:00 A.M. when President Kennedy emerged from the front doors of the hotel, flanked by Emory Roberts and Roy Kellerman.

Forty-eight-year-old Roy Kellerman was one of the most experienced agents on the White House Detail. He was in his twenty-third year with the Secret Service, having worked his way up from a shift agent to his current position as Assistant Special Agent in Charge. He'd served under Presidents Roosevelt, Truman, Eisenhower, and now Kennedy, and had earned his role in the top echelon of the Secret Service ranks through dedication and proven loyalty. In the past two decades he'd spent more time with heads of state than with his own daughters, who, he could hardly believe, were already seventeen and twenty.

Paul Landis met up with Emory Roberts, Kellerman, and the day shift agents in the lobby, and as the president walked across the street the agents created an envelope around him. Vice President Johnson, Governor Connally, Senator Yarborough, and several congressmen came trotting behind, trying to show a united front but, as the crowd of several thousand erupted into a cheer, it was clear that the only person they'd come to see was John F. Kennedy. Men yelled, women shrieked, and hands seemed to be flying out from everywhere, grasping at the president as he walked deliberately toward the mob.

The Secret Service agents scanned the mass of humanity that seemed to be closing in like a giant swarm. They looked at hands and faces for quick movements or quizzical looks—anything that seemed out of place. Their eyes gazed across the sea of people on the ground and up to the open windows in the buildings surrounding the lot. In the midst of the mayhem the agents were calm, but ready to react in a millisecond if anything got out of hand.

A temporary stage on the back of a flatbed truck had been prepared with a podium, microphone, and speaker system. Per the White House Advance Manual, the American flag stood to the president's right, the presidential seal flag to his left. When President Kennedy finally stepped up on the stand, Emory Roberts and Roy Kellerman moved into position, both in proximity to the podium, but careful not to appear as if they were hovering.

Emory Roberts's shift agents separated into their preassigned positions to cover the president's back and sides. Jack Ready and Don Lawton, the two senior agents, covered the front of the stage, while Paul Landis, Tim McIntyre, and Glen Bennett, the loaned agent from PRS, covered the rear. Agents from Vice President Johnson's detail were scattered at various posts in the open area.

Here in downtown Fort Worth, office buildings from six to ten stories high surrounded the open parking area. Even at this early hour people hung out of open windows, eager to catch a glimpse of JFK. Fifty yards away, the Washer Brothers building loomed like a giant, with dozens of windows overlooking the makeshift arena. The Boss relished these informal gatherings among the people. So different from the hundred-dollar-a-plate dinners for the wealthy privileged few. But behind any one of the open windows across the street a demented individual could be sighting in a rifle as he wrestled with the demons inside his head: Should he or shouldn't he? Was it the right time? What if he missed? And what if he hit him dead-on? Think of the fame he'd achieve by shooting that goddamned Negro-loving commie president.

It was no secret there were plenty of people in Texas who hated everything President Kennedy stood for.

As the president stepped up to the podium, the agents signaled each other with their eyes or a nod of their head to take notice of a man with his hands in his coat pockets, or a woman who looked like she might lunge toward the stage. And constantly, they scanned the windows overhead.

If President Kennedy had any fear at all, he sure didn't show it.

"There are no faint hearts in Fort Worth!" he announced into the microphone. The crowd cheered. Before he could speak again, a woman yelled out, "Where's Jackie?"

President Kennedy got that look on his face he had when creating a clever, humorous response and, after the briefest hesitation, he answered, "Mrs. Kennedy is organizing herself."

He paused for effect and then, trying to hold back a smile, he added, "It takes her a little longer." The crowd broke into simultaneous laughter. Now, grinning, he added the punch: "But of course she looks better than we do when she does it."

The crowd loved it. They loved him.

He kept his remarks brief—just long enough to make the people feel like the long wait in the drizzle had been worthwhile—then stepped down from the podium and returned to the hotel for the formal breakfast.

In Dallas, Special Agent Win Lawson had risen early and was sitting in his hotel room at the Sheraton going over the itinerary one last time. Every second of the visit was mapped out, and he carried the master plan.

When Win Lawson had first seen the schedule for the three-day Texas trip, he'd wondered how on earth they'd have enough agents to cover Love Field, the motorcade, and the luncheon at the Trade Mart. Even with temporary agents called in for backup, everybody was going to be working double shifts. The past three years had been brutal, and the pace was about to pick up. Win's personal record was 120 hours of overtime in one month—and with the 1964 campaign just around the corner, *that would be the norm.*

Agent Lawson peered out the window, looking up to the sky. Despite the thousands of details he'd arranged, the one thing he couldn't control was the weather. The issue of whether there would be a hardtop, bubble top, or no top at all on the president's car was determined by weather conditions and presidential preference. President Kennedy loved the convertible and preferred to use it whenever possible. The hardtop would be used only if it were raining, snowing, or the Kennedys were headed to a formal function and Jackie was worried about her hair being mussed.

The motorcade route was designed to weave through the streets of downtown Dallas during the lunch hour, on a weekday, when the office buildings would be full. Maximum exposure. Undoubtedly even the Goldwater supporters would be curious to get a glimpse of the president. It was politics on parade. The entire week he'd been working the advance, Lawson's looming concern was the number of tall buildings along the motorcade route that would have a bird's-eye view of the president in his convertible. Even though many buildings had air-conditioning, the majority of office windows could be opened. He and Dallas police chief Jesse Curry had discussed it several times and had agreed there was no way to physically secure every office building on the route, and no way to monitor every window. But Chief Curry was confident that his officers, strategically placed along the motorcade route, could handle any situation that might arise. There'd be two hundred Dallas police officers between Love Field and the Trade Mart, along with sixteen Secret Service agents in the motorcade. Securing the Trade Mart, with its numerous entry points and catwalks, had required dozens of the police officers available. There was only so much manpower.

Win Lawson carefully placed the stack of typed reports and handwritten notes into his briefcase. As he stood up, a ray of sunshine broke through the blue gray sky, casting a spotlight into the room.

Lawson looked at his watch and realized Agent Dave Grant would be showing up any minute. He realized he'd better use the bathroom; it could be evening before he got the chance again.

Two minutes later, Grant was knocking on the door.

"Come on in," Lawson said as he removed the chain and opened the door.

Special Agent Grant was dressed in a charcoal gray suit from Louie's, nearly identical to Win's, and had his tan trench coat draped over his arm.

"I think we're all set," said Win as he walked back into the room. "Let's go to the Trade Mart first and check things out."

"Sounds good to me," Dave said. "Looks like the rain is letting up. Any word on the bubble top?"

Before Win could answer, the phone rang.

"That's probably Kellerman now," Win said as he walked toward the phone on the nightstand.

"Hello?"

"Good morning, Win." It was ASAIC Roy Kellerman. "I just talked to Ken O'Donnell. He wants to know what the weather looks like over there."

Holding the phone to his ear, Win looked out the window and said, "It's still drizzling on and off, but it actually looks like it could clear up."

"Well, you know what that means," ASAIC Kellerman replied.

Win nodded and looked at Dave Grant. "No bubble top."

"That's the plan for now. We'll check back with you in an hour or so. We're running right on schedule and should land at Love Field at eleven-thirty."

"Okay. Thanks, Roy. I'll call Sam and let him know."

Sam Kinney had recently been promoted to the position of lead follow-up car driver and was responsible for the maintenance and transportation of the presidential cars throughout the Texas trip. He and driver agent George Hickey had accompanied the president's limousine and the Secret Service follow-up car in the C-130 from San Antonio. It took some effort to install the bubble top on the car and the earlier the decision was made, the better. Sam would be expecting Win's call.

After relaying the message to Sam, Win said, "Okay, Dave, let's get this show on the road." He picked up his briefcase and slung his coat over his arm.

Traffic was heavy this time of the morning, and with all the stoplights, it took Win and Dave more than ten minutes to travel the three miles from the Sheraton Dallas to the Trade Mart on North Stemmons Freeway. Underneath the large MARKET HALL sign at the front entrance, an electronic billboard spelled out, in red lights, WELCOME PRESIDENT AND MRS. KENNEDY. Police officers surrounded the building and stood post at every street corner. It looked like Chief Curry was coming through on his promises.

Inside the Trade Mart there were rows and rows of long tables covered in white tablecloths and set with fine china, facing a head table on a raised stage at the end of the massive room. The room had been locked and guarded by several Dallas police officers overnight. In about three hours, it would be filled with 2,600 people who'd be waiting for President and Mrs. Kennedy's arrival, promptly at 12:30. When the time came to serve lunch, one of the Kennedy Detail agents would randomly select a prepared plate from the kitchen and watch as it was served to the president.

Convinced that everything was under control at the Trade Mart, Agent Lawson left Dave Grant in charge and drove to Love Field along the same route the motorcade would take after the luncheon. He'd driven it half a dozen times in the past week. The politicians wanted the route to wind through the most populated sections of Dallas for maximum exposure and it was Win's job to anticipate every possible security threat along the way. He'd arranged for police officers to be posted in the most congested areas; police motorcycles would lead and drive alongside the motorcade; and of course the Kennedy Detail agents would be riding in the Secret Service follow-up car. But still, as he drove the route for the last time, he was consciously aware of every building, every intersection, and every overpass. Lawson and Chief Curry would be in the lead car of the motorcade precisely because they knew the route so well. For the rest of the drivers—including Secret Service agent Bill Greer in the president's limousine and Agent Sam Kinney in the Secret Service follow-up car—when they drove from Love Field to the Trade Mart and back it would be the first time on any of these roads. The lead car was their guide.

As Agent Lawson pulled onto the tarmac at the airfield, he realized he hadn't needed to use the windshield wipers at all. The sky had changed from dull gray to a crisp blue. There were just a few wispy clouds floating toward the horizon.

The presidential party could easily have driven from Fort Worth to Dallas in half an hour, but Ken O'Donnell had vetoed that idea early in the preparations, opting instead for a thirteen-minute flight between Carswell Air Force Base and Dallas's Love Field. O'Donnell knew that the image of the president stepping out of Air Force One, waving to an enthusiastic crowd of supporters, was a photo opportunity that couldn't be passed up. The local news stations loved this stuff. They'd have a full staff of cameramen and reporters on hand to air the arrival "live," and again on the evening news. And so the schedule called for the vice president and Mrs. Johnson to arrive first, on Air Force Two—the official designation while the vice president was aboard—just in time to get in place to greet President Kennedy and Jackie as they stepped off Air Force One, acting as if they hadn't just seen each other less than an hour earlier back in Fort

Worth. Great for politics, but for the Secret Service it had created one additional stop that needed to be advanced and staffed by agents, spreading the manpower even thinner.

When Agent Lawson arrived at Love Field around 9:30 A.M., he was pleased to see that the local law enforcement had already shown up and were at their posts along the fence, where a crowd of people had already begun to gather.

Meanwhile, back in Fort Worth, the president was getting ready to make his entrance into the Grand Ballroom of the Hotel Texas for the Chamber of Commerce breakfast, when he realized Jackie still hadn't appeared.

The crowd had been waiting and the president was already ten minutes overdue, so he entered the ballroom from the kitchen as the Eastern Hills High School Band played "The Eyes of Texas." The two thousand people in the audience stood and clapped, but there were visible looks of disappointment on the faces of many of the women, who had come mainly to see Jackie. It did not go unnoticed by the president.

The president turned toward Agent Bill Duncan, who'd handled the Fort Worth portion of the advance, and said, "Bill, call Clint. I want Jackie to come down to the breakfast now."

Special Agent Clint Hill had managed to get about five hours of uninterrupted sleep, and after a hot shower, two cups of coffee, and a room service breakfast of bacon and eggs, he was ready for the hectic day ahead. He wondered how Jackie would feel this morning. She wasn't used to the nonstop schedule of these trips and she'd clearly been exhausted when they finally arrived at the hotel last night.

Clint knocked on the door of the Presidential Suite.

"Mrs. Kennedy," he said, "the president wants you down at the breakfast. Are you ready?"

"Come on in, Mr. Hill," she answered in her soft velvet voice.

Mary Gallagher, her personal secretary and assistant, was helping her button her white wrist-length gloves. As Clint walked into the room, Jackie looked at him and smiled. Always cognizant of her appearance, she had seemed to be particularly focused on her clothing selection for fashion-conscious Dallas. Dressed in a two-piece rose pink Chanel suit

with a navy blouse and matching pillbox hat that was perched on her perfectly coiffed hair like a subtle crown, she looked lovely.

"Good morning," he said, returning the smile. "I hope you slept well.
We've got another long day ahead."

"Yes, I never realized how tiring campaigning could be," she said as she
took one last look in the mirror. "I guess I didn't do too much of it the last
time," she added, with what sounded like a hint of regret.

She'd been pregnant during the 1960 campaign and had delivered
John, Jr., just two weeks after her husband won the election. If Patrick
hadn't died, she most likely wouldn't have come on this trip, either, Clint
thought to himself. He was amazed at the strength of this woman he protected. She was thirty-four years old, had lost a baby just three months
earlier, and here she was, the dutiful politician's wife, waving and smiling
to the state of Texas, as if she were the happiest woman in the world.

As Clint led Jackie into the elevator, gently touching her elbow, he
sensed her excitement for the day ahead. Over the past three years he'd
learned to anticipate her needs before she voiced them, and he knew that
despite her outward graciousness, she despised crowds. He needed to
make sure she didn't get overwhelmed.

In the ballroom on the ground floor, the host of ceremonies was introducing the Texas politicians who were seated at the head table, while
the empty place next to the president left the audience wondering whether
Jackie was going to appear.

As Clint escorted her into the room the audience stood, applauded,
and cheered with a rousing Texas welcome. Clint stayed close to her as
they made their way toward the head table, where President Kennedy was
standing and applauding with as much pleasure as anybody in the room.

Oh, isn't she lovely? the women whispered. *Don't you just love the color
of that suit? Look at the way she walks. What class!*

The president smiled broadly. It had been such a long time since they'd
traveled together in public, and judging from the overwhelming welcome
Jackie was getting, Agent Hill had no doubt this would be a recurring
episode in the year ahead. As Jackie took her seat, Clint stood as incon-
spicuously as possible, just a few feet away, and focused his attention on
everybody *but* the first lady, scanning the room for anything or anybody
that seemed out of place.

A half hour later, the breakfast was over, another item marked off the agenda. It was just after ten o'clock in the morning, and already the president had appeared before six thousand people. Ken O'Donnell and Dave Powers were thrilled. Everything was going like clockwork.

After escorting President and Mrs. Kennedy back to Suite 850, Emory Roberts realized he needed to hand out the assignments to his shift for the arrival at Love Field in Dallas. As the shift supervisor it was his responsibility to assign the positions as suggested by the Preliminary Survey Report and make sure that all his men were physically and emotionally capable of performing their duties. Yesterday had been an exceptionally draining day and even though Emory had slept soundly, he knew a lot of the guys often had trouble winding down after so many hours of non-stop, adrenaline-pumping activity. He didn't know that some of them had gone to the press club, but that didn't matter. His agents had all reported for duty on time and had handled the speech and the breakfast flawlessly. Emory Roberts had no reason to doubt any of his men.

He pulled out the motorcade plan he'd been given the night before and looked at where Win Lawson, the Dallas advance agent, had posted the men on his shift. With Sam Kinney driving and Emory Roberts in the front passenger seat, there were eight more spaces available in Halfback, the follow-up car. Ken O'Donnell and Dave Powers would be in the jump seats, as they often were, leaving two places for agents in the backseat with four agents standing on the running boards.

Because agents had to have at least six months of experience on the White House Detail to conduct an advance, four of Emory's senior shift agents had been sent on the advances in Houston, San Antonio, and Austin, stripping his shift of resources. Jack Ready, Don Lawton, and Tim McIntyre were his only regular shift agents available on this trip, and one of them had to stay at Love Field to handle the advance for the president's departure later that afternoon to Austin, which left only two agents available for the follow-up car.

For Christ's sake. How much longer can we go on like this? Emory thought as he reviewed the report.

Dallas advance agent Win Lawson had come up with the most sensible plan, based on the manpower at hand. Thank God, Mrs. Kennedy had come on the trip and Clint Hill and Paul Landis were here.

Jack Ready, as the most senior of Emory's agents available, would cover the president in the motorcade; Don Lawton was the only other agent with enough time on the detail to do an advance, so he'd have to stay at Love Field. Win Lawson had placed Clint Hill opposite Jack Ready, on the left front running board behind Mrs. Kennedy, with Tim McIntyre, the brand-new guy on the shift, directly behind him. McIntyre at least had worked the Tampa motorcade four days earlier, so he wasn't totally green.

Win had stationed Paul Landis on the right running board behind Jack Ready, behind the president.

At first Emory thought about switching him around and moving him behind Clint on Mrs. Kennedy's side of the car, since he was on the First Lady's Detail, but then he realized why Win had put Landis behind Jack. Landis had a lot more experience than McIntyre—he had been on the detail since the Eisenhower administration—so it made sense for him to be on the side with the president. Emory left him there.

What both Emory and Win had failed to realize, however, was that while Landis had been on the White House Detail for nearly four years, he had never worked the follow-up car in a motorcade before. Paul's first assignment was with the Eisenhower grandchildren, and then, after Kennedy's inauguration, he was assigned to Glen Ora for several months. He had traveled with Clint Hill and Paul Rundle to Italy with Mrs. Kennedy in 1962 and had spent much time in Hyannis Port and Palm Beach filling in for the Kiddie Detail before Clint asked him to join Mrs. Kennedy's detail on a permanent basis. Of course, he had gone through motorcade training in Secret Service school, but this was going to be his first presidential motorcade. Emory Roberts had no idea.

Just three more agents were available to his shift for staffing the follow-up car: Hank Rybka, George Hickey, and Glen Bennett. Rybka and Hickey were both driver agents and Glen Bennett was a temporary agent on loan from the Protective Research Section. Hickey had filled in on the follow-up car in Tampa, but Rybka had never worked follow-up, other than driving. Lawson had assigned Rybka to assist Don Lawton at Love Field, and in the backseat of the follow-up car would be PRS agent Glen Bennett on the right, and driver agent George Hickey stationed at the AR-15.

The AR-15 was the loaded .223 rifle that was stored in the locked gun cabinet behind the front seat of the Secret Service follow-up car. Hickey would remove the weapon and place it on the floor, out of sight, but within reach, behind the jump seat, where President Kennedy's aides would be sitting. There'd never been an occasion for the rifle to be used, but every agent on the detail could shoot it with pinpoint accuracy. Proficiency with firearms was mandatory for all agents on the White House Detail, including drivers.

It was a requirement for all agents to maintain an "expert" status with their handguns, and in order to make it convenient for regular practice there was a tunnel that led from the White House to the Treasury pistol firing range. Rifle and shotgun practice was conducted at the outdoor range on a quarterly basis. God have mercy on you if you were the target of the AR-15.

Emory Roberts put the report on top of the stack on his clipboard and made the rounds to give the agents their assignments.

The midnight shift agents settled into their seats on the National Guard plane for the short flight to Austin. Sitting next to a window, Agent Jerry Blaine took a deep breath and closed his eyes. All he wanted to do was sleep.

Across the aisle, Bob Faison nudged Ken Giannoules, who was seated next to him.

"Hey, Ken. Did you see this?"

Faison held up a copy of the *Dallas Morning News*, opened to a full-page advertisement that said WELCOME MR. KENNEDY TO DALLAS. The ad, placed by the "American Fact-Finding Committee," basically called President Kennedy a traitor and accused him of supporting communism. The border of the sarcastic invitation looked like black funeral draping—as if it were a death announcement.

Special Agent Win Lawson had no time to read the newspaper that morning, so he didn't see the advertisement. But he was well aware of the circular that had been handed out a few days before, accusing President Kennedy of treason. Lawson hadn't taken it as a serious threat, but he'd asked Forrest Sorrels to check it out. The district attorney had verified that while it was certainly in poor taste, the circular wasn't a violation of local or federal law. It was all part of the balance of living in a free country. Americans had freedom of religion, freedom of speech, freedom of the press, the right to bear arms.

Lawson had made one final call to the Protective Research Section to make sure no new threats had come in overnight. PRS hadn't received any new names; there were just the regulars, the ones the agents all carried on index cards in their jacket pockets.

At Love Field, driver agents George Hickey and Sam Kinney had checked over the White House cars, making sure there had been no security breaches, and then washed and detailed the cars thoroughly before driving them to the designated staging area where the president would arrive on Air Force One. The rest of the vehicles in the motorcade were leased Lincolns and Fords.

Driver agent Bill Greer was coming in on Air Force One and would drive SS100X, the president's car, as usual, while Sam Kinney would drive the Secret Service follow-up car. They knew the drill, had done it hundreds of times. The only variation was the addition of the vice president's car and his Secret Service follow-up car, both standard convertibles.

President and Mrs. Kennedy's Secret Service agents had split up between two airplanes, while the Johnson agents flew with the vice president on the plane he was using for the Texas trip from Fort Worth to Dallas. ASAIC Roy Kellerman, day shift supervisor Emory Roberts, and Special Agents Clint Hill, Jack Ready, and Bill Greer were on Air Force One; the rest of the Kennedy Detail agents were traveling on the president's backup plane, which also carried members of the press.

On Air Force One, the mood was jubilant. ATSAIC Roberts could hear laughter coming from the front of the plane, where the president sat with Jackie, Dave Powers, Ken O'Donnell, Evelyn Lincoln, the president's secretary, and Admiral George Burkley, the president's private physician. The warm welcomes they'd received in Houston, San Antonio, and Fort Worth seemed to have put everybody at ease.

DALLAS MOTORCADE CONFIGURATION

Lead Car Unmarked White Ford (Hardtop)

Dallas police chief Jesse Curry	SS advance agent Win Lawson
Sheriff Bill Decker	Dallas field agent Forrest Sorrels

Presidential Limousine SS100X
1961 Lincoln Continental Convertible

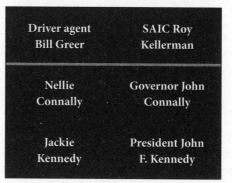

Driver agent Bill Greer	SAIC Roy Kellerman
Nellie Connally	Governor John Connally
Jackie Kennedy	President John F. Kennedy

Secret Service Follow-Up Car
"Halfback" Convertible

SS agent Clint Hill	Driver agent Sam Kinney	ATSAIC Emory Roberts	SS agent Jack Ready
	Pres. Aide Ken O'Donnell	Pres. Aide Dave Powers	
SS agent Tim McIntyre	AR-15 rifle		SS agent Paul Landis
	Driver agent George Hickey	PRS agent Glen Bennett	

12

Six Seconds in Dallas

The courage of life is often a less dramatic spectacle than the courage of a final moment; but it is no less a magnificent mixture of triumph and tragedy.
—JOHN F. KENNEDY

When the president's backup plane arrived at Love Field, Paul Landis from Mrs. Kennedy's detail was the first one off the plane. He was surprised to see the large crowd lined up behind the five-foot chain-link fence. There had to be about two thousand people gathered to greet the president. Wasn't Dallas a Republican stronghold?

When Emory Roberts had told him he'd be working the follow-up car today, he was more than a little surprised. He had just assumed that as the number-two man for Mrs. Kennedy, he would be sent to the Trade Mart. It wasn't normal to have two agents from the First Lady's Detail on the follow-up car.

Landis was known for his practical jokes and good sense of humor, and he decided to have a little fun. He walked over to driver agent Sam Kinney, who was standing right next to the Secret Service follow-up car.

"Hey, Sam," he said with a quizzical look on his face, looking everywhere but at the car directly in front of him. "I'm supposed to be in the follow-up car. Do you know where it is?"

Sam laughed and played along.

"Yeah, I think I saw it way over there," he said, pointing back toward the airplane hangar, several hundred yards away. "You better get on over there."

Meanwhile, Win Lawson walked calmly alongside the fence, scanning the enthusiastic crowd. He too was surprised at how many folks had shown up and were waiting in anticipation for what would likely be a once-in-a-lifetime glimpse of John F. and Jacqueline Kennedy. Most of the spectators looked as if they had taken great care with their appearance for the occasion. Men were dressed in suits and ties, their shoes polished to a high shine, while the women were nearly all wearing knee-length dresses or skirts with high heels. One young man in a plaid button-down shirt stood atop a platform at the back of the crowd, holding a huge Texas flag. Farther down, another man waved a Confederate flag. A dozen or so people held signs welcoming Jackie and President Kennedy to the Lone Star State but there were also a few, scattered throughout the crowd, raising handmade signs with slogans like YANKEE GO HOME and YOU'RE A TRAI-TOR. Clearly these were anti-Kennedy folks, but rarely did somebody with a picket sign pose a serious threat to the president. Sure, they could agitate the rest of the well-meaning crowd but in reality it was the hidden loner the Secret Service agents worried about most, the individual who'd come alone and whose eyes revealed the intense determination of someone who wanted to make a name for himself.

Lawson looked up and saw Paul Landis walking toward him.

"Win, Emory told me I'm supposed to man the follow-up car. I just wanted to double-check. Is that right?" Paul asked.

Win looked at his advance report. "Yep. That's right."

The vice president's plane had arrived, and a minute later Air Force One came into view. Slowly, gracefully, the elegant silver, blue, and white airplane landed on the runway, a picture-perfect grand entrance for the television cameras that were broadcasting live on the local Dallas and Fort Worth TV stations. The animated crowd clapped and hollered right on cue.

As the plane taxied to a stop less than fifty yards from the gaping crowd, Agent Win Lawson walked toward the stairs where the president and Mrs. Kennedy would descend from the plane. His eyes scanned the crowd, watching for anything unusual, anybody moving suddenly to the front of the fence. The president and Jackie would walk down the stairs, unguarded by any Secret Service agents, so the cameras could capture the couple alone. They'd been told not to dawdle, to move quickly to the bottom of the stairs, where Win and the other agents would suddenly appear at their sides.

The back door of the airplane opened, and as Jackie emerged, with the president directly behind her, the crowd went into an absolute frenzy. Standing at the top of the steps, the couple paused for just a split second to look at the impressive crowd on the other side of the fence. Then, smiling as if they were truly thrilled to be arriving in the great city of Dallas, the president and his wife quickly and deliberately descended the portable metal staircase. The spectators were so focused on Jackie in her bright pink suit and the president, looking so tanned and handsome, that they probably hadn't noticed the Secret Service agents disembarking from the front of the plane, moving rapidly toward the rear stairwell.

As soon as Jackie stepped onto the pavement, Agent Clint Hill was within an arm's length of her. ATSAIC Emory Roberts and ASAIC Roy Kellerman seemed to appear out of nowhere and were suddenly inches from President Kennedy. Straight-faced and serious, Emory Roberts darted eyes unseen behind his black sunglasses as Roy Kellerman moved in tandem with the president down the reception line. Clint Hill watched as the Dallas mayor's wife, Dearie Cabell, handed Jackie a huge bouquet of red roses. It was a bit strange, he thought; at every other stop the people had brought yellow roses, the famous yellow roses of Texas. Jackie, of course, made no mention of the fact and accepted the flowers gracefully, like it was the most extraordinary bouquet she'd ever been given.

Win Lawson looked toward the row of parked cars and made eye contact with Bill Greer, who was just stepping into the driver's seat of the presidential limousine. Sam Kinney was already at the wheel of the follow-up car, with the engine running.

The onslaught of noise was overpowering. Beyond the engines, whistles and yells seemed to come from every direction.

"Welcome to Dallas, Mr. President!"

"Jackie! Over here! Look over here!"

Lots of people had brought their Brownie cameras and were holding them above their heads, hoping to get a decent shot over the crowd.

The schedule called for the entourage to move through the official greeters and proceed directly to their assigned cars, and for a brief moment, Win thought the president was actually going to follow the plan. But when President Kennedy turned toward the eager crowd and saw the hands reaching out toward him, the voices urging him to come and say hello, Win knew it would be at least a few more minutes before the motorcade was on its way.

Agents Jack Ready, Paul Landis, Glen Bennett, and Tim McIntyre sprung into action as the president walked deliberately to the fence and began shaking the outstretched hands. The crowd was going wild—people were moving closer and closer together, vying for the prime spots next to the fence. In the agents' minds, any one of these people could have a gun or a knife. Agents Don Lawton and Hank Rybka, who would be staying at the airport to keep it secured for the president's departure, stayed farther away from the president, as a second perimeter of protection.

Jack Kennedy was in his element. He loved being among the people—the closer the better. Jackie, not knowing what else to do, followed her husband's lead and offered her own white-gloved hand to the adoring crowd.

Emory Roberts, Roy Kellerman, Clint Hill, and Paul Landis moved along with the Kennedys, their eyes watching every hand as it was held out, ready to jump if they saw so much as a flicker of metal or a grasp that held on a second too long.

Win Lawson took a deep breath as he surveyed the scene, making sure the agents were spread out effectively and the cars and other passengers in the motorcade were ready to go as soon as President Kennedy gave the word. This is where the detail teamwork was essential. With no portable radios, the agents relied on hand signals and eye contact to point out targets that the roaming agents could respond to.

Vice President and Lady Bird Johnson waited near the leased Lincoln convertible that would follow the Secret Service follow-up car; Governor John Connally and his wife, Nellie, stood near the presidential limousine. They'd be sitting on the fold-down seats in between the front and rear bench seats but it wouldn't be appropriate for them to take their places before the president was in the car. There still seemed to be the same confusion as in Fort Worth regarding whether Senator Yarborough would ride with the Johnsons, but that wasn't Win's problem. He'd let the political aides deal with the bickering politicians.

As the Kennedys walked along the fence, driver agent Bill Greer inched the presidential limousine forward alongside them. If the situation turned dangerous, he needed to be as close as possible so they could jump in the car for a quick getaway. The Irish-born Greer had been John F. Kennedy's driver since the day he was elected and he knew this car better than anybody. He knew precisely how much pressure he needed to put on the gas pedal when there were four passengers versus two, and how much more pressure was required when two agents were standing on the back platform. He knew that because of the weight and length of the car, he had to slow down when turning a corner so the passengers in the back didn't get thrown to the side. And, God forbid, if he ever did have to make a sudden getaway, he knew the 7,500-pound car with its 300-horsepower engine just didn't gather speed as quickly as he would like.

Finally, the president shook one last hand, thanked the crowd for coming out, and looked toward Jackie, signaling her with a quick nod. He'd had enough and was ready to go.

Governor Connally entered the president's limo and pulled up the jump seat so the Kennedys could slide into their positions in the back. Clint Hill, always anticipating where he should be to best protect Mrs. Kennedy, walked around to the left side of the car and stood at the fender, scanning the crowd as she sat down and smoothed out her skirt. She placed the bouquet of red roses on the seat next to her and looked up at Clint Hill with a smile, raising her hands to her eyes to shield them from the blinding sun, which was almost directly overhead. There was not a cloud in the sky.

Roy Kellerman held the door for President Kennedy and noticed him wince ever so slightly as he stepped into the back of the limousine next to Jackie, on the right-hand side of the car. Once the president and Jackie were settled, Governor Connally and Nellie flipped open the jump seats and sat down, with Nellie on the left, directly in front of Jackie, and the governor on the right, in front of the president. Sometimes President Kennedy would raise the hydraulic lift, elevating him another ten inches so he was even more visible, but this crowd, he knew, had come to see

Jackie as much as they'd come for him. He wasn't about to block their view. Still, with his height and the way the car was designed, he sat a good three or four inches higher than Governor Connally.

Jackie pulled out her sunglasses from her small handbag and put them on. The president looked at her and shook his head.

"Jackie, take those off," the president said, slightly irritated. "The people have come to see you."

Roy Kellerman sat down in the front passenger seat of the presidential limo, picked up the radio receiver, and pressed the transmission button.

"Lancer departing," he said, relaying to Win Lawson, who held a portable radio in the lead car directly in front of him.

Win Lawson took his seat in the white unmarked Ford sedan as Chief Curry put the car in gear and began following the police motorcycles in front of the procession. Win looked at his watch: 11:55 A.M. Just five minutes late. With any luck they might be able to make up some time along the way and still be at the Trade Mart by 12:30.

As the lead car pulled away, Bill Greer shifted the limousine into drive, took his foot off the brake, and eased down on the gas pedal. He was careful not to make any sudden lurches, always cognizant that the life of the President of the United States of America was in his hands. Even though he was not leading the motorcade, Greer controlled the pace. It was Win Lawson's job in the lead car to keep a close eye on the presidential limousine behind him and relay instructions to Police Chief Curry as to whether they needed to speed up or slow down.

Agent Greer looked in his rearview mirror to make sure the follow-up car was moving, and it was, almost as if there were an invisible five-foot chain connecting the two cars. Glen Bennett and George Hickey were seated in the backseat, with Dave Powers and Ken O'Donnell in the jump seats. As Sam Kinney kept the car moving at the same pace as the president's limousine, Jack Ready, Paul Landis, and Tim McIntyre dropped back to their positions on the running boards.

In his left-side mirror, Bill Greer saw Clint Hill still jogging alongside the car with his hand resting on the side of the midnight blue limousine, inches behind Jackie, even as the car sped up.

On the right side, Don Lawton, the designated departure advance agent, slipped into position next to the president as Jack Ready dropped back to the follow-up car and trotted along, like Clint, with a big grin on his face. On the trips to Tampa and San Antonio, Don Lawton had worked the follow-up car, but now he was relegated to handling the departure. He might as well enjoy the honor of working the motorcade, briefly, before he started the advance.

Finally, Clint Hill dropped back into position on the left running board of the follow-up car as Bill Greer picked up the speed. Don Lawton was still jogging alongside. Emory Roberts stood up and motioned him back with a *Lawton! What in the Sam Hill are you doing?* kind of look. The motorcade was just starting and the last thing Roberts wanted was the president getting upset over an agent blocking the view for the people who had come to see Jackie and him. Lawton turned to the follow-up car with a big grin and put up his arms in mocking protest as he dropped back to the sidelines.

"Okay, I've done my job, guys," Lawton said. "It's all yours now. Now go on and get out of here so I can have some lunch."

This was typical Don Lawton. He was joking, but the other agents could tell he'd rather be working the follow-up car than staying at Love Field with Rybka advancing the departure.

Sam Kinney, driving the follow-up car, focused on the back of the presidential limousine and its passengers, keeping as close to its rear bumper as possible to prevent another vehicle or even a person from separating the two cars. He also had to keep an eye on the agents hanging off the sides of Halfback. If an agent jumped off the running board headed for the president's car, Sam had to react in a heartbeat. The job of the team was to protect the president but, for God's sake, he didn't want to run over a Secret Service agent, either. For Bill Greer, Sam Kinney, and the other Kennedy Detail Secret Service agents, the rest of the motorcade behind them was inconsequential. Their sole purpose, and the role for which they'd been handpicked and highly trained, was to make sure nothing happened to the man and woman seated in the backseat of that dark blue convertible limousine. Nothing else mattered.

The motorcade proceeded like a long, slithering snake, traveling between twelve and fifteen miles an hour until it left the airport grounds and headed onto Mockingbird Lane to Lemmon Avenue. The four police motorcycles escorting the president's limousine were strategically placed according to the White House Advance Manual—two on each side, positioned between the rear tires of the limousine and the front tires of the follow-up car—so as not to impede the movements of the follow-up car agents. The loud roar of the motorcycle engines, however, made normal conversation between the passengers in the cars nearly impossible.

There were few spectators on this stretch of road, so Win Lawson told Chief Curry he could pick up the pace.

"Keep it between twenty-five and thirty until we start to see some crowds," he said. He knew that as they got closer to downtown, the sidewalks would be filled—the publicity in the local news media had guaranteed that—and inevitably the procession would slow down. He had to keep an eye on the timing to make sure they didn't get too far off schedule.

Bill Greer and Sam Kinney sped up at the same rate, maintaining a consistent distance between the vehicles.

Clint Hill tightened his grip on the handhold as the car gained momentum. He moved his head constantly: his eyes scanning along the left side of the road, up ahead, and then back again, the pink hat always within his gaze. She was no more than five yards in front of him, but she might as well have been on the other side of Dallas. *I shouldn't be this far away. I should be on the back of that limousine.*

The procession went along for several miles in this manner, passing used car lots, junk dealers, and auto parts stores. Every so often there'd be a handful of people waving or holding up a sign, and the president, Jackie, and Governor and Mrs. Connally would all wave back.

As the motorcade got closer to the city proper, the crowds multiplied—all of a sudden, it seemed—until there were people standing two and three deep along both sides of the road.

"Okay, let's slow it down," Win Lawson directed to Chief Curry. Lawson turned around and Bill Greer was already doing the same. The police chief gradually reduced the speed until he was going twelve miles an hour. The rest of the parade followed suit.

Up ahead, Agent Lawson saw a group of children standing next to a large sign, about the size of a full-size bedsheet, on which was hand-painted, "Please, Mr. President. Stop and shake our hands."

Lawson had worked enough motorcades with Kennedy to know that the president responded to signs like this and often he would indeed ask

Bill Greer to stop the car. As they passed the group, Lawson looked back to the president's car.

Sure enough, as soon as President Kennedy was close enough to read the sign, he said, "Bill, stop up here. Call these people over and I'll shake their hands."

As Bill Greer slowed down to a complete stop directly in front of the sign, ASAIC Roy Kellerman opened the front right door and jumped out, standing firmly next to the president with his legs spread and his arms ready to fend off anybody who pulled a weapon or tried to jump into the car. A woman who was holding up one side of the sign squealed, "It worked! Our sign worked!"

Suddenly the crowd surged forward as children and adults alike raced toward the limousine. The policemen on the motorcycles had to stop abruptly to avoid hitting anybody. Within seconds the well-meaning police officers were surrounded, unable to move.

As Sam Kinney slowed down in unison with Bill Greer, the agents on the running boards—Clint, Jack, Paul, and Tim—leapt off the follow-up car. It took each of them just a couple of strides to reach the rear doors of the limousine, acting as a human barrier between President Kennedy on one side and Jackie on the other, seconds before the first spectators bombarded the car.

President Kennedy stood up, leaned out the side of the car, and shook one hand after another, laughing as the children screeched with delight, while Jackie remained seated, offering a smile and a wave to the crowd that seemed to envelop the car. Clint Hill could see the unease in her eyes even as she tried valiantly to smile to the crowd. He moved in close and as she glanced at him, her anxiety seemed to disappear.

"He shook my hand! The president shook my hand!" a little boy squealed.

In the follow-up car, Dave Powers was recording some of the scenes with his home movie camera. He couldn't have scripted a better political commercial if he had tried.

After just a few seconds President Kennedy turned to Bill Greer and said, "All right. Let's travel on." Greer looked in his rearview mirror and saw the president wince as he sat back in his seat. He could tell Kennedy was wearing his back brace but still, he was obviously in pain.

ASAIC Roy Kellerman held the radio to his mouth and said, "Proceeding, Halfback."

As the procession took the slight right turn onto Turtle Creek Boulevard, the crowds continued to multiply. Men, women, and children were spilling over the sidewalk into the street, leaving barely enough room for the motorcade to pass. Jacqueline Kennedy was smiling and waving to the crowds on the left while the president worked the right-hand side. The procession had slowed to about six miles an hour and the four motorcycles at the sides of the presidential limousine were being squeezed between the spectators and SS100X on Jackie's side of the car. They had no choice but to drop back. The cutback in the roar of the motorcycles only stimulated the crowds, who rushed forward, shouting, "Jackie! Mr. President! Welcome to Dallas!"

Clint Hill jumped off the left running board of the follow-up car, ran to the back of the limousine, and hopped onto the back foot stand. President's orders or not, his job was to protect Mrs. Kennedy. Crouching down in an uncomfortable squat, he hung on to the small handrail and scanned the crowd.

As the cars moved through the downtown area, the agents' eyes darted from the thousands of people standing alongside the road, up to the windows of the high-rise buildings, where people were hanging out windows, waving, and holding signs, and back to the street level. At times it was a carnival-like atmosphere, with the motorcycle engines bleating, people whooping and hollering and sounding off noisemakers, trying to get Jackie or the president to look their way for a snapshot they could show their grandchildren someday. In the midst of the commotion Paul Landis noticed a group of people standing on the roof of an apartment building.

"Look, Jack!" he yelled to Agent Jack Ready. "There are even people on the roof of that building."

They didn't appear to be harmful or threatening, but if any one of them had a gun, they'd have a clear shot at the boss.

As the motorcade rolled along, the crowd would thin, and Clint Hill would drop back to the follow-up car when the motorcycles were able to maintain their positions between the spectators and Jackie. But then there'd be another patch where the people would be yelling and moving toward the car, reaching out their hands to the woman in the bright pink hat with the glamorous smile, and Clint would jump back onto the foot stand, poised like a guard dog daring anybody to come any closer. A couple of times he saw President Kennedy glance at him, but that didn't bother Clint. If he had to explain his actions, he'd be perfectly prepared. His job was to protect Mrs. Kennedy, and not even the President of the United States could keep him from his mission.

Turtle Creek Boulevard turned into Cedar Springs Road, and then jogged onto Harwood. When the motorcade made the right-hand turn from Harwood onto Main Street, the crowd was so thick that people were standing shoulder to shoulder, covering the sidewalks on both sides of the street, overflowing onto the pavement. The people clapped and cheered as the president's limousine came into view and, once more, the motorcycles were surrounded.

Bill Greer kept his eyes on the lead car, maintaining a constant speed between twelve and fifteen miles an hour. His goal was to keep four to five car lengths behind so that if he ever needed to speed up all of a sudden, he had enough room to get out. In his rearview mirror he could see Clint Hill, once again crouched on the back bumper.

Behind Greer, Sam Kinney kept his eyes on Jackie's pink hat directly in front of him and inched closer to the president's limousine. When the crowds were this thick the protocol was to keep as little space as possible between the follow-up car and SS100X. The last thing you wanted was for some crazy son of a bitch to charge in between the two cars, or have a car at an intersection separate the president from his protection. But Greer and Kinney had worked this exact formation hundreds of times and were so used to driving with each other that they could almost read each other's minds. They'd never had an incident they couldn't handle and always remained calm under pressure. Both men had remained in these jobs precisely because they were the most trusted, most competent drivers in the Secret Service.

For a city that hadn't much cared for Kennedy in the 1960 election, the size of the crowds was surprising to everybody, including Dave Powers and Ken O'Donnell. From the time they'd left Love Field there had to have been at least one hundred and fifty thousand people who had used their lunch hour for a chance to see the president.

Suddenly, on the right-hand side of the street, a teenage boy broke through the crowd and yelled, "Slow down! Slow down!" as he lunged toward the car. Agent Jack Ready jumped off the running board and shoved the boy as hard as he could, down onto the curb, causing a number of people to fall into each other. That wasn't Jack's problem. He knew he might be criticized by the president later for this, but he had to make a snap decision.

Without missing a beat, Agent Paul Landis quickly moved to cover the president the instant Jack jumped toward the teenager. Sweat dampened his face as he jogged alongside the presidential limousine, his suit coat flapping with each stride. Landis continued for a few hundred yards until Jack was back on the running boards, then he was able to slow down and resume his position on the rear of Halfback.

Sitting in the front passenger seat of the follow-up car, ATSAIC Emory Roberts was pleased with the way the agents were handling the motorcade. Every time he saw Clint Hill jump onto the back of the president's car, he swallowed hard, fighting the urge to call him back. The president's orders replayed in his mind. *Keep the Ivy League charlatans off the back of the car!* But Emory remained silent. Clint was doing his job, and doing it damn well.

The procession continued smoothly down Main Street. As Forrest Sorrels had predicted, this is where the crowds were heaviest. Agent Hill stayed on the back of the limousine, poised to react in an instant. The people were just too close to Mrs. Kennedy. He didn't like the situation at all.

Finally, as they neared the end of Main Street, neared the intersection of Houston and Main, the crowds thinned and the motorcycles were able to resume their proper positions. With fewer people on the sidelines, and farther from the car, Clint felt as if it was safe to return to the follow-up car. He jumped off the midnight blue limousine and in one fluid movement hopped back onto Halfback's left running board. Beads of sweat formed on his forehead. Keeping a loose grip on the handrail with one hand, he used the other to wipe his brow.

With the Old Court House on his left and the County Criminal Courts Building on his right, Bill Greer eased off the gas and applied just the gentlest touch to the brake as he turned the wheel to the right, onto Houston Street. Surprisingly, as soon as he made the turn, the number of people diminished dramatically. There were no people spilling into the street as on

Main. Here the people stood in small clumps. A couple of women standing together, a little boy sitting on top of his father's shoulders. There were buildings on the right and at the intersection just ahead, but to the left was a small park, where just a handful of people lounged in the grass.

As Clint scanned his eyes to the left, he saw the triple overpass, and across the plaza, a sign for the entrance to Stemmons Freeway. With the thinning crowd and freeway just ahead, Clint knew that this was the end of the downtown political tour and that the car would be picking up speed. It was standard procedure—regardless of the president's request— for all agents to fall back to the follow-up car in this situation. Otherwise an agent could be stranded on the back stand as the limousine sped up on the freeway, with no opportunity to drop back to the follow-up car. The last thing you wanted was an agent hanging on to the trunk of SS100X for dear life, at highway speeds.

Directly ahead was a seven-story brick building: TEXAS SCHOOL BOOK DEPOSITORY, it said over the doorway. A bright yellow Hertz billboard was mounted on the roof, angled toward the freeway, with a large digital clock that read 12:30. Clint noticed some open windows on the upper floors of the building. Nothing unusual. There had been open windows on the upper floors of buildings all along the route, with people waving and shouting from above. He turned his gaze to the left and saw several more groups scattered on a mound of grass, beyond which was the overpass and Stemmons Freeway.

Sitting in the right jump seat of the follow-up car, Dave Powers had come to the end of the roll of film that was in his camera. He would put in a new roll at the Trade Mart. Fortunately, he'd already gotten a lot of excellent footage.

Up ahead, the three lead motorcycles turned the corner—left onto Elm Street—just in front of the brick Texas School Book Depository building. In the lead car, Win Lawson saw the overpass and knew that the entrance to Stemmons Freeway was just beyond it. He turned to Chief Curry and said, "We're about five minutes away from the Trade Mart at this point. Is that right, Chief?"

"Yup. That should be just about right."

Win turned his head back to check once again that Bill Greer was in line behind him, four car lengths away, and just as the white Ford made the sharp left turn, he picked up the handheld radio. It was customary to advise the agents at the next stop when the president was five minutes from the destination. His transmission would be heard by the Dallas White House switchboard and they would call the telephone that had been installed at the Trade Mart. He looked down at his watch and pushed the transmission button.

"Five minutes away," he announced, just as the car turned left onto Elm Street.

Back in Washington, D.C., Special Agent Tom Wells stood on the South Portico of the White House with five-year-old Caroline Kennedy and her best friend, Agatha Pozen. The White House school had ended its daily session at 1:15, or 12:15 Dallas time, and the girls were chatting excitedly about the afternoon's activities. With both her parents away, Caroline had been given permission to spend the night at Agatha's house. She'd never spent a night away from relatives and she was absolutely giddy. Dressed in a powder blue coat and new red lace-up shoes, Caroline clutched her overnight bag in one hand and her favorite stuffed bear in the other as the girls waited for Agatha's mother to pick them up.

Tom knew that Jackie wanted her children to lead as normal an existence as possible, so he'd agreed to let Caroline ride with Agatha and her mother while he followed in a Secret Service car that was equipped with a radio link to the White House network. It was, of course, an off-the-record visit. Absolutely no press.

It was just before 1:30 when Liz Pozen entered the Southwest Gate in her Country Squire station wagon and pulled up to the South Portico.

"Sorry I'm late," she said to Agent Wells as she got out of the car.

"No problem," Wells said. "The girls are so excited, they hadn't even noticed."

As the girls tumbled into the backseat of the car, Wells explained that he'd follow behind her. If there were any problems, she'd signal and pull over. It wasn't a long drive, traffic shouldn't be heavy at this time of day, and neither of them anticipated any problems.

Upstairs in the family quarters of the White House, the children's nanny, Maud Shaw, was trying to get two-year-old John, Jr., to settle down for his nap. He was such an active boy—so different from quiet, demure Caroline—and he'd recently insisted on bringing a toy truck or helicopter into his crib. He'd cried for an hour when his mother and father left the day before—he so wanted to go with them in the big plane. Maud had been grateful when Agent Bob Foster suggested a trip to the toy shop on Wisconsin Avenue as a distraction.

"Mommy and Daddy will be back soon," Bob had assured John, Jr., as they walked through the aisles hand in hand. "Just in time for your birthday."

On November 25, John would turn three years old.

The flags on the front hood of the president's limousine flapped wildly as Bill Greer drove the short block on Houston Street. To his left was Dealey Plaza, a three-acre, triangular-shaped park of well-manicured grass, accented with concrete pergolas and walkways. Houston Street formed the base of the triangle and up ahead, Greer saw the lead car making a sharp left turn. He'd studied the map and knew it was Elm Street, but having never driven the route before, he found the size and locations of the buildings, as well as the gradient of the roads, to be completely foreign. What he did know was how his behemoth limousine took turns, which was not very gracefully.

The four passengers in the back of the limousine had been bantering back and forth for the past six miles. Nellie Connally turned around in her seat and looked at Jack Kennedy.

"You sure can't say Dallas doesn't love you, Mr. President," she said with a smile.

"No, you can't," he replied. He'd had a permanent smile on his face since he got off the plane at Love Field. Maybe the pollsters had been wrong about Texas after all.

Bill Greer slowed down, almost to a crawl, conscious of the comfort of his passengers as he rounded the hairpin turn, 135 degrees to the left. The road sloped down ever so gradually, and he accelerated once again as soon as the car was on the straightaway.

A woman in a red coat yelled out, "Hey, Mr. President! Look over here!"

In the follow-up car, Sam Kinney navigated the turn just as easily as Greer. Sitting in the front passenger seat, Emory Roberts heard Win Lawson's radio transmission that the motorcade was five minutes away, and glanced at his watch. He looked down and wrote 12:35 on his itinerary. The time they'd arrive at the Trade Mart.

"What a great crowd!" Ken O'Donnell said to Dave Powers.

"Sure is," agreed Dave. The 8mm movie camera was sitting in his lap.

The agents in the follow-up car, like the drivers, had never driven this route before, but when they saw the freeway entrance up ahead, combined with the dwindling crowds, they knew the vehicles were about to increase their speed. Standing on the running boards of the follow-up car was exactly where they were supposed to be.

On the front left running board, Clint Hill focused on the overpass ahead, looking for signs of anybody who might attempt something from that ideal vantage point. About ten people and two police officers. No problem. He moved his gaze to the left, to the flat grass area that formed Dealey Plaza, where just a few people were standing and waving.

Directly across from Hill, on the front right running board, Agent Jack Ready was scanning the clusters of people standing on the sidewalk and seated on another grassy slope on the right-hand side of the street. The four motorcycle police were back in position, a few yards from the agents, their growling engines drowning out the cheers and greetings from the few spectators.

Suddenly, above the noise of the motorcycles and beyond the screams of the adoring crowd, a sharp crack blistered through Dealey Plaza.

The triangular canyon of buildings created an echo chamber that masqueraded the sound such that even many of the Secret Service agents, all of whom were expert marksmen with high-powered rifles, didn't recognize it as gunfire. Bill Greer, driving the president's limousine, thought one of the motorcycles had backfired or that he had a blowout. He quickly tapped on the brake to see how the car would respond, but the car remained stable, so he continued on.

"What was that?" Agent Jack Ready blurted out. "A firecracker?"

Paul Landis, standing just behind Ready on the right running board of the follow-up car, was one of the few who recognized immediately that a rifle had been fired. Ironically, the night before in Fort Worth, he'd had a conversation with police officers who were talking about deer hunting. His thoughts had flashed back to the conversation, so when he heard the sound, he immediately recognized it as gunfire.

His eyes went directly to President Kennedy, who, about twenty feet in front of him, appeared to be turning his head toward the right, in the direction from which the sound had come. Paul swung his head around over his right shoulder and looked back toward the innocuous brick building they'd just passed. He didn't notice anything unusual, so he scanned the small clusters of people on the grassy hillside, his gaze moving quickly to the latticed design wall and fence at the top of the hill. Still, there was nothing that seemed to have caused the loud crack. He began to think that perhaps the sound had been a firecracker after all.

Clint Hill heard a sudden explosive sound from the right and to the rear. He instinctively moved his head in that direction. As his gaze crossed from left to right, he saw President Kennedy lurch forward, grab at his neck in a sudden strange motion, and then slump to his left. The average person might have screamed a profanity, but all Clint could think was *Oh God*.

He leapt off the running board of Halfback, as he'd done countless times before, his body reacting as it had been trained. In that terrible, unforgettable moment, Clint Hill had but one purpose: he had to reach Mrs. Kennedy and the president, and shield them. His powerful legs propelled him toward the pink hat that seemed to be moving farther and farther away each time his foot landed on the pavement. If only he could reach the back of the car, his legs knew the exact height of the rear step; his hands knew exactly where to grasp the hand grip. As he bounded toward the limousine, which had slowed to about seven miles an hour around the corner but was starting to pick up speed, he had to run at the breakneck speed of nearly fifteen miles an hour to adjust for the speed and the distance between the two cars. As his feet propelled him toward the moving car, Clint Hill was so focused on reaching his target that he didn't even hear the second shot.

On the right front running board of the follow-up car, Jack Ready had instinctively turned his head toward the Texas School Book Depository at the sound of the first shot. He was scanning the people on the right side of the street just as the sound of a second distinct rifle shot filled his ears. He whipped his head around and saw Clint running desperately toward the limousine.

Follow-up car driver Sam Kinney's responsibility was to maintain his focus on the president's car. He saw Kennedy's reaction to the first shot and then saw Clint leap onto the pavement a split second later. He immediately turned the follow-up car slightly to the right to clear a path for Clint to reach the president and first lady. His eyes were still focused on President Kennedy when he heard the second shot and saw Governor Connally slump toward his wife.

Just as Clint's system rejected the sound of the second shot, so did Governor Connally's. When the first shot was fired, Connally immediately recognized it as a rifle shot; the sound came from behind. He looked back in a reflexive motion over his right shoulder to where the sound had originated but saw only a few men, women, and children standing on the grassy knoll alongside the street. There was nobody holding a gun, and the sound seemed to have come from farther away. He turned forward again and was just about to look over his left shoulder to make eye contact with President Kennedy when he felt a crippling blow to his back. Like Clint, the adrenaline coursing through his veins threw his system into such shock that he never heard the sound of the second shot, the very shot that hit him.

The instant Nellie Connally heard the first shot, she turned her head to look over her right shoulder—the sound had come from the right rear of the car—and saw President Kennedy draw his hand to his throat. She turned to her husband just as the sound of the second shot permeated the car. Immediately the governor doubled over, blood spilling from his chest. "Oh no, no, no, no!" he yelled as he slumped toward Nellie. "They're going to kill us all!"

ASAIC Roy Kellerman was sitting in the front passenger seat of the presidential limo, directly in front of Governor Connally. He heard the first loud pop over his right shoulder and as he turned his gaze back and to the right, he thought he heard the president say, "My God, I am hit." He swung around to his left to look into the back of the car and saw President Kennedy grasping at his neck.

Kellerman grabbed the radio, turned to Bill Greer, and said, "Let's get out of here! We are hit!" He pushed the transmission button and there was no mistaking the urgency in his voice: "Lawson, this is Kellerman. We're hit. Get us to the nearest hospital! Quick!"

As he was relaying the message, he heard one bang, and then another, and as Greer tramped down on the accelerator, Kellerman felt the car burst forward with such thrust he felt like it was jumping off the god-damned road.

Up ahead the lead car was nearing the overpass when the first shot was fired. Through the open windows of the sedan, Agent Win Lawson heard the sharp report and turned to look back through the rear window. He could see some commotion in the president's car behind him. Then Kellerman's voice over the radio. "We're hit!"

Lawson turned to Chief Curry and said, "Get us to the nearest hospital. Quick!"

Sitting in the front passenger seat of the Secret Service follow-up car, ATSAIC Emory Roberts was recording the arrival time at the Trade Mart on his notepad when he heard the first shot. He looked up and saw the president slump five yards in front of him. Clint Hill practically flew off the left running board and in the same instant the car swerved a little to the right, creating a clear path for Clint to reach the limousine. Emory was focused on Clint—*Faster, faster! Come on, Clint!*—when the second shot filled his ears. A feeling of dread washed over him as he saw Governor Connally double over.

Standing on the front right running board, next to where Emory Roberts was seated, Jack Ready had one objective: to get to the president. He bent his knees and let go of the hand grip as his eyes focused on the back of President Kennedy's head.

Emory could tell that Jack was about to leap. But the follow-up car was veering to the right. If Jack jumped, he'd be jumping directly into the path of his own car. Sam Kinney was focused on Clint and would probably hit Jack dead-on. A sniper with a high-powered rifle had zeroed in on the open-top car, and Emory knew that the only hope for the president was either for Clint to reach him or for Bill Greer to get the hell out of there.

"Wait, Jack!" Emory called out, just as the third shot echoed through the canyon of buildings.

With one hand on the rail, poised to save the president, Agent Jack Ready watched John Kennedy's head explode into a grisly fountain of brains, bone, and blood. Behind him, Paul Landis sucked in his breath as the horrific image became forever etched into his soul.

In the driver's seat of the follow-up car, Sam Kinney clearly heard the loud crack of the third shot. Like Jack Ready, his gaze was transfixed on the president's head. When the bullet met its mark, he heard a sickening sound, like a melon shattering onto the pavement, and then Sam Kinney felt the warm blood of the president's head as it sprayed over the top of his windshield.

Jacqueline Kennedy was facing to her left when the first shot was fired. As she turned to the right, toward the sound, the president slumped to the left. Not knowing what was happening, she reached her right arm behind him, around his shoulders, just as the second shot hit the governor. She was staring into her husband's face just as the third and fatal shot hit the back of his head and splattered his brains in every direction.

Clint Hill was just feet from his goal, his eyes focused on Mrs. Kennedy, when he heard the third shot and the gruesome thump of President Kennedy's head exploding.

In one last desperate attempt, he stretched out his arms and wrapped his fingers around the handle as his foot found the step. His heart was pounding. He had made it . . . a split second too late.

Paul Landis had been looking right at the president and trying to calculate whether or not he could get there. A million thoughts were swirling in his head. But Clint was already on the way. *Go, Clint. Go! Clint, go!* And then he saw and heard the impact of the third shot.

When Bill Greer had accelerated suddenly, he didn't realize that Clint was hanging off the back. The extra weight forced the car to lurch forward and Clint's foot slid off the step, back to the pavement. Still holding tight to the hand grip, Clint raced to keep up with the car as it gained speed.

Jackie was screaming. "They've killed my husband! They've shot his head off!" She held out her white-gloved hand and yelled, "I have his brain in my hand!"

Good God! What is she trying to do? She had jumped out of her seat and was climbing toward Clint onto the trunk of the car, her brown eyes filled with terror. She looked like she was going to leap onto the pavement, like she was searching for something. For God's sake, a sniper was shooting at the car! He had to get to her. Nothing else mattered.

Clint lunged, and as the car sped toward the overpass his foot landed on the footstep one more time. He thrust his body forward onto the trunk, grabbed at Jackie's arm, and desperately pushed her back onto the seat. She slid back inside the car and collapsed. Clint was clinging to the back of the seat, his body spread-eagled across the trunk of the car as it raced onto the freeway. He sucked in his breath as he saw the horrific scene inside the limousine. Fragments of gray brain and white bone were splattered around the car like vile confetti. A pool of blood covered the floor. And slumped across the seat, President Kennedy lay unmoving, a bloody, gaping, fist-sized hole clearly visible in the back of his head.

Clint, now desperately holding on to the top of the rear door with all the strength in his hand, with one leg hooked down into the rear seat and one foot outside the car, placed his body so it covered Mrs. Kennedy and the president. He turned back to the agents in the follow-up car and, with a look of complete hopelessness, shook his head and gave them the thumbs-down sign with his one free hand.

"To the hospital! To the hospital!" he yelled to the lead car at the top of his lungs. And then his expression turned from despair to frustration as he pounded his fist onto the metal trunk again and again and again.

Agent George Hickey, stationed at the AR-15 in his first presidential motorcade, had picked up the rifle as soon as he registered that shots were being fired and immediately pulled back the lever to inject a shell from the clip into the chamber. He was just about to lift himself off the seat when the fatal shot hit the president. As the motorcade sped toward the triple underpass, Hickey stood up, released the safety, and looked back desperately into the windows of the buildings behind him, searching for the assassin.

Driving the presidential limousine, Bill Greer had glanced back after the second shot, saw Governor Connally slump, and realizing they were under attack, had tamped on the accelerator and hit the siren. In the same instant, Roy Kellerman, seated next to him, had yelled, "We are hit! Get out of here fast!" Suddenly he heard the third shot, just as the car lurched, as if it were being pulled back, rather than speeding forward. *What the hell was going on?* With his eyes focused on the road ahead, he had no idea that the 170-pound Clint Hill had just grabbed on to the back of the trunk.

The engine revved and the car suddenly propelled forward, leaving the side motorcycle escorts looking as if they were standing still.

Chief Curry, driving the lead car, saw the president's car barreling toward him in his rearview mirror. He quickly veered left as the lead motorcycle escort, unaware of what had just happened, peeled off toward Stemmons Freeway to clear the way to the Trade Mart.

Bill Greer skillfully maneuvered the accelerating limousine alongside the lead car and yelled out, "Take me to the hospital! Quick!"

Sam Kinney, driving the follow-up car, was still right on Greer's bumper. He had anticipated Greer's acceleration and now the vice president's Lincoln and the rest of the motorcade were far behind them. Somehow he kept his focus on driving—as he was trained to do—even with the harrowing sight of Clint Hill directly in front of him, sprawled across the bodies of Jackie and President Kennedy. Looking through his own blood-spattered windshield, the sirens blaring in his ears, Kinney couldn't even begin to imagine the horrific sight that must be inside the back of the car ahead.

In a sudden unforeseen tragedy such as this, everyone hears, sees, and reacts differently. People's responses will vary dramatically depending on their location or vantage point, their relationship to the victim or victims, and their emotional makeup. The mind and senses can absorb only so much in the scant moments of a traumatic event, especially if the individual is at the center of the disaster.

There would be marked variances in recollection over the coming days and weeks, and indeed, of all the people who witnessed the assassination, only two were able to observe and recall those five seconds with constant clarity—Sam Kinney and Nellie Connally.

Sam Kinney's responsibility as the Secret Service follow-up car driver required his eyes to remain focused on the presidential limo. And Mrs. Connally, seated to the left of one victim and diagonally in front of the other, had the calmness of character to respond without panic, carefully absorbing the tragedy as it unfolded before her eyes.

The way the rest of the Kennedy Detail agents responded depended entirely on their vantage points. With the sound and sight of the third shot hitting its mark and blowing the president's head apart, every agent in the follow-up car knew that the president's wound, if not fatal, would undoubtedly prevent him from functioning as president. Amid the chaos, everybody who had witnessed the terror had questions swirling in their heads. Who had fired on them? Was it one assassin? Or were there many? Were they after only President Kennedy, or were they on the hunt for Vice President Johnson, Governor Connally, or God knows who else?

The follow-up car agents were engulfed in despair. Guilt, helplessness, and emotional trauma seized them as they sped away from Dealey Plaza.

The agents in the presidential limo—driver Bill Greer and ASAIC Roy Kellerman—responded completely differently. They knew, of course, that shots had been fired and they'd heard Mrs. Kennedy's chilling screams, but from their vantage point they had no idea as to the extent of the injuries, as they had not seen the bullets hit their marks. Their only choice was to evacuate the scene and get to a hospital as quickly as possible. As Greer sped down the highway at eighty miles an hour, Roy Kellerman looked back and all he could see were the four passengers crouched down in the seats behind him, with Clint Hill sprawled out, like a human shield, across the president and Mrs. Kennedy. Kellerman knew the president had taken a bullet and now the mission was to save him.

Five or six yards behind Roy Kellerman, ATSAIC Emory Roberts knew the torch had passed. From his front-row seat in the follow-up car, there was no doubt in his mind that the third shot was fatal. His duty now was to protect Vice President Lyndon B. Johnson and he had to get the message to Agent Rufus Youngblood, who was sitting in the front seat of Johnson's car. Emory pressed the button on his radio and said, "Rufus, cover your man."

Unbeknownst to Emory Roberts, Youngblood was already lying on top of Lyndon Johnson, shielding the vice president's body with his own.

Every man on the Kennedy Detail would relive those six seconds in Dallas a million times over. For the rest of their lives, they would be defined by the assassination of JFK, questioned and blamed for failing to achieve the impossible.

As the clock on top of the Texas School Book Depository stood still at 12:30, Bill Greer raced to Parkland Hospital, leaving a trail of chaos in his wake.

13

Breakdown

*Those who make peaceful revolution impossible will make
violent revolution inevitable.*
—JOHN F. KENNEDY

NOVEMBER 22, 1963

There are moments in history that change the world forever. Time is suspended when an event occurs that is so shocking, so unexpected, so inexplicable that from that moment forward nothing can ever be the same. In the blink of an eye, on that dreadful day in Dallas, the hopes and dreams of the nation and the world were shattered.

At the Dallas Trade Mart, 2,600 people were seated, anxiously awaiting the arrival of President and Mrs. Kennedy. Agent Dave Grant was at the entrance with Trammell Crow and John Stemmons, the two co-owners of the Trade Mart, discussing the proper procedure for greeting the president and escorting him to the head table. The White House telephone had been installed just inside the front entrance of the Trade Mart and at 12:30, the phone rang. Grant walked inside, picked up the phone, and the switchboard operator told him the motorcade had given the five-minute signal.

"Great," he said as he looked at his watch. They were just five minutes behind schedule. He went back outside to wait with Crow and Stemmons for the arrival of the motorcade.

A few minutes later the sound of sirens could be heard in the distance, getting louder and louder. Suddenly Dave Grant saw the motorcade racing by the Trade Mart at about eighty miles an hour.

What the hell? The president's convertible looked empty in the backseat—and there was a person sprawled out across the trunk of the car.

Grant ran inside and called the White House switchboard.

"What's going on with the motorcade?" he asked breathlessly.

On the other end of the line, the switchboard operator said he had heard on the base radio that the president had been "hit" and that the motorcade was heading for the nearest hospital.

The operator didn't know which hospital, nor did he know the extent of the president's injuries.

Grant immediately thought of the overpass just before the Stemmons Freeway. Someone must have thrown a rock or a stick or something.

Grant found ATSAIC Stewart Stout inside the Trade Mart and told him what he'd learned.

They didn't know the extent of the injuries but decided that they and the other agents should remain at the Trade Mart in the event the president wasn't seriously hurt and might be returning to the Trade Mart after treatment.

Soon people started arriving at the Trade Mart who had been part of the motorcade and Grant learned that there had been some shooting and the president had been wounded.

Oh my God. When he had heard the word *hit* from the operator, he hadn't imagined gunshots. Suddenly securing the Trade Mart was irrelevant. As soon as they found out that the president had gone to Parkland Hospital, the agents scrambled to find available cars to take them there.

Dave Grant looked up to see Admiral George Burkley, carrying his black medical bag, rushing toward them. He had just arrived on the VIP bus moments earlier.

Breathing heavily, he asked, "What hospital is the president going to?"

"Parkland Hospital. Apparently it's not too far from here," Grant replied.

"I have to get to him quick. I have his medication," Burkley said with a look of panic on his face. Admiral Burkley was both anxious and irritated. Normally the admiral rode in a staff car in the motorcade, or in the rear seat of the follow-up car, but he and the president's secretary,

Evelyn Lincoln, had misjudged the timing of the motorcade's departure from Love Field and wound up scurrying to the VIP bus. He was furious for not having been in his normal seat but had nobody to blame but himself. His sole purpose for being in the motorcade was to be close to the president in case anything happened, but who could have predicted this?

ATSAIC Stout was standing nearby with Agent Andy Berger.

"Andy, go outside and find a ride to the hospital for you and the admiral. We'll follow as soon as we can round up some cars," Stout directed.

Burkley had been the president's personal doctor since October 1961 and was the only one who knew all the medications Kennedy was taking, not only for his severe back pain but also for Addison's disease—something that was known only by Kennedy's closest circle, including the agents.

Andy and the doctor moved quickly to the main entrance and looked outside. There was a police car with an officer standing next to it, parked out front.

"Come on, Admiral," Andy said.

The two men picked up their pace toward the car. As they were approaching, the officer started toward them.

"Hey, I just heard over the radio that the president was shot," the officer said.

Andy reached for his commission book and flipped it open. "I'm with the Secret Service and this is Admiral Burkley, President Kennedy's doctor. We have to get to Parkland Hospital right away."

"Hop in," the officer said as he ran around to the driver's side. He climbed in, started the car, and picked up the mike to call dispatch to let them know what he was doing.

Andy climbed into the front seat, and as the admiral was getting into the back, a Washington newspaper reporter rushed up and asked if he could go with them.

"No!" Admiral Burkley yelled as he slammed the door in the reporter's face.

During the drive to Parkland, which seemed to take forever, twenty-six-year-old Andy Berger sat in stunned silence. His entire body was trembling. He felt as if he should be able to control himself, but it was as if his mind and body no longer had a connection. Andy looked over and saw Admiral Burkley's hands. They too were shaking.

PARKLAND HOSPITAL
12:36 P.M.

Six minutes after the shots were fired, Chief Curry's lead car, the president's limousine, and the Secret Service follow-up car screeched up to the emergency entrance at Parkland Hospital. The agents from the follow-up car leapt off and swarmed the president's limousine even before the cars had come to a stop. No attendants from the hospital were in sight.

As Clint Hill slid off the back of the limousine, Roy Kellerman bolted out of the front seat and yelled, "Somebody get us two stretchers on wheels!"

Win Lawson sprang from the lead car and barreled through the double glass doors into the emergency room corridor. An orderly was awkwardly trying to push two gurneys by himself, and having a tough time keeping them moving in the same direction. Chief Curry had radioed the Dallas police headquarters and they'd called Parkland Hospital. *So why the heck weren't these gurneys waiting outside?* Win grabbed the two gurneys, one in each hand behind him, and raced back down the corridor. He hadn't seen the president, didn't know the extent of the injuries, but he knew every second mattered. Several hospital personnel came flying out the door with him.

Emory Roberts flung the back door open. He had heard the fatal shot, seen the president's head explode, but nothing could have prepared him for the gruesome scene inside the back of the limousine.

Mrs. Kennedy, dazed and in shock, huddled over her husband, who was lying faceup in her lap, with his eyes open. A chunk of his hair-covered skull was on the seat next to him. In front of the Kennedys, in the jump seats, Governor Connally was semiconscious, doubled over on his wife, Nellie. Fragments of gray tissue and white bone were splattered on everyone's clothes, while the entire back compartment of the car was completely awash with thick, red blood.

"Mrs. Kennedy," Emory said as gently as he could, "let us get the president."

Her eyes were glazed over and she clutched her husband even tighter, unwilling to let go. Clint Hill edged in next to Emory.

"Mrs. Kennedy, please . . . ," Clint pleaded in a guttural voice.

Dave Powers had jumped out of the follow-up car and as soon as he saw the president, lying lifeless in the backseat, he began sobbing. "Oh, Jack . . ."

There was no doubt in Emory Roberts's mind that the president was dead. With the experience of having protected four presidents and an innate ability to make astute decisions in the face of disaster, Emory Roberts knew what he had to do next. His duty now was to protect the next in succession—Vice President Johnson.

"You stay with the president," he said to Roy Kellerman. "I'm taking some of my men for Johnson."

To some his announcement may have appeared abrupt, but given the realities of the situation and the responsibility of the Secret Service, it was exactly the right thing to do. It was very rare for both the president and vice president to be together at the same time in the same place, and Emory was extremely concerned that whoever shot President Kennedy might also be targeting the vice president. There were more than enough agents to protect President Kennedy in the hospital, Emory thought, but a couple more agents could make the difference between life and death for Lyndon Johnson.

The way the jump seats folded out, Governor and Mrs. Connally were blocking the path to the president. They had to get Connally out first.

Despite his severe injuries, Governor Connally heard the discussion around him and mustered up every amount of strength possible to raise himself from his wife's lap, but he got only halfway and slumped against the door.

"Governor, don't worry," Kellerman said as he and Hill lifted him up. "Everything's going to be all right."

The governor nodded as two other sets of hands helped lift him out of the limo, placed him on a gurney, and rushed him into the emergency room. Clint Hill and Roy Kellerman helped Mrs. Connally get out of the car. She was unharmed, and despite what she'd just witnessed, was incredibly calm.

Mrs. Kennedy still had not budged.

Clint could tell she was in shock; she couldn't be expected to make any sensible decisions. But knowing her as well as he did, he knew that if anything, she was concerned with maintaining some semblance of dignity for her husband. There was nothing Clint could do to conceal the blood splattered on the pink designer suit Mrs. Kennedy was wearing, or the blood and bits of tissue, brain matter, and bone sprayed inside the car. The best he could do now was get the president inside the hospital with the remote hope there was something that could be done to save his life. He removed his suit coat and placed it over the president's head and upper chest to shield onlookers from the gory sight.

He looked at Jackie, looked into the beautiful brown eyes now filled with unbearable sadness, and said, "It's okay now, Mrs. Kennedy. Let us get him into the hospital."

She looked at Clint, and slowly nodded. Clint's jaw twitched as he struggled to force back the emotions that threatened to break through at any moment. Gulping hard, he turned to Win Lawson and said, "Win, move his feet. They're stuck under the seat."

Agents Hill, Lawson, Kellerman, and the sobbing Dave Powers lifted the president out of the limo and placed him on the gurney as Bill Greer steadied it.

When Agent Paul Landis helped Mrs. Kennedy out of the car he saw a bullet fragment in the back where the top would be secured. He picked it up and put it on the seat, thinking that if the car were moved, it might be blown off. And then he saw a bloody Zippo lighter with the presidential seal on it. He picked it up and put it in his pocket. He picked up her hat and purse and brought them inside.

The governor was already in Trauma Room No. 2, on the left side of the hallway. The agents could hear his groans as they jogged the president's stretcher into the open room on the right, Trauma Room No. 1, with Jackie clutching the side of the stretcher. She couldn't bear to let go. She had to stay with him.

Trauma Room No. 1 was suddenly filled with white-coated doctors and orderlies. The small room was packed and with the doctors needing to get to work immediately, the agents realized they needed to give the doctors space. Clint Hill urged Mrs. Kennedy to step outside with him, but she refused.

"I'm staying in here with him," she said. Hill nodded and as he walked out, Roy Kellerman said, "Clint, contact the White House. And keep the line open."

Hill had been thinking the same thing. They needed to notify Washington. What he and Kellerman hadn't realized, however, was that even though it had been less than ten minutes since the president had been shot, the news was already spreading around the world. UPI reporter Merriman Smith had sent out the first bulletin at 12:34.

Hill asked Lawson for the number of the Dallas White House switchboard, which had been installed by the White House Communications Agency, and Lawson immediately handed him a card with the contact number. On a hallway phone close by, Clint dialed the special Dallas operator.

"Dallas White House," the switchboard operator answered.

"This is Clint Hill. Give me Jerry Behn's office in Washington and keep this line open."

There was a click on the line and then Eve Dempsher's voice. "Jerry Behn's office."

"Eve, it's Clint. I need to talk to Jerry."

Eve could tell by the tone in Clint's voice that the call was urgent. She patched the call through to SAIC Behn.

Just then Roy Kellerman came out of the trauma room and took the phone from Clint.

"Jerry, this is Roy."

A medic came rushing out a second later and asked if anybody knew the president's blood type. Every agent carried a card with the president's vital signs, and as Lawson and Hill reached for their wallets, Roy Kellerman blurted out, "O. R-H positive."

Out of the corner of his eye, Hill saw Mrs. Kennedy walking out of the trauma room, alone. She looked as if she might faint, so he rushed over and grabbed her by the arms.

"Somebody get a chair for Mrs. Kennedy," Paul Landis called out as he rushed to help.

I'm not leaving Mrs. Kennedy no matter what, he thought. Hospital staff seemed to be coming in from everywhere, gawking, and Landis felt he had to do everything he could to protect her from them. He was traumatized. As he looked at Clint and the blood-covered Mrs. Kennedy standing there, he couldn't get the image of Clint lying across the trunk of the car out of his mind. It was as if he were still on the running board, as if time had been suspended and he was in some kind of surreal nightmare. Clint kept shaking his head back and forth, back and forth, and when he gave the thumbs-down sign, it was as if the world had come to a complete stop.

Agents and policemen were everywhere, but nobody knew quite what to do. It was chaos.

On the other end of the telephone line, Jerry Behn heard the commotion and asked, "What's going on?"

"Jerry, there's been a double tragedy," Kellerman said. "Both the president and Governor Connally have been shot. We're in the emergency room of the Parkland Memorial Hospital. Mark down the time." It was 12:39.

A medic burst out of the trauma room and instinctively Clint Hill took a step toward Mrs. Kennedy. "He's still breathing," the man said as he rushed past.

Mrs. Kennedy stood up. "Do you mean he may live?" she asked.

No one answered.

Paul Landis couldn't bear to tell her what he was thinking. *There is no way President Kennedy is alive. . . . People are talking about hope, but there is no way. I saw it. If he survives he won't have any semblance of mental capacity.*

Kellerman handed the phone back to Hill and rushed back into the trauma room.

"Clint, what happened?" Jerry Behn asked earnestly.

"Shots fired during the motorcade," Clint said as he kept an eye on Mrs. Kennedy across the hall. "It all happened so fast. We were five minutes away from the Trade Mart. . . . The situation is critical. Jerry, prepare for the worst . . ."

The operator cut into the line. "Attorney General Robert Kennedy wants to talk to Agent Hill."

"What's going on down there?!" Bobby Kennedy demanded.

"Shots fired during the motorcade," Clint repeated. "The president is very seriously injured. They're working on him now. Governor Connally was hit, too."

"Well what do you mean seriously injured? How serious?"

Clint swallowed hard. It was all he could do to keep it together. How could he tell the attorney general that his brother was dead? That he'd seen his brother's head explode before his eyes. He had to tell him something.

Clint closed his eyes and said, "It's as bad as it can get."

Meanwhile, the vice president and his detail had arrived moments after the president's limousine and his Secret Service follow-up car. Agents Tim McIntyre and Glen Bennett, standing on the curb, still in shock, joined Rufus Youngblood and his shift agents assigned to the vice president. They quickly assisted Vice President and Mrs. Johnson out of the vehicle and immediately surrounded LBJ. One of Johnson's agents, Warren "Woody" Taylor, grabbed Mrs. Johnson, and as the whole group proceeded inside, George Hickey scanned the area with the stock of the AR-15 on his shoulder and the barrel high, in a ready-to-fire position.

At the emergency desk, Emory Roberts requested a room for the vice president. The receptionist pointed one out, but there were two people in there.

"You need to get out," Woody Taylor said as he escorted the male patient and a secretary into the hallway, while Agents Youngblood, Kivett, McIntyre, and Bennett stayed put with the Johnsons.

The vice president and Mrs. Johnson were told to stay low, in the corner of the room, while the agents closed all the blinds.

Emory Roberts directed Glen Bennett—his temporary agent on loan from PRS—to stand post outside the door, and told Rufus Youngblood, the vice president's Special Agent in Charge, not to allow anyone in the room to see Johnson unless he knew them personally.

"I don't care what kind of ID they show you, if you don't know them, they don't get in."

Emory entered the room and approached Johnson.

"President Kennedy has been very badly injured, and his condition is not good. I believe it would be best if you went back to Washington as quickly as possible. Air Force One could depart immediately. Right now it is the safest place for you to be and you will have secure communication," Emory said.

Youngblood was nodding in agreement as Emory spoke, but Johnson disagreed.

"No. It would be unthinkable for me to leave with President Kennedy's life hanging in the balance."

The vice president looked to his trusted agent, Rufus, and asked, "What do you think?"

"I think you need to think it over, Mr. Vice President."

"I need confirmation from Ken O'Donnell or Dave Powers," Johnson said. "I can't just take Air Force One."

Emory strode off to find O'Donnell and left Youngblood in charge. The lines of authority had already begun to blur.

Mrs. Kennedy sat in a straight-backed folding chair outside the trauma room where doctors were doing everything they could to keep the president alive. Her eyes were glazed over, with no expression on her face whatsoever. Paul Landis and Clint Hill stood next to her, silent, focused on everything going on around them. Clint felt strange without his jacket on, but if he allowed himself to think about the jacket, his mind wandered to where it had gone, and he had to quickly snap his attention back to protecting Mrs. Kennedy.

Win Lawson, as the lead advance agent for the Dallas trip, tried to maintain his composure as he walked through the hospital and followed up on every detail he could think of. He made sure there were agents posted to provide the maximum coverage possible, that the emergency area was secured, and that the police outside the hospital were keeping the public away from the immediate area.

Emory Roberts had instructed George Hickey to secure the AR-15 back in its cabinet in the backseat of the follow-up car, and after doing so, Hickey walked into the emergency area. Agent Jack Ready was stationed at the doors leading to the hallway where Clint and Mrs. Kennedy waited in silence.

George had been able to hold his emotions in check thus far, but when he saw Jack Ready, he nearly lost it. Jack was in a stupor, his eyes so filled with pain it was almost unbearable to look at his face. George knew what he must have been thinking. *Could he have made it? Could he have saved the president? If he had jumped, maybe the bullet would have hit him instead of the president.*

But George had seen everything from the backseat. He'd seen Clint jump off and Sam Kinney swerve the car. Emory had been right to tell Jack not to jump. Kinney would have hit him for sure. But looking at Jack's sickened expression, George could tell that Jack didn't see it that way at all.

George wanted to tell him it was okay. That it wasn't his fault. There was nothing he could have done. The bullet came from above. Everything happened so fast.

Before George could speak, President Kennedy's aide Dave Powers approached from the other side of the hallway. His face was red, his eyes bloodshot. He looked at Jack Ready and said, "Jack, I need you to find a priest."

Emory Roberts took Ken O'Donnell into the room with Vice President and Mrs. Johnson. As he'd been searching for O'Donnell, Roberts realized there was something else that needed urgent attention. The president's limousine. It was still outside. Someone needed to secure it right away. When the horror subsided, there would be an investigation, and the car would be evidence.

While O'Donnell and the vice president were talking, Emory asked Lemuel Johns, one of Johnson's agents, to make sure the president's limousine was impounded.

Ken O'Donnell agreed with the Secret Service agents' recommendation that Johnson should return to Washington as soon as possible and that yes, he should leave Dallas on Air Force One. Woody Taylor was told to call the Dallas White House switchboard and have them notify Colonel Swindal, the commander of the aircraft, to be prepared to take the vice president back to Washington, D.C., as soon as possible.

Decisions needed to be made rapidly. The security of the country was at risk as President Kennedy's life hung in the balance. Nobody knew who was behind the shootings, or whom they might target next. Agent Rufus Youngblood realized Johnson's daughters needed to be protected. Lucy Johnson was at the National Cathedral School in Washington, D.C., Lynda

Johnson at the University of Texas. Youngblood told Jerry Kivett to make a call to Washington to get agents with them immediately.

Emory Roberts told Dallas police officials standing in front of the hospital that he needed to have an unmarked police car waiting for the vice president in front of the hospital and two more cars for other passengers and Secret Service agents to take Vice President and Mrs. Johnson to the airport. The press was not to be notified.

Vice President Johnson was still unsure of what to do. How could he take the presidential plane back to Washington? He wasn't the president. How would it look? What about Mrs. Kennedy? What about President Kennedy?

When Emory Roberts returned to Johnson's room, Lyndon Johnson asked Emory to double-check with Ken O'Donnell that it would be okay to take the president's plane.

WASHINGTON, D.C.

Jerry Behn sat in his office, stunned. He was supposed to be on vacation, but he'd come into the office for just a couple of hours. He couldn't believe what Roy Kellerman and Clint Hill had told him. In the past three years, Behn and President Kennedy had become such good friends that receiving that call was the same as if someone had told him an immediate family member had been killed. He was sickened.

Although Jerry was anxious to hear the details, he was enough of a veteran to not jump to conclusions until all the facts were in. He slumped in his chair for a second, but then pulled himself back to an upright position. He had to contact Jim Rowley, the director of the Secret Service. But Rowley was attending a graduation luncheon for Secret Service school attendees at O'Donnell's Sea Grill restaurant.

Behn scrambled to find the telephone number of the restaurant to get the message to Rowley.

At the restaurant, Kennedy Detail agent Toby Chandler was in the middle of giving the graduation speech when he saw Rowley's administrative assistant, Walter Blaschak, walk briskly into the room and whisper in Rowley's ear. The director stood and held up his hand for Chandler to stop.

Rowley could scarcely believe what he was about to say. Calmly, he said, "The president has just been shot in Dallas. We all need to get back to the White House immediately."

Agent Floyd Boring was relaxing at home on a rare day off when he got the call from SAIC Jerry Behn.

As Floyd drove immediately to the White House he wondered what could have happened in Dallas. The president's trip to Florida the week before crossed his mind. He couldn't help but wonder if JFK's request had unnecessarily exposed him to danger.

PARKLAND HOSPITAL
12:39 P.M.

Cecil Stoughton, the White House photographer, had arrived, as had a growing crowd of reporters and cameramen. Like everyone else, he was consumed by grief, but he also knew the Kennedys on a much more intimate level, and like Clint Hill, he knew the president's dignity had to be protected.

"No picture, no pictures," he said loud enough for everyone to hear. The horrific scene of the bloody limousine was something Mrs. Kennedy would not want the public to see.

Within five minutes after the president's limousine arrived at the hospital, the police cruiser pulled up with Andy Berger and Dr. Burkley. As Berger and Dr. Burkley rushed inside, another agent directed them to Trauma Room No. 1. Berger's heart pounded as he looked at the hallway floor and realized they were following a trail of blood.

Dr. Burkley entered the room and wedged himself in among the Parkland physicians treating the president on the stretcher. After checking the president's physical condition, Dr. Burkley knew immediately that there was no way President Kennedy could survive. He was still breathing, but he had a gaping hole in the back of his head. Death was certain and imminent. Still, Dr. Burkley felt compelled to do what he could.

He confirmed the president's blood type and handed them some adrenal medication to place in the intravenous blood and fluids, as he asked them about their procedures. It was clear that they were doing everything possible, and correctly, despite the fact that there was no hope the president could be saved.

Standing outside the room where the president was being treated, Andy Berger felt devastated. He didn't know where to go or what to do. Since the vice president was adequately guarded, Roy Kellerman told him to protect the lobby area leading to the trauma rooms.

Agents and policemen were everywhere and there was a sense of paranoia throughout the hospital. Andy tried to imagine what could have happened. *Who had shot the president? Was it part of a larger plot?*

An FBI agent showed up saying he'd received a call from J. Edgar Hoover. He immediately produced his credentials and said, "Hoover wanted me to let you know I'm available."

Andy checked his credentials and recorded his commission book number, then directed him to Roy Kellerman. A representative from the CIA appeared a while later, and again Andy followed the procedure.

Andy took a deep breath and looked around the lobby. He remembered the last time he had been in a hospital, in September, when his son Andrew was born. Andy was in Hyannis Port with the president when his wife, Dolly, went into early labor, in New York. Their son was born with the same respiratory ailment that had caused the death of the president's newborn son a month earlier. The heartbreaking memories of the president sobbing heavily on the day of Patrick's burial at Brookline Cemetery were still fresh in Agent Berger's mind when Dolly had called him. Her cries were painful to hear over the phone. As with Patrick, the chances for Andrew's survival were slim.

When President Kennedy was told about the situation, he immediately arranged for a military aircraft to fly Andy to New York to be with his wife and son at the hospital.

By the time Andy arrived, the baby's condition had improved, and miraculously, Andrew survived. A few weeks later, while working the 4:00 to midnight shift at the White House, Andy was informed that the president wanted to see him.

"My son didn't make it," President Kennedy said to Andy, "but your son did." He handed Andy an etching of the White House that was engraved for his son: "Andrew Paul Berger from the President and Mrs. Kennedy."

Now Andy thought about Caroline and John-John growing up without their dad. It was too much. He fought to hold back the tears.

WASHINGTON, D.C.

Pulling away from the White House in the Secret Service unmarked Ford, Agent Tom Wells could see Caroline's head bobbing up and down in the backseat of Liz Pozen's station wagon as she talked animatedly with her girlfriends. He unlatched the microphone from his radio and pushed the button to make contact with the control room at the White House. "Crown, Crown," he said, using the code name for the mansion. "This is Dasher. Lyric is en route to her destination."

Wells followed closely behind the station wagon, through the streets of Washington, making sure that no car could come between them. He had the car's radio tuned to a music station. Halfway between the White House and the Pozen residence, on Connecticut Avenue, just in front of the National Zoo, the programming was interrupted with a news alert that shots had been fired at the president's motorcade in Dallas.

No! Oh Christ! No!

He flashed his lights—a previously arranged signal—for Mrs. Pozen to pull over.

Mrs. Pozen had just heard the same news bulletin and had quickly turned off the car radio so Caroline wouldn't hear it. When she saw the flashing lights behind her, she knew it must have something to do with the report, so she pulled over as soon as she could. She rolled down the window as Wells walked up to the car.

Wells bent over and through the open window looked into the backseat, where Caroline and the other girls had gotten suddenly quiet. He hoped to God Caroline hadn't heard the news. "Did you have your radio on?" Wells asked Mrs. Pozen.

"Yes, I heard the bulletin and then I immediately turned it off."

"Okay, good," he said as he glanced back again to Caroline. It didn't appear that she'd heard anything. "Let me get more information and if plans change, I'll flash again."

Wells started the ignition and picked up the radio. "Crown, Crown.

This is Dasher. Request immediate instructions regarding Lyric in view of the present situation in Dallas. Over."

There was no immediate response. He was about to relay the message again when he heard, "Stand by."

By this point the radio station had begun continuous coverage from the White House news pool in Dallas, but the reports were sketchy. The situation didn't sound good, but nothing had been confirmed other than that the president and Governor Connally had been shot and had been taken to a hospital.

Wells still had not received word from the White House, but he was getting more and more nervous about Caroline being in the car ahead of him, rather than with him as she normally was.

"Crown, Crown from Dasher. Request immediate—repeat immediate—instructions in connection with previous inquiry. Contact Dresser or Duplex immediately. Over."

"Dresser" was Bob Foster's code name. Wells knew his supervisor was at the White House with John-John. "Duplex" was Jerry Behn, and Wells was certain he had to have been notified of the situation, even though he was supposed to be on vacation.

Finally Wells got in touch with Foster.

"Dasher to Dresser. I feel the danger has grown. We don't know whether this is an isolated incident, a plot, or a coup. I want Lyric back in a secure setting. Unless I hear anything to the contrary, I'm taking Lyric back to Crown."

On the other end, Foster couldn't help but agree. He knew the decision was going to break Caroline's heart, but Wells was right. Foster went upstairs to inform the children's nanny, Maud Shaw, while Wells once again flashed his lights to signal the station wagon in front of him.

The two cars pulled over and Wells turned off his radio before turning off the car. He hoped to God that Caroline hadn't heard anything and he wondered how he was going to explain to her that the sleepover had suddenly been called off.

Wells walked up to Liz Pozen's car and said, "I have to take Caroline back to the mansion."

This was not what Mrs. Pozen wanted to hear. "Why?" she questioned indignantly.

"Security reasons."

The girls in the backseat were silent but listening closely. Caroline looked as if she were about to burst into tears.

Mrs. Pozen tried to argue that Caroline would be better off at her house. "No one would ever know she's there," she whispered. "It's safer for her."

She doesn't understand, Wells thought. He was responsible for Caroline's life. He was the one making decisions here, not her.

Curtly, Wells said, "It's not my decision," and then he opened up the back door and said softly to Caroline, "Caroline, we have to go back to your house. Bring your bag with you for now."

Tears welled in her eyes as she leaned away from him. "I don't want to go."

"We don't have a choice, Caroline. Come on now. Something has come up." And then he added, "Maybe you can go back later." He, more than anyone, hoped that was true. He hoped the news reports were mistaken. But right now he had to do what he thought was best.

Sullenly she got out of her friend's car and into the backseat of the Secret Service car. Her mother and father didn't tolerate disrespectfulness, and they'd told the Kiddie Detail agents early on not to spoil the children. Right now Wells was grateful for that advice. Other than the first brief outburst, Caroline didn't make a fuss.

They got into the car and Wells radioed to Dresser that Lyric was with Dasher, on the way back to Crown. At one point Caroline asked, "But why? Why do we have to go home?"

Wells looked in his rearview mirror and realized he owed the teary girl an explanation. "Mummy is coming back early. She's changed her plans and she wanted you and John to be home."

Wells couldn't tell if Caroline believed him. He wondered if she'd heard the radio report, but he didn't dare ask.

During the drive along Rock Creek Parkway someone in a green Studebaker sedan recognized Caroline in the backseat of Wells's car. The driver sped up to stay even with them and kept looking over at Caroline. This was a common reaction whenever any member of the Kennedy family traveled. In fact, there had already been several accidents when agents were traveling off the record with the Kennedy children. Drivers would recognize them, become distracted, and run into the car in front of them. Agent Wells didn't want this to happen, especially on this day, so he sped up and zipped in and out of traffic, to lose the Studebaker. A few minutes later they arrived at the White House, and after Wells got Caroline inside, he phoned his wife, Shirley.

"Pack a suitcase and bring it to the Southwest Gate for me," he said. "I don't know when I'll be home."

AUSTIN, TEXAS

The agents on the midnight shift had checked into Austin's Commodore Perry Hotel around 11:00 A.M., which left them with a chance to rest and relax before the president arrived later that day. Like Jerry Blaine, most of the agents wanted nothing more than sleep, and after breakfast everybody but Bob Faison and Jerry O'Rourke retired immediately to their shared rooms. O'Rourke had an errand to run, and Faison was still searching for a pair of cowboy boots for his young son. He hadn't found any that he'd liked in Fort Worth.

There was a Western store not far from the hotel, and fortunately they had exactly what Faison had in mind, and at the right price. He couldn't wait to give them to his son.

He went directly back to the hotel and, as he was walking through the lobby, a television blared from the adjacent bar.

"President Kennedy has been shot in his Dallas motorcade . . ."

Faison rushed to the room he was sharing with Art Godfrey. Godfrey was sound asleep.

"Art! Art! Wake up!" he said as he shook his supervisor. "The Boss has been shot in Dallas!"

Art pulled on a pair of pants and rushed down the hall, still in his white undershirt, and banged on the door of Blaine's room so hard he almost splintered the wood. Blaine was in a deep sleep.

"Jerry! Wake up!" he yelled. "Wake up!" Finally, after what seemed like several minutes, Blaine groggily opened the door.

"Jerry, the president's been shot in Dallas. Turn on the television and get dressed. I've gotta tell the others."

Blaine tried to clear his head as he walked back to the bed and sat down, not knowing if he was awake or having a nightmare. Several minutes later the agents gathered in Godfrey and Faison's room.

Sitting on the beds, they watched the television coverage in silence. Individually their minds raced as they tried to make sense of what was being reported. They couldn't imagine what their colleagues must be going through in Dallas. It was unfathomable.

Details being broadcast on television about what had happened in Dallas were sketchy, but it was reported that an agent had been killed and the condition of President Kennedy was unknown. Still, they said nothing. Each man focused on his own scenario about what might have gone wrong.

Clearly all plans had changed, so Art Godfrey called the White House switchboard to find out what they should do. He hung up the phone and said to his silent, distraught men, "Pack your bags. We're going to Bergstrom Air Force Base and catching a plane back to Washington. Immediately."

PARKLAND HOSPITAL
12:50 P.M.

Because Dr. Burkley was not a member of the medical team administering emergency treatment to the president, and he could see they were doing everything that would be expected under such circumstances, he did not interfere. He needed to let Mrs. Kennedy know that it wasn't looking good.

He stepped out of the room but before he could say anything, Mrs. Kennedy stood up and said, "I'm going in there."

A nurse inside had heard her and suddenly appeared at the door. Tersely she said, "You can't come in here."

Mrs. Kennedy was undeterred. "I'm coming in and I'm staying," she said as she attempted to push past the nurse.

Admiral Burkley decided to take charge. Mrs. Kennedy was right. Her husband's death was imminent, and she should be in there with him when he died.

"I'm bringing her in," Burkley said to the nurse defiantly as he pushed through the swinging doors. Roy Kellerman, standing nearby, followed Dr. Burkley and Mrs. Kennedy back into the emergency room.

A small army of doctors hovered over the president, still working valiantly to keep him alive. Burkley stood stoically next to Mrs. Kennedy, wondering if he should put his arm around her. He'd never done it before, so it seemed inappropriate. Suddenly she knelt down and prayed.

As Mrs. Kennedy stood up, one of the doctors said, "It's no use. His life is gone."

Dr. Burkley edged in between two doctors and checked the president's vital signs. He took a deep breath, turned around, and stepped over to Mrs. Kennedy, who was looking at him with hope in her eyes.

"I'm sorry, Mrs. Kennedy. The president is dead."

She'd known he couldn't have survived. She'd held a piece of his brain in her hand. But still, to hear the words. Softly she began to weep.

The door opened and two priests walked in. They'd arrived a moment too late but they immediately began to administer Last Rites. The doctors moved away so that Mrs. Kennedy and Dr. Burkley could stand with the priests, and together they prayed.

John Fitzgerald Kennedy, the President of the United States, was dead.

Roy Kellerman, the acting Special Agent in Charge of protecting the president on this fateful trip, walked out of the room and closed the door gently behind him.

Clint Hill, still holding the phone, with Jerry Behn on the other end of the line, saw Roy come out, and from the obvious expression of pain on his face, he knew that the president was gone.

"Clint, tell Jerry that this is not for release, and is not official. But the man is dead."

Clint took a deep breath and relayed the message to Jerry Behn.

There was only silence on the other end of the phone.

Clint couldn't see him, but Jerry Behn, normally unshakable, had slumped over the desk, like a broken man.

Clint was struggling to remain composed, to be professional, to think rationally, but hearing SAIC Behn's broken gasps for breath was tearing him apart.

"Jerry," he said, "I think you should advise the attorney general and the other members of the president's family immediately so that they don't hear it through the news media. I don't know how long it will be before the word gets out."

Finally, Behn spoke. "Yes. Yes, I'll do that." After he hung up the phone, Behn sat, staring at his desk. Cecil Stoughton, the White House photographer, had dropped off a few photos for him before he'd left for Texas. Stoughton was great about that. If he'd caught a shot of an agent with the president or Jackie or the kids, he always made an extra copy to give to the agents in the photo. As Behn picked up the black-and-white glossy photograph on the top of the stack, which showed Behn standing behind the smiling president outside the White House a few weeks earlier, just one thought kept repeating itself in his mind.

If only I'd been there. If only I'd been there . . .

He'd taken his first vacation in four years, and the president had been assassinated. His journey down a path of unforgiving guilt had only just begun.

HYANNIS PORT, MASSACHUSETTS

Agent Hamilton P. "Ham" Brown, assigned to Ambassador Joseph Kennedy—who had suffered a severe stroke early in his son's presidency— was sitting in the Secret Service trailer in the compound when Ann Gargan, the ambassador's niece, called from the house in a panic.

Ham rushed into the residence to find Ann standing with Rita Dallas, the ambassador's nurse, and Frank Saunders, Rose Kennedy's driver. They all seemed to be holding their breath.

"Ham, we've just heard that the president has been shot," Ann said. Before Ham could react, Rose Kennedy, the president's mother, came into the room.

"Aunt Rose," Ann said, "Jack has been shot."

"Mr. Brown"—Rose Kennedy turned to Ham, her face contorted into a mother's look of despair—"what do you know of this?"

"I don't know what the details are, Mrs. Kennedy. I've just heard it myself. I'll make a call and let you know right away."

Ham ran to the phone that connected him to the White House. Secret Service agent Stuart Knight answered the call.

"Stu, I'm with Rose Kennedy and she would like to know what's happening. Was the president shot?"

Stu Knight, who had earned a Silver Star in World War II, was Vice President Johnson's Special Agent in Charge. He'd just been promoted and reassigned, which was why Rufus Youngblood had taken over the Texas trip.

"Yes, I am afraid it is true, but I have no further details," Knight said. "I'll call you back as soon as I know more."

Ham Brown went to Mrs. Kennedy's room and told her what he knew. By then she had been on the phone to her youngest son, Senator Ted Kennedy.

"Ham, Ambassador Kennedy is not to be told until the rest of the family arrives," Rose Kennedy said. She was afraid the news would literally kill her already fragile husband. "They'll all be here by tomorrow."

Ham immediately disabled the radios and televisions in the house and told the maids not to let the ambassador see any newspapers.

PARKLAND HOSPITAL
1:00 P.M.

As soon as Ken O'Donnell was informed of the president's death, he walked up to Clint Hill. It looked like O'Donnell had aged ten years in the past half hour. His face was ashen, his eyes lifeless.

"Clint, I need you to call a funeral home. We need to get a casket so we can get the president's body back to Washington as quickly as possible."

He had to get a casket for the body of the president. A casket for the body of the president. At least he had a task. As long as he had a task for his mind to focus on, the other thoughts could be pushed further away.

Two minutes later he was in a small office, on the phone with someone from the Oneal Funeral Home. One of the hospital administrators had told him they were the best.

"I need a casket delivered to Parkland Hospital's emergency entrance. Right away. The best one you have," he said. "It's for . . ." His voice started to break. *Stay on task, stay on task.* "It's for the president."

Clint hung up the phone and was standing, looking at nothing, seeing nothing. He walked back into the hallway and saw Mrs. Kennedy coming out of the swinging doors of the trauma room, followed by two priests. Paul Landis had not moved from his position outside the trauma room.

"Mrs. Kennedy, why don't you sit down," he said as he guided her toward the chair in the hallway. She reached for the chair as if to steady herself, and then sat down. Her shoulders drooped, and then she sat up straight and tilted her head up to the priests, and thanked them for being there. For praying for the president.

She was calm, but there was something different about her. What was it? Had she changed her clothes? And then Clint realized. The blood on her suit and her face and her hands and her legs had begun to dry and was turning from liquid red to crisp brown.

Clint heard Emory Roberts giving orders for some agents to get to Love Field, to secure the area around the presidential planes.

"Clear all the buildings, hangars, warehouses, everything," Emory demanded. "I don't want any people there but our agents and local law enforcement. Call Colonel Swindal and tell him we're heading back to Washington."

We're heading back to Washington. Clint looked at his watch and realized the casket would be coming in a few minutes. And then the two thoughts collided. *We're heading back to Washington. The casket for the body of the president. Oh God.*

His chest tightened as he strode back to the room with the phone. He took a few deep breaths as he waited to be connected to the White House. *Another phone call. Another task.*

"This is Clint Hill," he said as soon as he was connected to the White House. "I need to speak to Bob Foster, immediately."

The White House was certainly the safest place for Caroline and John-John, both agents agreed. But in the end it was decided that they should be moved to Mrs. Kennedy's mother's home in Georgetown. If John-John were at the White House he'd hear the helicopter landing on the lawn and would be expecting to see his daddy. But this time, his daddy was coming home in a casket.

14

The Unimaginable

For time and the world do not stand still. Change is the law of life. And those who look only to the past or the present are certain to miss the future.
— JOHN F. KENNEDY

In another corner of the hospital, Vice President Johnson was in the secured room with his wife, his executive assistant Cliff Carter, and Agent Youngblood, and still debating whether to take the president's plane back to Washington.

When Emory Roberts walked in with Mac Kilduff, the assistant White House press secretary, and Ken O'Donnell, Johnson could tell by the looks on their faces that now it was a moot point.

"President Kennedy has died," Emory said.

"We need to discuss when and how to announce it," O'Donnell added.

Emory glanced at O'Donnell, then turned his attention back to Johnson and added, "Keeping in mind that right now, the most important thing is your security . . ." He almost added "Mr. Vice President," as he normally would, but right now he didn't know what to call him. He was, for all intents and purposes, the President of the United States. He decided not to call him anything for the moment. "We still don't know who is behind this thing."

After a short discussion it was decided that for security reasons Kilduff would not publicly announce President Kennedy's death until Vice President Johnson, who was constitutionally now the President of the United States, had left the hospital.

"Mrs. Kennedy is insisting on staying with the president's body, but we need to get you back to Washington."

"I can't leave her behind," Johnson said. "I won't do it."

The various options were discussed and Vice President Johnson finally agreed that he and Mrs. Johnson would go to Air Force One, but they would not allow the plane to leave without Mrs. Kennedy.

Back at the entrance to the lobby outside the trauma rooms, where Agent Andy Berger was on post, a tall man in a gray suit had somehow managed to get past the outer security and was barreling his way into the lobby, nearly knocking over a nurse as he shouted, "I'm FBI!"

The man appeared violent and distraught. *Yeah, right, you're FBI.* Before he could get any farther, Andy knocked him to the ground and held him down.

Sprawled on all fours, and enraged but unable to break free, the man growled, "You're not in charge now! What's your name?"

"My name?" Andy asked incredulously as he pressed hard into the man's chest. "What the hell's your name? If you're FBI show me your goddamned identification!"

It turned out the man was indeed a Dallas FBI agent, but at this point Andy had no respect for him. Every agent—FBI, CIA, Secret Service— knew the protocol, and this guy had completely ignored it.

Andy let the man go but refused to allow him inside. Finally the FBI agent realized he wasn't getting anywhere and angrily walked toward the exit. Glaring at Andy, he yelled, "J. Edgar Hoover will hear about this!"

George Hickey had been redirected outside to assist Sam Kinney in securing the motorcade vehicles parked by the emergency entrance. Sam was just finishing attaching the bubble top. As he pulled the pieces out of the trunk and attached them, he couldn't help but think of the irony. The clear plastic dome was meant to shield the passengers from the weather— he could count on one hand how many times it had been used—but now its purpose was to protect the evidence of a crime scene. Hickey and Kinney were instructed to drive the cars nonstop to Love Field and immediately load them into the Air Force cargo plane that had delivered them. With a police motorcycle escort for additional security, Kinney would drive the limo, and Hickey the follow-up car. After the cars were loaded and the plane was secured, the two drivers would accompany the vehicles back to Andrews Air Force Base.

As Hickey and Kinney were getting ready to depart, Clint Hill walked out the door to meet the people from Oneal's who were delivering the casket. When he saw the president's limousine, now with its bubble top on, he flinched. *Stay on task. Stay on task.* To his left he saw a hearse approaching and looked down at his watch: 1:20 P.M. An hour ago the president was in front of him, waving to the cheering crowds. Now Clint was signing for his casket.

Clint helped roll the four-hundred-pound bronze coffin into the trauma room. Paul Landis and Ken O'Donnell saw the casket coming and tried to turn Mrs. Kennedy's attention away, but she immediately realized their humble attempt at a ruse.

"I want to go in," she said. "Please let me go in."

"No, Mrs. Kennedy . . . I don't think . . ."

She'd already made up her mind. This was her husband. She had to be with him one last time before he was gone forever. She forced her way back into the trauma room and watched as her husband was moved from the stretcher into the satin-lined casket.

Four sheets had been wrapped around the president's head and still the blood continued to soak through. The nurse who had tried to keep Mrs. Kennedy from entering the room had brought in a plastic mattress cover to be placed in the casket, under the body, so the pale-colored interior wouldn't be spoiled.

How odd, Agent Roy Kellerman thought as the president's body was lifted into the coffin. Our president is dead, and the nurse is worried about stains.

Meanwhile, Win Lawson had asked Sheriff Bill Decker to make the arrangements necessary for the president's body to be removed from Dallas and flown to Washington, D.C. Protocol had to be followed.

Tensions were mounting from every angle. Still, nobody knew who was behind the assassination. The Kennedy Detail agents needed to get Lyndon Johnson and Mrs. Kennedy the hell out of Dallas. But Mrs. Kennedy wasn't leaving without her husband's body, and Lyndon Johnson wasn't leaving without Mrs. Kennedy. They had to get the casket out of the hospital and onto Air Force One as soon as possible.

Roy Kellerman was waiting for the death certificate when a man barged into the trauma room, and after introducing himself as Dr. Earl Rose, the Dallas County medical examiner, he said, "You can't take that body. There's been a homicide here. We have to do an autopsy."

"Sir," Kellerman said as he walked toward the man, "with all due respect, I'm the Special Agent in Charge of the White House Detail of the Secret Service. This is the body of the President of the United States and we are taking it back to Washington."

Roy Kellerman towered over the medical examiner, but neither his six-foot-four frame nor his title seemed to intimidate Earl Rose.

"This homicide happened in Dallas County," Rose insisted. "Under the law there must be an autopsy."

"We are taking the body!" Admiral Burkley said defiantly, as he strode toward the two men.

"Certainly this part of the law can be waived," Kellerman said. He was trying to remain diplomatic but he was quickly losing patience.

"If you want a waiver, you'll need a judge to overrule me," Rose said. "But I'm telling you, you can't break the chain of evidence. The autopsy must be performed here."

Kennedy's advisors—O'Donnell, O'Brien, and Powers—couldn't take this nonsense. Did this lowly Dallas official realize who he was dealing with? Mrs. Kennedy had thus far been able to remain composed and was holding herself together remarkably well, but she was still in shock. She wasn't leaving Texas without her husband's body and if they waited to perform an autopsy, who knew how long it might take? It was completely irrational.

But Dr. Rose was adamant. "Texas law is clear when it comes to violent crimes. This was a homicide and there must be an autopsy."

"Oh for God's sake," Ken O'Donnell said as he paced back and forth. "This is not just a homicide, Dr. Rose. This is the President of the United States. Do you realize what Mrs. Kennedy has been through? Certainly you don't expect her to wait around here for an autopsy?"

The tension and tempers escalated as O'Donnell stormed out to make some calls.

Meanwhile, the afternoon shift leader, Stewart Stout, had ordered the Oneal Funeral Home driver to get out of the hearse.

"We're taking over now," he said unequivocally. He told Andy Berger to get in and be ready to drive the hearse to Love Field as soon as the president's casket was loaded.

Clint Hill had taken charge of securing the corridors between the trauma room and the loading dock for the hearse. The debate about whether the president's body could be removed had reached a crescendo and it looked as if people were about to start throwing punches. Neither side was willing to back down but at this point the Secret Service agents decided it was time to take control and worry about Texas laws later.

Hill walked into the trauma room where Kellerman was still with the president's body and told him everything was clear for departure.

WASHINGTON, D.C.

Agent Lynn Meredith, another member of the children's detail, was at home in Arlington, Virginia, on his annual leave. His wife had been watching *As the World Turns* when Walter Cronkite interrupted the program and announced that the president had been shot in Dallas.

Meredith immediately called Bob Foster, who told him they'd just decided to take the children to Mrs. Auchincloss's home in Georgetown.

"I'm coming over," Meredith said. "Do the kids know?"

"No," Foster said. "We're not telling them. That would be great if you could come in. The plan is to take John-John to the park this afternoon. Try to keep him in his routine. Caroline is with Mrs. Auchincloss. She seems to have no idea."

PARKLAND TO LOVE FIELD

At 1:35 P.M. agents surrounded Vice President Johnson and accompanied him out of Parkland Hospital to a waiting unmarked police car driven by Dallas police chief Jesse Curry. The idea was to get the president to Love

Field with as little notice as possible, so he was told to lie down on the seat below window level. Mrs. Johnson was in a separate police car with the same instructions. In an unmarked follow-up car, Emory Roberts drove with agents Jack Ready and Tim McIntyre and Chief Warrant Officer Ira Gearhart, the man holding the nuclear defense code "football." Gearhart had been with the motorcade through Dallas and had stayed in a secluded area of Parkland Hospital.

Agent Don Lawton and driver agent Hank Rybka, whom Roberts had initially assigned to handle the planned departure of President Kennedy, were still waiting at Love Field. A number of agents had been sent to help secure the aircraft and were posted strategically in and around the plane when the vice president, Mrs. Johnson, and the agents accompanying them arrived.

It was approximately 1:40 P.M. The Secret Service agents immediately closed all window blinds on the aircraft as the vice president called Attorney General Robert Kennedy to ask about the legal aspects of taking the oath of office. *Jesus Christ.* LBJ had never imagined he'd be in this situation. He needed somebody to tell him what the hell to do. What was the oath? Who could administer it? Johnson had often imagined himself becoming president, but never in his wildest dreams had he envisioned this scenario.

Back at Parkland Hospital, the situation over the removal of President Kennedy's body had escalated. Tempers flared and obscenities laced the conversation. The problem, it seemed, was that the murder of the President of the United States was not a federal crime. Thus it had to be treated as an ordinary homicide in the state of Texas. In truth, Dr. Earl Rose had the law on his side.

Admiral Burkley had called a justice of the peace in the hopes that he could overrule the medical examiner. But when the justice of the peace, Theron Ward, arrived, he agreed with Rose. In a homicide case, he had no choice but to order an autopsy. The good news, he said, was that it should take only three hours.

Three hours? Clearly Justice Ward did not realize who he was dealing with.

"You can't make an exception?" O'Donnell implored. "This is President Kennedy, for God's sake."

The young justice looked toward Dr. Rose and replied, "In the eyes of the law, it's just another homicide."

O'Donnell was incredulous. *Just another homicide?* That did it.

"Let's go," he said to Roy Kellerman. "We're leaving. And we're leaving now." Everybody in the presidential party agreed. They didn't have to put up with this crap.

Kellerman, O'Donnell, Powers, and O'Brien forced their way through the futile barrier of Dr. Earl Rose, Justice Ward, and a lone policeman. Clint Hill and Paul Landis stayed close to Mrs. Kennedy as the group marched through the empty hallways toward the hearse waiting in the bay outside.

Justice Ward stormed off to call Dallas County district attorney Henry Wade.

At the other end of the hall, the personnel officer of Parkland Hospital approached Agent Dick Johnsen and handed him an expended bullet that one of his employees had found on a stretcher near the elevator. Johnsen looked at it quickly, saw that indeed the end of the bullet had the telltale markings of one that had been fired, and realized it could be an important piece of evidence. Ordinarily Johnsen would have immediately written his initials on the bullet to show the chain of evidence, but with the chaos surrounding the removal of the casket, he took the bullet, wrapped it in his handkerchief, and stuffed it in his pocket. He would write his initials on it, but right now there simply wasn't time.

After the agents and President Kennedy's advisors had moved the heavy casket into the back of the hearse, Mrs. Kennedy declared she was going to ride in the back with her husband.

"Mrs. Kennedy, we can follow in another car," Clint suggested.

"I'm riding with him," she said. Indeed Andy Berger, Stewart Stout, and Roy Kellerman felt the same. They weren't about to desert President Kennedy.

Clint was trying to figure out how to handle the situation when Justice Ward came out and sheepishly announced that, yes, they could take the body. District Attorney Wade had agreed that if Dr. Burkley accompanied the body from Parkland back to Washington, and stayed with the body during the autopsy, *and* agreed to return to Dallas to testify, Wade would allow the president's body to be released.

This added a new dimension to the problem at hand. Admiral Burkley had to be in the hearse with the president, too. *Stay on task. Stay on task.*

There was no other choice. Andy Berger was at the wheel, with Stewart Stout and Roy Kellerman next to him in the front seat. In the back wagon portion of the hearse, where there were no seats, Admiral Burkley climbed in first, then Clint helped Mrs. Kennedy and climbed in behind her, and together they sat on their knees—she still in her bloodstained pink suit, he with a borrowed coat he hadn't even remembered borrowing—and rode in the back of the hearse, next to the dead president in the bronze casket, from Parkland Hospital to Love Field.

The hearse arrived at Love Field at 2:14 P.M. Andy Berger drove directly to the back steps to Air Force One. The Kennedy Detail agents who were present removed the heavy casket from the hearse, and then heaved it, step by step, toward the rear door of the plane. The agents were covered in sweat as the weight of the casket bore down on them, threatening to topple at any moment. And through the entire ordeal, nobody said a word.

Paul Landis was nearing his breaking point as he stood with Mrs. Kennedy at the bottom of the portable staircase, watching the unfathomable scene.

Several seats had been removed from the back of the plane to make room for the casket, but as the agents struggled to balance the nearly six hundred pounds on their shoulders, when they got to the top of the stairs, the casket wouldn't fit through the door of the plane.

The frustration of the moment was almost too much to bear. They had to get the casket on the plane. Somebody on the sidelines realized that it was merely the brass handles sticking out from each side that made the casket too wide for the door opening. And so they jammed the casket through the door, breaking off the handles and scraping the sides. There was no choice. The Secret Service agents had been trained to think of every possible scenario, to plan for every detail, to the minute, but nowhere in any training or manual was it ever mentioned that the width of the door on Air Force One was just a few inches too narrow for a casket.

15

Darkness Falls

In the long history of the world, only a few generations have been granted the role of defending freedom in its hour of maximum danger. I do not shrink from this responsibility—I welcome it.
—JOHN F. KENNEDY

As soon as Vice President Johnson had been evacuated from Parkland Hospital, Mac Kilduff, the White House assistant press secretary, held a press conference and announced to the media that President Kennedy had died at 1:00 P.M. Dallas time.

Already, less than an hour since the president had been shot, two-thirds of the adults in America had heard about it. Now the news was spreading around the world. From New York to London to Rome to Berlin to India, it seemed that time had stopped. People listening to their car radios pulled over and sobbed; stores closed; doctors canceled appointments; people gathered in coffee shops and living rooms—anywhere there was a television—and tried to comprehend how such a thing could have happened. For the first time ever, the three television networks halted normal programming and ran constant feeds from their newsrooms. The whole world seemed to be holding its breath. Nothing else mattered.

2:36 P.M.

On Air Force One, Lyndon B. Johnson was about to take the oath of office with Dallas federal district judge Sarah Hughes presiding. Twenty-five people had already crowded into the small stateroom of the presidential plane to witness the swearing-in ceremony, but Johnson wouldn't begin until Mrs. Kennedy came in.

She'd gone into the presidential cabin to compose herself and after combing her hair, washing her hands, and wiping the bits of blood off her face with a Kleenex, she'd asked for someone to get Clint Hill.

"Yes, Mrs. Kennedy?" he asked as he walked into the room. "What do you need?"

She turned to him, grabbed his hands in her own, and looked up at him with hollow brown eyes.

"What's going to happen to you now, Mr. Hill?"

Tears welled in Clint's eyes. It was all he could do to hold it together. After all she'd just been through, how could she be worried about him?

He inhaled through his nose, and swallowed hard.

With trembling lips he said, "I'll be okay."

Ken O'Donnell walked into the room and said gently, "Mrs. Kennedy, the vice president is waiting for you. He's ready to take the oath."

As she walked out of the small bedroom, Jackie glanced back at the casket. Admiral Burkley hadn't moved. He had vowed to remain with the president's body, and he wasn't about to leave his post. Dave Powers was now seated next to him.

"I'll stay here with the president," Powers said. He had no desire to see Lyndon Johnson take the oath of office. He still couldn't believe his best friend Jack was gone.

As soon as Paul Landis got on the plane he just broke down. He had been trying so hard to keep his emotions in check, but now, suddenly, as he sat down in an empty seat, he began sobbing uncontrollably. Glen Bennett was sitting in the seat next to him, calmly making notes about everything. *He's keeping a clear head. Why can't I keep a clear head?* But no matter how hard he tried, the young Agent Landis couldn't control his heaving sobs.

Then Roy Kellerman came up and said, "Paul, pull yourself together.

You're witnessing history. Come in here." Paul wiped his eyes and nose and followed Kellerman. Standing in the doorway of the cramped room, he watched the swearing in of a new president.

At 2:38 P.M. White House photographer Cecil Stoughton captured the surreal scene of Lyndon Johnson, his hand on John F. Kennedy's Catholic prayer book, taking the oath of office as Mrs. Kennedy stood next to him. Outside the scope of the lens, Clint Hill stood in the background with Paul Landis as Johnson became the thirty-sixth President of the United States.

Ten minutes later, the plane left Love Field and headed for Washington, D.C.

Stewart Stout's afternoon shift took over duty to protect President Johnson while Emory Roberts and his traumatized day shift agents flew on the backup plane.

On all the other trips, Vice President Johnson, his staff, and his agents had been on a separate aircraft. Now they were here on Air Force One, along with Stout's agents—all of them protecting President Johnson. The lines of loyalty and authority that had been so clear when they left Fort Worth in the morning were now a muddled blur.

Even though the afternoon shift—Stout, along with Andy Berger, Ernie Olsson, Dick Johnsen, and Sam Sulliman—had been stationed at the Trade Mart during the time of the assassination, they were all mired in grief. They still didn't know exactly what had happened. Nobody had spoken of the incident. All they knew was what they had heard from police and newsmen—that a sniper with a high-powered rifle had fired three shots—and now President Kennedy was dead. As they tried to keep their emotions in check, the same thoughts replayed over and over in each of their minds. To a man, they all wished they'd been there.

In the back of the plane, Mrs. Kennedy sat in a seat next to her husband's coffin, with Admiral Burkley and Dave Powers next to her, and Agent Dick Johnsen—with the bullet in his pocket—close by. Admiral Burkley had been trying to get her to take a sedative ever since he arrived at Parkland Hospital, but she'd refused. She didn't want anything to drink or eat. At one point someone brought her some coffee, and she occasionally took a few sips.

Burkley explained that it was mandatory to have an autopsy, but they had a choice of where it could be done. He could do it at the Army hospital at Walter Reed, or at the Navy hospital at Bethesda, or any civilian hospital.

"But really," the admiral said, "your husband was the President of the United States and was therefore the commander in chief of the military. I feel that it should be done at a military hospital."

"Jack was a Navy man," she said. "Let's have it at Bethesda."

Powers said he'd call ahead to make the arrangements. As he walked to the front of the plane, he stopped at where Roy Kellerman was sitting.

"Roy," Powers said, "Mrs. Kennedy has decided to have the autopsy at Bethesda."

Kellerman nodded.

"And she's requested that you and the agents who were with the president carry him from the plane. She wants Bill Greer to drive." Dave Powers had been holding it together, but now his voice broke as tears streamed down his face. "She said how much Jack loved Mr. Greer, and all of you, and she knows how much you're suffering."

Art Godfrey's midnight shift agents in Austin were headed back to Washington, D.C., on a Strategic Air Command KC135 that had departed Bergstrom Air Force Base at 3:00 P.M. They'd rushed from their hotel to the base, and by the time they had boarded the plane, they still didn't know whether President Kennedy was alive or dead. The military had all their units on radio silence because of a Strategic Air Command order, and except for the droning of the engines and occasional bits of information gleaned from commercial radio reports heard by those in the cockpit and passed back to them, there was complete silence during the long flight to Washington. As a group the agents were in emotional despair and even though they had not been in Dallas there was a sense of tremendous failure. When they landed at Andrews Air Force Base and found out that President Kennedy was dead, they were devastated.

Driver agents Sam Kinney and George Hickey flew a similarly lonely and grim flight on the Air Force C-130 that carried the Secret Service follow-up car and the bloodstained SS100X limousine, while still a third plane carried Emory Roberts and the follow-up car agents—minus Paul Landis and Clint Hill. Still stunned by the day's events, and now suddenly with nothing to do, they were lost in sorrow. Nobody said anything. There was no discussion of what went wrong, what might have been done differently. There was only silence.

All they could do during those seemingly endless hours in the air was try *not* to think about what had gone wrong, not now; they had to keep their emotions in check.

DALLAS

Agents Win Lawson and Dave Grant had watched Air Force One take off from Love Field carrying the newly sworn-in President Johnson and the body of President Kennedy. This was not anything they had anticipated during their intricate advance planning for that day's events in Dallas. They were both in agony, but there was no time to pause. They still had a job to do.

They'd been instructed to report directly to the Dallas police headquarters to observe the questioning of a suspect who had already been captured. Although seeing Lee Harvey Oswald's arrogant behavior and hearing his snide remarks to Dallas investigators' questions triggered their anger, Win and Dave refused to let it influence their judgment about whether Dallas police had the right man. Lee Harvey Oswald certainly did fit the classic profile of an assassin driven by a fanatical desire for recognition, but the seasoned agents knew physical evidence was also needed to prove Oswald's guilt.

Charlie Kunkel had been one of the Kennedy Detail agents who had requested a transfer due to the overwhelming hours and long stretches away from home. His transfer back to the Dallas Field Office had come through as soon as he'd returned from Berlin with President Kennedy four months earlier. By sheer coincidence, he'd been attending Secret Service school in Washington and was at the luncheon when Director Rowley broke the news of the shooting. He'd gotten on the very next flight to Dallas.

Kunkel had also gone to the police station where Oswald was being held and had walked into a chaotic scene. Members of the press were everywhere, packing the hallways and lobby, while overzealous citizens surrounded the station, demanding to see the man everybody believed had killed President Kennedy.

Meanwhile, Forrest Sorrels, the SAIC of the Dallas Secret Service office, had gone to the sheriff's office at about the time Oswald was picked
up. It too was filled with reporters. *Dallas Morning News* reporter Harry
McCormick had just gotten a tip he thought Sorrels might need to know
about.

"Forrest," he said, "you may want to come with me. I've just learned of
a man who got pictures of this whole thing."

They walked the short block to the Dal-Tex Building, which happened
to be directly across the street from the Texas School Book Depository,
and went up to the office of a man named Abraham Zapruder. Zapruder,
already surrounded by a few other reporters, was distraught beyond
words. He'd been standing on a pedestal in Dealey Plaza, alongside Elm
Street, holding his movie camera up to his eye when the president's motorcade drove past at 12:30. He'd captured the assassination on color film.

Sorrels asked Zapruder if it would be possible for him to make a copy
of the film for the Secret Service and Zapruder agreed. McCormick, eager for a story, offered to develop the film at the *Dallas Morning News,* but
when they took the film there, no one was willing to tackle the job. Sorrels ended up taking the film to the Eastman Kodak Company to be developed. As it turned out, he met a man there who had seen some still
pictures from around the time of the assassination and Sorrels arranged to
get copies of those as well.

WASHINGTON, D.C.

Lyndon B. Johnson was now the President of the United States, but the
White House was still the residence of the Kennedy family. Johnson would
meet with his staff there as soon as he arrived, but he couldn't stay the
night in the mansion. It wouldn't be right. Johnson had decided he would
stay at his home the Elms until Mrs. Kennedy had time to move out, but
this created yet another urgent and unprecedented situation for the Secret
Service. The Elms was located in an upscale neighborhood called Spring
Valley, in northwest Washington, D.C., and due to the unusual circumstances, it required an immediate upgrade in security.

Lee Harvey Oswald was in custody in Dallas, but even if he was the
man who'd killed President Kennedy, there was still the very real possibil-

ity that he was part of a bigger conspiracy to eliminate other government leaders.

Paul Rundle, the agent who'd come from the Denver office prior to Blaine and Hill, was put in charge of securing Johnson's residence. There would be three perimeters of security. The first, outer layer would be manned by the D.C. metropolitan police, the next perimeter would be manned by the National Guard, and the third and final layer of protection would be the Secret Service agents from the presidential and vice presidential details, supplemented by agents from nearby field offices.

At the White House, the switchboard was on overload. Agent Toby Chandler, who had been making the speech at the Secret Service school graduation, was one of the agents assigned to help field incoming phone calls. In the hours after the assassination, Chandler handled calls from nearly every agent who had ever worked on the Kennedy Detail: Ken Wiesman, who had transferred off the detail a week before and had just reported in to the Sacramento Field Office; Ed Tucker, who'd been on the children's detail and was now in Chicago; Bob Lilley in Boston; Bill Skiles, now in Oklahoma; Harry Gibbs in New York. The list went on and on. Everybody wanted to come back and do whatever they could to help with what they knew were going to be some of the most difficult days the Secret Service had ever faced.

ANDREWS AIR FORCE BASE
5:58 P.M.

Several thousand Air Force personnel had gathered for the arrival of Air Force One at Andrews Air Force Base, along with senators, congressmen, members of the Kennedy family, and a throng of newspaper reporters and television crews. Unlike the cheering spectators who had greeted the silver, blue, and white plane earlier in the day, this crowd was nearly silent.

A minute later the presidential helicopter landed on the tarmac nearby.

Despite the huge numbers of people, security was exceptionally tight. Secret Service director Jim Rowley had supervised and scrutinized the arrangements himself, and when the plane arrived in the darkness at 5:58 Eastern Standard Time, Rowley was there alongside Attorney General Robert Kennedy.

The instant the portable stairwell was moved into place at the front of the plane, the attorney general bounded up the stairs. He flew down the aisle to the back of the plane, greeting no one—not even President Johnson. He cared only about getting to Jackie.

The agents had opened the rear door of the plane and a forklift with a roofed, two-sided cubicle used for catering was being rolled up to the opening. Clint Hill, Paul Landis, Roy Kellerman, and the president's aides struggled to lift the heavy casket onto the forklift. Not only was it extremely heavy, but now with its side handles broken off it was like moving a six-hundred-pound boulder. Once the casket was in place, Bobby Kennedy held Mrs. Kennedy by the arm and the whole entourage joined the casket onto the elevator-type apparatus. Millions of Americans watched the unprecedented event unfold live on their television screens as the crowd on the sidelines stood in silent reverence.

A Navy ambulance backed up to the forklift as the large open cubicle was slowly lowered. The apparatus hadn't been made for this purpose, however, and its lowest point was still nearly five feet above the ground. Now the men who just four and a half hours earlier had seen the back of President Kennedy's head blown off hauled the casket holding his dead body off the forklift and into the waiting ambulance. They didn't even notice the television cameras and the gaping crowd.

Bill Greer got into the driver's seat. Bobby Kennedy had assumed that he and Mrs. Kennedy would fly in the helicopter to the White House, but she wouldn't leave the casket. She wanted to go to Bethesda, and once again she insisted on riding in the back of the hearse with the casket. The attorney general crawled in the back with her, as did General Godfrey McHugh, President Kennedy's Air Force aide. It was dark, and everybody was in a daze. Roy Kellerman, Admiral Burkley, and Paul Landis joined Greer in the front of the hearse, leaving no room for Clint Hill. He jumped into the follow-up car with Dave Powers, Ken O'Donnell, and Larry O'Brien.

The whole procedure had taken only twelve minutes. At 6:10 P.M. a motorcycle escort led the somber motorcade away from Andrews Air Force Base.

Finally, with the world watching, President Johnson appeared in the open door of Air Force One and walked down the steps, followed by his wife, Lady Bird, and members of his staff and Secret Service.

SAIC Jerry Behn and ASAIC Floyd Boring immediately flanked Johnson as supplemental agents from Secret Service headquarters and the Washington Field Office spread a wide shield around him.

A row of press microphones had been set up at a podium with the assumption that the new president would make a statement to the American people, and Johnson was guided toward them. At first he seemed flustered. Nothing could have prepared him for this. Like everybody who had witnessed the horror only a few hours earlier, Johnson was still in a state of shock.

Standing with Lady Bird by his side and Air Force One illuminated with the black sky behind him, Johnson waited until the television cameras were in place and then read the statement written by his executive assistant Liz Carpenter during the flight.

"This is a sad time for all people. We have suffered a loss that cannot be weighed. For me, it is a deep, personal tragedy. I know that the world shares the sorrow that Mrs. Kennedy and her family bear. I will do my best. That is all I can do. I ask for your help. And God's."

President Johnson stepped away from the microphones, and after greeting several members of Congress and the Senate, boarded the military green Marine helicopter with the band of white at the top signaling that it carried the President of the United States, and departed for the White House.

The forty-five-minute drive from Andrews Air Force Base to Bethesda Naval Hospital seemed interminable. Every so often Roy Kellerman saw Bill Greer take a hand off the wheel and wipe away a tear. In the follow-up car, Dave Powers's shoulders would suddenly start shaking with unstoppable grief.

There was a presidential suite on the seventeenth floor of the hospital, and as Bill Greer, Roy Kellerman, and Admiral Burkley accompanied the casket to the morgue for the autopsy, Clint Hill and Paul Landis escorted Mrs. Kennedy and her brother-in-law the attorney general to the suite.

Landis and Hill secured the area and set up a checkpoint for visitors. It wasn't long before the Kennedys' close friends—including Ben and Tony Bradlee—and immediate family members started arriving.

Meanwhile, discussions ensued about a new casket. The President of the United States couldn't be buried in a damaged casket. Bobby Kennedy wanted to be involved, but in the end he stayed with Mrs. Kennedy while Ken O'Donnell and Dave Powers set off for Gawler's funeral home, where they picked out a mahogany one. Mahogany seemed more fitting for Jack than bronze anyway.

It was 7:30 P.M. when Jerry Blaine finally got home to his Larchmont Village apartment in Alexandria. Because he hadn't been in Dallas, he felt oddly removed from the assassination and still there were so many unanswered questions. He hugged his two kids, Scott and Kelly, kissed Joyce, ate dinner, and talked with Joyce about the day's events. In many ways, for the first time Joyce knew more than he did, simply because she had been watching the news on television while he'd been in virtual lockdown on the flight from Texas. He had just a few hours before he needed to report for the midnight shift at the Elms, and while he tried to sleep, it was futile. Instead, he wrote down his thoughts on his daily report:

> *Even though there was little that could have been done—it is next to impossible to prevent an assassination with the President riding in an open top automobile—all of the agents are suffering from acute guilt and failure. The coming weeks of analysis and finger pointing will undoubtedly be an ordeal. There is always a search for the scapegoat and I know we are going to be the target.*
>
> *President Kennedy was great to work for. He was a courageous man who had a magnificent sense of humor and respected the agents of the Secret Service. This loss is personal. We not only lost a President, we lost a personal friend.*

He tried to get a few hours of sleep, but the unanswered questions kept replaying over and over in his mind.

WASHINGTON, D.C.
7:55 P.M.

The Air Force cargo plane carrying the president's limousine and follow-up car landed at Andrews Air Force Base and was met by agents from the Washington Field Office and several police motorcycles. Sam Kinney and George Hickey drove the cars directly to the White House garage with the motorcycle escorts. For Sam, the thirty-minute drive was nearly unbearable. With the bubble top on the car, the smell of death permeated the interior. He couldn't bear to look in the rearview mirror, to the empty, untouched, still blood-covered seat in the back. He struggled to keep his eyes and mind on the road, softly weeping in the solace of the last place President Kennedy had been alive.

At the garage, White House police and Secret Service agents set up an all-night watch over the cars, securing them for the pending investigation.

Meanwhile, Stewart Stout's 4:00 to midnight shift agents—who had started their day at 7:15 A.M. to secure the parking lot outside the Hotel Texas in Fort Worth, had gone to the Trade Mart and then on to Parkland Hospital, had helped with the loading of the casket onto Air Force One, and had flown back with the grieving Mrs. Kennedy—were now officially on duty to protect President Johnson. Agents Andy Berger, Sam Sulliman, Dick Johnsen, and Ernie Olsson went with President Johnson on Marine One from Andrews Air Force Base to the White House and stayed with him as he met with White House staff and key members of Congress at his offices at the Executive Office Building.

The rest of the White House Detail agents, with the exception of the midnight shift and those with Mrs. Kennedy and the children, jammed into the supervisor's office with Director Rowley. For about twenty minutes Rowley gave what could only be called a pep talk. He spoke about how they were professionals and would continue to do the job and be better than before. There was no feeling that he blamed anyone or that the assassination could somehow have been prevented. It was therapeutic for many of the men, and was the closest thing to counseling they would receive.

Afterward, the supervising agents who had been on the Texas trip were requested to stay and, while the memories were still fresh, type up their recollections of everything that had happened that day. There would of course be an investigation and Rowley knew his men would be at the center of it.

At 9:25 P.M. the afternoon shift traveled with President Johnson to the Elms at 4040 Fifty-second Street, just five minutes from the White House, where Agent Paul Rundle was waiting to brief them on the new security.

"Listen," Rundle said. "There are rumors flying all over the place but the truth is, nobody knows who might have been behind the assassination. They've got this guy Oswald in custody in Dallas, and while he could easily just be a deranged sociopath, there's still the chance that he was part of a bigger conspiracy. Could be Cuban, Mafia, or some Soviet-backed plan to overthrow the government. It's just too early to know, but the orders we've been given are to be excessive in our protective measures."

None of these Kennedy Detail agents had ever even been to Johnson's residence before, so Rundle gave them a quick tour. Every half hour the agents would rotate posts in a counterclockwise direction, just as they did at the White House—with one major difference. Tonight, along with the .38-caliber revolver each agent always carried, every security post would be armed with a Thompson submachine gun.

Exhausted and emotionally drained, Agents Stout, Sulliman, Johnsen, Olsson, and Berger took their posts around the house. Two and a half hours later, the midnight shift arrived to take over. They'd done this transition a thousand times, the shifts knew each other like brothers, and there were always a few minutes where they shared jokes or necessary information. But tonight was like no other. The agents on the 4:00 to midnight shift were emotionally destroyed and as their replacements came, they merely pointed to the Thompson gun and walked away.

Back at Bethesda, Mrs. Kennedy, surrounded by friends and family, suddenly realized that she wanted the children to be at the White House when she got there. Mr. Hill of course took care of it. He called Agent Bob Foster and around ten o'clock, the sleeping Caroline and John, Jr., were taken—in a carefully orchestrated and surreptitious movement—back to

out ok. **019**
r library to saed $2...
this year. ...ve save...
Title...
ID: 000...y detail...
Due: Tuesd...s brea th...ret
Messages: ...0 ...ce
Item checkout ok. ...**9, 2019**
using your library toda...t saed $2...
$1,210.66 this year. ...ha...e save...

Total items: 3
Account balance: $0.00
Tuesday, June 11, 2019 10:58 AM
Checked out: 4
Overdue: 0
Hold requests: 1
Ready for pickup: 1
Messages:
Patron status is ok.

Thank you for using the library!

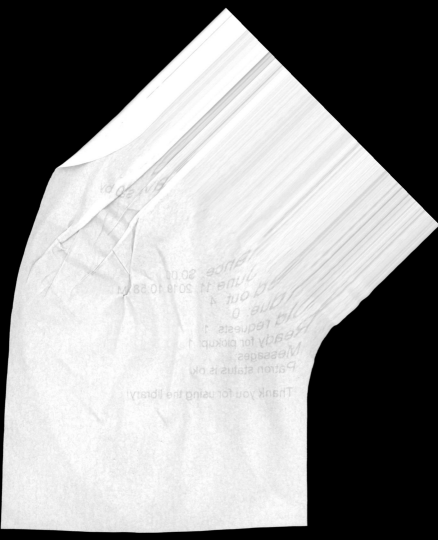

Balance $0.00

June 11 2019 10.58 M

...ed out 4

June 0

...ld requests 1

Ready for pickup 1

Messages

Patron status is ok

Thank you for using the library!

their bedrooms at the White House. The helicopter had come and gone. It hadn't brought their daddy home after all.

It was nearly two o'clock in the morning when Andy Berger finally walked through the door of his Hyattsville, Maryland, apartment with his trench coat draped over his arm. His wife, Dolly, had been sitting in the living room with friends, waiting the anxious hours for Andy to come home. Still dressed in the dark suit he'd put on in Fort Worth that morning, twenty-six-year-old Andy Berger sat down on the living room sofa, put his head in his hands, and cried and cried and cried.

16

No Time for Tears

History is a relentless master. It has no present, only the past rushing into the future. To try to hold fast is to be swept aside.

—JOHN F. KENNEDY

WASHINGTON, D.C.
NOVEMBER 23, 1963
2:15 A.M.

Standing outside in the pitch-black darkness, Agent Jerry Blaine tried desperately not to yawn. He was on post at the rear corner of President Johnson's large two-story French chateau–style house close to the back door, and with the exception of the forty-five-minute nap in Austin and some catnaps on flights, it had now been nearly sixty hours since he'd had any sleep. Blaine was almost to the point where he was hallucinating.

When he'd taken over from Andy Berger just before midnight, the two had simply looked at each other without saying anything. What could be said?

Blaine had been at this particular post for about fifteen minutes when he suddenly heard the sound of someone approaching from the clockwise direction. It wasn't rotation time, and he knew a Kennedy Detail agent would never approach from that direction.

Instinctively Blaine picked up the Thompson submachine gun and activated the bolt on top. The unmistakable sound was similar to racking a shotgun. He firmly pushed the stock into his shoulder, ready to fire. He'd expected the footsteps to retreat with the loud sound of the gun activating, but they kept coming closer. Blaine's heart pounded, his finger firmly on the trigger. *Let me see your face, you bastard.*

The next instant, there was a face to go with the footsteps.

The new President of the United States, Lyndon Baines Johnson, had just rounded the corner, and Blaine had the gun pointed directly at the man's chest. In the blackness of the night, Johnson's face went completely white.

A split second later, Blaine would have pulled the trigger.

President Johnson looked at Blaine, said nothing, and turned around and went back in the house.

Jesus Christ! I almost shot the new president. What the hell was he coming around the wrong way for?

With all the new security measures put into place that night, in the chaos nobody had thought to inform President Johnson about the standard counterclockwise movement protocol.

Blaine struggled to regain his composure as the reality of what had just happened washed over him. Fourteen hours after losing a president, the nation had come chillingly close to losing another one.

BETHESDA NAVAL HOSPITAL
2:45 A.M.

Clint Hill was standing outside the Presidential Suite when he got a message that Roy Kellerman needed him to come down to the autopsy room. Leaving Paul Landis in charge on the seventeenth floor, he stepped into the elevator, and as he looked at all the numbers on the panel, for a moment he was disoriented.

Stay on task. Stay on task.

He looked at his watch and realized that it was no longer November 22, the day President Kennedy had been assassinated. Time was moving forward. He hit the down button and the elevator doors closed.

Roy Kellerman was waiting for him in the stark hallway outside the autopsy room. "Clint," he said, "before the autopsy is closed, I need you to come in and view the president's body."

Clint's eyes were as hollow as Mrs. Kennedy's. He clenched his teeth, and his jaw twitched as he nodded.

"I know this isn't going to be easy, but we decided that since you are the closest to Mrs. Kennedy, it's important for you to see the body, in case she has any questions."

Kellerman opened the door and they walked in together.

Bill Greer was there, and General McHugh. There were doctors and other people Clint didn't recognize. And lying on the table was the naked body of President Kennedy, covered delicately with a white sheet. At first glance it looked like he was sleeping. There wasn't a mark on his face.

A man in a white coat pulled the sheet down and Clint saw the wound in the throat, where the doctors at Parkland had done a tracheotomy. More hands touched the pale, lifeless president and turned him to the side so Clint could view the back.

Six inches down from the neckline, just to the right of the spinal column, there was a small wound, a hole in the skin. Clint might not have noticed it had the man in the white coat not pointed it out. All Clint could see was that the right rear portion of President Kennedy's head was completely gone.

Clint grimaced and took one long look so that if Mrs. Kennedy ever asked—which he knew she never would—he could tell her what anybody who had been in the follow-up car could tell her. They'd all seen it, heard it. There wasn't any doubt what had happened. A sniper had shot the president from an upper window. *And I didn't get there in time to stop it.*

The president's body was placed in the new mahogany casket from Gawler's funeral home and Clint Hill returned to the seventeenth floor, where Paul Landis was still on guard. When Clint got word that the casket was being transferred to a U.S. Navy ambulance, he solemnly told Mrs. Kennedy that it was time to return to the White House.

Mrs. Kennedy and Attorney General Kennedy climbed into the rear of the ambulance with the casket. Bill Greer drove President Kennedy one final time, home to the White House.

A White House limousine followed directly behind with Clint Hill in the right front seat. When the motorcade arrived at the White House at

4:24 A.M., there was a unit of U.S. Marines waiting at the Northwest Gate. The squad, in full military dress, marched solemnly at port arms ahead of the body-bearing ambulance, escorting the fallen commander in chief to the North Portico, the sound of their boots on the pavement like a drumbeat. The stoic young men were surely glad for the darkness, for it hid the steady stream of tears none of them could control.

A military honor guard from Fort Myer had assembled outside the North Portico. In the black of night, the military body bearers carried the casket into the East Room, with the small procession of Secret Service agents following Mrs. Kennedy and the attorney general behind it.

In the hours since the president's death, Sargent Shriver—the husband of JFK's sister Eunice and the man President Kennedy had appointed director of the Peace Corps—had been working with the White House staff to prepare the East Room for the president's casket. Shriver had found an engraving of how the room had looked when Abraham Lincoln's body had been brought there, and he was striving to duplicate it. A replica of the catafalque used for Lincoln, and which had been used for the remains of the Unknown Soldier buried at Arlington Cemetery, had miraculously been located. Shriver had it placed in the identical spot in the East Room where Abraham Lincoln's body had lain nearly a century before. A staff member had found yards and yards of black crepe fabric and had draped it elegantly around the mantel, the drapes, and the large crystal chandelier. Keenly aware of Mrs. Kennedy's taste, Sargent Shriver made sure the room looked elegant and respectful without being garish or morbid.

Agent Paul Rundle was waiting at the White House, and when he saw Clint in his wrinkled, stained shirt, the stubble of a beard on his normally clean-shaven face, and the desolate look in his eyes, the reality of what his friend had been through hit him like a punch in the gut.

"Clint," Rundle said, "is there anything I can do?"

Clint seemed to look right through him and merely shook his head. *What can anybody do now? The president is dead. Oh, dear God. The president is dead.*

As Paul Landis followed Mrs. Kennedy into the White House, he suddenly remembered that the Zippo lighter he had retrieved from the limousine was still in his pocket. Provie, Mrs. Kennedy's Dominican attendant, was standing nearby.

He walked over to her and, his voice cracking, he handed her the lighter and said, "Provie, I don't know what to do with this. It was on the backseat of the car."

Paul didn't know whose lighter it was. Mrs. Kennedy didn't carry a lighter. Perhaps it had fallen from Clint's pocket, or from the president's. Tears welled in both their eyes as Provie took the blood-encrusted lighter and clutched it in her hands.

With her husband's body back home in the White House, Mrs. Kennedy finally felt as if she could try to get some sleep. Once Agent Hill was assured that Mrs. Kennedy was safely settled into her private quarters, he walked out of the White House and drove home.

Agent Joe Paolella had been working the evening shift at Atoka and was assigned the task of guarding the presidential vehicles and overseeing staff members from Bethesda Naval Hospital who would be arriving to search the presidential limousine and collect scalp, brain tissue, and bone matter. Paolella shook his head with disbelief at the gory sight inside the car. The thought of what had happened sickened him as his eyes moved through the interior of the once-pristine vehicle. It was then that he noticed what appeared to be a chip and a bullet fragment in the front windshield on the driver's side, and an indentation on top of the windshield frame. The inside of the windshield was spattered with blood, and as his mind started imagining the horror of the assassination, he quickly looked away.

7:15 A.M.

Emory Roberts and his day shift agents who had been in the follow-up car in Dallas showed up at the Elms forty-five minutes before their shift was to start. Art Godfrey briefed Roberts on the posts and the Thompson submachine guns and quietly mentioned the near accident that Jerry Blaine had reported to him.

"Everybody's exhausted, Emory," Godfrey said. "And you guys, more than any of us, have been through hell. Just tell your men to be cautious with the weapons."

The Secret Service badge as it appeared on the commission books of the Kennedy Detail agents. A new badge was created in 1971 and again in 2003. (PERSONAL COLLECTION OF GERALD BLAINE)

Caroline attempts to make a funny face for the photographer—encouraged by SA Bob Foster. (PHOTOGRAPH BY CECIL STOUGHTON, WHITE HOUSE, JOHN F. KENNEDY PRESIDENTIAL LIBRARY AND MUSEUM, BOSTON)

President Kennedy bursts into laughter at the sight of John and Caroline in their Halloween costumes in the Oval Office, October 1963. (PHOTOGRAPH BY CECIL STOUGHTON, WHITE HOUSE, JOHN F. KENNEDY PRESIDENTIAL LIBRARY AND MUSEUM, BOSTON)

President Kennedy looking across to East Berlin near the Brandenburg gate. Guards onthe other side of the Berlin wall carried their standard weapons, creating a security risk. (PHOTOGRAPH BY ROBERT KNUDSEN, WHITE HOUSE, JOHN F. KENNEDY PRESIDENTIAL LIBRARY AND MUSEUM, BOSTON)

SAIC Jerry Behn gives SA Clint Hill instructions after the loss of the Kennedys' newborn baby Patrick. (PHOTOGRAPH BY CECIL STOUGHTON, WHITE HOUSE, JOHN F. KENNEDY PRESIDENTIAL LIBRARY AND MUSEUM, BOSTON)

1961 Inauguration photo of agents called to Washington, D.C., to handle security. The entire Secret Service consisted of 278 agents at that time and nearly all worked President Kennedy's Inauguration. (OFFICIAL SECRET SERVICE PHOTO)

UPI reporter Merriman "Smitty" Smith and ATSAIC Art Godfrey share a laugh on a military helicopter. (PERSONAL COLLECTION OF GERALD BLAINE)

Mugsy O'Leary, ATSAIC Stewart Stout, SA Ken Giannoules, and SA Jerry Blaine in Venezuela. (PHOTOGRAPH BY CECIL STOUGHTON, WHITE HOUSE, JOHN F. KENNEDY PRESIDENTIAL LIBRARY AND MUSEUM, BOSTON)

Agents didn't always travel in the presidential helicopter. Left to right: Crew chief, SA Paul Burns, Driver Tom Shipman, Dr. George Burkley, SA Jack Ready, and SA Jerry Blaine. (PERSONAL COLLECTION OF GERALD BLAINE)

Posing with "The Singing Cowboy," Gene Autry. SA Win Lawson, friend of Autry, Gene Autry, SA Jerry Blaine, ATSAIC Art Godfrey, and SA Dennis Halterman. (PHOTOGRAPH BY CECIL STOUGHTON, WHITE HOUSE, JOHN F. KENNEDY PRESIDENTIAL LIBRARY AND MUSEUM, BOSTON)

As President and Mrs. Kennedy forge their way through a crowd, Agents Harry Gibbs (left) and Ken Wiesman (right) stay close. (OFFICIAL WHITE HOUSE PHOTO/PHOTOGRAPHER UNKNOWN)

The agents struggle to contain their emotions after the funeral of President Kennedy's newborn son. Left to right: SA Paul Burns, ASAIC Floyd Boring, Frank McDermott (SAIC, Boston Field Office), Dave Powers (in hat), SA Ron Pontius, JFK, SA Jerry Blaine. (PHOTOGRAPH BY CECIL STOUGHTON, WHITE HOUSE, JOHN F. KENNEDY PRESIDENTIAL LIBRARY AND MUSEUM, BOSTON)

Agent Ron Pontius stops an overzealous fan from getting close to JFK as he enters St. Ann's Catholic Church in West Palm Beach. Typically thoughtful and appreciative of his agents, JFK signed the photo for Pontius. (COPYRIGHT BY ASSOCIATED PRESS)

Agents Win Lawson, Jerry Blaine, Bob Burke, and Sam Sulliman scan the crowd during a motorcade in Ireland. (PHOTOGRAPH BY CECIL STOUGHTON, WHITE HOUSE, JOHN F. KENNEDY PRESIDENTIAL LIBRARY AND MUSEUM, BOSTON)

John Kennedy, Jr., waits to salute his father, the Commander in Chief, at Arlington National Cemetery on Veterans Day 1963. Two weeks later, JFK is buried there. (PHOTOGRAPH BY CECIL STOUGHTON, WHITE HOUSE, JOHN F. KENNEDY PRESIDENTIAL LIBRARY AND MUSEUM, BOSTON)

President Kennedy inspects the Freedom 7 space capsule flown into space by John Glenn, who is standing to the president's right. (PHOTOGRAPH BY CECIL STOUGHTON, WHITE HOUSE, JOHN F. KENNEDY PRESIDENTIAL LIBRARY AND MUSEUM, BOSTON)

Four days before the assassination, Special Agents Chuck Zboril and Don Lawton crouch on the rear steps of the presidential limousine during the 28-mile motorcade through Tampa, Florida. (PHOTOGRAPH BY THE TAMPA TRIBUNE)

Jerry Blaine and Art Godfrey pose in their newly purchased Western hats in front of the Hotel Texas, where JFK spends his final night. ATSAIC Stewart Stout in background on right. (PHOTOGRAPH BY CECIL STOUGHTON, WHITE HOUSE, JOHN F. KENNEDY PRESIDENTIAL LIBRARY AND MUSEUM, BOSTON)

(Left) Secret Service agents scan the huge crowd and open windows above as President Kennedy speaks outside the Hotel Texas in Fort Worth, just hours before the assassination. (PHOTOGRAPH BY CECIL STOUGHTON, WHITE HOUSE, JOHN F. KENNEDY PRESIDENTIAL LIBRARY AND MUSEUM, BOSTON)

(Right) SA Jack Ready keeps a watchful eye on the crowd as JFK speaks outside the Hotel Texas with Governor Connally, VP Johnson, and other dignitaries behind him. (PHOTOGRAPH BY CECIL STOUGHTON, WHITE HOUSE, JOHN F. KENNEDY PRESIDENTIAL LIBRARY AND MUSEUM, BOSTON)

Departing Love Field for the Trade Mart in Dallas on November 22, 1963. Agent Clint Hill directly behind Jackie Kennedy, SAIC Roy Kellerman in the front passenger seat. (TOM DILLARD COLLECTION, *DALLAS MORNING NEWS*/THE SIXTH FLOOR MUSEUM AT DEALEY PLAZA)

People hung out of windows, stood on balconies, and overflowed into the street as JFK's motorcade traveled down Main Street in Dallas on November 22, 1963. (PHOTOGRAPH BY *THE DALLAS MORNING NEWS*)

Despite orders to stay off the limousine, Agent Clint Hill crouches on the rear step, because of the large crowds, as the car turns onto Main Street in Dallas.
(DARRYL HEIKES, PHOTOGRAPHER, *DALLAS TIMES HERALD* COLLECTION/THE SIXTH FLOOR MUSEUM AT DEALEY PLAZA)

The traumatized and grief-stricken Secret Service agents feel the weight of the world on their shoulders as they struggle to load President Kennedy's casket onto Air Force One while Jacqueline Kennedy watches from below.
(PHOTOGRAPH BY CECIL STOUGHTON, WHITE HOUSE, JOHN F. KENNEDY PRESIDENTIAL LIBRARY AND MUSEUM, BOSTON)

Newly sworn-in President Lyndon B. Johnson addresses the nation upon arrival at Andrews Air Force Base, hours after the assassination. (PHOTOGRAPH BY CECIL STOUGHTON, WHITE HOUSE, JOHN F. KENNEDY PRESIDENTIAL LIBRARY AND MUSEUM, BOSTON)

The Honor Guard stands vigil over President Kennedy's casket in the East Room of the White House. (PHOTOGRAPH BY CECIL STOUGHTON, WHITE HOUSE, JOHN F. KENNEDY PRESIDENTIAL LIBRARY AND MUSEUM, BOSTON)

Agents Tom Wells and Bob Foster escort Caroline and John, Jr., in the funeral cortege to St. Matthew's Cathedral for the funeral of their father. (PHOTOGRAPH BY CECIL STOUGHTON, WHITE HOUSE, JOHN F. KENNEDY PRESIDENTIAL LIBRARY AND MUSEUM, BOSTON)

Mrs. Kennedy insisted on walking from the White House to St. Matthew's for her husband's funeral procession, creating a security nightmare for the Secret Service. Agent Paul Landis is on the far right. Agent Clint Hill, unseen in this photo, is behind Mrs. Kennedy. (PHOTOGRAPH BY ROBERT KNUDSEN, WHITE HOUSE, JOHN F. KENNEDY LIBRARY AND MUSEUM, BOSTON)

Foreign dignitaries, including President Charles de Gaulle of France and Emperor Haile Selassie of Ethiopia, offer their final salute to slain President John F. Kennedy. (PHOTOGRAPH BY CECIL STOUGHTON, WHITE HOUSE, JOHN F. KENNEDY PRESIDENTIAL LIBRARY AND MUSEUM, BOSTON)

The military honor guard prepares to fold the flag that covered the casket of President John F. Kennedy as Mrs. Kennedy, other members of the Kennedy family, and foreign dignitaries watch in silence. (PHOTOGRAPH BY CECIL STOUGHTON, WHITE HOUSE, JOHN F. KENNEDY PRESIDENTIAL LIBRARY AND MUSEUM, BOSTON)

For Paul Landis -
with deep appreciation for all your help
to us for three years
Jacqueline Kennedy

Mrs. Kennedy signed this photo for her loyal agent Paul Landis when he left the Secret Service not long after the assassination. (PHOTOGRAPH BY CECIL STOUGHTON, WHITE HOUSE, JOHN F. KENNEDY PRESIDENTIAL LIBRARY AND MUSEUM, BOSTON)

Agents Bob Foster and Tom Wells with John, Jr., Caroline, and nanny Maud Shaw as they move out of the White House following the assassination. (PHOTOGRAPH BY CECIL STOUGHTON, WHITE HOUSE, JOHN F. KENNEDY PRESIDENTIAL LIBRARY AND MUSEUM, BOSTON)

John F. Kennedy, Jr., had two passions: helicopters and playing soldier. It was in this outfit at ATOKA that he learned to salute in preparation for Veterans' Day at Arlington National Cemetery, two weeks prior to his father's assassination. (PHOTOGRAPH BY CECIL STOUGHTON, WHITE HOUSE, JOHN F. KENNEDY PRESIDENTIAL LIBRARY AND MUSEUM, BOSTON)

Nothing more was said between the agents. They were all walking zombies—mentally and physically drained—but still they had a job to do. Their job was to protect the President of the United States. The agents were filled with grief, anger, fatigue, and so many questions, but nobody said a word. It was as if the assassination were a forbidden subject.

After being relieved, the midnight shift agents drove straight to the White House and assembled in the Secret Service office in the West Wing. President Kennedy's body would be placed in the Capitol rotunda for viewing by the general public, but Mrs. Kennedy had requested that her husband lie in state in the East Room of the White House for twenty-four hours so that the staff and administrative officials who had served him so loyally could pay their personal respects.

Somberly the agents walked out of the Secret Service office. Rather than take the direct route to the walkway between the West Wing and the residence, the group took the longer path to pass by the Oval Office. They felt compelled to pay their respects.

But as they walked past the open door, they could see a tearful Evelyn Lincoln, President Kennedy's secretary, and some other White House staff members busy packing President Kennedy's personal items. Blaine, for one, was incensed and the anger over the assassination surged through him.

ATSAIC Art Godfrey led the shift past the Rose Garden and into the long hallway of the executive mansion.

Death was not new to Art Godfrey, Jerry Blaine, Ken Giannoules, Paul Burns, Bob Faison, or Jerry O'Rourke, but this death was different. The mission of the White House Secret Service detail was simple. Their sole responsibility was to protect the President of the United States. And they had failed. Even though the midnight shift had been miles away when the assassination occurred, they all felt an overwhelming sense of responsibility for the loss of a gifted world leader whom they'd also considered a friend.

With their heads bowed, the agents filed into the East Room. Directly beneath the ornate crystal chandelier in the middle of the white-walled room, President Kennedy's flag-draped casket lay in the same location where President Lincoln's had rested nearly one hundred years before, and on the same bier that had been used for the Unknown Soldier. There was already a line starting to form. Soft cries, sniffles, and heaving sobs echoed through the vast wood-floored room as the White House cooks, maids, gardeners, secretaries, and policy advisors circled the casket. Seeing the outpouring of grief by the other staff members suddenly brought rise to new emotions in the agents: guilt and shame. They stood back from the line, hoping not to be noticed, and after a while they looked at each other and silently walked out of the East Room.

Gwen Hill had barely slept. She couldn't turn away from the television. She still hadn't spoken to Clint, but, thank God, Eve Dempsher had called to tell her that the rumors of the Secret Service agent being shot were untrue. Clint was unharmed.

But nothing could have prepared her for how her husband looked when he walked in the door of their house at six o'clock in the morning.

His eyes. Oh God, his eyes. They were empty, lifeless. He looked as if he'd been to hell and back. No, that was wrong. He looked like, wherever he'd been, he had yet to return from it. She wrapped her arms around him and hugged hard, but it was as if he were catatonic. It was as if he weren't even there.

"Oh, Clint. Oh, Clint . . . ," she cried.

And Clint just let her hug him. It was a small piece of comfort, but inside he was wondering how he would go on. He had told Mrs. Kennedy he would be okay, but really, he didn't know how anything could ever be okay again.

Somehow he managed to go through the motions of showering and shaving and eating. Did he eat? He couldn't remember. And then, dressed in a clean shirt and tie and suit, he drove back to the White House.

When Jerry Blaine walked into the apartment sometime around 9:00 or 10:00—who knew what time it was? did it matter?—Joyce had breakfast prepared, but Jerry wasn't hungry. He headed for the bedroom and collapsed on the bed.

He'd just fallen into a deep sleep when he dreamed that the phone was ringing. And then Joyce was shaking him.

"Jerry, Jerry, wake up."

Jerry opened his eyes. Maybe it had all been a nightmare.

"Jerry, Jerry Behn is on the phone," Joyce said. "He says it's urgent."

Jerry got out of bed and walked groggily to the kitchen. He picked up the receiver.

"Hello?"

"Hi, Jer, how're you doin'?" Behn asked. "I know you were probably sleeping, but I need to give you an assignment."

"Sure, what do you need, Jerry?" Blaine asked dutifully.

"I need you to advance a reception at the State Department. We have dozens of world leaders coming for the funeral, and the president— President Johnson, that is—wants a reception for them immediately following the funeral. I hate to do this to you, but this is important."

Blaine felt as if he'd been punched in the gut. He had been with President Kennedy since the day after he was elected, traveled everywhere with him, and now Jerry Behn was telling him he would have to miss the funeral and burial in order to do the advance.

"When is the funeral?" Blaine queried.

"Monday. Two days from now."

"Not much time," Blaine answered. He was feeling more and more like he was being handed a punishment he didn't deserve.

"That's why I called you. I know this is a lousy assignment, but it needs to be done right. We have a lot of exposure responsibility. Almost every leader in the world is attending. Eve has the information, so you can pick it up this afternoon," Behn said.

"Okay," Blaine said, then hung up the phone. What else could he say?

Blaine knew that the SAIC was suffering, just as they all were. This had to be the toughest day of Jerry Behn's long career with the Secret Service. He was receiving orders from Johnson's staff while simultaneously trying to handle the Kennedy family requests. Even though there were agents flying in from all over the country to help, the only agents he could count on with absolute assurance were the agents on the Kennedy Detail. He had no alternative. Jerry Behn was now the Special Agent in Charge of the Johnson Detail.

• • •

A burial site had to be chosen for the president. The Kennedy family assumed he would be buried in the family burial site at Brookline Cemetery, outside Boston, but Jackie believed her husband was more than a Kennedy—he belonged to the American people. She was insistent that he should be buried at Arlington National Cemetery, in a state funeral befitting the commander in chief.

At two o'clock, just over twenty-four hours after President Kennedy was assassinated, Agents Clint Hill and Paul Landis accompanied Mrs. Kennedy to Arlington to choose a grave site for her husband. *To choose a grave site for the President of the United States.*

Stay on task. Stay on task.

The attorney general—the president's brother—was by her side, along with two of the president's sisters, Jean Kennedy Smith and Patricia Kennedy Lawford, and Secretary of Defense Robert McNamara. It didn't take long for Jackie to find the perfect resting place for her husband. As she stood on the hillside looking back over Memorial Bridge to the lovely, serene view of Washington, D.C., in the background, she envisioned a simple marker with an eternal flame, so that John F. Kennedy would remain alive in the hearts of the American people forever. The funeral would be Monday, here in the same cemetery where President Kennedy had placed the wreath at the Tomb of the Unknown Soldier, and had brought his son John to see the soldiers, exactly two weeks earlier.

When they returned to the White House, plans for the funeral continued. Tomorrow morning the casket would be taken from the East Room in a procession down Pennsylvania Avenue to the rotunda of the Capitol building, where President Kennedy would lie in state for twenty-four hours. On Monday, the day of the state funeral, the casket would again be placed on the horse-drawn caisson and travel from the Capitol back to the White House, on to St. Matthew's Cathedral for a requiem Mass, and finally on to its final resting place at Arlington Cemetery.

The outpouring of grief was overwhelming. Mrs. Kennedy was getting telegrams and telexes from all over the country, from all over the world. People from New York to Rome to Pakistan to Japan to Tibet to the Soviet Union were gathering in the streets, making impromptu floral temples to the slain president. In Berlin, where President Kennedy just five months earlier had stood and proclaimed *Ich bin ein Berliner*, thousands gathered again to mourn together and vowed to rename the huge public square John F. Kennedy Platz.

But even as commerce and entertainment and politics came to an abrupt halt as the world collectively mourned the beloved president, those closest to him had to focus on the days ahead. Dozens of world leaders and their representatives were flying in from all over the world, and the Secret Service was working nonstop with the State Department security staff to figure out how to handle the influx of dignitaries, where they would stay, how they would participate.

Mrs. Kennedy was deeply involved in the planning of the state funeral and wanted the ceremonial details to be modeled after President Abraham Lincoln's funeral. The Office of the Chief of Protocol and military staffs were working around the clock to get everything in place by Monday, and while Mrs. Kennedy left the majority of the planning to others, there was one thing on which she insisted: on the day of the funeral, after the president's body had lain in state at the Capitol, as the caisson traveled from the White House to St. Matthew's Cathedral, Mrs. Kennedy wanted to lead the procession of dignitaries, on foot.

It was just eight blocks, but to the White House Secret Service detail, who still felt as if they were living in a nightmare, the notion of Mrs. Kennedy walking through the streets of Washington, D.C., accompanied by President Johnson, leading members of Congress, and dozens of prime ministers, presidents, and representatives from other countries was beyond the bounds of reason.

The President of the United States had just been assassinated, world leaders were coming in from all corners of the globe—France's Charles de Gaulle, King Baudouin of the Belgians, Queen Frederika of Greece, Irish president Eamon de Valera, the Duke of Edinburgh, Ethiopian emperor Haile Selassie. It was a security nightmare even if everyone were to be in closed-top cars. Walking was a *bad* idea. Everybody agreed. Everybody, except Mrs. Kennedy.

She refused to compromise and in the end nobody was willing to stand up to the grieving widow. Chief Rowley and SAIC Jerry Behn wouldn't sleep until the funeral was over.

• • •

That morning in Hyannis Port, at the Kennedy compound, Special Agent Ham Brown and the Kennedy family went through their normal routine. Ambassador Kennedy had breakfast, a stroll outside in his wheelchair, and a nap. When Senator Ted Kennedy, his wife, Joan, sister Eunice Kennedy Shriver, and several other family members arrived, it was time to break the news. Rose Kennedy and her children gathered around the helpless ambassador and, holding him in their arms, they told him that his son, the President of the United States, had been killed. It was the saddest thing Ham had ever seen.

John and Caroline had been brought back to the White House and had been told their father was dead—a bad man had shot him. The helicopter had come and gone, and now their daddy was in a box with an American flag on top of it, in the big ballroom downstairs with soldiers guarding him. There was going to be a funeral and a lot of people were coming because their daddy had been so special. Everybody was very, very sad.

SUNDAY, NOVEMBER 24, 1963

In Dallas, Lee Harvey Oswald had been charged with the murder of President John F. Kennedy and was being held under tight security. Secret Service agents Forrest Sorrels, Win Lawson, and Dave Grant had all spent time observing Oswald being interrogated by FBI agents and Dallas police investigators. A receipt that had been found in Oswald's possessions had been traced to the same rifle that police found stashed in a corner on the sixth floor of the Texas School Book Depository. Additionally, Oswald's fingerprints matched those found on boxes near the window where a sniper's nest had been formed out of stacks of book boxes. There would have to be a trial, of course, but everybody who'd questioned Oswald had no doubts that he was the assassin. The bigger law enforcement concern now was that with so much public hatred and rage directed toward Oswald, somebody might try to take the law into his own hands and kill him before he could stand trial.

WASHINGTON, D.C.
12:15 P.M.

After attending Mass in the East Room with members of the family, friends, and household staff shortly after 11:00 A.M., Mrs. Kennedy returned to the second-floor living quarters. Special Agent in Charge Jerry Behn had summoned Clint Hill to his office, and Hill realized this would be the only time he'd have to meet with Behn before the procession started toward the Capitol in an hour.

Everybody was traumatized but SAIC Behn realized the men in the follow-up car were going through things nobody else could even imagine. Now, as Behn looked at Clint Hill sitting across the desk from him, his face sullen, his eyes devoid of the twinkle that had been a window into his fun-loving nature, Behn knew that nothing he could say would be of much comfort. From everything Jerry Behn had heard about the tragedy in Dallas, nobody was to blame. It had all happened so fast. Every advantage had gone to the shooter. Of course, there would be an investigation, but Behn knew his men, knew their dedication and the quality of their work. And by all accounts Clint Hill had saved Mrs. Kennedy's life. For that he should be commended. But Behn knew the only thing going through Clint's mind was that he had failed to save the president. It was the same thing every agent on the Kennedy Detail felt, himself included. But as Behn looked at the shattered man sitting before him, it was evident that nobody's pain could match that of the men who'd been in the follow-up car.

Behn had been speaking to Clint for several minutes—speaking to him, not really sure that Clint was even hearing what he was saying—when Eve Dempsher buzzed in on the phone.

"I'm sorry to disturb you, Mr. Behn," she said. "But General McHugh is on the line for Mr. Hill."

"Put him through," said Behn as he handed the phone to Hill.

"This is Clint Hill," Hill said into the phone.

General Godfrey McHugh, the Air Force aide to President Kennedy, said, "Clint, Mrs. Kennedy wants . . . she wants the casket open. She wants to see the president. I think you better get down here."

Oh God.

Exhaustion had prevailed and Jerry Blaine woke up to discover he had slept until noon. Joyce and the kids had gone to church and the apartment was quiet. Blaine could smell the coffee in the kitchen, so he got up and poured himself a cup. He couldn't believe how long he'd slept, but finally, for the first time in four days, he felt rested. It was going to be yet another long day; he still had plenty of details to arrange for the advance of the State Department function.

He walked into the living room and turned on the television. All normal programming had ceased as the network news agencies struggled to keep the public informed about the investigation of Oswald and the arrangements for the president's funeral.

Blaine sat down on the sofa and sipped the hot coffee as the television warmed up and the screen slowly came into focus. His television was tuned to NBC, which was just wrapping up a report from the Kennedy compound at Hyannis Port.

Suddenly the image on the screen switched to a shot of the basement of City Hall in Dallas, where newspaper reporters and photographers were crowded into an area outside the ground-floor elevator. The news anchor's voice announced that Lee Harvey Oswald was about to be transferred from the city jail to the county jail, and as soon as he said it, Oswald, handcuffed to a man in a white Stetson hat, stepped out of the elevator doors. The newspaper reporters started yelling questions at Oswald, who remained glibly silent as he was marched toward the waiting armored truck.

A man in a black hat lunged toward Oswald.

Bang!

Oswald collapsed to the ground as pandemonium broke.

"Oswald's been shot!" the news announcer declared. "Oswald has just been shot!"

Blaine was stunned. Before his very eyes, the one man who could explain why he'd taken President Kennedy's life was now being rushed to the hospital.

"Damn. That son of a bitch better live," he said to no one as he slammed his fist on the coffee table.

Several miles away, Win Lawson was sitting in his living room, holding his baby daughter in his arms—he'd just flown in from Dallas—when he saw Oswald get shot on live television.

"Oh crap," he said as his heart dropped into his stomach.

"Barb!" he called to his wife. "Come here. I've got to get back to work. Oswald's just been shot."

And then the announcer said something that made Lawson's stomach turn.

"Oswald is being rushed to the hospital. We're being told he's going to Parkland Hospital   "

12:34 P.M.

General Godfrey McHugh was waiting for Agent Hill on the first floor of the mansion. They walked together toward the East Room, where Mrs. Kennedy and Attorney General Robert Kennedy were standing near the doorway.

"Yes, Mrs. Kennedy?" Clint asked as he walked briskly toward the first lady. "What do you need?"

She was wearing a black suit, with a tailored jacked and knee-length skirt, and her hair was covered by a black lace veil. Clint tried to look into her eyes, but they'd gone numb. Her eyes were numb.

Standing next to her, her brother-in-law the attorney general, dressed in a charcoal-colored suit, was staring blankly into the East Room at the flag-covered casket.

"We want to see him. Bobby and I want to see the president."

Oh God.

Hill turned to General McHugh, who had met him on the first floor, and gave a brief nod.

Hill and McHugh walked into the ballroom, which was empty but for the casket perched atop the black funeral stand in the middle of the room, and the honor guard—the servicemen from each branch of the military who had faithfully been keeping watch since the president had been lying in repose.

General McHugh walked over to the commander of the honor guard.

"Commander, will you please have your men leave the room for a few minutes?"

Mrs. Kennedy interrupted, "No, it's fine. Let them stay."

Still, the commander gave an order for the guard to do an about-face, and they stepped away from the casket to give Mrs. Kennedy some privacy.

General McHugh carefully folded the flag back over itself to expose a portion of the mahogany wood, and opened the casket to reveal President Kennedy's upper body.

Mrs. Kennedy and the attorney general approached the casket and stared, solemnly, at the president. Clint Hill looked away. His chest tightened with pain; his brow furrowed as he willed the emotions deeper and deeper.

Mrs. Kennedy turned her head toward Clint, and in a voice now as numb as her eyes, she asked, "Mr. Hill? Will you please get me a scissors?"

Clint turned and let out the breath he hadn't realized he'd been holding. He walked down the hall to the usher's office.

Oh God.

A few minutes later he was back in the East Room, handing her the scissors, looking at her, trying to avert his gaze from the interior of the casket. He turned and as he took a few steps back, he heard the snip of the scissors as Mrs. Kennedy cut a lock of her husband's hair. And then the only sound that could be heard in the cavernous room was the inconsolable cries of two people in sheer agony.

Breathe, Clint told himself. Breathe. He couldn't break down. *He had to be strong, for her.*

Robert Kennedy reached for the lid of the casket and slowly closed it, for the last time. Clint looked at his watch. 12:46 P.M.

1:00 P.M.

The three television networks had set up their cameras outside the North Portico of the White House to show live coverage of the president's casket being transferred from the White House to the Capitol rotunda, where, for the next twenty hours, the president's body would lie in state.

The military honor guard carried the flag-draped casket back out the way it had come in, down the short flight of stairs at the North Portico door, and placed it in the waiting artillery caisson that would be led by six white horses to the Capitol. Holding her children's hands, Mrs. Kennedy walked behind the casket, down the stairs. Robert Kennedy, a few other family members, and Clint Hill came next, with President and Mrs. Johnson trailing behind.

They climbed into a procession of cars that was lined up behind the horse-drawn gun carriage, followed by Black Jack, the black stallion that was used for military funerals at Arlington National Cemetery. Saddled, with boots facing backward in the stirrups, the riderless horse was an enduring tradition that symbolized a fallen leader who will ride no more. The escort exited out the East Gate of the White House. Bill Greer drove the black hardtop Cadillac limousine with SAIC Jerry Behn in the front seat and the awkward group of President and Mrs. Johnson with Mrs. Kennedy, Robert Kennedy, John, and Caroline in the back. Following closely behind were two cars of Secret Service agents on high alert.

Pennsylvania Avenue had been blocked off and was empty of traffic, but on either side, as far as the eye could see, were people standing in the cold, somber-faced or weeping. Three hundred thousand people had come to pay their respects to the grieving first lady and her family, and to the president they had loved. Eerily, the huge numbers of people were dead silent along the entire route and the only sound you could hear, over and over again, was the clop-clop of the horses' hooves and the muffled drums of the military drum corps going *boom boom ba boom tadadada*. Clop clop clop. Boom boom ba boom tadadada. Along with the hundreds of thousands who felt compelled to pay their respects, millions more around the country watched the heartbreaking scene on television. There was no other programming, no businesses were open, sporting events had been canceled—the country had shut down. Nothing else mattered.

The television cameras followed the widow as she stepped out of the car. Clint Hill, somber, his eyes scanning the crowd, was immediately by her side as she reached for her daughter with one hand, her son with the other, while SAIC Jerry Behn and an army of White House Detail agents, all wearing black trench coats, moved into place around President and Mrs. Johnson.

They waited outside the Capitol as the formal military honors were granted the dead president and the caisson rolled toward the steps. With Bobby Kennedy on one side and Clint Hill on the other, the solemn-faced Mrs. Kennedy stood and watched with grace. But when the military band broke into "Hail to the Chief," she suddenly bowed her head, and with frail shoulders shaking, she began to sob.

Finally it was time to go inside. The Secret Service agents were tense and ready to move in a millisecond. Nine military pallbearers lifted the flag-draped coffin off the caisson. Standing next to Mrs. Kennedy, Clint Hill could see the strain on the men's faces as they started up the steps. Four men on each side and one at the foot, they were fighting gravity, struggling to keep the nearly half-ton mahogany case steady. Suddenly the casket wobbled.

Oh God, Clint thought. *Don't drop it. Oh please, whatever you do, don't drop it.* He knew that getting it up the stairs was taking every ounce of strength they had. He knew exactly how heavy it was. Two days earlier he'd been in their shoes.

Mrs. Kennedy waited until the pallbearers were halfway up the thirty-six steps, then, clutching the hands of her two children, she followed slowly, gracefully up the endless stairs of the Capitol.

Finally the casket was laid in state in the rotunda, under the huge Capitol dome, and after more pomp and circumstance, Senate Majority Leader Mike Mansfield from Montana proceeded to give a moving eulogy that would resonate forever in the hearts and minds of all those who heard it.

"There was a sound of laughter," Mansfield began, in a somber voice. "In a moment, it was no more. And so she took a ring from her finger and placed it in his hands.

"There was a wit in a man neither young nor old, but a wit full of an old man's wisdom and of a child's wisdom, and then, in a moment it was no more. . . ."

Mansfield spoke of how John F. Kennedy had left behind some priceless gifts—gifts of laughter, wit, kindness, strength, courage.

In closing, Mansfield posed a question not only to the politicians who surrounded him, but to all Americans glued to their televisions that day. "In leaving us these gifts, John Fitzgerald Kennedy, President of the United States, leaves with us. Will we take them, Mr. President? Will we have, now, the sense and the responsibility and the courage to take them? I pray to God that we shall and under God we will."

After being so good, doing all day what the grown-ups had wanted him to do, finally John, Jr., who would turn three the next day, just couldn't stand it anymore. The sad eyes, the silence, the slow walking. Everybody was acting so strangely. Almost as soon as the ceremony began, John began fidgeting, moving his hands through the air like airplanes, his mouth pouted to make the sound of the engine.

Agent Bob Foster squatted, grabbed John's hand, and gave him a look that said, *Come on. Let's get out of here.*

Mrs. Kennedy nodded her approval as Foster led John out of the rotunda into an adjacent room. Tom Wells followed and stood outside the room. The door was cracked ajar and he heard John's tiny little-boy voice ask, "Mr. Foster, what happened to my daddy?"

Wells struggled to control his emotions as he glanced into the room. Bob Foster had squatted to John's eye level and was trying to explain, in words John could understand, why his daddy hadn't come home in the helicopter like he usually did. Nobody knew about the heartbreaking question that had just been asked by the president's son, but outside the door, an equally unforgettable moment was being shared with America as Mrs. Kennedy and Caroline, hand in hand, walked up to the casket, knelt, and placed their lips on the coffin for a final good-bye.

And from one person to the next, from the stoic and wizened men of Congress to the dutiful secretaries and wives, to the millions watching on television, the tears were unstoppable.

On his way to the State Department, Jerry Blaine had heard on the radio—before the station started carrying live coverage of the procession to the Capitol—that a man named Jack Ruby, a Dallas nightclub owner, was being held for the shooting of Oswald. Then suddenly, just ten minutes after Jackie and Caroline Kennedy had kissed JFK's coffin, came an unnerving news bulletin. Lee Harvey Oswald, the man investigators believed to be President Kennedy's assassin, had just died at Parkland Hospital.

Oh my God.

The Diplomatic Reception Room, where the function for the visiting dignitaries would be held, was located on the top floor of the State Department, overlooking the Lincoln Memorial and Memorial Bridge. On any other day it was perhaps one of the best views in Washington, but today the only place Jerry Blaine wanted to be was with the procession going from the White House to the Capitol. He couldn't even see it from here.

Blaine went through the security details with the State Department security and staff and after a few hours had a plan in place. Fifty world leaders in one room. It was perhaps the most important advance Blaine had ever been assigned and while he'd gone through the entire checklist, he realized now that no matter how much planning went into an event, you could never plan for the unexpected.

He still had to type up the Preliminary Survey Report, so he drove straight to the White House. By the time he walked into the West Wing, the somber silence of the morning had turned to pandemonium. Johnson's staff was moving in as Kennedy's staff was moving out, plans were being made for tomorrow's state funeral, and now, when everybody was on emotional overload, the shocking news of Oswald being shot had put tensions over the edge.

Blaine typed up the report and dropped it off at SAIC Behn's office, then stopped by the shift office in the West Wing to check his mailbox. In it was a sealed envelope.

Blaine ripped it open. He was requested to attend a brief meeting in Chief Rowley's office the following morning at 8:00 A.M. Blaine's mind raced. He couldn't remember the last time he'd been summoned to Rowley's office. Was this about his confrontation with Johnson at the Elms?

As he drove home down Shirley Highway back to the comfort of his small apartment, Blaine wondered how things could get any worse.

17

Burial

Our most basic common link is that we all inhabit this planet. We all breathe the same air. We all cherish our children's future. And we are all mortal.
—JOHN F. KENNEDY

MONDAY, NOVEMBER 25, 1963

Immediately after the ceremony in the rotunda, after Mrs. Kennedy and President Johnson and the rest of the entourage had departed, the Capitol was open to the public and police and security guards were faced with a tidal wave of people who wanted to pay their respects to President Kennedy. Barriers were put in place and within a couple of hours the queue—in many places eight to ten bodies wide—wrapped around the Capitol, had spread beyond the enormous complex, and was overflowing onto streets in all directions. The mourners were young and old, black and white, dressed in mink coats and hand-me-downs. Traffic was jammed around the city as people came from the suburbs and neighboring states. There seemed to be an inexplicable compulsion for people to be there. Nothing else mattered.

The plan had been to keep the doors of the Capitol open until 9:00 P.M., but by then there were people who had been waiting since midnight the night before who still had not gotten in. And still, there had to be two hundred thousand more standing in the cold, dark night, knowing they would wait in line for hours to have no more than a few seconds to walk past the casket.

Meanwhile, representatives from countries all over the globe were flying in to attend the funeral, along with members of the Kennedy family. Jackie's sister, Lee, and Lee's husband, Prince Stanislaus Radziwill, arrived late from London. "Stash," as he was known to family and close friends, wanted desperately to go to the rotunda, so Clint Hill personally escorted him, cutting ahead to the front of the line. None of the mourners who happened to be filing past the casket recognized Prince Radziwill, but when he was allowed to step beyond the velvet rope and kneel by the casket for several minutes, nobody said a word.

By midnight, one hundred thousand people had filed through, and the line of those still waiting was more than three miles long. The guards urged people to move faster.

As the sun rose on Monday, on what had been declared a national day of mourning, throngs of people clamored for space along the streets between the Capitol and the White House and Arlington Cemetery to view the funeral procession.

By now, the fatal shooting of Lee Harvey Oswald had added a new dimension to the country's grief, and mixed with the universal cries of "How could this happen in America?" was the sudden unsettling feeling that the assassination was part of a larger conspiracy. The front pages of newspapers around the country carried side-by-side photos of the incredible events that had happened within minutes of each other in Dallas and Washington, D.C. There was the heartbreaking image of the kneeling Mrs. Kennedy and Caroline kissing the flag-covered casket in the rotunda, and right next to it, on every newspaper in America, was the shocking picture of the president's alleged assassin, Lee Harvey Oswald, at the moment he was shot by Jack Ruby. Now there could be no trial for Oswald and perhaps his motive would never be known. What was coming to the surface, however, was that Oswald's background was filled with connections to the Soviet Union, Cuba, and communism.

The Secret Service, the FBI, and the CIA were deeply concerned about the potential for another assassination attempt at President Kennedy's state funeral.

8:00 A.M.

Jerry Blaine had written down everything he could remember about the Saturday morning incident with President Johnson at the Elms and had arrived early for the meeting with Secret Service chief James Rowley.

"Good morning, Walter," Jerry said as he greeted Walter Blaschak, Rowley's secretary.

"Mr. Rowley's not quite ready yet," Blaschak said curtly. "Why don't you go ahead and take a seat in the conference room. The others will be here shortly, I'm sure."

At 7:55 A.M. Assistant Special Agent in Charge Floyd Boring arrived, along with ATSAIC Emory Roberts.

What are they doing here? Blaine wondered as he stood up to greet the two senior agents.

Two minutes later, ATSAIC Stewart Stout and SAIC Jerry Behn walked in.

Blaine was getting more and more nervous. He was here with every supervising agent, with the exception of Roy Kellerman. *What was going on?*

Chief Rowley had arrived at the office at 6:00 A.M. He'd barely slept more than a couple of hours in the last two days, and the lines of fatigue had settled into his face. He was still trying to work the security planning for today's funeral, and the fact that Mrs. Kennedy insisted on walking from the White House to St. Matthew's was merely the icing on the cake. There were so many exposures with the scenario today, it was almost beyond comprehension. And while Rowley was normally confident in the abilities of his men, the assassination was so fresh, so raw, that he was overseeing every detail himself.

Blaschak walked into his office just as the wall clock chimed.

"Everybody's assembled in the conference room," he said.

Director Rowley walked in and closed the door behind him.

"Good morning, gentlemen," Rowley said as he sat down at the head of the conference table. "We've got an extraordinary day ahead, so let's get right down to it."

He flipped open a file folder and turned to Floyd. "Floyd, do you want to give me a brief recap of President Kennedy requesting the agents drop back to the follow-up car in Tampa?"

"Absolutely," Floyd replied. "Because we were faced with a long motorcade, limited agents, and expected large crowds, it was recommended that we have coverage on the back of the car."

"Was that the recommendation of the advance agents?" Behn asked.

"Yes, sir," Blaine spoke up. "I was the lead advance agent. We had over twenty-eight miles to travel and were expecting demonstrations. We also had two PRS subjects incarcerated."

"I understand your reasoning and I am not faulting anyone. I believe it was a reasonable request." Jim Rowley never second-guessed his White House Detail agents, since he thoroughly understood their thought processes. He'd had a lot of input into the Secret Service training programs. The only thing he would not tolerate was an agent being lax in his responsibilities.

Blaine had relaxed a little bit. *So this wasn't regarding the Johnson near incident after all. It was about Tampa. But why was he so concerned about Tampa now?*

Rowley nodded. "Go on, Floyd. So what happened?"

Floyd recounted how Agents Chuck Zboril and Don Lawton were posted on the rear steps of the limousine throughout much of the motorcade; the heavy crowds; the small group of protesters.

"Everything was going along fine, but I noticed the president continually glancing back at the agents standing behind him," Floyd said. "And then he made an unusual request."

"And what exactly did he say?" Rowley asked.

"He was standing up and he leaned toward me . . . I, of course, was sitting in the front passenger seat, while Bill Greer was driving," Floyd said. "So, he leaned toward me and said, 'Floyd, have the Ivy League charlatans drop back to the follow-up car.'"

The statement made Rowley's mouth turn up in a slight smile, even as he blinked back a tear. He could hear the president saying that. *Ivy League charlatans.* God, he was going to miss JFK.

Rowley blinked and continued the questioning.

"Now, when he made this unusual request, was he angry? And what did you take it to mean?"

"No, no," Floyd began. "I didn't get the impression that he was angry. To be honest, I wasn't exactly sure what he meant by 'Ivy League charlatans,' but I sure as hell knew what he meant when he said to have them drop back to the follow-up car. I knew he felt like they were hovering a bit too close. And this being a political trip and all, I think he was very conscious of the appearance."

"And what about the crowds there in Tampa?" Rowley asked. "Were the crowds unruly, or did they seem threatening at all?"

"No, sir," Floyd answered. "They were great crowds. We'd been concerned, and perhaps Jerry can fill you in more on those concerns, but you know, with the large Cuban population down there, we just didn't know what to expect."

"Okay, so the president asked you to have the agents drop back to the follow-up car, and what did you do then, Floyd?"

"Well, sir, I got on the radio and radioed back to Emory, who was in the front seat of the follow-up car."

"And what did you tell Emory?"

"I repeated what the president had said to me," Floyd said with a slight laugh. "I repeated it exactly because I thought Emory would get a kick out of the president's phrase. I said, 'Halfback, Lancer requests the Ivy League charlatans drop back to your location.' "

Rowley looked at Emory Roberts. "Is that correct, Emory?"

"Yes, sir. That's exactly what he relayed over the radio."

Rowley turned to Jerry Blaine. "And Jerry, since you were in the lead car, did you hear this over your radio as well?"

"Yes, sir. I did. I heard exactly what Floyd just told you."

"And what did you do next?" Rowley asked Emory.

"Well, I tried motioning to Lawton and Zboril to get their attention, but because I was behind them—they were on the steps of the limousine looking forward, up and to the sides—they didn't see me motioning, so I let out a whistle."

Rowley was listening intently.

"They both glanced back and I motioned with my hands for them to come on back to the follow-up car. But just around that time, the crowds had really started thinning, and Bill Greer automatically sped up. So, just at the time when I wanted them to drop back, the car sped up, and really, it would have been dangerous for them to jump off at that speed."

"So then what happened?" Rowley asked.

Emory continued: "I radioed to Floyd that we were going too fast, that it wasn't safe for them to drop back. And I motioned to Lawton and Zboril to just stay low, to not stand up straight, but to stay low. Then, within another minute or two, the pace slowed down and they were able to jump off and drop back to the running boards of the follow-up car."

Rowley was nodding. "Okay. Now that I have a clear picture of what happened during the motorcade, what effect, if any, did the president's comments in Tampa have on the trip to Texas?"

"Let me jump in here, sir, if I may," said Floyd Boring. "When we arrived at our destination after this incident, the president pulled me aside and told me that this was a political trip and that he felt like the agents were being excessive in their coverage. He told me that the same goes for the upcoming trips to Texas and would I please relay his request to the other supervisors, which I did upon returning to Washington."

Chief Rowley turned to SAIC Jerry Behn. Rowley knew that Jerry Behn could not stop beating himself up over not being in Texas. Nobody blamed Jerry for taking his first vacation in four years, but the fact that the assassination had occurred when he wasn't there was already taking its toll. Added to the professional sense of failure was the fact that Behn and Kennedy had become close friends. Rowley knew Jerry was going through emotional hell.

"Jerry," Rowley said, "were the advance people in Texas notified about the request by President Kennedy?"

Jerry Behn looked directly at Rowley. "Jim, after Floyd told me about the incident, I told him to relay the information to the shift leaders—to Emory Roberts, Art Godfrey, and Stu Stout—and I know he did that. They in turn told the men on their shift, which included the agents out on advances."

Behn suddenly remembered his conversation with Ron Pontius, the advance agent in Houston. "I did mention it personally to Pontius in Houston when he called me about another matter. But other than that, the information was transferred by the normal chain of command."

"Okay. I understand," Chief Rowley said. He turned to Jerry Blaine.

"Jerry, I think your request was reasonable, but"—Rowley paused as he looked down and took a deep breath—"in light of the assassination, I am confronted with another issue."

What was he getting at? Blaine wondered.

Jim Rowley hesitated. This was going to be tough to say. "We are still trying to sort out Dallas. This is a terrible tragedy. I know we will be run through the gauntlet in the coming months, but we are going to have to take the hit and continue our mission to the best of our abilities."

The agents in the room nodded in understanding. There was no excuse the Secret Service could give. It was going to be a dark winter.

Director Rowley continued: "The problem is that the word about the request of the president in Tampa has spread to the whole detail and beyond and I want the issue closed right now. Since the president is dead it is inconsequential. We cannot say that the president's assassination was caused by his own actions—that he was somehow at fault. We all know from past experiences that presidents do not want it to appear that anyone or anything be allowed to come between them and the public, the voter. And from everything I've heard about what happened in Dallas, it sounds to me like the timing of the incident was such that no agents would have been positioned on the back of the president's car due to the sparse crowds and the anticipated increased speed of the vehicles due to the approaching freeway. This motorcade was no different from many previous motorcades we ran in various cities in the United States and throughout the world— except for the end result. I want you to pass the word to the agents to forget about Tampa and I don't want to hear any more discussion on the issue. Let's bite the bullet and move on. Is everyone in agreement?"

Rowley looked around from one man to the next and each one nodded, silently. Message understood.

"Okay, it's going to be a busy day," he said, and he turned and walked out of the conference room.

As they were moving out of the room Jerry Blaine pulled SAIC Jerry Behn aside.

"Jerry," Blaine said, "I would like to ask one favor."

"Sure, Jer. What is it?"

"Well, I've documented the advance at the State Department and will finish up the final arrangements later on. So, I was wondering, would it be possible for me to work the movement from the White House to the church? I hate to miss out on the whole funeral."

Behn looked at Blaine and sensed the isolation Blaine was feeling. He

knew that Blaine had been with JFK from day one. "Jer, I don't see a problem with that. You know what you have to do and only you can determine
if everything is ready to go at State."

"State will be ready to go."

"Okay. No problem."

At 8:30 A.M. the doors to the rotunda were closed. A quarter of a million people had filed past President Kennedy's casket in less than twenty-
two hours, and the line still stretched as far as the eye could see. Now they
were positioning themselves for a viewing of the funeral procession, and
each hour more and more people arrived by the busload.

By 10:00 A.M. the various ballrooms of the White House—the East,
Green, Blue, Red, and State Dining rooms—were filled with White House
staff, cabinet members, Kennedy family members, and close friends, along
with the largest number of foreign leaders ever assembled at one time.
The State Department was officially responsible for the security of visiting
dignitaries, but they were overwhelmingly understaffed for such a sudden influx. Many of the foreign leaders had brought their own security
people—the controversial Charles de Gaulle had twenty-two of his own
men—who were supplemented by the field Secret Service agents who had
flown in from around the country, along with more than one hundred FBI
and CIA agents and four thousand Pentagon and District of Columbia police officers.

The security logistics were complicated, and out of necessity had been
thrown together quickly. Everybody was on edge. For God's sake, the
President of the United States had just been assassinated and the man
who'd killed him had been gunned down—all within a matter of forty-
eight hours. And now, this unprecedented gathering would be walking
for over a mile, through the streets of Washington, D.C. It was a security
nightmare.

Indeed, the FBI and the CIA had received numerous threats—several
against de Gaulle alone—but nothing they could confirm as credible or
imminent. Secretary of State Dean Rusk and Treasury Secretary Douglas Dillon were desperately trying to convince President Johnson and the
other dignitaries to ride in limousines, but none of the men were willing

to give the appearance that they were the least bit afraid. As long as Jacqueline Kennedy was walking, they were walking with her.

In a last-ditch effort, Rusk and Dillon went to Special Agent in Charge Jerry Behn and urged him to step in. The only person who might stand a chance of convincing Jackie not to walk was Clint Hill.

SAIC Jerry Behn pulled Agent Hill aside.

"Clint," Behn said, "you know everybody is scared to death something is going to happen, but nobody—not Johnson, not de Gaulle, not even de Valera, the eighty-one-year-old President of Ireland—nobody will ride in a car as long as Mrs. Kennedy is walking. Do you think there's any chance of convincing Mrs. Kennedy to share a limousine with Johnson?"

Clint shook his head. "Everybody has told her this is a bad idea. Trust me. Everybody." Clint raised his eyebrows to make the point even stronger. "She wanted to walk the whole way—from the White House to St. Matthew's to Arlington. It's only because of the older men like de Valera that she agreed to go by motorcade from the church to the cemetery. But she's made up her mind. She's walking."

The sky was gray, and a light rain drizzled on and off, as if the heavens were grieving along with the rest of the world. At 10:30 A.M., Mrs. Kennedy, flanked by her two brothers-in-law, Robert and Ted, departed the White House in a motorcade for the Capitol. And less than twenty-four hours after it had been brought up the Capitol steps, the flag-draped coffin was carried back down, as the pallbearers again struggled to keep the casket steady.

A company of Marines led the horse-drawn caisson and the following motorcade back down Pennsylvania Avenue and into the Northeast Gate of the White House. Jerry Blaine, having just finished up the last-minute details of the State Department advance, arrived just in time to hear the Naval Academy choir singing "Eternal Father Strong to Save."

Secret Service agents were strategically placed around the forming procession of dignitaries who would be following Mrs. Kennedy on the one and a quarter-mile walk from the White House to St. Matthew's Cathedral. To Roy Kellerman and Emory Roberts and Stewart Stout, and all the agents who had just three days earlier witnessed how quickly a parade could turn to chaos, the walking procession was sheer madness. Gathered together in one small space were many of the world's most influential leaders and the entire structure of America's government, including the Supreme Court justices, Joint Chiefs, national security advisors, and the new President of the United States. For anyone who wanted to evoke change and was inclined to violence, this would be like shooting fish in a barrel.

The plan called for Mrs. Kennedy, Robert, and Ted to lead the procession, with President and Mrs. Johnson and the huge diplomatic entourage behind them. John and Caroline would be in a limousine with Agents Tom Wells and Bob Foster immediately following the walking diplomats.

As the procession was about to get under way, Mrs. Kennedy suddenly realized that the children's limousine would be far behind her and the rest of the family, separated by the huge contingent of world leaders.

"That's not right," she said. She wouldn't leave until the children's limousine was moved in the lineup so it was immediately behind her and the rest of the Kennedy family. To move the car at this point would require it to plow through the crowd of kings and queens and presidents and ambassadors who were already in their assigned places in the driveway. And that was exactly what Kiddie Detail agent Tom Wells decided he would do.

Tom Wells directed the White House sergeant who was driving the limousine with nanny Maud Shaw, John, and Caroline in the back to stay right behind him.

"Move aside! Move aside!" Wells repeatedly called out, waving his arms broadly, motioning the prime ministers and presidents out of the way. And amazingly, the people did as they were told. While some of the dignitaries even started helping the agents, Charles de Gaulle hesitated when he thought he was being moved from his position of prominence but when he saw the children, he moved aside, allowing the car to move into place behind the family.

The Scottish Black Watch bagpipes that had performed at the White House the week before the assassination began to wail, and so the procession began.

For the hundreds of thousands lining the streets, and the millions more watching it live on television, the funeral procession was an unforgettable sight. A company of Marines marched in front, followed by the Scottish Black Watch, in their red tartan kilts, their bagpipes filling the air with a surprising but poignant sound that seemed to be in perfect synchronization with the clop-clop of the horses that followed. The gray-and-white horses pulled the focal point of this parade—the artillery caisson rolling along on its four oversize wheels, carrying the mahogany casket containing the body of the dead president.

Behind the casket came the riderless horse Black Jack, led by his military trainer, who struggled to keep the skittish horse in line.

And then, the sight that brought the world to tears: Mrs. Kennedy, in her black suit, her expressionless beautiful face covered with a black veil, walking between her husband's brothers, Robert and Ted.

Just behind her, an arm's length away, Clint Hill, invisible to those who were focused only on the grace and dignity of the grief-stricken Jackie Kennedy, scanned the eyes and hands of the tearful crowd. President Johnson was also nearly invisible, surrounded by a swarm of White House Detail agents—Stout, Kellerman, Pontius, Roberts—and led by SAIC Jerry Behn.

The agents had not slept in four days, and right now they were facing the most nerve-racking security challenge imaginable: multiple protectees, bunched together, outside, in an announced, well-known route, walking slowly. From a security standpoint, this was about as bad a situation as there could be. Who among this throng of people has a problem or a grievance so serious that they are willing to commit a violent act? What about the copycat? Who among this sea of humanity is so mentally disturbed or deranged that they are willing to act on those sick thoughts?

As he walked just behind Mrs. Kennedy, Clint Hill searched the crowd, his adrenaline the only thing keeping him going. He could not think about why he was here, could not think about who was in the casket, and why Mrs. Kennedy—who rarely wore black—had lost her infectious smile and had her visage covered by a mourning veil. There was no room for emotion.

Be alert. Be aware. Stay on task. One explosive device thrown from the crowd will obliterate the whole group of walkers. There is no room for error.

Be alert. See everything. But don't overreact.

Why is that man raising his hand up to his head? What does he have in his hand? He's staring at her. Can't take his eyes off her. What does he have in his hand, Goddamn it?!

Okay. Relax. It's just a handkerchief. A handkerchief. He's wiping away his tears.

The limousine carrying the children came crawling behind with the Kiddie Detail agents walking solemnly next to it. Tom Wells was at the front left near the driver and Bob Foster walked alongside the left rear door. As soon as the bagpipes started playing, the back window rolled down and Caroline stuck out her hand, reaching for Agent Foster. He looked down at the precious girl, her hair pulled back from her face with a black headband, and as tears welled in his eyes, he grabbed her hand and quickly looked away. This is not the time for emotion. *Stay on task. Scan the crowd. Good God, you can't let anything happen to this little girl.* Still, he was grateful for the comfort of her hand. They proceeded like that for the entire way to the church, the steadfast agent and the fatherless daughter, hand in hand.

At St. Matthew's, the walking procession filed into the church to their preassigned pews. Cardinal Cushing had flown in from Boston to provide the Catholic Mass. It had been just three and a half months earlier that he'd tried to comfort the inconsolable President Kennedy after the loss of his newborn son. This was far more than one family should have to bear.

Mrs. Kennedy and the children sat in the front pew, just a few feet from the casket, which had once again been removed from the caisson and wheeled inside. Clint Hill was directly behind Mrs. Kennedy. She was a wreck. She was trying so hard to hold it together, to put on a brave face. The world was watching and she knew it.

The cardinal circled the casket three times, sprinkling it with incense and holy water, as the people recited the Lord's Prayer in unison. The cardinal followed with a prayer in Latin, and then suddenly broke into English.

"May the angels, dear Jack, lead you into paradise. May the martyrs receive you at your coming. May the spirit of God embrace you, and mayest thou, with all those who made the supreme sacrifice of dying for others, receive eternal rest and peace. Amen."

Jackie had been so stoic, so strong until, it seemed, the cardinal's mention of her husband's name. Everybody referred to him as "the president." It was respectful of course, but so distant to his wife. For to her, he was Jack, had always been Jack. And when Cardinal Cushing prayed not for "the president" but for "Jack," it struck a chord, and Mrs. Kennedy began to weep.

Sitting behind her, Clint Hill instinctively grabbed the handkerchief from his suit coat pocket and placed it in her hand.

Partway through the Mass, John, Jr., became bored and fidgety. Why was everybody crying? And where was his daddy?

Bob Foster picked him up out of his seat and carried him back to an anteroom. It was his birthday, after all. No little boy should have to attend his daddy's funeral on his birthday.

Foster was trying to distract John when a Marine colonel came in. John was infatuated with his medals for a short while, but quickly became bored.

"Let's practice your salute, John," Agent Foster said. "Why don't you give the colonel a salute?"

That perked up the little boy, but it had been two weeks since he was at Arlington Cemetery with his daddy and he suddenly went back to his old ways of using his left hand. The colonel gently corrected him, straightened his hand, and showed him how to stand at attention. After a few more tries, he had it down.

Finally the service was over. John stood with his mother and sister outside the church as she received the important people who had come to pay their respects. John was holding a pamphlet Bob had found for him to draw on and was waving it around, just as the casket was being brought out of the church.

Bob Foster was watching him, about to intervene when Mrs. Kennedy leaned over, whispered something into her son's ear, and took the paper from his hand. In one swift move—completely unexpected—three-year-old John Fitzgerald Kennedy, Jr., took one step forward, thrust his shoulders back, and just as his father's casket was passing in front of him, he raised his right hand to his forehead in a perfect salute.

Bob Foster heaved with emotion as tears streamed down his face. He was not alone. The salute had been captured by the television cameras, which were broadcasting live, and in an instant the impetuous three-year-old son of the slain president brought America to its knees.

• • •

The walk had gone remarkably smoothly and Mrs. Kennedy's bold decision had paid off in terms of helping a nation come together in its grieving. Still looming was the procession from St. Matthew's to the burial at Arlington Cemetery, and the reception for the visiting dignitaries.

Upon arriving at St. Matthew's, Mrs. Kennedy had decided that John and Caroline should be taken back to the White House rather than be subjected to the burial ceremony at Arlington. John clearly had no concept of what was happening, while Caroline was at such an impressionable age that her sad eyes were soaking up everything. But the sudden change of plans meant that the children needed a separate car. Every vehicle was already in use by VIPs, staff, and security personnel. Out of desperation, Agent Tom Wells ended up taking over a vehicle that had been used by the Joint Chiefs, leaving them to crowd into other cars for the ride to Arlington.

Special Agent Sam Sulliman had been assigned the advance for the burial at Arlington. Sulliman had been on the 4:00 to midnight shift in Dallas—first stationed at the Trade Mart, then to the chaos at Parkland Hospital. Like all the other White House Detail agents, he'd had little to no sleep since then. With all the world leaders attending the burial ceremony at Arlington, it was one of the more challenging advances of the day. The cemetery was covered with trees, monuments, headstones, and quite a number of areas where a person could conceal himself, but Sulliman had been told not to make it look like an armed camp. He called in some troops from Fort Myer and set them up in a perimeter around the area, out of view of the attendees.

Meanwhile, Jerry Blaine was busy completing the arrangements for the diplomatic reception at the State Department. He excused himself during a meeting with the protocol staff and walked out to the balcony, where he could get a view of the funeral procession as it passed over Memorial Bridge on the way to Arlington. The hundreds who had walked from the White House to St. Matthew's were now stuffed into an endless motorcade of black limousines that snaked its way for three miles, through Washington, over the Bridge, and finally to the cemetery on the hill. Blaine watched the slow, tragic procession for a few minutes, quietly said a prayer, wiped his eyes, and walked back to the meeting.

For the agents who had been on duty since the early morning hours, the day seemed endless. The multiple eulogies and hymns went by largely unnoticed as they continually searched the crowd, desperately hoping they wouldn't see a rifle or a handgun, but primed to cover whomever they were assigned to protect.

On the hill, at the grave site, the underground piping for the eternal flame had somehow been miraculously constructed overnight. There were more drums and prayers, a twenty-one-gun salute and a stunning, earth-shaking flyover at six hundred feet by Colonel Swindal at the helm of Air Force One. Finally, the trumpeter faced the black-veiled widow and played taps.

With that, the eight-man military team began folding the American flag that had lain on the coffin since it was closed at Bethesda into a thick, perfect triangle. There wasn't a dry eye among the generals and presidents and queens and kings. Clint Hill choked back the tears yet again, sup-pressed the emotions deeper inside as he tried to focus on everything but the fact that President Kennedy's body was being buried.

And then somebody handed Jackie Kennedy a lit taper, and she leaned over and ignited the flame that would burn forever on the hillside, the eternal reminder of a tragedy that changed a nation.

PART FOUR

OUR LIVES

18

The End of Camelot

As we express our gratitude we must never forget that the highest appreciation is not to utter words, but to live by them.

—JOHN F. KENNEDY

Immediately after the burial ceremony, Jacqueline Kennedy had returned to the White House and graciously hosted a small reception for President Charles de Gaulle, Ethiopian emperor Haile Selassie, Britain's Prince Philip, and Ireland's President de Valera, along with numerous close friends and family members. How did she do it? Three days earlier she'd seen her husband's head blown off and today she was leading the world in mourning. Everybody was emotionally and physically depleted.

Shortly before midnight on the day her husband was buried, Mrs. Kennedy called for Clint.

"Yes, Mrs. Kennedy?"

"Mr. Hill, Bobby and I want to go to Arlington. We want to see the flame."

Clint Hill could barely stand up, he was so tired.

"Certainly, Mrs. Kennedy. I'll get the car."

With no photographers, no television cameras anywhere in sight—thank God, finally they had gone—Clint Hill escorted Mrs. Kennedy and Attorney General Robert Kennedy back to Arlington. Bobby had been with her every waking moment since she'd arrived at Andrews Air Force

Base. They were both left with the same thoughts. How would they go on without Jack?

As they drove over Memorial Bridge, the flame flickered on the hillside directly in front of them. It was amazing. She had thought of it only two days earlier and there it was. Just like the one at the tomb of the unknown soldiers in Paris. It was the first eternal flame in America—a fitting tribute to her husband, a man who'd brought hope to so many people around the world, and whose magical life had been so unfairly and inexplicably cut short.

Mrs. Kennedy laid flowers on the grave and knelt in prayer, quietly grieving as the flames cast shadows across their tearful faces. They stayed just fifteen minutes. After being in the glaring spotlight for the past four days, she needed this private moment.

Immediately after the shooting of Oswald in the basement of the Dallas police headquarters on Sunday morning, rumors and conspiracy theories had begun to spread like a mutating virus. There was no doubt about who had killed Oswald—Jack Ruby had done it on live television in front of dozens of witnesses. The question was, why?

Like the majority of Americans, fifty-two-year-old nightclub owner Ruby was distraught over the assassination of President Kennedy, but the fact that it had occurred in his city seemed to make it all the more personal to him. Ruby's older sister Eva Grant told reporters, "He took Kennedy's death much harder than that of our father five years ago. He couldn't eat Friday, and he kept talking about Jackie and the Kennedy kids."

President Johnson realized the implications that Oswald's murder would have on the already traumatized nation. On the evening of President Kennedy's funeral, the White House announced that President Johnson had instructed the Department of Justice and the FBI to conduct a "prompt and thorough investigation of all the circumstances surrounding the brutal assassination of President Kennedy and the murder of his alleged assassin."

The media, however, was intent on doing its own investigations.

THANKSGIVING DAY
NOVEMBER 28, 1963

For the past six days, the Secret Service had been in something of a state of disarray as the Johnson Detail meshed with the Kennedy Detail agents. Three agents had been added to each shift, but with the funeral, and President Johnson still living at the Elms, most of the agents were still working double duty.

Because Johnson was staying in Washington for Thanksgiving, the agents who had planned to be in Hyannis Port with President Kennedy were now able to be in town with their families. After working from 9:00 A.M. until midnight on Wednesday, Jerry Blaine was given the good news that he could have Thanksgiving Day off. For the first time in three years, he was able to spend the holiday with his own family.

The Kennedy family had decided to gather together in Hyannis Port, at the large family compound, to mourn the loss of their beloved Jack. At 8:30 A.M. Agents Landis, Wells, and Meredith left Washington and flew to Otis Air Force Base on Cape Cod to establish security for the arrival of Mrs. Kennedy and the children. Meanwhile, Clint Hill and Bob Foster accompanied Mrs. Kennedy, Lee Radziwill, Caroline, John, Maud Shaw, and Provie Parades for one more visit to the Arlington grave site before flying on an Air Force aircraft to Otis. It was a bittersweet homecoming, and when Jackie embraced her wheelchair-bound father-in-law, Ambassador Joseph Kennedy, in the sprawling oceanfront mansion, tears streamed down the poor man's face.

For Clint Hill and the other agents, it was extraordinarily painful. While the Kennedys surrounded each other with love and support, the agents dealt with their grief silently, away from their own families for yet another holiday. The Kiddie Detail agents hadn't been in Dallas, and as much as they wondered what had happened, what had gone wrong, there was no way they could bring up the subject with Paul Landis and Clint Hill, who had been on the running boards of the follow-up car. Their grief was written all over their faces as they went through the motions of their jobs, more focused than ever on not making a single mistake, of documenting every little thing that happened. The subject of the assassination was never mentioned.

After the incredible outpouring of emotion from around the world, Mrs. Kennedy now seemed to be obsessed with how her husband would be remembered in history. Journalists were already chronicling his accomplishments, along with his failings, in an effort to condense his life into the space available in a few column inches, and Jackie realized that it was important for her to tell her husband's story, the way she wanted it to be told. She felt compelled to talk to someone, someone who would share her thoughts with the world. The day after Thanksgiving she summoned writer Theodore H. White to Hyannis for the first-ever interview following the assassination, for an exclusive essay that would appear in *Life* magazine. White had written a complimentary account of John F. Kennedy in his Pulitzer Prize–winning book, *The Making of the President, 1960*, and Jackie trusted him.

It was pouring rain when White arrived at the compound at 8:30 A.M. exactly one week after the president had been assassinated in Dealey Plaza. Jackie wanted to be alone with the journalist, so Dave Powers, Lee, Pat Lawford, Bobby—all the people who had been by her side for the last seven days—reluctantly let her be. Clint Hill stood outside the closed door as the two talked for hours and hours and hours. He could hear only muffled voices, but once or twice he heard her mention "Mr. Hill" and wondered what she could possibly be saying.

When the clock struck midnight, Clint Hill could barely keep his eyes open. Finally White came out and went into a servant's room and began typing. Mrs. Kennedy wouldn't go to bed until she read White's article, which he was going to phone in to the editors right away so it could be in that week's edition of the magazine. The tapping of the typewriter in the back room was grating on Hill's nerves. All he could think about was sleep. He had barely slept more than a handful of hours over the week, and Mrs. Kennedy had had little more than he.

After a half hour of the annoying tap-tap-tap-tap-tap, finally Hill could take it no longer. He burst into the little room where White was typing away.

"For Christ's sake, we need some sleep here. Mrs. Kennedy needs to get some rest."

It would be another twenty minutes before White finished and finally at 2:00 A.M., after Mrs. Kennedy had approved the lines, the article was phoned in and everybody went to bed.

When *Life* appeared on newsstands November 29, all anybody could talk about was how Mrs. Kennedy had compared her husband's presidency to Camelot.

She'd told White that after the assassination, something kept repeating itself in her mind, over and over like a broken record, a line from a song in *Camelot,* a musical comedy then playing on Broadway. Jack had loved the musical about the Knights of the Round Table, and in the theme song, he particularly liked the line at the end that went:

Don't let it be forgot, that once there was a spot, for one brief shining moment that was known as Camelot.

She wanted to make sure that the point was clear to the writer, so she added, "There'll be great presidents again—and the Johnsons are wonderful, they've been wonderful to me—but there'll never be another Camelot again."

Jackie hoped that by giving the interview, it would help quell the public's questions surrounding the tragedy. Unfortunately, the public would not be so easily satisfied.

Bizarre conspiracy theories were coming out in the press. President Johnson had been given a preliminary report by the FBI and was convinced that Lee Harvey Oswald acted alone, but there were still questions regarding Cuban or Russian involvement because of Oswald's connections to both. Johnson's biggest concern at this point was international peace. To put the public's mind at ease and to avoid potential military action, he appointed a presidential commission to investigate every aspect of the assassination.

Chaired by Chief Justice Earl Warren, the group that came to be known as the Warren Commission consisted of a bipartisan group of two U.S. senators—Richard Russell, a Democrat from Georgia, and John Cooper, a Republican from Kentucky; two U.S. congressmen—Hale Boggs, a Democrat from Louisiana, and Gerald Ford, a Republican from Michigan; the former director of the CIA, Allen Dulles; and John J.

McCloy, former president of the World Bank. Johnson purposely chose the highly respected and politically diverse group to avoid any appearance of bias. The hearings were closed to the public, but were not considered "secret," as the witnesses were free to divulge their testimonies, and all the testimonies would be recorded and subsequently published. President Johnson, more than anybody, wanted the country to move forward and was eager to put the outrageous claims of conspiracy to rest.

The media, however, was conducting its own investigations, which were far less thorough and had far less noble objectives.

SUNDAY, DECEMBER 1, 1963

San Francisco Chronicle columnist Drew Pearson was a muckraking "journalist" whose forte was digging up dirt on various government and political organizations. He knew members of the White House press corps and was well acquainted with the Kennedy Detail Secret Service agents and their stellar reputations. On December 1, 1963, Pearson wrote a scathing editorial in the *San Francisco Chronicle* demanding an investigation into the Secret Service and the role they may have played in the assassination of the president.

"Six Secret Service men," he wrote, "charged with protecting the President, were in the Fort Worth Press Club the early morning of Friday, Nov. 22, some of them remaining until nearly 3 o'clock. This was earlier in the same day President Kennedy was assassinated. They were drinking. One of them was reported to have been inebriated. When they departed, three were reported en route to an all-night beatnik rendezvous, 'The Cellar.'

"Obviously men who have been drinking until nearly 3 A.M. are in no condition to be trigger-alert or in the best physical shape to protect anyone.

"It has been stated that it was an impossibility for the Secret Service to check the occupancy of every building along the route. While this is true, it is also true that warehouse type buildings, such as that in which the assassin hid, should be searched, and the extra time spent by Secret Service men at the Fort Worth Press Club could have been spent in so doing."

The article sent immediate shock waves through the Secret Service, and the Kennedy Detail supervisors—Emory Roberts, Art Godfrey, and

Stewart Stout—were called into Chief Rowley's office and told to have every agent write a memo giving their whereabouts during the evening of November 21 and the early morning hours of November 22. The agents were to state if they consumed alcoholic beverages and what time they retired that morning.

For the agents still crippled by a guilt that had no words, it was as if Drew Pearson had ripped out their broken hearts; any semblance of healing that might have begun was instantly shattered.

Questions were asked about who was involved and who was inebriated. Nobody could remember anybody being drunk or slightly inebriated, but questions began to arise among the agents about who the culprit might be, despite the fact that the claims seemed preposterous. If any detail agent had been drinking heavily or had been intoxicated, the other agents would have heard about it because the agent would have been immediately dismissed and removed from the detail. Chief Rowley had no idea if the column was accurate, and immediately assigned Inspector Gerard McCann and SAIC Forrest Sorrels of the Dallas office to conduct a complete and thorough investigation into what had happened.

But the damage had been done. The accusations gained momentum and the idea that the Secret Service could somehow have been responsible for the president's death ignited a firestorm of new conspiracy theories.

Pearson's suggestion to check warehouses the night before was ludicrous. Neither Pearson nor the vast majority of the public had any idea that the "warehouse," as he called the Texas School Book Depository building, was kitty-corner from the Dallas County Jail, which was next to the county court complex. A search of the depository the evening prior would have revealed nothing out of the ordinary. The shots could have come from any one of a thousand buildings or locations as the president traveled through the streets of Dallas. The shots could have come from millions of similar buildings over the past three years during which President Kennedy traveled around the world in an open-top car. It had long been the Kennedy Detail agents' biggest concern. And the only safeguard was a bulletproof, closed-top vehicle.

The agents felt like they'd been stamped with guilt by an outsider, a muckraking journalist so intent on making a name for himself with a new angle to the biggest story of the century that he never bothered to check the facts or validate the claims that would haunt these already broken men for the rest of their lives.

Back in Arlington, Virginia, Clint Hill's wife, Gwen, was at home, surrounded by moving boxes, wondering how she was going to get everything transferred to the new apartment in Alexandria. It was as if a cyclone had hit the country and her husband was in the middle of it, and nobody knew which end was up. The lease was up, they had to move, and Clint was in Hyannis Port.

The doorbell rang and when Gwen opened the door, there were two young men who looked familiar. Did they work with Clint?

"Hello, Mrs. Hill. I'm George Dalton," one of them said. He turned to the man next to him and added, "This is Jim Bartlett. We're here to help you move."

"What?" Gwen couldn't believe it. "Really?" It was as if two angels had shown up on her doorstep just at the moment when she thought she couldn't handle any more.

The two guys were Navy men who worked in the military aide's office. Bartlett handled all the boats for President Kennedy, while Dalton was the liaison between the naval aide's office and the president. Clint had spent a lot of time with both of them at the Cape. He'd mentioned that he and Gwen were going to be moving, and hoped he'd be able to get home for a day off after Thanksgiving to move everything to the new place. Dalton and Bartlett hadn't seen Clint since the assassination, but they knew he had to be going through hell. The least they could do was step in and move the furniture and boxes for him. The very least. They wanted to do more, but what could you do?

They'd found a truck—rented it or borrowed it—and before Gwen could protest, they were loading the sofa and the kitchen table onto the truck. They wouldn't allow her to help. It was the least they could do, they kept saying. The very least.

By the time Clint returned to Washington with Mrs. Kennedy the next day, Gwen had already unpacked half the boxes in the new apartment. When he walked in the door of the new apartment, he was greeted by his two tow headed sons, seven-year-old Chris and two-year-old Corey.

"Daddy! Daddy!" they yelled in unison as they ran toward him. He looked down at their innocent faces, so blissfully unaware of how the world had turned upside down, and squatted down to hug them, one in each arm.

Gwen came walking in, hoping that some of the old Clint might be back, but his eyes were still so sad, devoid of the sparkle they used to have.

He stood up and gave her a kiss. He had some news.

He took a deep breath. "Well, you're finally going to get a chance to meet Jackie," he said.

DECEMBER 3, 1963

Two days later, in a conference room on the fourth floor of the Treasury Building, Gwen Hill did indeed get to meet Jacqueline Kennedy. Clint was being presented with a gold medal and a citation for "exceptional bravery" and Mrs. Kennedy had come with her sister, Lee, and two of her sisters-in-law, Pat Lawford and Jean Smith.

Dressed in a black two-piece suit, Jackie was gracious as Clint introduced her to his wife and their two sons, but this was not at all how Gwen had imagined their first meeting.

A podium had been set up at one end of the conference room and the folding chairs that filled the rest of the space were taken up with reporters and photographers. Secretary of the Treasury Douglas Dillon called Clint Hill up to the podium as Gwen stood next to the somber-faced Jackie Kennedy. Chris and Corey were dressed in suits and ties, and while Chris was old enough to understand that his father was getting something special, little Corey was finding it hard to keep quiet and stay still.

As Clint stood before the flashing bulbs, he vaguely heard what Secretary Dillon was saying. How he ran from his car . . . as soon as the bullets began . . . and jumped on the rear of the president's limousine . . . and then Dillon was handing him a box, a small velvet box with the lid open. Inside was a gold medal.

Clint took the box as Dillon kept talking. Out of the corner of his eye, Clint saw Corey moving around, Gwen trying to calm him, and Mrs. Kennedy standing there, looking straight ahead.

Dillon continued as the bright lights from the cameras glared: "His extraordinary courage in the face of maximum danger reflects great credit on the United States of America, which can produce such men."

The reporters stood up and were clapping. They wanted him to say something. He'd just received the Treasury Department's highest award—for exceptional bravery.

I don't deserve a medal. Why are they giving me a medal? The president is dead. His widow is standing right there. Can't you see? Don't you see?

He was filled with emptiness.

"Thank you," he finally said.

Corey, unable to stand still any longer, jumped up onto the small stage. The reporters laughed.

"Corey," Gwen whispered as she grabbed her son's hand. "Come on down."

Mrs. Kennedy cocked her head to the side and as Corey struggled to maneuver his short legs down the big step, suddenly her face broke into a smile.

DECEMBER 4, 1963

Letters addressed to Jackie Kennedy had been flooding into the White House since the day after the funeral. The mailroom had processed over two hundred thousand letters in the past week alone and the unopened envelopes were being stored in the East Wing of the White House, where the overflowing boxes were in six-foot-high stacks. Mrs. Kennedy had vowed to read each one personally, but she had so many other things that were taking priority with her time.

One of the first things she'd had to consider was where she and her children would live, and where Caroline would go to school. She and Jack had sold their Georgetown home shortly after moving into the White House, but Jackie had always loved that neighborhood. Almost immediately after the assassination, Undersecretary of State Averell Harriman, who had been a close friend to both her and the president, offered his redbrick Georgetown house at 3038 N Street to Jackie and the children so they would have an immediate home with as little hassle as possible. Jackie accepted the generous offer and began supervising the torturous task of packing up the family's belongings—along with her husband's papers and personal items.

Something else had also been weighing heavily on her mind: she wanted the remains of the two children she and her husband had buried to lie next to President Kennedy at Arlington Cemetery. Her brother-in-law Senator Ted Kennedy had made the arrangements and accompanied the two small caskets to Washington on the family plane, *Caroline.*

At 8:30 P.M. on Wednesday, December 4, a quiet procession left the White House and headed to Arlington National Cemetery, two miles away. In stark contrast to the massive and meticulously planned public ceremony nine days earlier, this was to be an intensely private service. Completely off the record.

President John F. Kennedy's eternal flame provided a glowing light in the darkness as Mrs. Kennedy, Clint Hill, and a handful of relatives and close friends gathered around the grave site. The two white caskets were placed in the ground next to the remains of the father they'd never known. The twenty-minute ceremony was simple, but no less heartbreaking than all the others had been. As Clint Hill watched the tears stream down Mrs. Kennedy's face, he wondered how much longer this nightmare could go on.

Meanwhile, President Johnson had requested the Secret Service to provide protection for at least a year to Mrs. Kennedy and her children. She could have requested any of the agents, and any of them would have stepped up to the task. But for Jackie Kennedy, there was no decision. She wanted Lynn Meredith, Tom Wells, and Bob Foster to remain with John and Caroline. For her own protection, she wanted Paul Landis and Clint Hill.

DECEMBER 6, 1963

Exactly two weeks after her husband had been assassinated, Jackie Kennedy and her children moved out of the White House and into the Harriman home in Georgetown. There was a two-wheeled bicycle, a couple of boxes filled with toy helicopters and airplanes and soldiers, and wardrobes filled with Jackie's clothes. Charlie the dog had come, while most of the other animals had been sent to the farm at Atoka. Clint Hill, Paul Landis, Tom Wells, Lynn Meredith, and Bob Foster had set up the security arrangements and supervised the entire moving process.

It seemed that somehow, time was moving forward. But even as Mrs. Kennedy, the children, and their five-man Secret Service detail began a new routine at the new address, the pain refused to go away. For Mrs. Kennedy, Caroline, and John-John, the agents were a source of comfort and indeed, the agents couldn't have imagined any other assignment. But for Clint and Paul, protecting the widow and her children, seeing their sad empty faces day after day, was a cruel irony—a constant reminder of their failed mission.

DECEMBER 10, 1963

Eighteen days after the assassination, Dallas SAIC Forrest Sorrels and Secret Service inspector Gerard McCann submitted their report on the agents' drinking investigation to Chief Jim Rowley. Rowley was pleased to see that the investigation was thorough and had been conducted professionally. Sorrels and McCann spent three days and nights talking with anyone who'd been around, including the management of both the Fort Worth Press Club and the Cellar. The questioning and interviews included members of the White House press corps, local press, hotel managers, Fort Worth police management, and the White House staffers who had been in attendance. Everyone submitted statements. The statements of the agents were reviewed by Sorrels and McCann and clarified if there was a question regarding their accuracy. The supervisors were interrogated about the habits of the agents, whether any had been involved in prior heavy drinking episodes, and if anyone had ever appeared to have a drinking problem.

McCann and Sorrels's investigation found that Pearson had grossly exaggerated the agents' behavior. Of all the people interviewed, all those who were in a position to know, not one would say that any of the agents had been intoxicated or acted in anything other than a proper manner. Of the nine agents who went to the press club, all were off duty at the time, and the amount of liquor consumed did not exceed one or two drinks or an equivalent amount of beer. And regarding the "Cellar" coffeehouse, there were no alcoholic beverages dispensed, and a total of ten agents had occasion to drop in for coffee and fruit drinks at various times throughout the night. The tempting factor, it seemed, was not drink, but the waitresses who wore nothing but underwear.

The inquiry found no evidence that any special agent of the Secret Service was inebriated as reported in Pearson's piece. Unfortunately, Pearson's unfounded article would remain in the public's consciousness far longer than the investigation that disproved the accusations. The damage had been done.

Even as outsiders and journalists were intent on laying blame, Jackie Kennedy felt compelled to honor the Secret Service agents who had become like family members. Three weeks after the assassination, she wrote a letter to Douglas Dillon, secretary of the Treasury, the man who had given the citation and gold medal to Clint Hill and who was ultimately responsible for the future of the Secret Service agents who had served on the Kennedy Detail:

> Dear Douglas:
>   I would like to ask you one thing that was so close to Jack's heart—he often spoke about it—It is about our Secret Service detail—the children's and mine. They are such exceptional men. . . .

The letter went on to say that the president had often remarked that before he left office, he would see that the men on the First Lady's Detail and the Kiddie Detail would be given the highest recommendation to advance in the Secret Service. He didn't want them to be stuck in assignments with children or future first ladies unless they requested it.

She was careful to be clear that this note was in no way speaking against the President's Detail and added how her husband had felt about his agents.

He was devoted to them all—so was I, and so were our children. She listed Jerry Behn, John Campion, who retired from the detail shortly before the assassination, Floyd Boring, Roy Kellerman, and Bill Greer, "who always drove the president." She assumed that the futures of these senior agents would be secure—that they'd always be on the President's Detail, but added, *If I am wrong in this, please do all you can for them because they were perfect and the President loved them.*

But the purpose of the letter was to express her wishes regarding the agents who had been responsible for protecting her and the children—the younger agents.

> *You cannot imagine the difference they made in our lives. Before we came to the White House, the thing I dreaded most was the Secret Service. How wrong I was; it turned out that they were the ones who made it possible for us to have the happy close life that we did.*

She remembered how she'd told the agents on the children's detail about her own experiences as a young girl, playing with Katie Roosevelt—the granddaughter of President Theodore Roosevelt—and how the presence of her Secret Service agents had made her feel "rather lonely and unique." She wanted to make sure that her children never felt that. And indeed, the agents on John and Caroline's detail were so exceptional that "I now have two unspoiled children," she wrote.

The four-page letter went on to say that neither she nor her husband would have been happy without knowing that these men's futures were assured. She went on to list the men whom she held in such high regard:

Clinton Hill, Paul Landis, Lynn Meredith, Robert Foster, and Thomas Wells.

She concluded the heartfelt letter by saying that these men had served the president as well as anyone in his government, and that *protecting his wife and children with such tact, devotion, and unobtrusiveness . . . made our White House years the happy ones they were.*

19

The Johnson Detail

In the blink of an eye the transition of the office of the presidency was over. Just as had happened three years earlier when John F. Kennedy took over from President Eisenhower, some shuffling occurred within the White House Secret Service detail. The Johnson and Kennedy details were integrated and two new agents were brought in from field offices so that each shift now had an additional three agents. But so much more had changed. Everything was different. The Kennedy Detail had become the Johnson Detail.

The integration of Johnson's detail with the former Kennedy Detail agents was not in any way seamless—assignments were made by seniority, and naturally Johnson felt more comfortable with his agents than with those who had been loyal to Kennedy. Tensions rose and tempers flared. The cohesiveness of the Kennedy Detail unraveled like a slow death.

There was no more kidding with the staff. The foolish requests the agents had tolerated before were shut down forcefully and swiftly. The joking and camaraderie between the agents disappeared instantly, and there was an intensity that made them feel isolated from each other. The only common bonds were grief, guilt, and paranoia. And while paranoia was part of the psyche of an outstanding agent, it was one of those things that if it went too far, it could send you right over the edge.

Every agent who had served an extended amount of time with

President Kennedy was suffering; whether they were still on the detail or had been transferred, they all felt an overwhelming sense of failure. Rationally, they could tell themselves that they had no intelligence of Lee Harvey Oswald and his presence in Dallas, and that they had limited control when it came to the president riding in an open-top car, but none of these excuses was acceptable to the former Kennedy Detail agents. They vowed to work twice as hard to tighten the ring of security around the president. There was no more double-checking, there was triple- and quadruple-checking. Nothing less than perfection was acceptable. The agents were determined that if they were to be labeled, the only labels would be that they were effective and efficient. The most important item on the agenda was to ensure such a disaster would not happen to another president while under their protection.

Exhausted and despairing, they mustered the energy to effectively handle their responsibilities, patiently waiting for the moment they could mourn their own personal loss and determine how to deal with the heavy guilt they had placed on themselves as a unit. The Drew Pearson article, despite the fact that it had been proven baseless, resulted in every off-duty action of the agents being scrutinized. The couples no longer gathered for dinner or friendly poker games. Everybody was struggling to find ways to deal with the guilt, the shame, the unbearable pain. A couple of them turned to alcohol when off duty; others threw themselves obsessively into the work. The one thing they needed most, the only thing that could help them heal, was the one thing none of them could do. While the nation and the world seemed obsessed with untangling the truth behind what had happened in Dallas on November 22, 1963, and could talk of nothing else, ironically the Secret Service agents who had been on the Kennedy Detail never discussed it at all.

Somehow the days turned into weeks, and suddenly it was Christmas. Clint Hill, Paul Landis, and the Kiddie Detail went to Palm Beach with Mrs. Kennedy and the children and spent another Christmas away from their own families. President Johnson decided to stay in Washington for the better part of December, and for the first time since Jerry Blaine had joined the White House Detail, he was able to spend Christmas Day with

Joyce and his two young children, Kelly and Scott. The family time was brief, however, for President Johnson would spend the next two weeks at his ranch in Texas. The chic and upscale Kennedy retreats of Hyannis Port and Palm Beach had been replaced by the Texas hill country, and at 5:00 A.M. on December 26 the Johnson Secret Service detail departed Andrews Air Force Base for Austin.

Sixty-five miles west of Austin, in west central Texas, is the town of Johnson City, which in 1964 had a population somewhere around seven hundred. The LBJ Ranch, a working cattle ranch on the Pedernales River, was located sixteen miles west of Johnson City, not far from where Lyndon Baines Johnson had been born fifty-five years earlier. It was a great place for President Johnson to rest up from the trauma of the assassination and focus on both his own future and the future of the country, surrounded by his family in the place he'd always called home. For the former Kennedy Detail agents the "Texas White House" was desolate.

When the agents were not on shift, they were holed up in the Hobbs Motel, owned and operated by Ernest and Teet Hobbs on the outskirts of Johnson City. The simple accommodations consisted of the Hobbses' living quarters and ten rooms, in which the agents stayed two to a room. The Hobbses were very accommodating and tried to make the agents' time there as comfortable as possible, but recreation for the most part was limited to a jog on a country road or a jaunt "downtown" to one of the few home-style restaurants. Most of the time the agents remained in their rooms with nothing to do but reflect.

The transition to the Johnson Detail was difficult on a number of levels. While the agents struggled to suppress their feelings of failure and frustration, they were also dealing with the operating style of the new president. While at the ranch, the Kennedy Detail agents had time to personally evaluate the new president. Before they had only heard stories. President Johnson's personality and demeanor were totally opposite to John F. Kennedy's. His vocabulary was littered with obscenities and his temper was quick and sudden. You never knew what kind of mood he would be in and what might suddenly set him off in a tirade. He was well-known for his face-to-face confrontations in which he'd grab you by the lapels or pound a pointed finger into your chest while verbally assaulting you. And while the mission of protecting the president remained the same, it wasn't the president's responsibility to adapt to his Secret Service detail; it was up to the agents to adjust to the new president's style.

Maybe it was the emotional pressure Johnson personally had experienced during the past month, but he was quick to fly off the handle to the agents, his staff, and even members of his own family. Agents Stuart Knight, Rufus Youngblood, and Paul Rundle had served on Johnson's detail when he was vice president and had learned how best to deal with his idiosyncrasies. Their advice was to stand up to him or he would bowl you over. He rarely apologized but would frequently come back with a compliment to balance a prior confrontation.

It didn't take long for stories about Johnson's unconventional behavior to circulate among the agents. The day shift reported the president was a fairly good marksman at shooting deer by sighting his telescopic rifle over the hood of the leased tan Lincoln convertible, which caused some of the agents to question his sportsmanship. And then there were the eyebrow-raising things they witnessed Johnson doing that Kennedy never would have done, things such as President Johnson relieving himself wherever and whenever he pleased, sometimes even in the presence of female press members. He had a larger-than-life personality and while he was not necessarily someone the agents could ever imagine as a friend—as they had with President Kennedy—Lyndon B. Johnson clearly understood the power of government and the office of the presidency. The man had an overwhelming responsibility ahead of him, and if he wanted to pee in the woods or wherever he got the urge, it wasn't the agents' job to judge.

Meanwhile, there had been rumors that the FBI would take over the presidential protection responsibilities from the Secret Service. It was no secret that Director J. Edgar Hoover wanted this responsibility for his agency, and since the Secret Service had lost a president this thought was undoubtedly on President Johnson's mind as well. As it was currently set up under the Treasury Department umbrella, the Secret Service did not have the resources to accomplish the task—meanwhile, the FBI had thousands of agents.

While they were at the ranch, Rufus Youngblood passed along to a few agents that President Johnson himself was considering the option, so clearly it was more than just a rumor. The White House Secret Service detail had no idea what the future held for them. That uncertainty combined with the overwhelming emotions from the assassination made the two weeks following Christmas 1963 at the Johnson Ranch two of the loneliest and darkest weeks any of the agents had ever experienced.

The agents felt like they were walking on eggshells with President Johnson, and they were overly sensitive to Jack Ready, Tim McIntyre, Emory Roberts, and Roy Kellerman, who had been on the front lines of the tragedy. There was also a sense of protectiveness around Win Lawson and Dave Grant, who were still filling out paperwork and follow-up reports and only beginning to deal with what would be endless questions about the Dallas advance.

Win Lawson had gone over his reports a thousand times already, wondering if there was something he'd missed, something he should have foreseen. The first thought that went through his head when he saw the president being lifted onto the gurney at Parkland replayed over and over in his mind. *I'm the first Secret Service advance agent to lose a president.* Indeed, although three other U.S. presidents had been assassinated— Abraham Lincoln, James Garfield, and William McKinley—President Kennedy was the first one since the Secret Service had been authorized as the protectors of the President of the United States.

The other agents who had been on the Kennedy Detail for much of his presidency knew what Win was thinking. It was the luck of the draw that he'd been assigned the Dallas advance. Any one of them could have been in his shoes. Individually, the agents felt compelled to let him know they didn't blame him. One by one they found a private moment to talk to him. And the message was always the same.

Win, I'm so glad it was you who did the advance. The first time he heard it, he didn't understand. And then it sunk in.

Win, if it had to happen, I'm glad it was you. We all know how conscientious you are, how detail-oriented. You never leave a stone unturned. We know since you were on the advance, it was done the best it could have been. Thank God it was you, Win. Thank God it was you.

Jerry Blaine was back on the midnight shift, and while standing post all night was never fun at any location, in the pitch-black darkness of Johnson's 350-acre ranch all you could do was get more and more depressed.

The rolling hills were dotted with live oak and pecan trees, but while the land was beautiful, to the agents from the Kennedy Detail it felt like another planet.

One night Blaine was walking from the command center to the first post to start the rotation for his shift when he heard a terrifying screech ring out in the darkness as something propelled toward him from a tree branch.

What the hell is that?

As the object hit the ground, Blaine instinctively reached toward his gun with one hand and waved his flashlight with the other, as his heart raced. *What kind of thing makes that terrible sound?* Suddenly his light caught sight of a huge bird fanning out its tail. It had scared the daylights out of him but turned out to be just one of the wild peacocks that roamed freely on the ranch. Peacocks, he decided, have two reasons for being. The first is to be magnificently beautiful and the second is to scare off strangers. Blaine wished somebody had warned him. The bird nearly gave him a heart attack.

A half hour later, when it was time to rotate posts, a new agent who'd joined Art Godfrey's shift from the Boston office, Dan Hurley, was mumbling as he walked up to relieve Blaine.

"That goddamn bird."

"Did he jump you, too?" Blaine asked.

"He totally pissed me off. I picked up a rock and threw it at him. Damned if I didn't hit him in the head."

"What did you do with it?" Blaine asked.

"It's still lying over there," Dan replied.

"I suggest you get rid of it," Blaine said. The last thing they needed was President Johnson finding a dead peacock in the morning.

Hurley walked away into the darkness.

About five minutes later he returned and said, "I threw it in the river."

Blaine laughed nervously as he moved to the next post, wondering what the president's reaction would be if he found one of his prize watch birds no longer on duty.

Later, as the sun came creeping over the horizon, Blaine looked up to see Hurley once again approaching for the rotation. Blaine had been thinking that if LBJ discovered what had happened to one of his peacocks, the FBI would probably be flying in here tomorrow. Hurley stopped and stared toward the river. Blaine turned to look in that direction. Staggering up the hill came the wet, scraggly peacock. *Well, look at that. Maybe we'll get another week before the FBI flies in,* Blaine thought to himself.

As it turned out, President Johnson realized during the weeks at the ranch that he did not want to turn his personal life over to J. Edgar Hoover—he recognized the inherent danger in having protection turned over to an agency responsible for internal investigations of the government. Meanwhile, the FBI was receiving far more flak than the Secret Service for the assassination, due to the Bureau's handling of Lee Harvey Oswald. It had come out shortly after the assassination that Oswald had been on the FBI's watch list because of his defection to Russia, and there was speculation about whether the information they had on him constituted a threat that should have been reported to the Secret Service. In reality, Oswald had never threatened the president, so there was no legitimate reason for the FBI to pass information to the Secret Service. For the time being it seemed that the Secret Service would remain the protectors of the president.

Meanwhile, President Johnson had a bigger and more urgent problem to deal with. In the aftermath of the assassination, the FBI had conducted an investigation and had determined that Lee Harvey Oswald was the sole assassin. The problem facing Johnson now was related to the facts that had come out of the investigation: not only had Oswald defected to Russia, but upon returning to the United States he had been involved with groups favorable to Cuba and Fidel Castro. Journalists were taking on the task of investigation and, like Drew Pearson, were igniting firestorms from all different directions. The case of who had killed President Kennedy was nowhere near closed.

JANUARY 1964

Emotionally the country had been turned upside down and the headlines were filled with new theories on who was behind the assassination: left-wing liberals; right-wing extremists; the CIA; the Soviets; the Cubans; the CIA in conjunction with the Cubans and the Soviets; J. Edgar Hoover and the FBI; President Johnson himself. The thought that such a heinous act could occur on our own soil was beyond comprehension, and most Americans simply couldn't come to terms with the notion that President Kennedy's death could have been the result of one sick individual who was merely desperate for attention. There had to be a more complex scenario. It just didn't make sense. What most Americans didn't understand was something of which the Secret Service was well aware—that an assassination was most likely to occur by a loner, an individual seeking infamy; these were the kinds of people they had on their index cards, the kinds of people who wrote letters and tried to climb the fence of the White House. A conspiracy involving two or more people was the most unlikely scenario of all.

Despite what the agents believed in their hearts, the White House Secret Service detail had no time to delve into investigations—they were busy protecting the new president. There was no way in hell this was going to happen again. Not on their watch. But until Congress approved more funds for more manpower, the only thing the assassination had accomplished was to increase the workloads of the already overloaded and exhausted White House Detail agents to ridiculous levels.

As the Warren Commission was beginning its investigations, the new president started traveling throughout the country to try to put confidence back into the hearts of the citizens. Johnson had witnessed how relatively easy it was for a sniper to eliminate someone, but he had to balance his personal fears with his role in leading the country back to some semblance of normalcy. At times he was very anxious for his own safety and would bark orders at SAIC Jerry Behn to stay close to him. At other times he would needlessly rush head-on into a large crowd to show that he was not afraid. It was a natural struggle, but he had to demonstrate to the American public and the free world that the assassination would not deter him or future presidents from making themselves available to the people.

The flurry of advances and protection assignments that kept the Johnson Detail agents operating at a fast pace in the weeks and months following the assassination were like painkillers—they dulled the pain temporarily, but did nothing to heal the wounds. On top of the day-to-day protection requirements, the agents were required to fill out individual reports and legal affidavits in relation to the Warren Commission's investigation. The daily shift reports that were typed out by the shift leaders and

Special Agents in Charge became like detailed diaries down to the minute of each day. The agents were scrutinized for every tiny decision, every movement.

One of the mandates of the Warren Commission was to investigate weaknesses in the Secret Service protection policies and to make recommendations. One change following the assassination, however, was immediate: the president would no longer travel in an open-top car. The Secret Service had always opposed presidents traveling in convertibles, but it had taken an assassination for the recommendation to resonate with the politicians. J. Edgar Hoover had three armored cars—including one that had been owned by Chicago gangster Al Capone—that were strategically located in the West, Midwest, and at FBI headquarters, and Hoover had recommended President Johnson use one of them. For the time being, however, Johnson decided to stick with hardtop Cadillacs.

There was a strange phenomenon that was occurring throughout America in the early months of 1964: people young and old, from all walks of life, were seeing doctors for sudden physical ailments. A national survey was conducted and showed that more than two-thirds of the American people were experiencing, or had experienced, some kind of physical illness and emotional distress as a direct result of the assassination. The same was true for the Secret Service agents. For a group that was rarely ill, sick days started to become more common as the agents went to their doctors for stomach problems, traumatic reactions, and uncontrolled emotions that were similar to what they'd felt in combat. Win Lawson developed a faltering kidney problem; Andy Berger, who had always been happy-go-lucky, had turned introspective and quiet; and Chuck Zboril suddenly lost a clump of hair that turned into a temporary bald spot the size of a silver dollar.

Blaine worked through his depression and feeling of failure by returning to a sport he had played in college—handball. Blaine would meet up with his friend Tom Rosenberg—who happened to be a contract psychiatrist working for the CIA—and pound out his frustration and anger by slamming the ball over and over and over against the cement wall of the court. Sweat would seep out his pores and the pain of the ball on his hand became like a drug. He began to crave the physical sessions on the court at the Pentagon and gradually the internal pain began to subside. Jerry believed it was the physical exertion that was making him feel better, but Rosenberg knew that what was really helping Jerry was the conversations they had on the court. Subtly, Rosenberg had found ways to get Jerry to open up and talk about the range of feelings he'd been holding inside. It made a world of difference.

For Tom Wells, Lynn Meredith, and Bob Foster on the Kiddie Detail, even though they had not personally witnessed the assassination, it impacted them dramatically. They loved John and Caroline like their own children, and day after day they had to watch the slow mourning process. Forty-year-old Lynn Meredith had lost his own father suddenly and tragically when he was the same age as John, Jr. It hadn't made a huge impact on him at that age, and he could see that John certainly didn't understand the true meaning of his own father's death, either. But now the president's death was affecting Lynn so deeply that every time he even looked at John, he had to choke back tears. John had idolized his father and Caroline had adored him. As the male figures who spent more time with the children than any others, the agents felt a tremendous responsibility not only to protect John and Caroline, but to be role models of which the president would have been proud.

Foster and Wells similarly found the Kiddie Detail assignment emotionally challenging in the aftermath of the assassination, but they couldn't imagine being anywhere else. As far as the effect on the children—it was difficult to gauge. John-John, despite his curiosity about his father's sudden disappearance, seemed for the most part unchanged. Caroline, on the other hand, seemed to repress the event. Out of necessity, the White House school Mrs. Kennedy had set up had to be dissolved, and Caroline was enrolled in a school at the British embassy. Not surprisingly, it was a difficult transition and she seemed much more withdrawn.

The Kiddie Detail agents often took Caroline and John to a local playground in Georgetown. One day Byron "Beano" Rollins, a longtime Associated Press photographer, went to the park with Foster and Wells to take photos of the children as a gift for Mrs. Kennedy. After running around and playing, John became thirsty and asked Bob Foster for a lift so that he could drink out of the fountain. As Foster held the tousle-haired little boy to the fountain, Beano snapped his picture. When Agent Foster put John-John back down on the ground, the boy looked at the photographer and asked, "What are you taking my picture for? My daddy is dead."

Both Foster and Rollins crumbled.

It seemed as if the president's death was a forbidden subject. Nobody knew what to say. Only John-John seemed unafraid to speak what was on his mind. He slowly learned that the helicopters no longer landed on the lawn, but his curiosity about them never ceased. And whenever he'd see a soldier or man in uniform, he was quick to practice his salute.

As the Kennedy Detail agents tried to move forward, tried desperately to go on with their lives, and tried to lock the images and feelings from the assassination deep inside themselves, there was always something that would take their minds back to that dreadful day in Dallas.

For the agents who lived in Virginia, as most of them did—Dave Grant, Jerry Blaine, Win Lawson, Paul Landis, Clint Hill, the list went on and on—the daily commute home from Washington took them over Memorial Bridge, and as they drove across the Potomac River the flame marking President Kennedy's grave at Arlington National Cemetery flickered on the hill directly ahead, an eternal reminder of their failure to protect the president.

20

The Pendulum Falls

Lyndon Johnson was still not emotionally or politically prepared to accept the presidency in the manner in which he had received it. Like the rest of the nation, he had gone through a period of shock, but he also had an immediate and enormous responsibility thrust on his shoulders. Not only did he inherit the issues Kennedy had left behind—civil rights; the Cold War and its ramifications with Cuba, the Soviet Union, and Southeast Asia—but it was now up to him to ease the sorrow of the nation and restore confidence to the American people. On a personal level, President Johnson had to win over the people who had loved Kennedy and had already elevated JFK to legendary status.

The new president was caught in the paradox of needing to be a fearless leader in a world in which his predecessor had been gunned down in broad daylight.

SOUTH BEND, INDIANA
APRIL 24, 1964

In an ambitious schedule to push civil rights and the newly conceived "War on Poverty" scheme, which was part of his Great Society program, President Johnson traveled to the economically hard-hit cities of Chicago,

326

South Bend, Pittsburgh, and Huntington, West Virginia, in late April. The 1964 presidential campaign was in full swing.

Johnson Detail agents Jerry Blaine and Walt Coughlin peered out the windows of the helicopter as the pilot circled over a high school stadium that had been selected as a landing site. Johnson's political aides had chosen South Bend so he could offer words of inspiration and hope to the community in which two thousand people had lost their jobs when the Studebaker plant shut down production a few months earlier. Five thousand people had come to greet the president and the stands were filled. The field was to be used to form the motorcade that would deliver the president to the speech site, and was supposed to be clear of people. But as the helicopter descended, the agents could see that hundreds of people—many of them students—had pushed beyond the meager rope barrier and had surged onto the field, in the exact spot where the helicopter needed to land. Marine One, carrying President Johnson, was circling nearby, facing the same problem. It was clear from this vantage point that there were far too few police officers on the ground to control the unruly crowd.

Blaine shook his head and turned to Coughlin with a look of disgust on his face. Over the noise of the chopper he asked, "I wonder who screwed this up?"

The president's hardtop stretch limousine and the Secret Service follow-up car were parked on the track that encircled the field, but were too far from the open space where the chopper was supposed to land. The situation was not set up anything like what the preliminary advance report stipulated.

Slowly the pilot lowered the helicopter toward the ground and as he got closer, the people moved away like rings of water when a stone is thrown into a pond. But still there was not enough room for Marine One to drop in. Blaine, Coughlin, and the three other agents in the chopper were going to have to first control the crowd and then move the horde of people back from the landing area.

Jerry Blaine felt his gut tighten. It had been five months since the assassination but the tension and anxiety still ached like a ball of lead in his stomach whenever the president was in public. Blaine looked over at Coughlin and could tell he was just as frustrated with the situation.

Remarkably, as the Warren Commission continued its probe into the assassination of President Kennedy with *an unlimited budget*, there had been no increase in resources, budget, or manpower to the Secret Service, whose mission it was to protect the President of the United States. If anything, the workload had in fact increased for the White House Detail agents, due in part to the ongoing investigation, yet also because the agents had placed such pressure on themselves to perform with perfection. They had to prove that they were capable and worthy of protecting the president—no way in hell was there going to be another assassination on their watch.

As soon as the helicopter touched ground, the agents piled out. They cleared the rotors and started moving the spectators back.

"Move! Get back!" they yelled as they waved their arms and physically pushed the throng of people. They had to get the crowd to the fringes of the field and place them behind the flimsy rope being held by a half-dozen police officers as a barrier. The dust and grass being blown by the descending helicopter carrying the president had temporarily forced the crowd back, but the people seemed ready to lunge toward it after it landed. The advance agent, who had been on Johnson's detail when he was vice president, was on the ground wondering what had prompted the cheering crowd to surge. There were definitely not enough security personnel for this number of people.

Marine One landed gently and settled to the ground.

"L-B-J!" they cheered. "L-B-J!"

The officers had no choice but to yield, and the crowd pushed closer toward the helicopter.

Driver Bill Greer and SAIC Jerry Behn stepped out of the aircraft, followed by a few members of Johnson's staff. Then President Johnson made his appearance. Instead of immediately walking down the stairs, he stopped at the top and waved at the crowd. This prompted another immediate surge, accompanied by screams and waving hands.

The president's face contorted nervously for an instant as he saw the rowdy herd of people trampling toward him. He put both of his hands in the air, gesturing for the mob to stay back. Surprisingly, it worked.

Perhaps it was the trauma to the nation of losing its president, but society seemed to be focusing on its leader more than ever. With Kennedy, the office of the presidency had achieved idol status and it had transferred to LBJ. At the same time, an unsettling change was occurring. Public demonstrations had proven to work in moving civil rights legislation forward, and now there were growing numbers of demonstrations against the buildup in Vietnam as well. The youth who had responded to John F. Kennedy's plea for change had started becoming more and more vocal. The younger generation, in particular, was completely devastated by JFK's death and now they'd become disenchanted with government as a whole. The response was anger and dissent. The division between liberals and conservatives had widened and as both faces of society focused on the president, the agents could sense it. With JFK there had been mostly adoration, with few protesters. Now the tide seemed to be turning. It almost seemed as if those six seconds in Dallas, that one fatal shot, had turned the world upside down, and it would never be the same again.

One result was that the number of flash cards increased. Threatening the president was increasingly in vogue. In fact a new card had been issued from PRS the day earlier, involving a threat from an ex-Marine in San Francisco.

The agents eased into their escort positions, surrounding President Johnson while giving him space. Their eyes scanned the unruly crowd, searching the eyes and the hands, looking for a glint of metal that shouldn't be there. They were still halfway between the chopper and the car.

As if a starter's pistol had fired, the crowd surged forward, pushing aside the police officers and heading directly for President Johnson.

Instinctively Blaine and Coughlin looked back at the president to see where he was headed, so they could protect him from the tidal wave of people that was about to overwhelm him. They could not believe their eyes. There was President Johnson beckoning with his hands for the crowd to come forward.

Jesus Christ! What the hell is he doing?

Clearly Johnson had never experienced the mob mentality with which the agents had become all too familiar when Kennedy was president. Suddenly there was a stampede. Everyone in the track of the stadium was headed in his direction.

A mob has no conscience, no common sense. Chaos reigns. The agents instinctively closed in on the president to protect him from the onslaught.

It was as if they were on the front line of a battlefield. The initial shock forced them to dig in and press against the crowd as the screaming men and women thrust out their arms to touch the president or try to shake his hand.

In front of Blaine a young mother carrying her young baby suddenly realized what was happening around her. People's elbows were banging into the baby's head. The baby was screaming and now the mother was panicked.

"No! No!" she shrieked as she tried to shield her child's head from the ravaging swarm.

Agent Blaine's job was to protect the president but he couldn't ignore the sight of the innocent baby being battered. By this time he could also sense the president was nervous for his own safety as the mob pressed harder. Blaine braced his front leg and bent into the crowd to push them back and away from the mother and the president, but his strength was no match for the wall of people slamming against him. In an effort to keep himself from being flattened, he thrust his right leg back, stomping his foot on the ground. Only it didn't meet the ground.

"Get off my toe, you goddamn son of a bitch!" the president bellowed.

Blaine whipped his head around to see President Johnson glaring at him with a combination of fear, panic, and rage.

For a second Blaine considered letting the crowd have him.

Now furious, Blaine started pressing even harder against the crowd. The three other agents were doing all they could as well, but the crowd wasn't responding.

"Somebody help get that woman and her child out of here before they get trampled to death!" Blaine yelled.

They were kneeing people in the groin, pushing people down, ready to throw punches if necessary. They used every tactic possible to move the crowd back.

Where is the mother with the baby? In the instant Blaine had turned around, he'd lost sight of her.

For Christ sake! Where is she? Blaine looked frantically around and finally caught a glimpse of two men who had come to their senses and were moving the woman out of the mob. Eventually the agents cleared the way for the president to make it to the car and he readily jumped in. Bill Greer pulled away as the agents jogged alongside, glaring at the still-cheering throngs of people.

Fortunately President Johnson suffered no more than a sore toe, and clearly he relished the attention. The three years as vice president had been tedious and had not provided Johnson with a sense of accomplishment, only frustration. He was now witnessing the power of the presidency and he loved it.

The next stop was Pittsburgh—another Democratic stronghold that would appreciate his War on Poverty message. Even though he was in a closed-top car, the streets leading into the city were filled with people pushing toward the president's limousine. Blaine and Coughlin were running along the side of the car, not only to shield the president but also to ensure nobody was injured. There weren't enough police officers to contain the crowd. It was insane.

Suddenly the limousine stopped.

What? We're nowhere near the speech site, Blaine thought as he looked around.

The president opened the door, popped out of the car, and began beckoning to the crowd. Instantly Jerry Behn, who was in the front seat, jumped out. Suddenly President Johnson and the agents were engulfed again. President Johnson had a huge smile on his face. He turned back to the limousine, hauled his six-foot, four-inch frame onto the trunk, and then stepped up onto the roof of the limousine. Immediately all eyes of the agents turned upward to the windows of the tall buildings overlooking the chaotic scene. People were hanging out of open windows and flashbacks of Dallas ran through everybody's minds. Only President Johnson seemed blissfully unaware. He was so enraptured with the adulation.

Finally Jerry Behn said forcefully, "Mr. President. Time schedule. Let's get back in the car."

President Johnson climbed back inside the car, and Blaine and Coughlin let out the breath they'd been holding in for the last ten minutes. They looked at each other and shook their heads. *What the hell was he thinking? For God's sake. What the hell?!*

On the way back to Washington on Air Force One, Blaine could not stop thinking about what had happened that day. His mind swirled at how easily he could have been in the same situation as Clint and Jack. A few times he'd thought he'd heard what sounded like a shot, then realized it was only his imagination. Were the endless nights at the ranch, staring into oblivion in total darkness, finally getting to him? Was he driven by a sense of accomplishment that had ended in failure? And was the job still worth the amount of time he had to be away from his family?

These thoughts had been creeping into his mind over the past few months, but when the President of the United States—whom he was trying his damnedest to protect—suddenly lashed out at him with a personal insult, it was as if he'd crashed into a brick wall. After five years on the detail, the love, dedication, excitement, and professionalism he valued so highly had culminated in the assassination of President Kennedy. Meanwhile, little had changed as far as resources and work hours. All that was left was a sense of futility. You could do only so much. But the one thing you couldn't do was protect the president from his own ego.

The Warren Commission was now deep into its investigation. Some—but not all—of the agents had been called into the private hearings, while others had been asked to file written affidavits on their every move for the two days prior to and including the assassination. Win Lawson, Dave Grant, and Dallas SAIC Forrest Sorrels—as had been expected—were put under intense scrutiny. It seemed that everybody assumed if there were someone to blame, it should be the agents who had done the advance. The White House Detail agents rallied around Lawson, Grant, and Sorrels because they knew differently. Any of the agents who had been with President Kennedy for any length of time knew that every outdoor appearance, every motorcade in every city around the world had had the same potential for disaster. With the number of agents they had available, combined with the president's political need and desire to mingle with the public, there had always been a calculated risk. There always would be. President Kennedy knew it better than anybody. It came with the job. In the weeks following the assassination, a story was passed throughout the detail that even the president himself had commented on how easy it would be for someone to assassinate him from an upper-floor window. He'd made the comment to Ken O'Donnell and Dave Powers in his suite at the Hotel Texas the morning of the assassination. The night before had been dark and rainy when they'd arrived in Fort Worth, and as the president jumped out of the car, disregarding the plan to move directly into the hotel, and looked up to see all the people hanging out of windows up above, he'd realized in that moment what an easy target he was. He knew his agents were loyal and were the best of the best. But common sense told you that with the power of rifles and scopes these days, it really wouldn't have been that difficult.

Clint Hill, Paul Landis, and the three members of the Kiddie Detail—Lynn Meredith, Tom Wells, and Bob Foster—continued to suffer through the days with Mrs. Kennedy and the children. After five weeks at the Harriman house, Mrs. Kennedy had purchased another redbrick Georgetown home on the same street so she and the children could have a permanent home. Unfortunately, the new residence became a tourist attraction. Tour buses would actually squeeze down the narrow streets of Georgetown to pass by her house at 3017 North N Street. She was incensed. She tried to get it stopped, but couldn't. For safety and privacy, she decided to move to New York City. Clint went house hunting with her, as both sounding board and bodyguard, and finally she decided to buy a large apartment at 1040 Fifth Avenue, across the street from Central Park. She stayed in a large suite at the Carlyle until the place was ready. Clint set up residence in a very small room at the hotel, which would be his home for the next several months. Along with his supply of suits and white shirts, Clint had all the boxes containing the protective equipment stuffed into the little room. It was the Carlyle, but it felt like he was living in a storage closet.

In reality, Mrs. Kennedy and the children didn't stay too long in one place those first few months. They traveled between New York and Atoka and Palm Beach and Hyannis Port, always surrounded by friends or the extended but close-knit Kennedy family. For Clint and the other agents, the constant travel was just as therapeutic as it was for Mrs. Kennedy. Being on the move, there were always arrangements to be made, logistics to coordinate. And the farther away they were from Washington, the less they heard about the ever-expanding theories surrounding President Kennedy's assassination.

MAY 1964

On May 7, 1964, Jerry Blaine was conducting an advance in Athens, Ohio, for President Johnson's appearance at Ohio University when he met a man named Jack Hight, who had worked in President Johnson's senatorial office at one time and was now working in government relations for International Business Machines Corporation. Hight and Blaine had dinner one night and Hight's enthusiasm about the future of IBM and the opportunities it presented was contagious. The company was best known for its typewriters but had become a leader in the growing mainframe computer industry.

Ever since the assassination, Jerry had had a rough time trying to envision his future with the Secret Service. Everything about the job that he had once loved seemed to have disappeared, yet still he was working the equivalent of two jobs, getting paid for one, and spent a good deal of time away from his wife and kids. The conversation with Jack Hight had got him thinking. Maybe it was time to consider leaving the Secret Service and pursuing a career in the private sector.

In late May, nearly six months after the assassination, in the midst of the Warren Commission hearings, a new theory emerged. This one seemed to be the most bizarre yet, since it was alleged by a Secret Service agent. An agent in the Chicago office by the name of Abraham Bolden, who had just been indicted on charges of soliciting a bribe from a defendant for documents related to a counterfeit case, held a press conference to announce that he was being framed. The reason for his indictment, he claimed, was that he had approached the Warren Commission to provide testimony about derelict behavior of Kennedy Detail agents—which included elaborate sex parties and on-duty drinking at Hyannis Port—that he had witnessed while serving a thirty-day temporary assignment on the White House Detail in the summer of 1961. The insinuation was that the Kennedy Detail agents may have been responsible for the president's death due to a laxness in their duties, and Bolden's arrest was an attempt to shut him up.

The claims were absurd. Certainly, it was strange that now, as he was being charged with conspiracy to sell government documents—a crime for which the Secret Service had a pile of convincing evidence against him—that he was suddenly coming forth with these preposterous accusations. On top of everything else, Bolden, an African-American, was claiming he'd been the subject of racism. He said he had logged a complaint with Chief Jim Rowley following his brief stint in Hyannis Port, which was never followed up on.

Most of the White House Detail agents had never even heard of Bolden, and those who had worked with him when he served the temporary duty nearly three years earlier remembered him only as an agent whose attitude interfered with group cohesiveness. He was no doubt a good investigative field agent who may just have decided to remain in the field. In any event, he was not transferred permanently to the White House Detail.

Bob Faison, who was transferred to the Kennedy Detail in September 1963 and was the first African-American to be a permanent White House Detail Secret Service agent, found Bolden's claims to be so ridiculous, he simply ignored them. He'd never experienced a drop of racism from his colleagues. Indeed, at the Hotel Texas in Fort Worth the day before President Kennedy's assassination, the agents on Faison's shift had put up a fight on his behalf when the hotel manager at first refused to allow him to stay. Bob Faison had never met Bolden, but he couldn't imagine any of his colleagues conducting themselves in the manner Bolden described.

Nonetheless, the Warren Commission initially took Abraham Bolden's accusations seriously and required every agent who had been on the same shift with Bolden on that thirty-day assignment in 1961 to write out a statement, under oath, about what they could remember of the July Fourth weekend activities.

In the end, the Warren Commission rejected Bolden's accusations against the White House Detail agents. What did seem clear was that Bolden was trying to divert attention from the crimes for which he'd been indicted.

For the majority of the White House Detail agents, the Bolden issue was but another baseless accusation for which they'd have to bite the bullet and remain silent. It was Secret Service policy for agents not to speak publicly about the inner workings of the agency, and in reality Bolden's allegations were so ludicrous that none of the Johnson Detail agents gave the issue another thought. They were consumed with the work of protecting the president, and trying to figure out what the future held for each of them individually.

JULY 1, 1964

It was the hardest decision Blaine had ever had to make. IBM had offered him a job as a salesman. He would have to complete the Systems Engineering course first, but it was a lucrative position with a virtually unlimited career path. The money wasn't the driving factor—Blaine had never cared much about money. He needed to do what felt right.

He knew he would never be in close association with a finer group of men than those with whom he worked in the Secret Service. Being on the small White House Detail was like being a member of an exclusive club that no outsider could ever understand. Their bond was a true brotherhood. They'd traveled together, laughed together, supported each other, and worked in the White House through one of the most turbulent times in the history of the United States. Being on the White House Secret Service Detail was an incredible honor. How could he walk away?

On the other hand, Blaine realized that not only had the job changed, but he had changed, too. His heart wasn't in it like it should be. Like it had to be. But was he capable of doing anything else? His entire life had been wrapped around his identity as a Secret Service agent, and out of necessity he had created a barrier between himself and the outside public. It was his job to be wary of people, to observe, evaluate, and move on to the next subject. Anybody was potentially dangerous. Nobody outside the inner circle could be trusted. Blaine was not at all certain that he would fit in on the other side of the fence.

Silence had become his habit, and talking to strangers was something he avoided. As a salesman for IBM's high-technology products, he would have to pass the rigorous training program. Right now the only piece of technology with which he was proficient was the Thompson submachine gun.

He'd spent two weeks of sleepless nights trying to make the decision he knew would change the entire direction of his life. Finally, on July 1,

1964, just shy of his fifth anniversary with the United States Secret Service, Blaine walked into Chief James J. Rowley's office and resigned.

It was terrifying and awkward. Jim Rowley was one of the finest men he'd ever met. Blaine felt like he was betraying his brothers.

"Jerry," Rowley said, "I wish you luck in your new job. We are really going to miss you."

Suddenly Blaine wanted to plead temporary insanity and take it all back. He had never been so torn.

"Jim," he said, "I have never pondered over a decision in my life like I have this one. My heart is here, but I don't see any alternative."

Rowley nodded. He understood completely. Everything had changed. Nothing was the same. They were all struggling. "Look, Jerry, you are always welcome to come back. There will always be a job for you here. But I have no doubt that you will be successful in whatever path you choose. Who knows? Perhaps at IBM you will come up with solutions that will help us in the long run."

Perhaps, Blaine thought. *Or perhaps I'm making the biggest mistake of my life.*

21

The Verdict

In President Johnson's first address to Congress, on November 27, 1963, the new president had told the legislators, "No memorial oration or eulogy could more eloquently honor President Kennedy's memory than the earliest possible passage of the civil rights bill for which he fought so long." It had not been easy to get the votes needed to pass the bill—one hundred years after the Civil War there was still a huge division in philosophy between the northern and southern states, between liberals and conservatives, that reached across political party lines—but Lyndon Johnson forged ahead, determined to make Kennedy's dream a reality. Finally on July 2, 1964, President Lyndon B. Johnson signed into law the Civil Rights Act. Containing the most far-reaching civil rights legislation since the Reconstruction era, in the 1860s, when slavery was abolished, the Civil Rights Act of 1964 made racial segregation in public facilities illegal, included provisions to help guarantee black Americans the right to vote, and outlawed a number of employment practices based on race, color, religion, sex, or national origin. Kennedy was gone, but his legacy would endure.

While Jerry Blaine had come to the painful conclusion that he had to leave the Secret Service, every agent who had served on the Kennedy Detail went through a similar struggle. It was a struggle each one of them dealt with individually. Still, none of them talked about the assassination with each other, and rarely with anybody else. Meanwhile, every agent had in the back of his mind anxiety about what the Warren Commission findings and recommendations would be.

WARREN COMMISSION REPORT
SEPTEMBER 24, 1964

On September 24, 1964, the Warren Commission presented its 888-page report to the president. After an exhaustive investigation that included testimonies and questioning from more than five hundred witnesses and would be supported by twenty-six published volumes of the hearings, the report began with the following:

"The assassination of John Fitzgerald Kennedy on November 22, 1963 was a shocking act of violence directed against a man, a family, a nation, and against all mankind. A young and vigorous leader whose years of public and private life stretched before him was the victim of the fourth presidential assassination in the history of a country dedicated to the concepts of reasoned argument and peaceful political change."

The Warren Commission jointly and unanimously concluded that:

1. The shots that killed President Kennedy, and wounded Governor Connally, were fired from the sixth-floor window at the southeast corner of the Texas School Book Depository.

2. President Kennedy was first struck by a bullet that entered at the back of his neck and exited through the lower front portion of his neck, causing a wound that would not necessarily have been lethal. The president was struck a second time by a bullet that entered the right-rear portion of his head, causing a massive and fatal wound.

3. Governor Connally was struck by a bullet that entered on the right side of his back and traveled downward through the right side of his chest, exiting below his right nipple. This bullet then passed through his right wrist and entered his left thigh, where it caused a superficial wound.

4. The weight of the evidence indicated that there were three shots fired.

5. The shots that killed President Kennedy and wounded Governor Connally were fired by Lee Harvey Oswald. This conclusion was based on the following facts: The Mannlicher-Carcano 6.5mm Italian rifle from which the shots were fired was owned by and in the possession of Oswald. Oswald carried this rifle into the Book Depository Building on the morning of November 22, 1963. Oswald, at the time of the assassination, was present at the window from which the shots were fired. Additionally, based on testimony of the experts and their analysis of films of the assassination, the commission concluded that a rifleman of Lee Harvey Oswald's capabilities could have fired the shots from the rifle used in the assassination within the elapsed time of the shooting. The commission concluded further that Oswald possessed the capability with a rifle to enable him to commit the assassination.

On top of the evidence above, Lee Harvey Oswald lied to the police after his arrest concerning important substantive matters and, seven months prior to the assassination of the president, Oswald had attempted to kill Major General Edwin A. Walker, thereby demonstrating his disposition to take a human life.

6. Oswald killed Dallas police patrolman J. D. Tippit approximately forty-five minutes after the assassination. This conclusion was based on the reports of nine eyewitnesses and corroborating evidence, including Oswald's possession at the time of his arrest of a revolver that matched the cartridge cases found at the scene of the shooting.

7. Regarding Oswald's interrogation and detention by the Dallas police, it was concluded that Oswald was not subjected to any physical coercion. He was advised of his right to counsel and rejected it. However, "newspaper, radio, and television reporters were allowed uninhibited access to the area through which Oswald had to pass when he was moved from his cell to the inter-

rogation room and other sections of the building, thereby subjecting Oswald to harassment and creating chaotic conditions which were not conducive to orderly interrogation or the protection of the rights of the prisoner."

The next line was of extreme importance: "The numerous statements, sometimes erroneous, made to the press by various local law enforcement officials, during this period of confusion and disorder in the police station, would have presented serious obstacles to the obtaining of a fair trial for Oswald. To the extent that the information was erroneous or misleading, it helped to create doubts, speculations, and fears in the mind of the public which might otherwise not have arisen."

8. Regarding the killing of Oswald by Jack Ruby on November 24, 1963, the commission concluded that there was no evidence to support the rumor that Ruby may have been assisted by any members of the Dallas Police Department in the killing of Oswald. Further, the commission admonished the Dallas Police Department's decision to transfer Oswald to the county jail in full public view, and during which the police department's arrangements for the transfer were inadequate. Of critical importance was the fact that news media representatives and others were not excluded from the basement even after the police were notified of threats to Oswald's life. These deficiencies contributed to the death of Lee Harvey Oswald.

9. The commission found no evidence that either Lee Harvey Oswald or Jack Ruby was part of any conspiracy, domestic or foreign, to assassinate President Kennedy. All the evidence before the commission established that there was nothing to support the speculation that Oswald was an agent, employee, or informant of the FBI, the CIA, or any other governmental agency. All contacts with Oswald by any of these agencies were made in the regular exercise of their different responsibilities.

10. In its entire investigation the commission found no evidence of conspiracy, subversion, or disloyalty to the U.S. government by any federal, state, or local official.

11. On the basis of the evidence before the commission it concluded that Oswald acted alone. "Therefore, to determine the motives for the assassination of President Kennedy, one must look to the assassin himself. Clues to Oswald's motives can be found in his family history, his education or lack of it, his acts, his writings, and the recollections of those who had close contacts with him throughout his life."

The commission admitted that it could not make any definitive determination of Oswald's motives, but it isolated factors that contributed to his character and might have influenced his decision to assassinate President Kennedy, including his deep-rooted resentment of authority, which was expressed in a hostility toward every society in which he lived; his inability to enter into meaningful relationships with people; his urge to try to find a place in history and his despair at times over failures in his various undertakings; his capacity for violence, as evidenced by his attempt to kill General Walker; his avowed commitment to Marxism and communism, which was expressed with antagonism toward the United States, even after his disenchantment with the Soviet Union, and by his frustrated efforts to go to Cuba.

12. Regarding the actions of the Secret Service, the commission recognized the various challenges faced by the Secret Service in performing its duties and boldly stated that "consistent with their high responsibilities presidents can never be protected from every potential threat. The Secret Service's difficulty in meeting its protective responsibility varies with the activities and the nature of the occupant of the Office of President and his willingness to conform to plans for his safety."

Further, the report stated, "In appraising the performance of the Secret Service it should be understood that it has to do its work within such limitations."

After these initial caveats, the commission concluded that the criteria and procedures of the Secret Service designed to identify and protect against threat suspects were not adequate prior to the assassination, and that the Protective Research Section "lacked sufficient trained personnel and the mechanical and technical assistance needed to fulfill its responsibility."

Additionally, the commission determined that there was insufficient liaison and coordination of information between the Secret Service and other federal agencies necessarily concerned with presidential protection, including the FBI.

When it came to the advance preparations in Dallas made by Win Lawson and Dave Grant, the commission concluded that the detailed security measures taken at Love Field and at the Trade Mart were "thorough and well executed." However, the commission noted that there were procedures in place and used by the Secret Service that were not well defined when it came to the responsibilities of police officials and others assisting the protection of the president. Further, the commission concluded that while the Secret Service, as a matter of practice, did not investigate or check any building located along the motorcade route, this was something that should be changed.

When it came to the agents and whether they should or should not have been on the back of the car, the report stated that "the configuration of the presidential car and the seating arrangements of the Secret Service agents in the car did not afford the Secret Service agents the opportunity they should have had to be of immediate assistance to the president at the first sign of danger.

"Within these limitations," the report continued, "the Commission finds that the agents most immediately responsible for the president's safety reacted promptly at the time the shots were fired from the Texas School Book Depository Building."

By this one statement, the Warren Commission exonerated Bill Greer, Roy Kellerman, Emory Roberts, Jack Ready, Paul Landis, Tim McIntyre, George Hickey, Glen Bennett, and Clint Hill. They had all done their jobs as best as could be expected in the situation. With their comments on the advance, the commission concluded that Win Lawson and Dave Grant also had done their jobs as flawlessly as could be expected, given the limitations of budget, resources, and cooperation with other agencies.

Based on the "limitations" of the Secret Service, the commission recommended a variety of changes, which included better communication between government agencies. It was noted that the Secret Service did not have sufficient personnel or adequate facilities at the time of the assassination and would need increased resources to achieve what was being recommended.

In a relatively short time, the Warren Commission had gathered and compiled the material evidence, had delved into almost every conceivable aspect of the lives of Lee Harvey Oswald and Jack Ruby, had conducted scientific evaluations using available technology, and had probed into every rumor and theory that had arisen since the assassination. Yet almost immediately there were cries of foul play and accusations of a cover-up. Authors and pundits began writing books and articles on their own theories and took great relish in pointing out any inconsistency that could be found in the commission's investigation. There were indeed discrepancies, but the majority of them were due to inconsistent memories and recollections and erroneous media reports that came out in the chaos of the minutes and hours following the tragedy. When something so unexpected, so horrific, and so tragic occurs the human mind must find a way to cope with the onslaught of sensory overload. No two people will react to or remember the events exactly the same. That was abundantly clear throughout the Warren Commission's investigation. But despite the lack of concrete evidence of a conspiracy, people still didn't want to believe that the death of their beloved President John F. Kennedy could have been the result of one mentally disturbed loner. So while the case should have been closed, instead a cottage industry sprouted with the intent of proving the Warren Commission wrong.

Meanwhile, the White House Secret Service detail agents struggled to perform their job of protecting President Johnson and tried to ignore the controversy.

Just as Jerry Blaine had come to the painful conclusion that the best thing for him to do was resign, four other agents came to the same conclusion within a year or two after the assassination. Frank Yeager, who had done the advance with Blaine in Tampa, had always wanted to coach athletics, so he went back to school and earned his master's degree in secondary education; Joe Paolella, who had come from Chicago, decided to return to his home city, and after a short stint as a loan officer in a bank, in which he realized a desk job was not what he wanted, started his own private investigation and protection company; Ed Tucker, who had worked on the children's detail early on but had transferred back to the Chicago Field Office, also left the Secret Service a couple of years later, to pursue a career in security in the private sector; and finally, Paul Landis, who had worked with Clint Hill on Mrs. Kennedy's detail and had been on the right running board of the follow-up car in Dallas, resigned in 1964.

The rest of the agents who had served on the Kennedy Detail chose to stay with the Secret Service until they were eligible for retirement, and many stayed on for much longer. Still, the assassination hung like an albatross around their necks as they suffered in silence, the haunting memories never far away.

The government had authorized Secret Service protection for Jacqueline Kennedy only for the year following the assassination. Finally, in November 1964, Clint Hill was left to wonder what the Secret Service would do with him, now that he was no longer required to protect Mrs. Kennedy.

The question she'd asked him with such concern, as they flew back to Washington on Air Force One with President Kennedy's body, resonated in his mind.

What will happen to you, Mr. Hill?

Oh, I'll be okay, he had replied.

Somehow he had made it through the year; somehow they'd both made it through the year. As long as he was busy, as long as he had a task—and he had had plenty with the move to New York and Mrs. Kennedy's constant traveling—the memories of that dreadful day in Dallas had remained buried.

After being by her side nearly every day for the past four years, all he could think was, *What will happen to you now, Mr. Hill? What will happen to you now?*

22

Confronting Conspiracies

The great enemy of the truth is very often not the lie, deliberate, contrived and dishonest, but the myth, persistent, persuasive and unrealistic.

—JOHN F. KENNEDY

GRAND JUNCTION, COLORADO
JANUARY 2004

When Jerry Blaine finally retired from the corporate world in 2004, at the age of seventy-two, he suddenly had what felt like endless time on his hands. With no pressing deadlines or assignments or business trips to attend, his mind started reflecting on the past. After leaving the Secret Service in 1964, he had thrown himself into his new career with IBM, and had suppressed the dark days of the assassination. He tried to cling to the fond memories of the days on the White House Detail, and the photos of him with JFK and Ike were always the first things he hung in his home office as he'd moved from Virginia to Connecticut to Texas and finally to Colorado. After all these years, he still remembered those as some of the best times of his life.

When Secret Service chief Jim Rowley had casually suggested to Jerry, on the day Jerry resigned, that perhaps he would find a way to help the Secret Service agency through his new career with IBM, Jerry had put the comment in the back of his mind, never imagining what might be possible. In his first year at IBM, Jerry was competing with trained and talented computer mathematicians who had graduated from MIT, Harvard, Yale, and other elite universities. What they had learned in Ivy League schools he had to cram in during a condensed training program. It was brutal, but he wasn't about to fail. He went on quota selling mainframe computers to the communications industry, and made the 100% Club in three months.

After just one year on the job, Jerry was approached by the Johnson administration about taking a one-year leave of absence to help train the Shah of Iran's bodyguards. The Shah was a close ally of the United States and had just survived an assassination attempt in which two of his bodyguards had been killed. If anything happened to the pro-Western Shah, Iran might be lost as an ally forever. IBM granted him a leave of absence and he attacked the assignment with zest. Most of the training was in Washington, D.C., but it also required trips to Tehran. The assignment made him realize that his heart and mind were still in the protection business.

Throughout that year he kept thinking about everything he'd learned at IBM. He realized that the technology he'd been selling to the communications industry could potentially be used in law enforcement to get access to information on a real-time basis. He could see that the old index filing system of tracking suspects could be put on a computer database and the information could be shared across agencies almost instantaneously.

Jerry contemplated his future with IBM and could focus on nothing but how he could develop the law enforcement and intelligence market. It so happened there were two other individuals who had the same vision. A new department was formed that included Blaine, an ex-police captain from Chicago named Dick McDonnell, and Phil Silver, formerly with the Los Angeles County sheriff's department.

The three former law enforcement specialists worked with systems designers to develop fingerprint scanners, mobile terminals, resource allocation programs, and court scheduling systems. Their objective was to create a total integrated justice system that could track offenders from arrest to final disposition. They also designed a computer-assisted dispatch system that could locate the closest available vehicle and assign cars according to statistical probability of where the most calls would originate.

Together Blaine, McDonnell, and Silver generated enormous computer sales to police and intelligence agencies worldwide, including Scotland Yard and numerous European nations. For their efforts they won an outstanding contribution award and were recognized worldwide as the experts in this field.

In the U.S. market Jerry worked on an information system for the CIA called "Walnut" and assisted the FBI with the design of the National Crime Information Center, which utilized an IBM mainframe. The NCIC system was compatible with the law enforcement communications network that linked state and local police departments together, while the mainframe located at FBI headquarters provided a database of wanted persons, stolen cars, firearms, and ultimately criminal histories. The database allowed police officers to immediately determine the status of an individual during an arrest or traffic stop. Jerry realized that if the Secret Service purchased an IBM system, it could be designed to tie into the FBI's system to track threat suspects.

If only we had had this capability in 1963.

As a result of the Warren Commission's recommendations, the Secret Service had hired a computer technician to build a computer system in an attempt to link the field offices and headquarters. As part of the bidding process, Jerry presented a proposal to sell one of IBM's systems that would link to the FBI's National Crime Information Center so that as people were queried on traffic stops or suspicious activity, the query could be run against the Secret Service file. He pointed out that if the president were going to Los Angeles, for instance, and a police inquiry came up on a traffic stop in that city that involved a person on the PRS threat list, the information would be immediately forwarded to Secret Service field offices. It was the ideal solution to the age-old problem of tracking itinerant threat cases.

Jerry never expected the response he got.

"That would be an invasion of privacy."

An invasion of privacy? What?

Jerry couldn't believe what he was hearing. An invasion of privacy? The Secret Service had never cared about that in the past. He thought perhaps the technology he was presenting was so futuristic—so far beyond the index card filing system—that perhaps it was being misunderstood.

And so he tried explaining it in a different way. The response was exactly the same.

Jerry was flabbergasted. The organization had been raked over the coals about the antiquated systems at PRS and he was offering an ideal solution. And then it dawned on him: It had nothing to do with the IBM system or its capabilities, or an invasion of privacy—the Secret Service had no intention of buying a system from him. He got the distinct feeling he was being viewed as a deserter. After President Kennedy's assassination, only a few agents had left—and he was one of them. To those who had stayed, it was like Jerry was coming back after all these years and trying to tell them how to run their business.

When a competitive system was chosen that did not have the same capabilities as the IBM system he was offering, Jerry couldn't help but feel that the decision may have been based not on pricing, but on the fact that he was the person pushing the solution. He was devastated. He had spent the last nine years working on something with the goal of helping the Secret Service and it had been rejected. Maybe it hadn't been personal, but the result was that the Secret Service agents who worked so hard to protect the President of the United States still didn't have the resources they needed.

In 1974, when IBM started having a number of trade secrets stolen, Jerry moved out of Industry Marketing and for the remainder of his career with IBM he was a director of security for numerous divisions and groups worldwide. He helped lobby for a federal trade-secret law, and in his last assignment, he was loaned to the U.S. State Department as a member of the Overseas Security Advisory Counsel, where he worked during the Persian Gulf War attempting to remove trapped oil workers in Kuwait.

After retiring from IBM he was hired by ARCO International as director of foreign affairs and security, responsible for international development, and traveled to virtually every country in the world to establish security protection programs and assess foreign operations. The operations included work in Algeria, Yemen, Egypt, Indonesia, and Africa during their various fundamentalist struggles. He attacked every assignment with the same relentless pursuit of perfection that he had in the Secret Service, and was proud that even though he'd been responsible for evacuating workers from numerous countries, he'd never lost an employee.

He'd always vowed to return to Colorado, the place he called home, and in 2004 he settled into retirement. After traveling all over the world, overseeing every type of security threat imaginable—from Colombia to the Congo—he was finally ready to confront the issue that had haunted him for forty years: he needed to revisit the events surrounding the assassination.

One day he started reading some of the blogs and articles on the Internet about President Kennedy's assassination. As he devoured the information, he didn't know whether to laugh or cry. Everybody and their brother, it seemed, had a theory on why JFK was killed, who killed him, and how many people were involved in the cover-up. The theories were endless. But what was most disturbing to Jerry Blaine were the accusations against the Secret Service—accusations that somehow the Secret Service was either responsible for JFK's death or had played a role in the assassination and alleged cover-up.

Where did they come up with this stuff?

He couldn't believe what he was reading—things like the Secret Service changed the route of the motorcade at the last minute so it would pass in front of the Book Depository, where Oswald was waiting; Secret Service agents "suspiciously" replaced President Kennedy's original casket and altered his wounds during the autopsy to conceal a shot from the front; Secret Service agents destroyed evidence of advance reports; Secret Service agent George Hickey accidentally killed JFK with the AR-15 rifle; Bill Greer purposely slowed down as the shots were being fired; and the craziest—Bill Greer turned around and shot the president as he was driving.

What? George Hickey? Bill Greer? Are you kidding me?

Jerry's heart was pounding. He felt as if he were going to explode. He couldn't believe the nonsense that was being published—not only on the Internet, but also by respectable book publishers. Outright lies had been published as if they were fact. Along with the outrageous conspiracy theories were the wildly inaccurate stories about President Kennedy's private life. It seemed the only thing that mattered was selling books or making a name for yourself on the Internet as some kind of "expert." It didn't seem to faze the authors and researchers and filmmakers that they were assassinating the characters of some of the finest men Jerry had ever known.

But beyond the personal attacks, the most disturbing aspect of the conspiracy theories was that factual history had been replaced with fiction. The unrealistic myths had been perpetuated for so long that they indeed had become the enemies of the truth.

Jerry devoured the material, became obsessed. He checked out books from the library, and with each one, became more and more frustrated.

How will future generations ever know the truth?

From the time the Warren Commission report was released in 1964, polls had been taken of the American public and consistently, a majority— some polls said as many as 75 percent—believed that there was a cover-up and a conspiracy in the assassination of John F. Kennedy. Yet still, more than forty years after the assassination, not one theory had been proven to be true. *Not one theory had proven to be true.*

In 1976 the U.S. House of Representatives formed the House Select Committee on Assassinations (HSCA) to investigate the assassinations of both President John F. Kennedy and Martin Luther King, Jr. The HSCA resulted from public demands in the aftermath of the hundreds of books and magazine articles that had tried to present cases of conspiracy in both assassinations. After two years of investigations, the HSCA presented its final report in 1979 and concluded that President John F. Kennedy was assassinated by Lee Harvey Oswald, just as the Warren Commission had found. But—and this was big—the committee concluded that President Kennedy was "probably" assassinated as a result of a conspiracy. *Probably. Not definitely. Not beyond reasonable doubt.* Unfortunately, this irresolute conclusion merely left the door wide open for more theories to be concocted.

But despite its statement of a "probable" conspiracy, the committee had been unable to identify other gunmen or the extent of the alleged conspiracy. Additionally, the HSCA made it clear that none of the following were involved in the "probable" conspiracy: the Soviet government, the Cuban government, the FBI, the CIA, nor the Secret Service. Additionally, the report concluded that anti-Castro Cuban groups and the national syndicate of organized crime—as groups—were not involved in the assassination, but it did not preclude the possibility that individual members may have been involved. The statement that there was a "probable" conspiracy combined with the "possibility" that some Cuban or mafia-related individuals could have been involved ensured that the cottage industry of conspiracy theorists would endure.

In the forty years since the heart-wrenching day Jerry had handed in his resignation to Jim Rowley, he had never lost touch with his brothers in the Secret Service. When he had a question about some of the disturbing things he was reading, he would call the agents. Additionally, as one of the founders of AFAUSSS—the former Secret Service agents' association—Jerry made it a point to attend as many of the annual conferences as possible, and inevitably he and the other Kennedy Detail agents would huddle together at these reunions. Everybody had the same frustrations. They had all been contacted by potential authors or people wanting the inside scoop. Most of the agents would be polite and helpful with innocuous questions that didn't violate the code, and whenever something controversial or questionable was asked, the replies were standard. If ever asked about whether JFK had ordered them off the back of his car, the answer was always, "Oh, no. President Kennedy was wonderful. He was very easy to protect. No, I don't remember him ever ordering agents off the back of his car."

At the reunions the subject of whether there might have been a conspiracy was often discussed, however, and of all the Kennedy Detail agents Blaine had spoken with over the years, none believed there had been a conspiracy. The people who made their living selling books and films and television documentaries were simply trying to come up with some magical answer that two lengthy and thorough government investigations had failed to prove.

Now that he was retired and had the time, Blaine started reviewing the "facts" that conspiracy researchers and authors used to support their theories.

One of the most popular theories was based on the belief that a shot was fired from the grassy knoll—"evidence" that Lee Harvey Oswald did not act alone. From where did this originate? It had come out during the Warren Commission's investigation that the number of shots witnesses heard had varied. Indeed, even those closest to the impact could not agree on the number of shots. Everything happened so fast. But the vast majority heard three shots that came from the direction of the Book Depository, and the three casings found in the sniper's nest on the sixth floor there provided validity. Agent Paul Landis, who had been on the right running board of the follow-up car, wrote in his original statement dated November 27, 1963, that he thought one of the shots might have come from the front—every other agent was confident that the shots all came from the right rear. But Landis's statement provided a spark for conspiracy theorists to jump on the possibility that there may have been another gunman.

Jerry knew—as any good investigator does—that when a sudden catastrophic event occurs, people will react, respond, and remember events inconsistently. The mind can handle only so much at one time. Combined with that is the fact that every individual comes to the scene with a completely different background and set of references. Paul Landis was an expert marksman with his revolver, and he recognized the sound of the rifle, but he had never worked a presidential motorcade before. His senses were on overload and the canyonlike configuration of Dealey Plaza created an echo chamber that distorted the sounds for many witnesses. Jerry knew that Paul had had an emotionally difficult time after the assassination, and like him, had chosen to leave the Secret Service in 1964.

It had taken Paul Landis a long time to get over the trauma of what he'd seen. And it wasn't until many years later that he was able to admit to himself that what he thought he heard and what he thought he saw in the chaos of those tragic moments had very simple explanations. He had said that one of the shots he heard seemed to have come from somewhere toward the front, but when he thought back with a rational mind, he believed it must have been an echo. It wasn't a shot from the front: it was the shot fired from behind him, echoing off the overpass directly ahead.

And he had seen a man running up the grassy knoll, away from the street, and with his rational mind he realized that if he had been a bystander and had heard the barrage of gunfire, had seen the president's head explode, he would have been running away, too. It was a natural human reaction—not evidence of a second shooter. He had made the statements five days after the assassination, still traumatized, and at the time he believed those statements to be true. He wished he had had the presence of mind then that he had now. He realized the effect of his statements, but what could he do now, after all these years? He too had been living with tremendous guilt and grief, on so many levels.

Another claim, in a book published in 1980, was that President Kennedy's body was kidnapped sometime between departing Parkland

and arriving at Bethesda and that the wounds were altered on the corpse to make it look like there was only one assassin. Absurd. Admiral Burkley was with President Kennedy's body from the time he arrived at Parkland Hospital until the casket was taken to the White House. Roy Kellerman, Clint Hill, Paul Landis, or other Kennedy Detail agents were always within sight of the president's body. Nothing could have happened without their knowledge. There wasn't one Kennedy Detail agent who would have allowed anything like that to happen. The only reason there was a change of casket was that the original bronze one was damaged when the agents had to force it through the doorway of Air Force One in what was a climactic traumatic moment on the worst day of their lives. The suggestion of agents being involved in something sinister was beyond comprehension and reason.

Another "fact" used as "evidence" of a Secret Service plot to have President Kennedy assassinated evolved from the erroneous directions and drawings in the various Dallas newspapers. These were publication errors. Once Win Lawson and Forrest Sorrels set the motorcade route, it never changed. There was simply no other logical route. Yet people on the Internet continued to argue that the route should have gone straight on Main Street and not taken the jog onto Houston and Elm Street. Clearly anybody who adheres to this theory has never been to the site. It would have been impossible.

The book that claimed George Hickey shot the president really riled Jerry Blaine. The author—who was a ballistics specialist and avid researcher—stated that the president was shot, albeit accidentally, by the agent manning the AR-15 rifle. When the book came out in 1992, Hickey of course knew the claim was ridiculous, but he took no action. His wife was very ill and he had no strength to file a lawsuit right away. Meanwhile, unbeknownst to Hickey, a television announcer named Gary Mack at KXAS-TV, the Dallas–Fort Worth NBC affiliate, had contacted the publisher of the book shortly after its release, because he knew of a home movie of the assassination—the Charles Bronson film—that showed Hickey was still seated in the backseat of the follow-up car when the third and fatal shot hit the president. This meant that Hickey would have had to fire through the front windshield of the follow-up car. Additionally, the shot would have gone through or between Ken O'Donnell and Dave

Powers, JFK's two closest friends. The publisher and author had viewed the film, yet still the book remained in print. Mack couldn't believe it. He called the Secret Service in Washington, D.C., and told the public affairs officer about the film. When the officer heard Mack's story, he said, "You have no idea how important your phone call is." Soon Mack received a phone call from George Hickey's daughter, nearly in tears, thanking him for coming forward.

Several years later, the book was still in print, and George Hickey became concerned that the theory was going to taint his family name. He didn't want his grandchildren faced with defending his innocence. In 1996 Hickey filed suit against the author and publisher. However, the judge stated that the statute of limitations had passed and threw the suit out. When the book was reprinted in a paperback version, that allowed the suit to be reopened. By this time, Gary Mack was the curator of the Sixth Floor Museum at the assassination site and agreed to be deposed. The publisher eventually settled with George Hickey after publication of the paperback and audio versions of the book appeared without any changes. Those books remain in circulation and people still debate the ridiculous theory.

When Jerry read that some "researchers" were claiming that Bill Greer and Roy Kellerman should be held accountable for President Kennedy's death, he nearly lost it completely.

Who are these people? What right do they have making baseless accusations about men who were loved by President Kennedy, and who would have happily given their lives for him?

It was maddening. Some people claimed that Greer slowed the car deliberately as the shots were being fired. Others claimed that Greer simply didn't react quickly enough to the shots. Bill Greer and Roy Kellerman were two of the most loyal, diligent, and conscientious men on the White House Detail. You didn't get to these kinds of positions unless you'd proven yourself time and time again. Both Greer and Kellerman did not recognize the first shot as rifle fire. The acoustics of the plaza, combined with the barrier of the windshield, the direction of the car, and the roar of the motorcycles, drowned out the sound of the first shot. The adrenaline level had dropped as the motorcade entered Dealey Plaza, with the dwindling crowds. Nobody was expecting to hear gunfire.

When Bill Greer heard the first unusual noise over the roar of the motorcycles, he thought he might have blown a tire. He turned his head around and simultaneously tapped his foot on the brake. He knew how the car reacted. It was as if the car were an extension of him. The car slowed for an instant—a split second—just enough time for Greer to realize that the tires responded normally to the brake. The sound had not been a tire blowout. Yes, Bill Greer put his foot on the brake after the first shot. But for God's sake, it had nothing to do with a conspiracy, or negligence—he was merely responding as any professionally trained driver would respond.

In 2005, a book was published that claimed "JFK was the target of an assassination plot during his long motorcade in Tampa, Florida, on November 18, 1963 four days before Dallas."

Oh really? Jerry thought. He bought the book to see what this author apparently knew that he hadn't known as the Secret Service agent who conducted the advance for that very trip. Once again he could not believe that stuff like this was being published. No wonder people believed in conspiracy theories. There was so much crap being put out with absolutely no validity to it, but this one was a real doozy.

The convoluted theory the author had come up with was beyond the realm of reason. The author claimed that the Secret Service's Tampa advance reports had been destroyed and that the Tampa plot was somehow connected to another plot by the mafia to assassinate President Kennedy in Chicago during his November 2, 1963, visit. The author claimed that JFK had canceled the Chicago trip at the last minute because the Secret Service had knowledge of a four-man hit team that was planning his assassination in Chicago, Tampa, or Dallas.

Blaine wondered where this theory cropped up, since he had been on all those trips; he had knowledge of every threat, everything that was known at the time. Blaine was incredulous. *Where did this guy come up with this crazy idea?* And then he read that one of the author's sources was "a Secret Service agent named Abraham Bolden."

Abraham Bolden? The name Bolden was vaguely familiar, but he couldn't place it.

And then he remembered: Bolden was the Secret Service agent from the Chicago Field Office who, after being charged with a felony several months after Kennedy's assassination, had made all those claims about the Secret Service agents being lax in their duties at Hyannis Port. Blaine had had to write a sworn statement and he remembered thinking at the time how absurd Bolden's claims were. Bolden's case was appealed all the way to the Supreme Court, but in the end he was convicted and sent to prison for offering to sell documents in a counterfeit case. Bolden—a convicted criminal—was the author's source of the plot in Tampa, which was based on a case allegedly reported to the Secret Service by the FBI involving an alleged four-man hit team that the Secret Service had allegedly covered up. Bolden continued to claim that he was sent to prison to shut him up. Once again it appeared to Blaine that Bolden was grasping at straws—and using JFK's assassination to try to get his record cleared.

Despite the earlier rejection of his allegations, Abraham Bolden was allowed to speak with HSCA investigators when the JFK assassination was reopened. Bolden told them that sometime before November 2, 1963, the FBI sent a Teletype message to the Chicago Secret Service office stating that there would be an attempt on Kennedy's life in Chicago on November 2 by a four-man hit team using high-powered rifles. The HSCA interviewed Ed Tucker and other agents who were working in the Chicago office at that time, and none of them could recall any such thing. The HSCA could not document that such a case existed and found that Bolden's story was of "questionable authenticity."

It had been a long time, but Blaine was compelled to pull out his files to make sure his memory was serving him correctly. Like any good investigator, he had kept all his personal reports for all these years. Every time they moved to a new house, with his various jobs, Joyce had asked him why couldn't he throw all that stuff away, but he'd insisted the boxes of files were important.

He found the box from 1963 and started going through it. It was all there. Pages and pages of information that refuted all the claims this guy was making. He was holding in his hands the Tampa advance report that had supposedly been destroyed.

Jerry remembered that the only possible threat investigation that occurred in Chicago before President Kennedy's assassination involved a man called Thomas Arthur Vallee. Indeed, Vallee was mentioned in the book as being somehow connected to this whole bizarre theory. His good friend Ed Tucker, who had been on the White House Detail during the early part of Kennedy's administration and had transferred back to the Chicago office, had handled the Vallee investigation with another Chicago agent, Thomas Strong.

Jerry remembered when Cecil Taylor in PRS had first told him about Vallee, when he was preparing for the Tampa advance. He had heard the details of the story many times over the years straight from Ed Tucker. Vallee was the Korean War veteran who had scribbled threatening comments all over the strange collage of pictures of Kennedy and other political leaders he'd pasted on the wall of his Chicago boardinghouse room. When his landlady had notified the Secret Service that Vallee was planning to take the day off from work the same day the president was to be in Chicago, Tucker had directed the police to send out an all-points bulletin. Vallee was stopped for making an illegal turn, and when the officers saw an illegal knife in the front seat, they popped his trunk and found an M1 rifle and a thousand rounds of ammunition. Vallee was immediately incarcerated and was monitored until an accurate assessment could be made.

President Kennedy did indeed end up canceling his trip to Chicago for the Army–Air Force football game, but it had nothing to do with Thomas Arthur Vallee or a four-man hit team, as Bolden had told the author. Blaine had been on post at the White House when President Kennedy was notified of the coup in Vietnam in which the Diem brothers were assassinated. The president immediately canceled the trip to Chicago and had meetings well into the night with every ranking member of his security, intelligence, and military staffs. The coup had global implications that needed to be addressed immediately. It was no time for the President of the United States to be attending a football game.

The only other case of a potential threat nature in Chicago in November 1963 happened *after* President Kennedy's assassination. An informant had stated that a threat had been made against President Johnson's life. However, the investigation determined there was no threat and Secret Service headquarters informed the Chicago Field Office to send all documentation to headquarters to be turned over to the proper enforcement agency.

Despite the fact that there was no corroboration of Bolden's stories, conspiracy theorists believed him—a convicted criminal—over the sworn testimonies of Secret Service agents who had proven to be Worthy of Trust and Confidence.

Jerry was chuckling with disbelief as he read how the author tried to connect dots that were not even on the same page, not even in the same realm. To call the book nonfiction was like classifying *Star Wars* as history. It was typical of these conspiracy theorists, he had realized. The more convoluted the alleged story was, the more convinced they were that there was a conspiracy. But with all the people this guy had working together to assassinate the president, it was like everybody in the CIA, the FBI, and the Secret Service was involved and had knowledge of a cover-up— including President Kennedy. The sad thing was, people read this kind of stuff and actually believed it. Myths were perpetuated, and twisted, and retold time and time again such that the lines between fact and fiction had become blurred beyond recognition.

Another theory involving the Secret Service circulated around one of the black-and-white television news videos that was taken as the motorcade was departing Love Field. It showed the agents jogging alongside the presidential limousine and Emory Roberts standing up in the follow-up car motioning to Don Lawton—the shift agent who had been assigned to stay at Love Field. Lawton raised his arms and in typical Don Lawton fashion said something along the lines of "It's all yours now, guys. I've done my job. Now get out of here so I can have some lunch." There is no sound to the video. None of the "experts" could know what was said; none of them knew what had gone on with the advance preparations. One self-described "Secret Service expert" used this five-second video clip with no sound to jump to the assumption that Emory Roberts was telling the agent to back off, that there was no room for him on the follow-up car. There were countless blogs debating the video in which the "expert" erroneously named the agent in the video as driver agent Hank Rybka. Yet Rybka doesn't appear anywhere in the video clip. Despite the incorrect identification of the agent, the problem with the theory is that neither Rybka nor Lawton was scheduled to be in the motorcade. The second agent allegedly being called off is Clint Hill, who was in the normal process of moving back to the follow-up car as the motorcade departed. The argument has no basis at all, yet people had been debating it back and forth on blogs and presenting the theory at conspiracy conferences *for years* as if it were some legitimate cover-up or a justifiable reason to place blame on the Secret Service.

This same "expert" who had been interviewed for many conspiracy theory books relentlessly blamed the Secret Service for JFK's death by using their own statements against them. In many cases he called agents and recorded their conversations without their knowledge. When asked whether President Kennedy had ever ordered the agents off the back of his car, the agents gave him the standard line that Chief Rowley requested they give. And as the agents upheld their code, Rowley's words from the day of President Kennedy's funeral forever resonating in their minds, the Secret Service "expert" turned around and used their words to stab them—and their brothers—in the back with baseless accusations.

If these "experts" and "researchers" had only read some of the documents that were released in 1992 and are available online, they would have found a letter from Chief James J. Rowley written in response to J. Lee Rankin, general counsel on the Warren Commission, in which Rowley admitted what he so desperately did not want to become public. He did not want it to look as if the Secret Service was in any way blaming President Kennedy for his own death. He and every other member of the Kennedy Detail had accepted responsibility, and they would live with the grief and sense of failure for the rest of their lives.

Rankin had requested further information concerning expressions by President Kennedy regarding the placement of Secret Service agents on or near his car during the motorcade, and on April 22, 1964, Rowley responded with a letter. Rowley attached statements from Jerry Behn, Floyd Boring, Emory Roberts, Jack Ready, and Clint Hill with the understanding that these documents would remain confidential.

Jerry Behn, Special Agent in Charge of the White House Detail, wrote:

> *The policy of special agents covering the presidential vehicle is flexible and is based on the speed of the motorcade; the amount and type of accompanying escort; the number, enthusiasm, and character of the people watching the motorcade and how well-controlled they are by the police; and finally, but certainly not least but perhaps the dominant factor, the desire or instructions of the President . . .*

> *On numerous occasions during motorcades where the pace was slow and crowds were fairly well-controlled by the police, but the agents were none the less in position around the presidential car, the President would either tell me to tell the agents, or he would attempt to tell the agents on his side of the car, to get back.*

Behn's letter described specific instances in Mexico City and Berlin in which SAIC Behn and agents on the follow-up car physically pushed people away from the car and President Kennedy requested them not to do so because "his feeling was that these people only wanted to shake his hand and should not be pushed away from him."

Assistant Special Agent in Charge Floyd Boring wrote:

> *I was on duty in Tampa, Florida, November 18, 1963 and was riding in the right front seat of the presidential limousine. . . . Special Agents Lawton and Zboril were working on the ground on either side of the limousine, as the crowds were heavy. As the crowds thinned out and the motorcade increased in speed, the agents jumped onto the rear steps of the limousine. Shortly thereafter the President requested the agents return to the follow-up car. The agents dismounted about three minutes later or as soon as our speed allowed.*
>
> *A similar request was made by President Kennedy to me on July 2, 1963 . . . in Rome.*
>
> *It was the understanding among the agents on the White House Detail assigned to the President that they should not jump onto the rear steps of the presidential limousine when the crowds along the route were sparse unless it was absolutely necessary.*

Assistant to the Special Agent in Charge Emory Roberts wrote:

> *On November 18, 1963 during Presidential motorcade in Tampa Florida, ASAIC Boring, who was riding in right front seat of the Presidential car, contacted me by radio, to get the men off the back of the President's car.*

Special Agent John "Jack" Ready, who had been on the right front running board of the follow-up car in Dallas, wrote:

> *It was common knowledge that among the majority of the White House Detail agents that President John F. Kennedy, on several occasions, had asked that agents not ride on the rear steps of the presidential limousine.*
>
> *Although I was not in Tampa, Florida, Monday, November 18, 1963, it was known to me that President Kennedy requested, through Assistant Special Agent in Charge Floyd M. Boring, that two agents be removed from the rear steps of the presidential vehicle during a motorcade in that city.*

And finally, Clint Hill, who had been on the left front running board of the follow-up car in Dallas, wrote:

> *I, Special Agent Clinton J. Hill, never personally was requested by President John F. Kennedy not to ride on the rear of the Presidential automobile. I did receive information passed verbally from the administrative offices of the White House Detail of the Secret Service from Agents assigned to that Detail that President Kennedy had made such requests. . . . No written instructions regarding this were ever distributed.*

Regarding the Tampa incident, Hill wrote that he was informed that on that November 18 trip, President Kennedy had requested that Special Agents remove themselves from the rear of the presidential automobile, and while he was not on that specific trip, he received this information sometime between November 19 and November 21, 1963.

Despite his knowledge of these instructions, Hill ended his letter with the following statement:

> *On November 22, 1963 during the Presidential motorcade in Dallas, Texas, prior to the assassination of President Kennedy, I did ride on the rear of the Presidential automobile on approximately four (4) separate instances. This was necessitated by the fact that*

motorcycles which were flanking the presidential automobile on the left side were forced to drop back from their normal positions because of the closeness of the crowd on this side which did not allow sufficient room for the motorcycles to continue moving. I did on these specific instances, move from my position on the front portion of the left running board to the left rear step of the Presidential automobile. I was not requested by anyone to do so, and there was not sufficient time involved for such a request to be made, but rather did so at my own discretion. I considered this action necessary because of the proximity of the general public to the left side of the Presidential automobile.

Those were the facts. But the Kennedy Detail agents had been told to keep quiet, to bite the bullet for the Secret Service. Jerry knew Chief Rowley could not have foreseen how his determination to protect President Kennedy would ultimately have devastating consequences in the lives of his agents. He couldn't have known. But the more Jerry delved into the lies that had been spread over the past four decades, he realized something had to be done.

There was no doubt that President John F. Kennedy had stood as an icon of hope and peace and change for many Americans, but the slim margin by which he'd won the election in 1960 was a clear indicator that Kennedy's idealistic views did not resonate with the entire nation. Still, in the short tenure of his presidency, he had developed into a larger-than-life idol whose image was perpetuated by the emergence of television and a global focus on America as a result of World War II. As an agent who was with him day in and day out, Jerry had never ceased to be amazed by the response of the crowds who clamored to be close to John F. Kennedy. Women would faint, shriek, and lunge recklessly in front of the president's moving car as if they were possessed by his magnetic smile. Men too were mesmerized by—and certainly envious of—JFK's charisma, his attractive wife, and his total self-confidence. So when President Kennedy was gunned down in broad daylight, the notion that one demented individual could have had the power to do such a thing seemed incomprehensible. It was too simple. There had to be a bigger explanation. And then, when Jack Ruby took it upon himself to kill the assassin who had shot down America's hopes and dreams, it was as if the world had gone mad. Nothing made sense. That kind of thing just didn't happen in America. The conspiracy theories—and that's all they were: theories, not fact—had been born out of the inability of people to cope with the simple truth.

The string of assassinations and assassination attempts that followed President Kennedy's tragic death was evidence that this kind of thing did happen in America. Three presidents had been assassinated prior to John F. Kennedy, and attempts have been made on every president since. It is the mission of the Secret Service to protect the occupant of the Office of the President of the United States, and on November 22, 1963, the Secret Service failed in its mission. But to lay blame on men who were dedicated beyond any doubt is criminal.

It is the policy of the Secret Service not to comment on issues surrounding its mission or its personnel. But Jerry realized it was time somebody spoke on behalf of the Secret Service agents who had been on the Kennedy Detail and who, like him, had had to live with the burden of failure for their entire lives.

He had reached the twilight years of his life, and Jerry Blaine realized it was time the story of the Kennedy Detail was told. However, he wouldn't do it unless he had the support of the other agents with whom he'd served and witnessed history. It had to be their collective story, not his.

In the fall of 2005, Jerry Blaine sent out a three-page questionnaire to every man who had been a permanent member of the Kennedy Detail, asking if they would be willing to contribute to a book about the Kennedy Detail. Many, of course, were already gone, so he sent the letters to their surviving family members.

And when the responses came flooding in—the emails, the phone calls, the long, heartfelt letters—Jerry realized there was no turning back.

23

Clint Hill:
Witness to History

Efforts and courage are not enough without purpose and direction.

—JOHN F. KENNEDY

The spring of 1964 was a blur as Clint Hill coordinated Mrs. Kennedy's move to New York. Security had to be set up in the sprawling four-bedroom apartment that occupied the entire fifteenth floor at 1040 Fifth Avenue, in between coordinating her constant travels between Atoka, Palm Beach, Georgetown, and New York. The move was difficult for everybody—Jackie, John and Caroline, Clint, the staff. Everything was different. Routines changed; the familiar surroundings of Washington were exchanged for the unknown of New York City. Temporary agents were brought in to fill in the shifts.

Fortunately, Mrs. Kennedy had retained some of her staff from Washington, including Nancy Tuckerman, who had been the social secretary during the final months of the Kennedy administration. Nancy was very knowledgeable and supportive and now, as Jackie's chief of staff, she was a tremendous help to Clint as well.

The days were busy—there was always something to do—but the nights were torturous. When Mrs. Kennedy's activities for the day were finished and she was safely in the confines of her residence, Clint would turn over security to the shift on duty and walk the three blocks back to the Carlyle, where he had his tiny room. There was a small café off the lobby of the hotel and Clint would sometimes stop in there before he headed to his room, to sit at the bar with a scotch. He'd try to focus on the plans for the days ahead, but as he stared into the glass, sitting all alone, the visions would inevitably creep into his thoughts.

When Tommy Rowles, the Irish bartender, first started noticing Hill coming into the bar, he tried to make conversation. He recognized the man—had seen him on occasion with Mrs. Kennedy. But it quickly became clear that the man who came in alone, and left alone, wasn't interested in conversation. The empty look in the man's eyes nearly broke Tommy's heart.

At the end of August, the Democratic National Convention was held in Atlantic City, New Jersey. Attorney General Robert Kennedy had lobbied to be Lyndon Johnson's vice presidential running mate, but President Johnson was worried that having Kennedy on the ticket would cost him votes in the South. Instead Johnson chose Hubert Humphrey, a U.S. senator from Minnesota. Robert Kennedy was slated to speak at the convention, and there was a great deal of concern that he would cause a disruption. When Jackie Kennedy decided that she too would like to make an appearance to thank the party for all the support they'd given her husband, Clint Hill worked with Nancy Tuckerman and Pamela Turnure, who had been Jackie's press secretary, on the security advance in Atlantic City.

As it turned out, former attorney general Kennedy did not upset the proceedings. When he appeared onstage, he received an uninterrupted standing ovation that lasted for nearly twenty-two minutes, and his heartfelt speech about how much his brother President John F. Kennedy had depended on and appreciated the support of the Democratic Party was the highlight of the convention. At the end of the speech he urged the party to offer just as much support to the 1964 candidates, President Lyndon B. Johnson and Hubert Humphrey.

During the moving speech, the eyes of those in the audience were often turned away from the stage and to an upper balcony where Jackie Kennedy sat, gracious as usual. And if anyone happened to glance to Jackie's left, they would have seen a handsome, dark-haired man standing solemnly, his empty, hollow eyes constantly scanning the room.

Shortly thereafter, Clint Hill was notified that immediately following the presidential election in November, he would be transferred. Mrs. Kennedy's Secret Service protection was meant to be only for a year, and the anniversary was approaching. There was no mention as to where Clint would be transferred, but he assumed he'd be sent to a field office— probably somewhere as far from Washington as possible. There was no way they would put him back on presidential protection. With any luck, perhaps they'd send him back to Denver. That might not be so bad. But really, he knew he had no choice in the matter. He'd go wherever the Secret Service decided to send him.

On what was to be his last day with Mrs. Kennedy, she and her staff hosted a farewell party for him in her office. There was much laughter as the small group shared stories about the many fun times they'd had together—times before the world had changed a year earlier. Finally, one of the staff members pulled Mrs. Kennedy aside and handed her a big cardboard poster. With as much fanfare as if she were bestowing on him another gold medal for bravery, Mrs. Kennedy presented the handmade gift to her devoted agent. The poster had an enlarged picture of the head of a random man depicting a Secret Service agent, complete with sunglasses. Above the photo, in big letters it said: MUDDY GAP WYOMING WELCOMES ITS NEWEST CITIZEN. Everybody had signed the poster, including Mrs. Kennedy, and Clint assumed that he was being sent to the boondocks.

When the party was over, Mrs. Kennedy hugged him and said, "Good luck, Mr. Hill. I'm going to miss you."

They'd been through so much together—more than anybody would ever know, more than anybody could ever imagine—and it took every ounce of strength for Clint to hold his emotions inside.

"I'm going to miss you, too, Mrs. Kennedy."

The next day, Clint flew back to Washington. He was looking forward to being back home with Gwen and his two sons, who were now three and eight years old, but he wondered what was going to happen next.

The next day Clint reported to the White House as directed, to get what he imagined were his walking papers. Jerry Behn was still the SAIC of record, but the White House Detail was actually being run by Rufus Youngblood, the agent who had been in Dallas with Vice President Johnson. When Youngblood told Clint that he was being transferred, not to Muddy Gap, Wyoming, or some other such faraway place, but to one of the shifts on the Johnson White House Detail, he couldn't believe it.

Clint's first trip on the Johnson Detail was to the LBJ Ranch over Thanksgiving. Whenever he was on duty and happened to cross paths with the president, Clint would notice President Johnson looking at him with a quizzical look. It wasn't long before Johnson realized why the new agent looked so familiar. He was furious. He told Rufus Youngblood to get Agent Hill removed from his protective detail. President Johnson didn't want Clint Hill anywhere close to him. It didn't have anything to do with Clint's ability to protect him—he seemed more worried about Clint's allegiances, and his closeness to Jackie and Bobby Kennedy.

Somehow Youngblood and his assistant, Lem Johns, convinced President Johnson that Clint was a professional—that personalities and political parties didn't matter to him. They'd known Clint for a long time and knew he was loyal to the Secret Service and its responsibilities to the Office of the President, no matter who occupied that position.

Johnson begrudgingly allowed Hill to stay.

MAY 1967

Over the next two and a half years, Clint was promoted through the ranks of the Secret Service. A year after joining the Johnson Detail, he became a shift leader with the title Assistant to the Special Agent in Charge; and one year later he was promoted to Assistant Special Agent in Charge. Along with the increased responsibility, he had received steady salary increases and finally, he and Gwen had saved up enough money for a down payment on a house. In May 1967, they were packing up everything in the apartment to move into the charming brick home they'd bought in a quiet Alexandria neighborhood, where Chris and Corey could each have their own room.

The work schedule had not slowed down much, but this time Gwen made sure that Clint was around to help her with the move. As they were filling the cardboard moving boxes with all their belongings, Clint came across the small box that contained the gold medal he'd received after the assassination. He'd shoved it in the bottom of a desk drawer along with the citation for bravery and hadn't looked at it in more than three years. He opened the box and as he read the inscription, *For exceptional service in the Treasury Department,* his jaw clenched. He promptly shut the box. And then Clint started rummaging through drawers, flipping through files that Gwen had put away—Gwen had taken care of everything the past several years—and found a stack of photographs and papers he'd brought home from his White House office after the assassination, after Mrs. Kennedy had moved out. There were photos that Cecil Stoughton had given him—photos of him with Jackie and with the children, photos of private moments, photos that captured the happy times. Clint leafed through them as the familiar pain in his chest returned.

Clint grabbed the box containing the medal, the citation for bravery, and all the photos and handwritten notes from Jackie and stuffed everything into an empty moving box. He found a roll of packing tape and wound the tape around the box, sealing it tightly. And then more tape, around and around. When he got to the new house, he took the box into the basement and shoved it into a dark corner.

On December 1, 1967, Clint Hill was promoted to be the Special Agent in Charge of the Presidential Protective Division protecting President Johnson. After the Warren Commission report there had been a number of changes to the Secret Service—one of which was changing the name of the White House Detail to the "Presidential Protective Division." As it had turned out, Johnson and Agent Hill had become pretty good friends over the past three years. They understood each other, and Johnson grew to respect the man who had acted so valiantly in Dallas. Clint Hill had become the number-one man in charge of protecting the President of the United States.

Less than three weeks into the new position, Hill was put to the test. On December 17, 1967, Harold Holt, the prime minister of Australia, drowned in the ocean outside his weekend home. Holt had recently visited the United States and had been a guest of President Johnson's at Camp David. The president felt compelled to attend the funeral, so off they flew on Air Force One. It was quite a trip. They flew to Travis Air Force Base in California to refuel, then departed for Honolulu. From there they went to Pago Pago, and on to Canberra, finally landing in Melbourne just in time for the funeral. After the funeral President Johnson decided that since he'd already flown halfway around the world, he might as well continue and go straight around rather than return the way they'd come. There was no advance planning. Johnson's Secret Service agents were on cargo aircraft that became "strike advance teams"—they'd sometimes arrive at the next destination and be getting off their aircraft as Air Force One was touching down on the runway. The trip went to Perth, Australia; then Korat, Thailand, to visit a U.S. Air Force unit returning from a bombing raid in Vietnam; and on to Cam Ranh, Vietnam.

From there the president stopped in Karachi, Pakistan, for a brief meeting with Ayub Khan in the airport terminal, then flew on to Rome, Italy. In Rome, on short notice, President Johnson flew by helicopter from the Rome airport to Porziano villa and met with Italian president Giuseppe Saragat and Prime Minister Aldo Moro. Then it was on to the Vatican, landing in the garden—in the dark—to meet with Pope Paul VI.

Finally, on Christmas Eve, they departed Rome and flew to the Azores to refuel. Everybody suddenly realized they had no gifts for their families, so the president's Air Force aide arranged to open up the post exchange— the Air Force base general store—in the middle of the night. President Johnson was sleeping, so Clint stayed aboard Air Force One with two agents and some Air Force security people while the rest of the agents, staff, aircrew, and the press people did some last-minute Christmas shopping. Clint was wondering what he was going to do about presents for Gwen and his sons when all of a sudden, President Johnson appeared in his pajamas.

"Where is everyone?" he asked.

Clint explained and Johnson said, "Good idea. Let's go."

So Clint commandeered an Air Force car and driver and off they went—Clint and LBJ, still dressed in his pajamas, beneath a raincoat— Christmas shopping in the PX at the Azores air base on Christmas Eve.

Finally, once everybody was aboard with all their packages, Air Force One returned to Washington, D.C. The journey home took the passengers over the International Date Line once, the equator twice, and took over 112 hours. By the time Clint Hill got home on Christmas Day, all he wanted to do was sleep.

1968

From then on, things just seemed to get worse. First, Robert Kennedy announced on March 16 that he was going to seek the Democratic nomination for president. There was no love lost between Robert F. Kennedy and President Johnson. They hadn't seen eye to eye when JFK was president, and since the assassination, what little trust or respect they had for each other had completely disappeared. Two weeks later, on March 31, incumbent president Lyndon B. Johnson announced that he would neither seek nor accept the nomination of his party to be President of the United States. With the antiwar movement growing, Johnson could not wage a war while facing Robert Kennedy in the Democratic primary. President Johnson had become a virtual prisoner in the White House, unable to campaign for another term due to increasingly violent protests against the unpopular Vietnam War. The war was being run from the White House war room as Johnson and his advisors actually picked bombing targets. He became weary of the burdens of the office as the country began to tear apart at the seams while fighting a war without an end in sight and antiwar candidates pushed forward in the Democratic Party.

Then, on the evening of April 4, civil rights leader Martin Luther King, Jr., was brutally assassinated in Memphis, Tennessee. The murder rocked the nation and shook President Johnson to the core. He appeared on television later that evening and while the president urged Americans "to reject the blind violence that has struck Dr. King, who lived by nonviolence," race riots around the country started almost immediately. A memorial service was planned for the following day at Washington National Cathedral, and Lyndon Johnson had said he would attend. The night of Dr. King's assassination, Clint was at home asleep when the direct line from the White House switchboard phone rang at 2:00 A.M.

He picked up the phone and President Johnson himself was on the other end of the line.

"Clint, about tomorrow. I want my car to stop as close to the entrance door to the cathedral as possible. And I want you so close to me it's like we're stuck together with glue."

Everybody was on edge as President Johnson's motorcade drove from the White House to the National Cathedral. In the car, Johnson reiterated to Clint that he wanted Clint to remain as close to him as possible. There would be other agents all around him, too, but he trusted that Clint would do whatever was necessary to protect him.

As it turned out, everything went fine and there were no incidents. But racial tensions grew across the nation. President Johnson ordered four thousand army and National Guard troops into Washington, D.C., and thousands more into cities around the country. Fires raged in the nation's capital and at one point rioters were within two blocks of the White House. The riots were contained after several days, but clearly the nation was in turmoil.

On June 5—another assassination. Clint was at home when he got the phone call from the agent on duty at the Secret Service desk at the White House. Robert Kennedy was campaigning in Los Angeles and had just finished a speech. As he exited through the hotel kitchen, a gunman shot him at close range. Clint was both shocked and saddened by the news, but everyone knew that Bobby Kennedy had a lot of enemies. He was very popular in some circles and hated in others. Kennedy had a former FBI agent who worked with him on security and was always with him, but no Secret Service people—the Secret Service did not protect presidential candidates.

President Johnson was legitimately concerned about his safety based on the two back-to-back assassinations. The Secret Service was also very concerned, so much so that Rufus Youngblood, now the deputy director of the Secret Service, joined the detail and traveled with the presidential party to New York, where Robert Kennedy's funeral was being held at St. Patrick's Cathedral.

Clint was deeply concerned about the president's exposure as he departed from St. Patrick's, but he was also worried about his presence at the funeral and the emotional impact it would have on the Kennedy family. If he were standing next to President Johnson at the funeral, it would undoubtedly add to the family's emotional turmoil by bringing back vivid memories of 1963. So Clint asked Rufus Youngblood, whom President Johnson trusted completely, to take his place close to Johnson in the confines of St. Patrick's while Clint checked all the security posts.

After the funeral services in New York, the Kennedy family and other dignitaries accompanied Robert Kennedy's casket by funeral train to Washington, D.C., while President Johnson and his agents flew back on Air Force One. When the funeral train arrived at Union Station in Washington, Clint once again remained close to President Johnson. He stood by, silently, as President and Mrs. Johnson spoke to members of the Kennedy family—including widow Ethel, Ted, and Jacqueline.

Robert Francis Kennedy was buried at Arlington Cemetery that night, not far from where his brother had been laid to rest four and a half years earlier. That was the last time Clint Hill saw Jacqueline Kennedy.

A direct result of Robert Kennedy's assassination was that President Johnson signed a presidential directive that from then on candidates for the Office of the President would be protected by the U.S. Secret Service. Agents were selected from all the various Secret Service offices to form details. The number of agents per candidate depended on the candidate's level of activity and the intelligence information regarding threats. Every candidate was protected—even those who didn't stand a chance of winning the nomination. The Secret Service was once again stretched to the limit, and so other agencies within the Treasury Department—including the ATF, Customs, and Internal Revenue Service—had to provide agents. The new directive caused many problems for the Secret Service, not the least of which was a drop in morale. Agents were gone for extensive periods of time from their families and were often working alone or in small teams.

The Democratic National Convention was being held in Chicago that year. President Johnson was at his ranch in Texas pondering whether to attend the convention to support Hubert Humphrey in his bid for the presidency. Dissent over the Vietnam War had reached a crescendo and antiwar groups were planning protests. So Clint went to Chicago to make sure the Secret Service knew as much as possible about what was going on there. The concern was that LBJ might decide to go to Chicago on the spur of the moment, because he often operated in that manner. The Secret Service had to be prepared for such an event. The Secret Service had a large number of personnel in Chicago protecting various candidates, including Vice President Humphrey, so they were typically spread thin. Clint remained in Chicago throughout the entire convention, but in the end Johnson did not attend.

Richard M. Nixon won the election and now the Secret Service faced another change in administration. It was decided that because Clint had been with Kennedy and Johnson, it would not be a good idea for him to be the SAIC of Nixon's Secret Service detail. So Robert H. Taylor, who had been one of the agents with then vice president Nixon when he was attacked in Caracas, Venezuela, in 1958, was selected for the position, and Clint Hill accepted a lateral transfer to the Vice Presidential Division as the SAIC for Vice President–elect Spiro Agnew.

When President Johnson found out that Clint was being moved to the Vice President's Detail, he called Clint into his office.

"Clint, would you be willing to come down to the ranch and be the SAIC of my detail?"

Johnson knew that Clint enjoyed the ranch—it reminded him of his youth, growing up in a small town in North Dakota. But Clint couldn't imagine it. He and Johnson had grown to become good friends, and he certainly respected the man, but the thought of spending years, rather than weeks, out there along the Pedernales River was not at all appealing.

Clint laughed and said, "That's not exactly the career path I had planned, Mr. President."

The president kidded with him and made a few crude remarks in typical LBJ style before finally saying, "I wish you luck, Clint. I really do."

Just over a year later, on January 11, 1970, Clint Hill was promoted to deputy assistant director of protective forces and was transferred to U.S. Secret Service headquarters. For the first time in his career with the Secret Service, Clint was in a strictly administrative position. Throughout the six years since the assassination, Clint had been so busy that he'd rarely had a chance to stop and think about anything outside his protective duties. He'd been kept very active both mentally and physically. Now he was at a desk job. Suddenly he had time to think.

The Zapruder film was being used for Secret Service training and sometimes Clint was called on to comment. Watching himself over and over was like reliving the nightmare. It went by so fast on the film, but in his mind it was always in slow motion—the car just out of his reach, the pink hat moving farther and farther, and then the explosive sound of the third shot. He knew the film was helpful for the young Secret Service agents—they had to know the very real situations they might face. But my God, to watch it over and over and over. It was pure torture. The feelings of failure and guilt began bubbling up to the surface and Clint settled into a deep depression.

By 1972, Clint had been promoted again—to assistant director of protective forces. He was one step below the highest position in the United States Secret Service. He'd come a long way from the orphanage where he'd been dropped off as a newborn, and had managed to avoid a transfer to Muddy Gap, Wyoming, so far. Clint asked his old pal Paul Rundle to be his deputy and Paul was thrilled. Paul and Clint and their wives had remained close friends throughout the years and Clint truly thought of Paul as a brother. He was without a doubt someone Clint could trust.

1972

Nineteen seventy-two was an election year and part of Hill and Rundle's responsibility was to beef up the security protection during the campaign. They were back to working eighteen-hour days, seven days a week.

On May 15, 1972, Clint woke up to find his wife, Gwen, in a coma. It turned out that she'd gone into a diabetic coma due to a mix-up in the medication she was taking. She needed to stay in the hospital for the night, so Clint drove home to take care of their boys. On the way home, driving in his official government car, he heard a radio transmission over the Secret Service channel. George Wallace, the governor of Alabama and a Democratic candidate for president, had just been shot.

Oh God.

Clint made it home and called the command post. He learned that along with Wallace, one of his campaign workers, an Alabama state trooper, and Nick Zarvos—one of Wallace's Secret Service agents—had also been hit in the barrage of gunfire. Clint had to get back to the office. He found someone to watch Chris and Corey and headed back to Washington.

Wallace had survived the attack, which took place in a shopping center in Laurel, Maryland, but he was paralyzed from the waist down. Clint went to visit Wallace in the hospital and expressed his regret on behalf of the Secret Service. Wallace was receptive and gracious, and placed no blame. When Wallace departed the D.C. area and flew to Montgomery, Alabama, Clint accompanied the Secret Service detail. And almost immediately, President Nixon granted Secret Service protection to additional candidates, as well as to Senator Ted Kennedy, even though he was not a candidate for president.

It was unusual for the Secret Service to be protecting a noncandidate for president, but in light of the Kennedy history, and the current wave of violence, Hill thought, perhaps this made sense. But when he got a call from the White House with further instructions, Hill realized the true reason behind Nixon's wanting to protect Senator Kennedy.

There was a specific agent who Nixon wanted to be in charge of Kennedy's protection, an agent who happened to be extremely loyal to the Nixon camp. Hill had to assume that Nixon was trying to use the Secret Service as a spying operation. He refused to put that particular agent with Ted Kennedy. Immediately another call came in from the White House. The voice at the other end of the phone said, "Either you put that man in the job, or your job is on the line."

Hill had no option but to do as he was being ordered. The decision weighed heavily on his mind. Of course, he couldn't be certain that the reason they were offering protection for Ted Kennedy was solely for this purpose, but he needed to take the decision a step further.

He went straight to Jim Burke in the Office of Investigations. The Office of Investigations is the real backbone of the Secret Service and is where the majority of manpower in the service is located. Generally speaking, it is the place where you enter the service and the place from which you retire. All the U.S. Secret Service offices throughout the world answer to the Office of Investigations and Jim Burke was the deputy assistant director. Clint knew Burke would take his concerns seriously.

"Let's take care of this right now," Burke said.

Burke called the agent and told him to report to his office immediately.

In no uncertain terms Burke and Hill told the agent they were aware of his relationship with the Nixon administration, yet he was still being assigned to protect Ted Kennedy. The Secret Service does not have political loyalties. However, if any information regarding any of Kennedy's activities were passed on in any way to the Nixon administration, the agent would be held completely responsible and would be dealt with accordingly.

The agent went on to protect Ted Kennedy, and fortunately no problems developed.

JUNE 17, 1972

From the time he started the desk job in 1970, Clint Hill had fallen into a downward spiral. The nightmares had returned and were more frequent and the only thing that eased the pain was his nightly scotch and soda. One turned into two, and sometimes two turned into three . . .

On this particular night, he was on round two when he got a call from the Intelligence Division. There'd been a burglary at Democratic National Headquarters at the Watergate Hotel. Several men were arrested and one of them had some identification on him that showed an affiliation with the White House and the Nixon reelection committee. Clint didn't recognize the name, but he said he'd make some calls and find out the story.

Oh, for God's sake. We can't save these politicians from themselves, Clint thought as he downed his drink.

He called Deputy Director Pat Boggs, who had a close relationship with the Nixon staff.

"Pat, this is Clint. Do you know somebody on the Committee to Re-elect named McCord?"

"Yes, of course. James McCord. He's the security director for the committee. Former CIA and FBI. Now runs his own private security firm."

Oh my God.

From that point on Watergate became a real problem for the Secret Service—from the securing of documents in the Old Executive Office Building to the revelation of the tapes in President Nixon's office.

By October 1973, the house of cards began to fall, and on October 10,

1973, Vice President Spiro Agnew resigned. He pled guilty to failure to report income received—but had been charged with extortion, tax fraud, bribery, and conspiracy. Hill had worked with Agnew for over a year as his Special Agent in Charge and was saddened by the outcome. The worst part about it, though, was how it affected Agnew's wife, Judy.

Judy Agnew was a lovely lady whom all the agents adored, and Clint had become good friends with her. When she called him in tears and asked, "Clint, what's going on?" it broke his heart. She had no inkling of what had happened, and Clint tried to explain what had brought about the vice president's legal problems.

That same month, Secret Service director James J. Rowley was retiring after a long and distinguished career. Clint Hill was one of those called in to interview for the job. In his mind, there could be no bigger honor—to be the director of the Secret Service would mean he'd reached the pinnacle. Apparently he'd been able to keep up a strong façade: for what nobody knew was how the dark abyss of depression had taken over his soul.

When he walked into the deputy secretary of the Treasury's office for the interview, he could hardly believe the words were coming out of his mouth.

"Please take my name off the list," he said. "I'm not physically or emotionally capable to be considered for the position."

The assistant secretary nodded and said he understood. H. Stuart Knight was named the director that month.

On December 6, 1973, Gerald R. Ford was sworn in as vice president.

On August 9, 1974, President Richard M. Nixon resigned, and Gerald Ford was sworn in as the thirty-eighth President of the United States.

In fifteen years, Clint Hill had witnessed four presidential transitions, one resignation, one attempted assassination, two assassinations of high-profile leaders, and the assassination of a president. And through it all, he'd been worthy of trust and confidence. It was a lot for one man to hold inside.

24

Clint Hill: Don't Call Me Hero

A man does what he must . . . in spite of personal consequences, in spite of obstacles and dangers, and pressures . . . and that is the basis of all human morality.
—JOHN F. KENNEDY

Clint Hill's health was rapidly deteriorating. He'd been having stomach problems for years, and when it finally started impacting his work, he went to a gastroenterologist. The doctor ran a bunch of tests, and then told him he really needed to see a neurologist. He had every test imaginable from top to bottom. His nerves were shot and soon he was really struggling to cope with the day-to-day activities. Thank God he'd named Paul Rundle as his deputy.

Rundle had never forgotten how Clint looked the morning of November 23, 1963, when he'd shown up at the White House with Jackie and the president's casket at four in the morning. Rundle had asked Clint then what he could do to help. At the time, Rundle had felt helpless. Finally, all these years later, he'd found a way to offer support to his oldest friend. Basically, Paul Rundle was quietly filling in the gaps during the times that Clint was incapable.

In March 1975, Clint went to Bethesda Naval Hospital for his annual physical. In the same hospital where he'd spent those interminable hours, where he'd had to examine the shattered skull of Mrs. Kennedy's husband, Clint Hill learned that he was in worse shape than he'd imagined.

Navy Captain M. William Voss was a physician who'd been a member of the White House physician's office, and had known Clint for many years. Regret was written all over his face as he showed Clint the results of the physical. At the very end of the report the doctor had written, "Not qualified for continued duty as a Secret Service Agent."

Clint was stunned. How could things have gotten that bad? What was he going to do now? He was just forty-three years old.

Clint sought legal advice to determine his options and learned that, based on the results of his recent physical exam, his medical history, and his Secret Service employment history, he could apply for retirement. It was a tough decision, but Clint felt as if he had no choice, and he advised Director Knight of his intentions. A board of physicians and government officials studied Clint's case and concluded that he should be retired. On July 25, 1975, the board issued an order: as assistant director in the United States Secret Service, having been found physically incapacitated for further duty, Clinton J. Hill is retired effective July 31, 1975.

Clint Hill packed the personal things he had in his office, said goodbye to his longtime administrative assistant, Eileen Walsh, and was driven to his home in Alexandria by two Special Agents. His life in the Secret Service was over.

Now, with nothing to get up for in the morning, all Clint could do was think about the past. If he continued like this, he knew he would go insane. He had the rest of his life ahead of him and he had to find a way to pull himself together. On August 12, the direct phone lines to the White House were removed from his home in Alexandria. And that's when it hit him hard. He had to get out of here. The only place he could think to go was back to his roots.

Two days later he flew to North Dakota, where his sister Janice lived on a farm with her husband. Their mother had passed away the year before and had left some acreage for Clint and Janice, adjacent to her and her husband's farm. And so he went to work. The land had been left unplanted, so Clint would get up at sunrise and head into the field alone, and for the next twelve hours he'd pick rocks off the summer fallow, preparing the land for seeding. It was hard labor and every muscle in his body ached, but when he was in the field, it was as if he were sweating out twelve years of pent-up feelings he'd buried deep inside, feelings he'd stuffed into a corner of his soul, like the photographs and memories he'd packed away in the box in the basement.

He'd come back to the house at sunset, caked with dirt and sweat, covered in the dust of the land, nearly unrecognizable. Janice would laugh hysterically every day when he walked through the door.

"The only way I know it's you is by the whites of your eyes," she'd say.

This went on for a few weeks, until it was time for the harvest. His brother-in-law didn't trust him with his expensive combine, so Clint ran the swather that cut the wheat into neat rows, and drove truckloads of grain to the grain elevator. Even as he was struggling to deal with the anger and guilt and frustration he'd locked away for so long, it felt good to work the land, to be with his sister, to be far away from Washington and politicians. There was a sense of accomplishment at the end of each day. But Clint knew he couldn't hide out forever. Sooner or later he was going to have to find a way to deal with the past that continued to haunt him.

The afternoon of September 5, when Clint returned to Janice's house after working in the fields all day as usual, his sister greeted him with a concerned look on her face.

"Clint, you better come in here. There was just a report on television that somebody tried to assassinate President Ford."

Clint shook his head and walked rapidly into the living room toward the television. Even out here in the plains of North Dakota, he couldn't escape.

The details were limited. Clint couldn't stand not knowing what had happened, so he called Gwen to see what she knew about the situation. For the first time, Gwen had more information than Clint.

A twenty-seven-year-old woman who was a follower of convicted murderer Charles Manson had tried to assassinate President Ford with a .45-caliber automatic as he shook hands with spectators near the state capitol in Sacramento, California. Secret Service agent Larry Buendorf had seen the gun and quickly threw the woman to the ground before the pistol could fire, while the other agents rushed President Ford into the capitol. Fortunately he was uninjured.

Hearing the still sketchy details from Gwen made Clint painfully aware that he was now on the outside. He was no longer in the middle of the activity, no longer able to make a phone call and get immediate information from the inside.

Gwen had some other news to share with Clint, too. The Secret Service was having a conference at the end of the month, and agents were coming from all the field offices. Additionally, they were planning a retirement party and Clint was to be the honoree. It was just the push he needed, so he made arrangements and returned home to Washington on September 19.

He'd been home three days, and then there was another assassination attempt on President Ford—also by a woman, also in California. As President Ford exited the St. Francis Hotel in San Francisco, a matronly woman named Sara Jane Moore fired a revolver at the president from forty feet. Just as the shot went off, a bystander managed to grab Moore's arm and the shot missed. Secret Service agents flung the president into the waiting limousine and raced away from the scene.

Again Clint felt himself yearning to be a part of the activity. It was in his blood. The only thing he knew was protection. What in God's name was he going to do with the rest of his life?

In truth, the two assassination attempts did not surprise Clint at all. He'd been in the business of protecting presidents long enough to know it was only a matter of time. No matter who was president, there would always be assassination attempts. Fortunately, in both these cases the attempts were unsuccessful.

Clint's retirement party was three days after the second attempt on President Ford's life. Clint had no idea what to expect—and wasn't even sure he wanted to go—but Paul Rundle and his wife, Peggy, picked up him and Gwen and headed downtown to the Washington Hilton hotel.

When Clint walked into the ballroom of the hotel, he was stunned. There had to be at least two hundred people there. Secret Service personnel from headquarters, protective details, and those who had come in from all over the country for the conference were there, and the rest of the guests read like a *Who's Who* of Washington.

Seventy-nine-year-old former first lady Mamie Eisenhower had driven down from her Gettysburg home with her Secret Service detail especially for the party. She spent some personal time with Clint and the other agents who had been in the Denver office watching over her mother al-most twenty years earlier. There was Hubert Humphrey, former vice pres-ident Spiro Agnew and his wife, Judy, and even Senator Ted Kennedy and Ethel Kennedy. Paul Landis, who had ridden on the other side of the follow-up car in Dallas and had resigned shortly after the assassination, had flown in from Cleveland with his wife. Clint was astonished and hum-bled. He couldn't believe that so many people had made the effort to come to a party in his honor. It was as if he were surrounded by everybody who had been a part of the last sixteen years of his life.

The only person missing was Mrs. Kennedy.

Not long after the retirement party, Clint got a call from Paul Loewen-warter, a producer for the CBS television newsmagazine *60 Minutes*. Loewenwarter wondered if Clint would consider coming on the program to talk about his life in the Secret Service. The call took Clint completely by surprise. With the recent assassination attempts, he knew that the sub-ject of Kennedy's assassination would undoubtedly come up, but twelve years had passed, and Clint was sure he could handle any question asked.

On October 8, Clint and Gwen met reporter Mike Wallace, Paul Loew-enwarter, and a bunch of the staff from *60 Minutes*, and the show was discussed in broad terms. It would be a taped interview—Gwen was wel-come to be there, too—and the focus would be on Clint's career in the Se-cret Service, which spanned five presidents over sixteen years. President Kennedy's assassination was barely mentioned, and by the time the meet-ing was over, both Clint and Gwen were looking forward to the interview. It sounded like fun.

On Sunday, October 12, Clint and Gwen drove to the Madison Hotel in Washington for the taping.

Before the interview began, Gwen pulled Mike Wallace aside.

"Mike," she said, "I know it's not apparent on the outside, but I just wanted you to know that Clint is emotionally fragile. Please take it easy on him. He's had a rough time recently."

Clint and Gwen sat together on a sofa, with Wallace to their left in a wingback chair. Clint lit up a cigarette as the taping began, and the inter-view started off just fine. Wallace made him feel completely at ease. There were questions about his background—why and when he entered the Secret Service—followed by a few questions about the recent assassination attempts on President Ford. Gwen's words must have had an impact on Wallace, because when he came around to asking about the Kennedy assassination, he merely glossed over it, and moved straight into how Clint wound up becoming the Special Agent in Charge of President Johnson's detail.

When the interview was finished, Clint breathed a sigh of relief and thanked Wallace and the rest of the crew. It had gone very well and Mike promised to call Clint to let him know when the story would air.

A few days later Clint was sitting at home when the phone rang.

"Hills," Clint answered.

"Hi, Clint, it's Mike Wallace."

"Hey, Mike. How are you?" Clint assumed Mike was calling to tell him when the interview would be airing.

"Well, I'm fine, Clint," Wallace began. "But it seems we've had a slight problem."

Wallace explained that when they went back and reviewed the tapes there were some technical problems and they needed to reshoot some portions of the interview. He wanted to set up a date—again at the Madison Hotel. Wallace would treat them to lunch beforehand. Clint didn't think anything of it, and readily agreed. Before Wallace hung up the phone he added, "Oh, and one last thing. Please be sure you and Gwen both wear the same clothes as you did for the first interview, as we'll be editing the two tapes together."

So when the day came, once again Clint put on his light gray plaid suit, a white shirt, and his rust-colored tie, while Gwen wore the powder blue two-piece pantsuit with the floral print blouse. At noon, they walked into the restaurant at the Madison Hotel and were surprised to see not only Mike Wallace and Paul Loewenwarter already seated at the table, but also *60 Minutes* executive producer Don Hewitt.

The menu featured steak tartare, which was one of Clint's favorite dishes. Mike Wallace ordered before Clint, and when he ordered the steak tartare, Clint laughed and said, "Well, that's exactly what I was going to have." The waiter told them it was a very large portion—enough to serve two people. So Wallace said, "Well, why don't we split it, then."

The conversation was casual and comfortable as the men from *60 Minutes* explained how the taping would work, while Clint and Mike Wallace shared their meal of raw beef and minced onions. They finished lunch and moved into the small banquet room, where the lights and equipment had already been set up.

When they walked into the same room where they'd done the first taping, everything looked exactly the same, with the exception that this time, Don Hewitt was there. Clint made a joke about how it felt like déjà vu, and they took their places—Clint and Gwen on the sofa, with Mike Wallace to the left in the wingback chair.

Once again Clint lit up a cigarette as the cameras started taping.

Wallace eased in with a few questions, similar to what he'd asked in the first interview and then, out of the blue, he said, "Can I take you back to November 22, 1963." It wasn't a question. It was a statement. Mike Wallace was about to take him back to that dreadful day in Dallas.

Gwen could sense Clint suddenly stiffen, and her heart started racing.

Oh no, she thought.

Clint took a deep breath and closed his eyes.

Without waiting for Clint to respond, Wallace continued, his voice coming out like rapid fire. "You were on the fender of the Secret Service car, right behind President Kennedy's car."

Clint turned his gaze down at his knees, unable to look at Wallace. His eyebrows shuddered as a pained expression washed over his face. The cameraman zoomed in for a close-up as Wallace's words hit Clint like a round from a machine gun.

"At the first shot you ran forward and jumped on the back of the president's car. In less than two seconds . . . pulling Mrs. Kennedy down into her seat, protecting her."

Clint reached for his cigarette and took a long drag. He blew out the smoke, and as he stared into nothingness, Wallace continued.

"First of all, she was out of the trunk of that car," Wallace stated.

Clint suddenly interrupted. "She was out of the backseat of that car, not out of the trunk of that car." His head was trembling and his eyes, his eyes had gone numb.

He still wouldn't—couldn't—look at Wallace or at the camera. His mind was back in Dallas, reliving those endless seconds.

Wallace attempted to clarify. "Well, she had climbed out of the back and she was on the way back, right?"

Still looking down, Clint nodded. His face had contorted into a pained expression, his brow furrowed, his cheeks taut.

Clint, visibly tormented, said, "And because of the fact that her husband's—part of her husband's head . . ." He paused, and his face winced into a painful grimace. ". . . had been . . . shot off . . . and had gone off into the street."

Incredulous, Wallace asked, "She wasn't trying to climb out of the car?"

Clint was shaking his head, still looking at the floor, his eyes reddening as the memory flashed like a vivid movie in his mind.

"She was simply trying to reach that head . . . part of that head."

The look on Clint's face was gut-wrenching. Gwen sat frozen. Her heart broke for Clint.

"To bring it back?" Wallace asked.

"That's the only thing," Clint said. His head dropped as he winced. Torment was written all over his face, as the emotions he'd suppressed for all these years came flooding out, in one sudden tidal wave. It was so poignant, so visceral, that Wallace himself had begun to tear up.

"Clint," Wallace said. "Let's take a break. Stop the cameras."

Clint stood up and took a deep breath. He didn't know what had come over him. He had to get control of himself.

He walked out into the hallway, away from the bright lights and the cameras, as Gwen followed behind. She didn't know what to say. She had never talked to Clint about the assassination. They had never discussed it. She had no idea he would react like this.

Wallace came into the hallway and offered some words of empathy. He knew how difficult this had to be for Clint, to talk about the tragedy in front of the cameras.

"It's not that," Clint said. Tears streamed down his face as he desperately tried to hold them inside. "I've never spoken about this to anyone. Not anyone. Not Gwen, not the other agents. You're the first person I've ever spoken about this to."

Wallace appeared shocked. It had been twelve years and Clint had never talked about the assassination with anyone? He'd been holding this inside for twelve tormented years? It was heartbreaking.

They talked for several minutes and finally Clint said, "Okay. Let's go back in and finish this."

"Are you sure you're ready?" Wallace asked.

Clint nodded.

They walked back into the room, took their places, and began again. Wallace eased into the questioning. He repeated some of the questions he'd asked before, asked them in a different way, and then went in a different direction.

"In the twelve years since that assassination, undoubtedly you have thought and thought and thought again about it. And studied it. Do you have any reason to believe that there was more than one gun, more than one assassin?"

Clint's head shook gently, his face contorted with pain, as Wallace continued: "Was Lee Harvey Oswald alone, or were there others with him?"

"There were only three shots." Clint shrugged. "And it was one gun. Three shots."

"You're satisfied Lee Harvey Oswald acted alone," Wallace confirmed.

Finally Clint looked directly at Wallace, and with one hundred percent conviction, he said, "Completely."

"You're satisfied," Wallace repeated, and then added, "Was there any way, anything the Secret Service or that Clint Hill could have done . . . to keep that from happening?"

The cameraman pulled the shot back, wider. The smoke from Clint's cigarette swirled around him.

Clint slumped back into the sofa and closed his eyes. What could he have done? Was there anything he could have done? It was a question he'd asked himself a million times. But he'd never answered it out loud. And as the words came out of his mouth there was a look of sheer torture on his face.

"Clint Hill . . . yes."

"Clint Hill, yes?" Mike Wallace asked. "What do you mean?"

Clint lifted his head and looked Mike Wallace straight in the eye. "If he had reacted about five-tenths of a second faster, or maybe a second faster . . . I wouldn't be here today."

"You mean you would have gotten there and you would have taken the shot?"

"The third shot. Yes, sir," Clint said, still looking at Mike to make sure there was no confusion about what he was saying.

"And that would have been all right with you?" Mike asked.

Clint shook his head, remorsefully. Tears welled in his eyes. "That would have been fine with me."

Wallace couldn't help but see that the man sitting in front of him was about to break down completely. "But you couldn't, you got there in less than two seconds, Clint. You couldn't have gotten there. You don't—surely you don't—have a sense of guilt about that?"

"Yes, I certainly do," Clint said. The sheer anguish of the moment transferred from him through the camera as he acknowledged out loud, for the first time, what he'd been holding in for twelve torturous years. "I have a great deal of guilt about that."

Mike Wallace was suddenly silenced by the broken man in front of him.

"Had I turned in a different direction, I'd have made it," Clint said. "It was my fault."

As Clint crumbled, emotionally defeated, Mike Wallace attempted to rescue him.

"No . . . No one has ever suggested that for an instant," Wallace said. "What you did was show great bravery and great presence of mind. . . . What was on the citation that was given you?"

The cameraman zoomed in close—Clint's pain spread out for the whole world to see, as Wallace tried to save him. "For your work on November twenty-second, nineteen sixty-three . . ."

Clint's face had completely transformed into the image of what could be described only as pure anguish. "I don't care about that, Mike . . ."

"Extraordinary courage and heroic effort in the face of maximum danger," Wallace rattled off as Clint violently shook his head.

"Mike, I don't *care* about that." He winced and Wallace let him continue. "If I had reacted just a little bit quicker . . . and I could have, I guess."

Clint let out a deep breath and in one last wrenching contortion of his face, he said, "And I'll live with that to my grave."

Finally, the questions stopped. The cameraman stopped recording. Gwen reached over and hugged her husband. She was so relieved it was over. It was heartbreaking to see Clint in such agony.

"Thank you, Clint," Mike Wallace said as he stood up and unclipped the microphone from his lapel. "I know that was so difficult for you. But thank you so much."

Gwen walked over to Don Hewitt and thanked him. It had been terribly rough on Clint, but she felt that Mike Wallace had handled the interview with compassion.

Clint stood up and steadied himself. He felt sick inside. He didn't know what had come over him. He shook hands with Mike Wallace and Don Hewitt, but he felt as if he were in a fog. He just wanted to go home.

Before they left, Gwen mentioned to Don Hewitt that she admired his sport coat. It was a caramel-colored ultrasuede jacket. Hewitt said it was one of his favorites, too—from Saks in New York.

Clint and Gwen drove home in silence and as soon as they walked in the door, Clint poured himself a strong scotch and soda. He had suppressed the memories for twelve long years and Mike Wallace had forced him to face his demons. He needed a drink.

Several days later, a package appeared on the Hills' doorstep. A box from Saks. Inside was the women's version of Hewitt's ultrasuede jacket with a note from Hewitt for Gwen. She couldn't believe it. Clint agreed it was a nice gesture and when Gwen said that now she just needed to buy the matching skirt, Clint rolled his eyes and agreed to take her to Saks.

On Wednesday, December 3, Mike Wallace called Clint and told him that his story was going to be airing that week, that Sunday evening.

"Well, we'll be sure to watch it," Clint said.

They called the story "Secret Service Agent Number Nine" and it was one of the most-watched episodes of *60 Minutes* ever. As Clint watched himself, as he saw his literal nervous breakdown on television, he gulped down a big ol' scotch and soda. When the show was over, the phone started ringing immediately and didn't stop for a week. His sister Janice called—she was so worried. After what she'd seen on the farm, and now this. She urged Clint to get help.

Paul Landis called, and Jerry Blaine and Paul Rundle. They stopped by the house. They needed to make sure he was okay. They were worried about him.

At CBS, the interview with Agent Number Nine had sparked a response in viewers the likes of which they'd never seen before. Letters came flooding in. Mike Wallace called Clint a week after the interview to see how he was doing. Even he was worried about him.

I'll be okay, Clint said. *I'll be okay.*

In the days that followed, his enjoyable scotch and soda became a necessity. Soon, after a few scotches, he'd start in with a sweet Rob Roy on the rocks. He didn't go outside, didn't want to see anyone. Day after day he lay curled up on the couch, drinking and smoking, and reliving those few seconds in Dallas, the torturous hour at Parkland Hospital, the long plane ride back to Washington, the funeral, and then back to the motorcade, and the shots, and the race to Parkland. Day after day, week after week, smoking and drinking, and thinking.

Finally Gwen convinced him to get help. The answer was Valium and later Elavil—neither of which, it turned out, mix well with alcohol. For the next seven years—*seven years*—Clint lived in the prison of his memories, barely surviving as he tried to dull the constant, searing pain with pills and booze.

In 1982, his doctor confronted him. "You're addicted to alcohol, Clint. You're killing yourself. If you don't stop drinking you will die."

The stark realization of what he'd allowed himself to become was shattering. He'd grown up in a home where neither alcohol nor tobacco was allowed, and look where he'd wound up. He was beyond disappointed in himself. He had reached the bottom.

It was not easy, but slowly Clint gave up drinking. Once he became sober, he tackled the cigarettes. He quit cold turkey and almost tore the pocket off his shirt reaching for what was not there.

Slowly, slowly, things started to get better. The nightmares became fewer and fewer. He began to exercise again. He started socializing.

In 1990, the Association of Former Agents of the United States Secret Service was holding its eighteenth annual conference in San Antonio, Texas. The organization, founded in 1971, had been Floyd Boring's idea.

After his retirement in 1967, Boring realized how much he missed the unique comradeship of the agents, and he envisioned a group with membership exclusive to former Secret Service agents and their wives. It would be a safe haven that would provide support and a place where memories could be shared in complete confidence. It was heartily approved by then director of the Secret Service Jim Rowley. Rowley provided Floyd with names and addresses for some of the agents who had recently retired or resigned in good standing. Eve Dempsher offered to help with the group's paperwork, and prospective members were sent invitations to become charter members. Jerry Blaine and former SAIC Jerry Behn were among the twenty charter members of AFAUSSS. Later the organization became open to Secret Service agents who had completed at least one full year of service and by 1990, membership had grown to over five hundred members.

During the summer of 1990, Clint and Gwen decided to attend the conference with Gwen's sister Gloria and her husband, Dave Grant, who had also retired from the Secret Service by this time. They would fly to Dallas, rent a car, and drive to San Antonio. On the way back they'd stay overnight in Dallas, where Gloria still had friends from her Braniff Airways days.

Besides wanting to see his old pals from the Secret Service at the conference, Clint had another intention, which he hadn't shared with anyone. He was ready to return to Dealey Plaza.

When Clint, Gwen, Dave, and Gloria were checking into the Marriott hotel adjacent to the River Walk in San Antonio, familiar faces began to appear. People Clint had not seen in fifteen years; people with whom he had served in good times and bad. Everybody was shocked to see him there. They'd all seen his appearance on *60 Minutes* and were aware that he had been going through an emotional deterioration since that time. The warm welcome they gave him, however, made Clint know that this was the right thing to do. He was back where he belonged—among friends, among family. Because that's what this was. It was more than a conference—it was a family reunion—the Secret Service family.

That evening, Clint and Gwen joined a large group for some of the Tex-Mex food for which San Antonio is so well-known. They were seated around a large table and as the waitress came around everybody ordered drinks to go with the nachos and tacos. Most were ordering beers or margaritas and when it came to Clint's turn, you could have heard a pin drop.

"I'll have iced tea," he said. Everybody breathed a sigh of relief and from then on, it was a fun evening filled with levity, remembrances, and true friendship.

Various activities were planned for the attendees and while some played golf, Clint and Gwen opted for a bus trip through the Texas hill country to the LBJ Ranch near Stonewall, for a tour of the Johnson home, which was now open to the public. On arrival at the ranch, they were met by Jim Hardin, the SAIC of Lady Bird Johnson's protective detail, a long-time friend and former coworker of Clint's. Another remembrance of times gone by, both good and bad.

The weekend seemed to fly by because of the wonderful camaraderie both Clint and Gwen enjoyed. Among the familiar faces were Art and Betty Godfrey; Joyce and Jerry Blaine; Paul and Peggy Rundle; Win and Barb Lawson; Walt and Ann Coughlin; Bob and Peggy Foster; Tom and Shirley Wells; Ham Brown—the list went on and on.

When the conference was over and all the hugs and handshakes had concluded, Clint got into the driver's seat with Gwen, Gloria, and Dave in the car, and drove to Dallas.

The year before, on Presidents Day in 1989, a nonprofit museum had opened at the site of the assassination. It was on the sixth floor of what used to be the Texas School Book Depository but was now the Dallas County Administration Building. The exhibits told what had happened starting with the early 1960s and the Kennedy presidency and continuing through the assassination and investigations. No theories, just history, with a lot of pictures, text, and videos.

Clint parked the car in the parking lot behind the brick building, and the four of them walked around to the front. As Clint stood at the intersection of Houston and Elm streets, the memories came flooding back, as he knew they would. But he was stronger now; he was ready to face them.

It was eerie to be back here after all these years, and Clint was struck by how little had changed. A few tall skyscrapers had gone up in the downtown area of Dallas, but here in Dealey Plaza, it looked almost exactly as it had in 1963. The only visible difference was that the trees had matured, and grown taller.

For nearly two hours, Clint walked around the area and went over the sight lines, the angles. He ignored the man on the corner hawking a brochure that claimed to tell the "real story" of the assassination—the conspiracy theories—complete with photos and analysis by "experts."

Back and forth he paced on the street, looking up toward the grassy knoll and back to the brick building. He walked back to Main Street and turned around, and as he turned the corner from Main onto Houston Street, following the same path he'd ridden nearly twenty-seven years earlier, he could hear the crowds, the motorcycles. There was so much noise.

And then he turned left onto Elm Street and passed in front of the brick building, and as he walked down the hill, as the road curved, in his mind he heard an explosive sound.

He was ready to go into the museum. His stomach was in knots. Gwen held his hand as they took the elevator to the sixth floor. There was no turning back.

As he walked through the exhibits, he was struck by how many pictures and references to him there were. There he was, frame by frame in still photos on the wall, racing toward the president's limousine. He looked so young. His chest tightened as he walked toward the lair that Oswald had built of book boxes—reconstructed as it had been found the day of the assassination. Clint looked out the window and saw the clear view to the street, saw how close it was. He shook his head. He was an expert marksman, and even without a scope could hit anything he wanted on the street below. It would have been easy—especially when the trees had been so much shorter. For Lee Harvey Oswald, having had military training in the use of firearms, and with the assistance of a scope, hitting the target would not have been difficult at all.

After walking the streets below and now seeing the clear view that Oswald had, Clint realized that even if he had been on the back of the president's limousine, Oswald could have hit the president as the car approached the intersection of Houston and Elm. The assassin had all the advantages that day. The Secret Service had none. But even knowing all this, the gnawing in the gut, the visual memory of the explosion of the president's head, the knowledge that he and the other agents had been responsible for President Kennedy's safety, still lingered. And he knew now, it would never go away. But at least he had reconciled with himself that he'd done the best he could.

As Clint neared the end of the exhibit, there was a guest book. He opened it and looked at all the people who had signed their names—they'd come from all over the world. He reached for the pen and wrote down a name. But it wasn't his name. He didn't want anybody to know he had been there.

EPILOGUE

By Gerald Blaine

We would like to live as we once lived, but history will not permit it.

—JOHN F. KENNEDY

ALEXANDRIA, VIRGINIA
2009

One day, after a particularly long and jovial phone conversation, Clint Hill hung up the phone and realized there was something he needed to do. He went down into the basement of his home in Alexandria—the same home where he and Gwen have lived for more than forty years—and searched through the dozens of boxes and piles of stuff that one accumulates over a lifetime, and back in the corner he found a box covered in tape. He hauled the box upstairs and set it on the kitchen table. He tried to rip apart the tape, but it had become almost like cement after all these years. He would need a pair of scissors.

His hands trembled ever so slightly as he cut through the tape and opened the flaps at the top of the box. Inside were the memories he'd packed away that day so long ago. There were stacks of papers and handwritten notes between him and Mrs. Kennedy, a citation from the Department of the Treasury, a small box, and a handful of eight-by-ten black-and-white glossy photos.

There was a photo from Italy—when he thought they were going to capsize in a rowboat as the paparazzi were standing nearby. He flipped through the photos as the memories came rushing back. There she was leaving the hospital, after John was born. There was the one of him in a tuxedo, grinning, walking just behind her, and she's turned her head toward him with a smile as if she'd just made a funny remark and wanted to get his reaction. She'd written on the photo in pen:

Mr. Hill—

Are you happy in your work? JBK

Clint chuckled as tears welled in his eyes. He could hear her voice, see her smile. They sure had had some fun times. But she was gone now, too.

He spent some time going through the notes, the cards—all the mementoes he'd saved. There were so many memories. It seemed like another lifetime. It was as if he had lived two lives—the one before the assassination, and the one after. Finally, after nearly fifty years, the nightmares had almost gone away, and he realized that he was laughing more these days. He too had begun calling his old Secret Service pals more often, and it felt great to be back in touch. It had been a long journey. He put everything back into the box. The last thing to go in was the picture of Mrs. Kennedy laughing, sitting in the boat. And as he looked at the picture, he thought to himself, *I'm okay, Mrs. Kennedy. I'm okay.*

As I type this story into my computer, my seventy-eight-year-old hands often having trouble finding the right keys, I realize that even though my time on the Kennedy Detail was but three years, those years had a dramatic influence on the course of my life. The writing of this book has not been an easy task. It brought about many emotions that I had suppressed for decades, including the anger at the character assassination and defamation of outstanding men who were ready to sacrifice their lives to protect the president; anger at the bogus claims of conspiracies involving members of the Secret Service—all of whom loved John F. Kennedy; and finally, frustration that so many books have been published with blatant disregard of fact, distorting history to the point of mockery.

Every agent who has ever served on the White House Detail knows that security relies on detailed planning, constant study of current events, understanding the makeup and mind of a potential assassin, teamwork, physical fitness, mental alertness, intelligence, and a lot of hard work. The safety of the president also depends on other factors.

For nearly one hundred and seventy-five years, Congress ignored the safety of the president. The subject was only ever debated after an assassination or an attempted assassination. It was in 1950, after the attempt on Harry Truman's life, that Congress officially recognized the Secret Service and provided additional manpower. That manpower stayed the same until the assassination of President Kennedy. In fact, it was not even a federal crime to murder the president, though it was a federal crime to kill one of his agents.

When a new president is elected, the presidential staff marches into the White House newly victorious, eager to make their mark on history and to better their own futures. They realize that if they are to succeed, their president must be successful. Success means getting reelected. To do this, overzealous staff overbook the president with constant travel and public appearances, much of it unnecessary, in order to ensure he has as much people exposure as possible. They soon realize they can throw the responsibility on the Secret Service, and if things go wrong, the Secret Service will take the hit.

The most important partner in protection is the president himself. I do not know all the ins and outs of how the Secret Service operates today, but I do know that the president can still override the Secret Service. The president is not legally bound to follow the directives of the Secret Service. The SAIC of the detail can recommend and advise, but if the president has his own agenda and is willing to take the risk, then he can countermand the recommendation. The Secret Service must then establish a security strategy to cover the president's decision.

Every agent also realizes that protection is not guaranteed. If a dedicated individual or group of individuals is intent on assassinating the president, has acquired the right weapon, and is not concerned with losing their own lives, the chances are they might succeed. When they strike, it is sudden and time is on their side regardless of counterassault teams or countersniper teams. If the hit is successful, these teams are irrelevant.

When protecting the president, there is something I call a "confidence factor." The confidence factor is the probability of success, which is dependent on how closely the president and the Secret Service work together, combined with the personality of the president.

President Eisenhower did not have a narcissistic bone in his body. He was a career military man and grew up with armed men around him. When he achieved commanding rank he had protection. He was elected after doing minimal campaigning compared to today's standards. He did not necessarily like crowds and did not feel that he had to run over and shake every person's hand. He rode in a closed-top car and did not like parade-type motorcades. He did not have an overarching mission besides bringing the nation back from World War II. He was noncontroversial. He went out of office with a 60 percent approval rating from the American people. Protecting Ike worked like clockwork. He was not warm and fuzzy with the agents, but he had confidence in his agents' ability and he understood unnecessary exposure. The confidence factor for protecting President Eisenhower was 95 percent. There was always the outside chance that someone would get lucky.

With President John F. Kennedy, a man whom all the agents admired and who took the time to know each agent's name and background, it was a different story. He loved motorcades in an open car. He loved to run over and shake people's hands. He was charismatic, had a beautiful wife and family, and ran on an accelerated agenda that included civil rights, which was a highly volatile issue at the time. He inherited the Cold War and was tested. He also failed in not supporting an exile invasion of Cuba. As a result, Kennedy was controversial. His political style for overcoming this was visible exposure and his personable attributes. The confidence factor with President Kennedy was 70 percent. Totally unacceptable.

Somehow, the election of 2008 reminded me, more than any other in the last four decades, of the year Kennedy changed America. President Barack Obama has entered the presidency in much the same vein as John F. Kennedy—young, charismatic, and desperate to convince the half of America that didn't vote for him that he is worthy—utilizing similar tactics as Kennedy did to build his political base.

I have no idea what the confidence factor is today, but what I do know is that the tools of the assassin are far more sophisticated. Sniper rifles can strike a person's head from over a mile away with accuracy. Missiles, radioactive materials, biological weapons, chemicals, explosive devices, and the dreaded nuclear weapon are available. The sophisticated unmanned aerial drones are becoming even more sophisticated and more readily available.

No longer is the norm a single assassin acting alone. Anwar Sadat was assassinated by an offshoot of the Muslim Brotherhood in 1981, and three years later the prime minister of India, Indira Gandhi, was assassinated by two of her own bodyguards. These were wake-up calls to the world that fanatical people could group together and conspire, which resulted in a complete reevaluation of protection methods.

In 1963 the Secret Service had an operating budget of about $4.1 million, three hundred agents nationwide, and forty agents protecting the president and his family around the clock. The White House Detail was small and extremely dedicated, but stretched to the limit. Prior to President Kennedy's assassination, Chief James J. Rowley had appeared repeatedly before Congress to request an increase in funding. Each time, because of partisan politics, it was denied.

The Secret Service is no longer under the auspices of the Treasury Department, but is now part of the sprawling Department of Homeland Security. Today, in 2010, the Secret Service has around four thousand agents plus technical specialists, uniformed personnel, sophisticated tools, armored cars, a dedicated training center, and a budget that will undoubtedly pass 2009's budget of $1.6 billion. Along with increases in resources and budget, however, have come drastically increased responsibilities. Besides providing protection for the president, the vice president, the president-elect, vice president–elect, and their immediate families, the Secret Service is responsible for protecting former presidents and their spouses; children of former presidents until age sixteen; visiting heads of foreign states or governments and their spouses; other distinguished foreign visitors to the United States; official representatives of the United States performing special missions abroad; major presidential and vice presidential candidates and their spouses within 120 days of a general presidential election; other individuals as designated per executive order of the president; and so-called National Special Security Events—such as the Olympics or state funerals—when designated as such by the Department of Homeland Security.

Of this I am certain: The Secret Service still has extremely dedicated men and women agents who never take their job lightly and are working every day to ensure the people they are charged with protecting are covered. They are ready to sacrifice their own lives to carry out their mission. I am also certain that if someone takes advantage of the confidence gap, which goes along with exposure, the Secret Service will take the hit. That is part of the job description.

I hope to God that the partnership between the president, his staff, Congress, and the Secret Service is solid and never varies. The United States of America cannot afford another assassination. It would tear apart the very fabric of our nation.

November 8, 2010, marks the fiftieth anniversary of President John F. Kennedy's election. Without doubt, the researchers and "experts" and filmmakers will exploit the anniversary to focus on their baseless and unreasonable conspiracy theories. But this futile debate merely distracts from the more important and intelligent discussions that should be taking place—to examine the lessons learned from President Kennedy's assassination so that history will not repeat itself.

When I made the decision to become an agent with the Secret Service I made it with total commitment. The organization is the epitome of integrity, dedication, and loyalty. Agents abide by a code that was developed to allow the White House Detail to perform its mission without embarrassing or compromising those they protect, regardless of political views or personal traits. The Secret Service is there to protect the office of the President of the United States. The code should always be at the forefront of the agents' thoughts.

That code extends to protecting the president's private life. Just as those of us who served on the Kennedy Detail have had to remain silent in the face of conspiracy theories, we have also had to remain silent in the face of rumors even though the rumors are false. As is often the case with rumors, they grow and spread like an uncontrolled epidemic and before long they are accepted as fact. The bigger the name affiliated with the story, the more lurid the details. An example is the widespread rumor of JFK's alleged affair with movie actress Marilyn Monroe.

Let the record state that I was on duty the night of the May 19, 1962, Democratic fund-raiser celebrating the president's birthday at Madison Square Garden. The treat of the evening was watching Marilyn Monroe sing "Happy Birthday" to the president. Marilyn was also present in the president's suite at the Carlyle Hotel, as one of many guests, including Bobby Kennedy, Jean Smith, the president's sister, other family members, White House staff personnel, and other entertainers. Miss Monroe left before the other guests.

To my knowledge, the only other time Marilyn Monroe was in the president's company had been in Santa Monica, at the home of Peter and Pat Lawford, during one of the president's visits to the Los Angeles area in 1961. The president stayed long enough to enjoy a brief swim and greeted the public on the beach area before we departed.

These were the only two times that I or any of the agents I have discussed this with remember Marilyn Monroe being in proximity to the president.

There will always be speculation on the private life of America's first families, but the reality is that it is the responsibility of the Secret Service to ensure that the first family has the ability to have privacy. The family quarters of the White House are sacred unless an agent is requested to respond. What happens when the family retires is private, and the Secret Service has an obligation and duty to protect that privacy.

In my five years on the detail I do not remember a conflict between agents permanently assigned to it. The group was cohesive, professional, loyal, and always available during moments of crisis as well as joy.

I am proud to have served as an agent of the United States Secret Service and I have nothing but total admiration and respect for every man and woman within the organization. I am also confident that the same dedication and values guide the agents' actions today as they have guided them in the past. These brave men and women operating in silence are a resource that the United States of America desperately needs, and will always be dedicated to their mission.

ACKNOWLEDGMENTS

The writing of this book has been a journey in so many ways, and the authors would like to acknowledge those without whom it would not have been possible. First, we thank the surviving Kennedy Detail agents, and the families of those who are deceased, for providing their stories and memories, and for allowing us to share them. Their overwhelming support has been humbling. To Gary Mack, the curator of the Sixth Floor Museum at Dealey Plaza, his insight, expertise, and willingness to share the historical information of the museum so freely were invaluable. To Ken Atchity, our literary manager, his guidance and belief in this story have been ceaseless and we thank him for bringing everything together in a way that has surpassed our expectations. To Mitchell Ivers, our editor at Gallery Books, who had the same passion for this story as we did from the outset, we thank him for his insight in helping to shape the book, and for his quiet work behind the scenes that has resulted in not only a book of which we are proud, but a book brought to life with new technology.

GERALD BLAINE

Special recognition goes to my wife, Joyce, and children, Kelly and Scott, who lived this event and who have made my life so very special. A special recognition to fellow agent Paul Rundle's wife, Peggy, who courageously fights for her life against cancer, yet has provided support and encouragement for this book. Thanks to Beth Morris for her initial encouragement. A special thanks to my sister, Judith Prescott, for special counsel and editing, and to Gwen Colfer for editing my first efforts. Special thanks to Fred Morache for his counsel and to Jeff Beyer and his talented staff at Big Rig Media for the wonderful Kennedy Detail website.

To Lisa McCubbin, my undying gratitude for her natural talents and her insight as a reporter and writer whose understanding of the publishing world made this book possible. To her I give total credit for the heart of this book. Her ability to tackle an event that occurred before she was born, yet interpret the vivid emotions and internal feelings of those who lived it, is truly amazing. She has the soul and compassion of my fellow agents. A special thanks to Wyman Harris, Lisa's father, for sharing his insight and memories of the Kennedy years.

LISA McCUBBIN

The writing of this book has been an extraordinary process, and I am forever grateful to Jerry Blaine for trusting me and allowing me to be a part of it. Your vision never wavered, despite many obstacles, and it is only because of your persistence that we were able to bring your incredible story to life. It has been an honor, a pleasure, and truly, one of the most rewarding experiences I have ever had.

To my husband, Brent, and my two wonderful sons, Connor and Cooper—thank you so much for your sacrifices during the many months in which I was engrossed in this project, and for your constant support and love. I couldn't have done it without you. To my mother and father, Gay and Wyman Harris, thank you for your encouragement and perspective throughout this process. Dad, you are an editor extraordinaire.

To my dear friends—Teresa Unnerstall, Jessica Blakemore, Joanne Blakemore, Elizabeth Cattan Pilar and John Proctor, Larry and Karen Bailey, Joy Bacon, Lia Zaccagnino, Frances Johnson, Jadzia Olson, and Shelly Sorem—whether it was a listening ear, an extra set of eyes, or a shared glass of wine, you were always there when I needed you.

And finally, to Clint—thank you for placing your trust in me. You are a remarkable man, and I cherish our friendship. To me, you are a hero.

LIST OF ABBREVIATIONS
AND CODE NAMES

AFAUSSS	Association of Former Agents of the United States Secret Service
ASAIC	Assistant Special Agent in Charge
ATSAIC	Assistant to the Special Agent in Charge (Shift Leader)
BOSSI	Bureau of Special Services and Investigations
EOB	Executive Office Building
SA	Special Agent
SAIC	Special Agent in Charge
PRS	Protective Research Section
WHCA	White House Communications Agency

RADIO CODES:

Chief's Office

Chief Rowley	*Domino*
Deputy Chief Paterni	*Diamond*
Asst. Chief Wildy	*Debate*

Washington Field Office

SAIC Geiglein	*Diesel*
ASAIC Dahlquist	*Driftwood*

405

First Family

President	*Lancer*
Mrs. Kennedy	*Lace*
Caroline	*Lyric*
John, Jr.	*Lark*

Vice President's Family

Vice President	*Volunteer*
Mrs. Johnson	*Victoria*
Lynda Johnson	*Velvet*
Lucy Johnson	*Venus*

White House Detail

SAIC Behn	*Duplex*
ASAIC Boring	*Deacon*
ASAIC Kellerman	*Digest*
ATSAIC Stout	*Dipole*
ATSAIC Roberts	*Dusty*
ATSAIC Godfrey	*Dangle*
ATSAIC Rodham	*Dogwood*
SA Clint Hill	*Dazzle*
SA Paul Landis	*Debut*
SA Lynn Meredith	*Drummer*
SA Bob Foster	*Dresser*
SA Mugsy O'Leary	*Dapper*

Vice President's Detail

SAIC Stuart Knight	*Dividend*
ASAIC Rufus Youngblood	*Dagger*
SA Paul Rundle	*Dixie*
SA Jerry Kivett	*Daylight*
SA Lemuel Johns	*Dandy*
SA Glen Weaver	*Derby*

Aircraft

Presidential	*Angel*
Vice Presidential	*Angel Two*

Boats

Crashboat PT 109	*Novice*
Honey Fitz	*Nomad*
Patrick J	*Neptune*
Marlin	*Marlin*
Presidential chase	*Horsewhip*
Jet boats	*Guardian 1 & 2*
86' Coast Guard	*Waterwagon*
33' Navy	*Rockfish*
Vice President	*Vanguard*
VP Chase	*Village*

Cars

Pres. Follow-up	*Halfback*
VP Follow-up	*Varsity*
Bomb Disposal	*Hammer*
Bomb Patrol	*Halo*

Helicopters

Army-Davidson Field	*Pat*
Army-Anacostia	*Alpha*
Marine-Anacostia	*Nighthawk*
Airforce	*Botany*

Staff & Aides

Kenneth O'Donnell	*Wand*
Pierre Salinger	*Wayside*
Andrew Hatcher	*Winner*
Malcolm Kilduff	*Warrior*
Evelyn Lincoln	*Willow*
Dr. George Burkley	*Market*
Secretary Dean Rusk	*Freedom*
General Chester Clifton	*Watchman*
Captain Tazewell Shepard	*Witness*
General Godfrey McHugh	*Wing*
Walter Jenkins	*Vigilant*

Locations

Andrews AFB	*Acrobat*
Auchincloss Estate	*Hamlet*
Camp David	*Cactus*
Site R-Ft Ritchie	*Cosmic*
Glen-Ora	*Chateau*
High Point	*Crystal*
Net Control—WHCA	*Crown*
Olmstead AFB	*Astro*
Washington Field Office	*Hedge*
VP EOB Office	*Valdosta*
VP Capitol Office	*Vendor*
VP Senate Office	*Valentine*
VP Residence	*Valley*

advance work: manual for, 75–76, 140, 167, 185, 204; purpose of, 58–59. *See also specific person or trip*

AFAUSSS. *See* Association of Former Agents of the United States Secret Service

Agnew, Judy, 378, 383

Agnew, Spiro, 374, 378, 383

Air Force One: and Dallas advance, 195; and Dallas welcome, 198–99; and Jackie's return to D.C., 244, 246, 250; and JFK burial at Arlington Cemetery, 297; and JFK Cape Cod trip, 127; and JFK Chicago trip, 95; and JFK Dallas trip, 97, 98, 189; and JFK Florida campaign trip, 145, 146, 149, 150; and JFK Fort Worth trip, 173, 174, 182; and JFK Houston trip, 159, 168, 169, 173; and JFK Italy trip, 81; and JFK New York trip, 16, 24, 25; and JFK San Antonio trip, 160, 166, 167; and LBJ at Kennedy (Robert) funeral, 373; and LBJ return from Dallas to D.C., 228–29, 230, 231, 244, 246, 255, 258–59; LBJ round-the-world trip on, 370–71; LBJ swearing-in ceremony on, 252; and return of JFK body to D.C., 244, 246, 250, 255, 257–59, 271, 354; state-of-the-art equipment on, 24

Air Force Two, 189

Alliance for Progress, 171

American Fact-Finding Committee, 194

American Newspaper Publishers Association, 90

Andrews Air Force Base: agents' return from Texas to, 254; LBJ return to, 245, 257, 258–59; presidential cars return to, 254, 261; return of JFK body to, 245, 257–59

AR-15 rifle, 193–94, 196, 217, 228, 229, 350, 354

Aragon, Ernie, 64

ARCO International, 349

Arlington National Cemetery: eternal flame at JFK grave in, 297, 302, 311, 325; JFK burial at, 272, 297; John Jr. at, 72, 295; Kennedy children's burial at, 311; Kennedy (Robert) grave at, 373; motorcade from St. Matthew's to, 284, 296; Tomb of Unknown Soldier at, 71, 72, 267, 269, 272; Veterans Day ceremony at, 72, 295

Ashoka Hotel (New Delhi, India), 107, 110

assassination: difficulties of stopping, 397–98; JFK comments about, 93, 332–33; loner theory of, 322; and mission of Secret Service, 364; sophistication of tools of, 399. *See also specific person*

assassination, JFK: Blaine decision to tell about, 364; films of, 256, 340, 375; and Oswald shooting of JFK, 211–19; public belief in cover-up of, 351; public reaction to, 272–73; scapegoat for, 260. *See also* Warren Commission; *specific person or agency*

Association of Former Agents of the United States Secret Service (AFAUSSS), 352, 390–92

Athens, Ohio: Blaine advance in, 334
Atoka (JFK Virginia retreat), 1, 57–58, 64, 65, 71, 106, 268, 312, 333, 365
Auchincloss, Hugh, 129
Auchincloss, Janet Lee Bouvier, 242, 247
Augusta, Georgia: Eisenhower in, 37–38, 41–42
Augusta National Golf Club, 37–38, 40
Austin, Texas: and agents learn about JFK assassination, 237–38; JFK planned trip to, 18, 159, 161, 181
autopsy, JFK, 246–47, 248–49, 253–54, 265–66, 350
Azores: LBJ in, 370–71

back-of-the-car issue: agents' response to questions about, 352, 360; and Dallas advance, 101; and Dallas motorcade, 208, 232, 360, 362; and features of presidential cars, 79–80; and Houston advance, 162–63; and JFK Fort Worth trip, 183–84; and JFK San Antonio trip, 168; JFK Tampa statement about, 148, 149, 150–51, 162, 208; and JFK Tampa trip, 74, 139–40, 142–45, 147–49, 150–51, 162–63, 285–89; and leasing of presidential cars, 163; and purpose of agents, 139–40, 145; Rowley-agents discussion about, 285–89; Rowley-Rankin correspondence about, 360–63
Bales, Arthur, 173
Bartlett, Jim, 308
Batista, Fulgencio, 69
Baudouin (king of Belgians), 273
Baughman, U. E., 39, 42, 43, 44, 104
Bay of Pigs, 17, 69–70, 97, 138
Behn, Jerry: and AFAUSSS, 391; appearance of, 16; and back of the car issue, 286, 288, 360–61; and Berlin advance, 91; and Blaine assignment to State Department reception, 271, 282; Blaine learns of JFK Florida-Texas itinerary from, 16, 17–18, 19, 21, 30; and Blaine request to work JFK funeral procession, 289–90; code name for, 235; and Dallas advance, 86, 90–91, 92; and Hill transfer to LBJ detail, 367–68; and Houston advance, 162–63; and Jackie-Dillon letter praising White House Detail, 313; and Jackie's India-Pakistan trip, 107; and JFK death, 239–40; and JFK funeral, 273, 275, 291, 293; and JFK Italian motorcades, 82; and JFK Tampa trip, 67; JFK views about, 16–17, 288; LBJ relationship with, 322; and LBJ return from Dallas to D.C., 259; and LBJ South Bend trip, 328, 331; motorcade role of, 16; and news about JFK assassination, 226, 227, 235; and Patrick Kennedy birth and death, 127; personality and character of, 17; reaction to JFK assassination by, 231, 240; resemblance to JFK of, 16; and Rowley-agents meeting, 285, 286, 288; as SAIC for JFK, 16, 51; as SAIC for LBJ, 271, 322; staffing concerns of, 20, 92; tells Boring about JFK assassination, 232; time off for, 19, 21, 144, 163, 240; and transfer of JFK body from White House to Capitol rotunda, 279
Bennett, Glen, 174, 176, 177, 185, 193, 196, 200, 202, 228, 252, 343
Bennett, John Francis, 63
Berger, Andy: birth of son of, 233; Dallas assignment of, 177; grief of, 253, 263; health of, 323; and JFK Fort Worth trip, 176, 177; and JFK Palm Springs trip, 120, 121–23; JFK relationship with, 123, 233; and LBJ security, 261, 262, 264; and motorcade from Parkland Hospital to Love Field, 250; and news of JFK assassination, 222; at Parkland Hospital, 222–23, 232, 233–34, 244, 247, 249; personal and professional background of, 120, 123; personality and character of, 123; and return of JFK body to D.C., 247, 249, 250; Sinatra discussion with, 121–22
Berger, Dolly, 120, 233, 263
Bergstrom Air Force Base (Texas), 182, 238, 254
Berlin, Germany: building of wall in, 69, 95; JFK trip to, 91–92, 184, 361; reaction to JFK assassination in, 272–73
Berman, Stanley, 63
Bethesda Naval Hospital: Hill physical exam at, 379–80; and JFK autopsy, 254, 258, 259–60, 265–66
Birdzell, Donald, 35–36
Black Jack (riderless horse), 279, 293
Blaine, Howard, 38
Blaine, Jerry: and AFAUSSS, 352, 391, 392; awards and honors for, 348; call to Joyce about celebrity party from, 55; commitment to Secret Service of, 400–401; "confidence factor" of, 398–99, 400; as "deserter" from Secret Service, 349; and difficulties of stopping assassinations, 397–98; early career of, 39–40; first joins White House Detail, 15, 39–40; Grant relationship with, 40; as handball player, 323–24; Hill relationship with, 21–22, 105–7, 389–90; at

IBM, 346–49; job concerns of, 331–32, 334, 336–37; job demands of, 30, 64, 181; joins Secret Service, 39; Joyce's relationship with, 55, 56, 154–55, 181, 260; and LBJ Athens, Ohio trip, 334; LBJ comments to, 330; and LBJ gun incident, 264–65, 268, 282, 285, 286; at LBJ ranch, 316–17, 319–21; and LBJ South Bend trip, 327–28, 329–32; and LBJ White House Detail, 260, 316–17, 319–21, 331–32; marriage of, 39; mission of, 9; motorcade concerns of, 74, 84–85; nuclear attack concern of, 96; off-duty time of, 270–71, 303, 316–17; and Oswald shooting, 276, 281; papers and reports of, 357–58; and peacock incident, 320–21; personal and professional background of, 11, 38–39; personality and character of, 15, 38; and presidential–Secret Service relationship, 397; and private life of presidents, 400–401; and relationship among members of White House Detail, 336; resignation from Secret Service of, 337, 344; and responsibilities of Secret Service in modern society, 399–400; retirement from corporate world of, 346, 349–50; and Rowley-agents meeting about back of the car issue, 282, 285–87, 288–89; Rowley first meeting with, 39; Rundle relationship with, 39; and Shah of Iran's bodyguard, 347; and State Department reception advance, 271, 277, 282, 289, 290, 291, 296; and technology development for law enforcement, 346–49; training of, 9–10; Zboril relationship with, 2, 11. *See also specific person or topic*

Blaine, Jerry, and JFK Detail: Behn review of JFK Florida-Texas itinerary with, 16, 17–18, 19, 21, 22, 30; and Dallas advance, 17, 30; and decision to tell about JFK assassination, 364; eternal flame as reminder of failure for, 325; first assigned to JFK Detail, 42; and Grant as replacement for Dallas advance, 30; and JFK-Blaine Easter golfing story, 88–90; and JFK Cape Canaveral trip, 17; JFK concerns about family of, 96; JFK first meeting with, 31; and JFK funeral procession, 289–90, 291; and JFK Miami trip, 172; and JFK Tampa trip, 17, 18, 19, 30, 58–64, 65–71, 72–74, 77–81, 84–85, 88–90, 93–94, 97, 135–49, 150, 151, 162, 193, 357, 358; reactions to JFK assassination by, 237–38, 260, 269, 323–24, 325, 396; revisiting of JFK assassination by, 350–64; and viewing of JFK casket at White House, 269

Blaine, Joyce Hazlett: and AFAUSSS meeting, 392; and demands of Jerry's job, 30, 64, 181; and Jerry off-duty, 270–71, 276, 317; and Jerry's advance work for Tampa, 58, 64, 73; and Jerry's concern about nuclear attack, 96; and Jerry's papers and reports, 357; Jerry's relationship with, 55, 56, 154–55, 181, 260; marriage of, 39; and news about JFK assassination, 2–5, 260

Blaine, Kelly, 3, 64, 96, 260, 317

Blaine, Scott, 2, 3, 64, 260, 317

Blair House: assassination attempt on Truman at, 34–36

Blaschak, Walter, 231, 285

boat capsizing incident, JFK–White House Detail, 123

Boggs, Hale, 305

Boggs, Pat, 377

Bolden, Abraham, 334–36, 356–59

Boring, Floyd: and AFAUSSS, 390–91; and back of the car issue, 144–47, 148, 149, 150–51, 162, 232, 285–88, 360, 361, 362; and balance of politics and protection of president, 146, 147–48, 149, 150–51; and Behn time off, 18; and Jackie-Dillon letter praising White House Detail, 313; and JFK Florida campaign trip, 19, 74, 143, 144–47, 148, 149, 285–88, 361, 362; and JFK inauguration, 54; and JFK Palm Beach trip, 42, 44, 46, 47, 49; and JFK Palm Springs trip, 120, 121; and LBJ return from Dallas to D.C., 259; learns about JFK assassination, 232; retirement of, 391; and Roosevelt Detail, 34; and Rowley-agents meeting, 285–88; and Truman–Blair House assassination attempt, 35, 36

BOSSI. *See* New York City Bureau of Special Services and Investigations

Boston Children's Hospital, 128

Bradlee, Ben, 260

Bradlee, Tony, 260

Brookline Cemetery (Massachusetts), 128, 233, 272

Brookman, Carl, 63

Brooks Air Force Base (Texas), 159, 168

Brown, Gloria, 30–31

Brown, Hamilton P. "Ham," 240–41, 274, 392

Buendorf, Larry, 381

bullets, JFK assassination: Johnsen find of expended, 249, 253; Landis finds fragment of, 225; Paolella finds fragment of, 268

Bundy, McGeorge, 62, 94

Burke, Bob, 27–28, 76, 94

Burke, Jim, 376–77

Burkley, George, 195, 221–23, 232–33, 238–39, 246, 248–50, 252–54, 258, 259, 354
Burns, Paul, 82, 163, 165–66, 175, 269

Cabell, Dearie, 199
camel: Jackie's ride on, 112–13
Camelot: and White-Jackie interview, 305
Campion, John, 313
Cape Canaveral: JFK visit to, 17, 140–41, 145
Cape Cod: Hill family on, 125–26. See also Hyannis Port
Capitol, U.S.: JFK body in rotunda of, 269, 272, 273, 278–81, 283–84, 290
Carlyle Hotel (New York City), 23, 25, 26, 28–29, 141, 142, 333, 366, 401
Caroline (airplane), 46, 49, 311
Carpenter, Liz, 259
Carpenter, Scott, 140
Carswell Air Force Base (Texas), 173, 174–75, 189
Carter, Cliff, 243
Castro, Fidel, 33, 69–70, 321
CBS: announcement of JFK assassination by, 4. See also 60 Minutes; specific person
Cellar (Fort Worth coffee shop), 177, 178, 306, 312–13
Central Intelligence Agency (CIA): assassination concerns of, 284; and Bay of Pigs, 69; and Blaine-IBM development of law enforcement technology, 348; and HSCA investigation, 351; and JFK funeral, 290; at Parkland Hospital, 233, 244; and theories about JFK assassination, 321, 351, 359; Warren Commission report about, 341
Chandler, Toby, 231, 257
Chicago, Illinois: JFK trip to, 61–62, 95, 161, 357–58; LBJ trip to, 326; and theories about JFK assassination, 356–58
Chicago Police Department, 62
Christina (Onassis yacht), 132–33
Churchill, Winston, 33
civil rights, 9, 18, 32, 85, 159, 326, 329, 338, 398
Civil Rights Act (1964), 338
Coast Guard, U.S., 145
code names, 24
Coffelt, Leslie, 35–36
Cold War, 33, 398
commission books, 13, 15
"confidence factor," Blaine's, 398–99, 400
Congress, U.S.: and funding for Secret Service, 86, 397, 399; LBJ address to, 338; official recognition of Secret Service by, 397

Connally, John: and Dallas motorcade, 196, 200, 201, 202, 204; Dallas shooting of, 214, 215, 216, 217, 219, 235; and JFK assassination, 4; and JFK Fort Worth trip, 184; and JFK Houston trip, 170; and JFK San Antonio trip, 159, 167; at Parkland Hospital, 223, 224, 225, 227; and Texas politics, 77; Warren Commission report about, 339, 340
Connally, Nellie: and Dallas motorcade, 196, 200, 201, 204, 211; and JFK San Antonio trip, 159, 167; at Parkland Hospital, 223, 224; recollection of shootings by, 218; and shooting of Connally, 214
conspiracy theories: and HSCA investigation, 351–52; prevalence of, 302, 305, 321–25, 333, 350–64; Warren Commission report about, 341, 344. See also specific person or theory
Cooper, John, 305
Cooper, L. Gordon, 140
Coughlin, Ann, 392
Coughlin, Walt, 12, 23, 30, 151, 160, 327, 329–30, 331, 392
Cronkite, Walter, 2, 4, 5, 6, 247
Crosby, Bing, 3, 120, 121
Crow, Trammell, 220
Cuba: and challenges facing JFK, 33; and challenges facing LBJ, 326; and HSCA investigation, 351; and JFK assassination, 262, 342, 351; and JFK inauguration, 284; and Oswald, 321, 342. See also Bay of Pigs; Cuban Missile Crisis; Cubans, anti-Castro
Cuban Missile Crisis, 62, 69, 94–97, 120, 138
Cubans, anti-Castro: and Caroline kidnapping rumor, 138–39; and challenges facing JFK, 398; and HSCA investigation, 351; and JFK election concerns, 18; and JFK Miami trip, 150; and JFK Tampa trip, 64, 68–70, 94, 138–39, 142, 145, 147, 287; and theories about JFK assassination, 321, 351; and threats against JFK, 64
Curry, Jesse: and Dallas advance, 87, 99, 100, 102, 155–56, 168–69, 187, 188, 189; and Dallas motorcade, 196, 202, 204, 209; and motorcade from Parkland Hospital to Love Field, 247; at Parkland Hospital, 223; and protests in Dallas, 155–56; and shooting of JFK, 215, 218; statement to people of Dallas by, 156
Cushing, Richard, Cardinal, 128, 294–95

Dallas: advance for, 30, 31, 64, 75–76, 85–88, 97–102, 151–56, 161, 168–69, 173, 177–78, 186–90, 192–94, 343; anti-Kennedy feelings in, 194–95, 198; Behn-Blaine discussion about JFK trip to, 17, 30; Curry statement to people of, 156; elections of 1960 in, 207; Hill return visit to, 392–94; integration in, 85–86; JFK assassination comments in, 332–33; and JFK Texas itinerary, 159; JFK welcome in, 197–202; newspaper editorials in, 155; Oswald arrest and questioning in, 255–56; politics in, 156; Preliminary Survey Report for, 154, 192; protests in, 155–56; questions about advance in, 319, 332; Stevenson in, 18, 85, 99, 156. *See also* Dallas Police Department; motorcade, Dallas; Parkland Hospital; *specific person*

Dallas Morning News, 194, 256

Dallas motorcade: AR–15 base in, 193–94, 196, 217, 228, 229, 350, 354; and back of the car issue, 208, 232, 360, 362; configuration for, 196; and Dallas advance, 18, 86, 91, 98–102, 169, 182, 183, 186, 188, 189, 192, 193–94, 195; leasing of cars for, 195; from Love Field to downtown, 359; motorcycle escort for, 169, 189, 202, 203–4, 205, 206, 209, 212, 218, 363; from Parkland Hospital to Love Field, 247–50; pictures of, 359–60; route for, 152–53, 187, 354; Rowley comments about, 289; shooting of JFK during, 211–19; start of, 199–202; teenager incident during, 207–8; and Texas School Book Depository, 209–10, 213–14, 219; and theories about JFK assassination, 354, 359–60; weather conditions for, 186, 188

Dallas Police Department: and Dallas advance, 87, 153, 168–69, 190; and Oswald arrest and questioning, 255, 274; at Parkland Hospital, 231; Warren Commission report about, 340, 341. *See also* Curry, Jesse

Dallas, Rita, 240

Dalton, George, 308

Daniels, Russell "Buck," 43

Davidson, Joseph, 35

Davis, Sammy Jr., 120

de Gaulle, Charles, 273, 290, 291, 292, 301

Decker, Bill, 196, 245

DeFreese, Bert, 73–74, 136–37, 151, 161, 162, 163, 173

Democratic National Convention (Atlantic City, 1964), 366

Democratic National Convention (Chicago, 1968), 373–74

Dempsher, Eve, 58, 67, 75, 76, 226, 270, 271, 275, 391

Dickinson, Angie, 55, 120

Diem brothers: assassination of, 62, 358

Dillon, Douglas, 290, 291, 309–10, 313

District of Columbia Police Department, 54, 136, 290

Doud, Elvira M., 39

driver agents, Secret Service, 136, 193. *See also specific person*

duck hunting, Rundle's, 109

Dulles, Allen, 305

Duncan, Bill, 27, 76, 161, 164, 190

Eastman Kodak Company, 256

Edinburgh, Duke of, 273

Eisenhower, Dwight D. "Ike," 15, 16, 32, 36–38, 39, 40, 42, 47, 89, 111, 184, 193, 315, 347, 398

Eisenhower, Mamie, 382–83

Elder, Bill, 66–67

elections of 1960, 32–33, 77, 85, 159, 169, 191, 207, 363, 400

elections of 1964, 17, 20, 134, 159, 186, 327

elections of 1968, 371, 373–74

elections of 1972, 375–76

elections of 2008, 398

elephant: Jackie's ride on, 112

Elms (LBJ Georgetown home), 256–57, 260, 262, 264–65, 303

eternal flame: at JFK grave (Arlington National Cemetery), 297, 302, 311, 325

Faison, Bob, 163–64, 165–66, 175, 194, 237, 238, 269, 335

Fay, Anita, 129–30

Fay, Paul "Red," 129–30

Federal Bureau of Investigation (FBI): assassination concerns of, 284; and Blaine-IBM development of law enforcement technology, 348; Bolden allegations about, 357; conspiracy theories about, 321; and Dallas advance, 155; and HSCA investigation, 351, 357; investigation of JFK assassination by, 302, 305, 321; and JFK funeral, 290; and JFK Tampa trip, 93; and NCIC system, 348; and Oswald murder charge, 274; at Parkland Hospital, 233, 244; rumors of takeover of presidential protection by, 318–19, 321; and theories about JFK assassination, 351, 357, 359; Warren Commission report about, 341, 343 film/pictures: by Jackie about president's murder, 130–32; of JFK assassination, 175, 256, 375

flash cards, 13–14, 60, 63, 329

Flores, Peppi Duran, 63

Florida: Behn-Blaine discussion about JFK trip to, 17, 18, 19; Boring as SAIC for JFK trip to, 144; civil rights in, 85; risks of JFK appearances in, 17–18; threats to JFK in, 136–37, 138–39; and White House Detail turnover, 65. *See also specific location*

Ford, Gerald R., 305, 378, 381–82, 384

Ford Motor Company, 79, 80, 161

Fort Worth Press Club, 174, 176, 192, 306, 312

Fort Worth, Texas: advance in, 161; JFK trip to, 159, 163–66, 173–78, 181–86, 190–92, 195; motorcade in, 17, 174–75, 183–84; and Sorrels-McCann report about Secret Service in, 307, 312–13

Foster, Bob: and AFAUSSS, 392; code name for, 235; and continuation of protection for Kennedy children, 311; Hill conversation about return of JFK body with, 242; impact of JFK assassination on, 324, 333; Jackie-Dillon letter praising, 314; and Jackie return to D.C., 262; and Jackie visits to Arlington Cemetery, 303; and JFK comment about not voting for him, 50; and JFK funeral, 292, 294, 295; JFK tells Foster to take care of John Jr., 158; and JFK Texas flight, 158; and John Jr. at toy store, 211; and John Jr. at Veterans Day ceremony at Arlington Cemetery, 71–72; and John Jr. helicopter fascination, 71, 157, 158; and John Jr. salute at JFK funeral, 295; and John Jr. speaking about JFK death, 325; and Kennedy family in Georgetown, 312; and Kiddie Detail on Cape Cod, 126; Kiddie Detail transfer of, 50; and news of JFK assassination, 235; relationship between Kennedy children and, 324; and telling Caroline and John Jr. about JFK death, 247, 281; and transfer of JFK body from White House to Capitol rotunda, 281

Foster, Peggy, 392

funeral, JFK: Arlington advance for, 296; and concerns about another assassination attempt, 284; John Jr. salute at, 295; motorcade to Arlington Cemetery for, 296–97; plans for, 272, 273; procession for, 273, 284, 285, 289–94, 296; security for, 285, 290–91, 296; St. Matthew's service for, 294–95. *See also specific person*

Gainey, Wayne, 60–61, 62, 63, 68, 137

Galbraith, John Kenneth, 105, 107, 110, 111, 112

Gallagher, Mary, 50, 190

Gandhi, Indira, 399

Garelick, Sandy, 24–25, 26, 27, 28, 81

Garfield, James, 319

Gargan, Ann, 240

Gates, Thomas, 42

Gawler's Funeral Home (Washington, D.C.), 260, 266

Gearhart, Ira, 248

Georgetown: Jackie and children at Harriman home in, 310–12, 333; Jackie home in, 333, 365; JFK home in, 56, 105

Giannoules, Ken, 12, 23, 30, 163, 166, 175, 194, 269

Gibbons, Sam, 147

Gibbs, Harry, 23, 28, 47–49, 257

Gies, Morgan, 136

gifts on international trips, 112, 113

Gleason, John, 72

Glen Ora (JFK Virginia home), 105–6, 114, 193

Glenn, John, 140

Godfrey, Art: and AFAUSSS meeting, 392; appearance of, 22; and back of the car issue, 288; and Blaine-LBJ gun incident, 268; and competition among White House agents, 123–24; and Dallas advance work, 31, 86; and Jackie at Hammersmith, 130, 132; and JFK Fort Worth trip, 163, 165, 166, 175, 182, 183; and JFK Italian motorcades, 81, 82, 83, 84; and JFK New York City trip, 12, 22, 23, 24, 25, 26, 27, 29; and LBJ security, 268, 320; learns about JFK assassination, 237–38; and Pearson Secret Service article, 306; personal and professional background of, 22; personality and character of, 22; return from Austin to D.C. of, 254; and viewing of JFK body at White House, 269

Godfrey, Betty, 392

Goldwater, Barry, 159, 187

golfing story: Blaine-JFK, 88–90; Jones-JFK, 124–25

Grant, David: and AFAUSSS meeting, 391; agents' relationship with, 319; and Behn-Blaine discussion of JFK itinerary, 30; and Blaine advance in Tampa, 65; Blaine relationship with, 40; Brown relationship with, 30–31; and competition among White House agents, 123; and Dallas advance, 31, 86, 151, 152–54, 155, 168–69, 176, 177, 182, 187, 188, 189, 319, 343; early career of, 40; eternal flame as reminder of failure for, 325; and Hill return visit to Dallas, 392; and Jackie India-Pakistan trip, 107, 111; and JFK Fort Worth trip, 176, 177; and JFK Italian motorcades, 82, 83, 84; and JFK New York City trip, 12, 23–24, 29, 30, 31; and news of JFK assassination, 220–21; and Oswald, 255, 274; retirement of, 391; and Warren Commission, 332, 343

Grant, Eva, 302

Grant, Gloria, 391, 392

grassy knoll shot: conspiracy theory about, 352–53

grave, JFK, 297, 302

Great Society, 326

Greece: Jackie trip to, 132–33

Greer, Bill: at Bethesda Naval Hospital, 266; and Dallas advance, 189, 195; and Dallas motorcade, 196, 202, 203, 204, 205, 207, 208, 209–10, 211, 212; and Dallas welcome, 199, 201; as driver of JFK body to Bethesda Naval Hospital, 254, 258, 259; grief of, 259; and Jackie-Dillon letter praising White House Detail, 313; and JFK at Veterans Day ceremony, 72; and JFK flight to Texas, 158; and JFK Florida trip, 145, 147, 149, 286, 287; and JFK Houston trip, 170; and JFK Italian motorcades, 82; and JFK New York City trip, 25, 26, 27; JFK relationship with, 201, 254; and JFK San Antonio trip, 167–68; and LBJ South Bend trip, 328, 330–31; at Parkland Hospital, 219, 225; and return of JFK body to White House, 266–67; and shooting of JFK, 212, 214–15, 216, 217–18, 219; and theories about JFK assassination, 350, 355–56; and transfer of JFK body from White House to Capitol rotunda, 279; and Warren Commission Report, 343

Guthrie, Forrest, 46, 108, 112–13

Hackworth, Johnnie Mae, 63

hair, JFK: Jackie cuts lock of, 278

Hall, Ned, 76

Halterman, Dennis, 76, 95, 160, 161, 166, 167

Hammersmith Farm (Newport, Rhode Island): Jackie at, 129–33

Hardin, Jim, 392

Harriman, Averell, 310

helicopters: and JFK Texas trip, 161; John Jr. fascination with, 20, 71, 126, 157–58, 325; and LBJ return to White House, 259. See also Marine One

Hess & Eisenhardt, 79

Hewitt, Don, 384, 389

Hickey, George: and Dallas advance, 173, 188, 193, 194, 195; and Dallas motorcade, 196, 202; and JFK San Antonio trip, 160; and JFK Tampa trip, 136, 142, 148, 193; lawsuit of, 355; memories of, 229–30; at Parkland Hospital, 228, 229–30; and return of presidential cars to Andrews Air Force Base, 254, 261; securing of Dallas motorcade vehicles by, 244, 245; and shooting of JFK, 217; and theories about JFK assassination, 350, 354–55; and transport of presidential cars, 136; and Warren Commission Report, 343

Hight, Jack, 334

Hill, Chris, 40–41, 43, 103, 104, 125–26, 308–9, 368, 376

Hill, Clint: administrative position of, 374; and AFAUSSS meeting, 391–92; as Agnew SAIC, 374, 378; appearance of, 40; awards and honors for, 309–10, 313, 369, 388, 395; and back-of-the-car issue, 360, 362–63; Baughman discussion with, 42, 43, 104; Blaine relationship with, 21–22, 105–7; Blaine thoughts about, 331; considered for Secret Service directorship, 378; Dallas return visit of, 392–94; depression of, 375, 377, 378; drinking by, 377, 389, 390; early career of, 40; and Eisenhower Detail, 40, 41; and Eisenhower-JFK transition, 41–42; and elections of 1972, 375; and eternal flame as reminder of failure for Hill, 325; family moves of, 308–9, 368–69; and Ford attempted assassination, 381–82; and Grant-Brown relationship, 30; grief/guilt feelings of, 254–55, 267, 303, 388; health of, 379–80; Hickey memories about, 230; impact of JFK assassination on, 254–55, 267, 303, 325, 375, 377, 378, 388, 389, 390; on JFK Detail, 22; and JFK Tampa trip, 362; joins Secret Service, 41; and LBJ at Kennedy (Robert) funeral, 372–73; and LBJ at King memorial service, 371–72; and LBJ Azores Christmas stop, 370–71; at LBJ Ranch, 368; LBJ relationship with, 368, 369, 372, 374; and LBJ round-the-world trip, 369–71; as LBJ SAIC, 369–70, 384; and LBJ swearing-in ceremony, 253; and Nixon-Kennedy (Edward) protection situation, 376–77; in North Dakota, 380–82; papers and photos of, 369, 395–96; personal and professional background of, 40–41; personality and character of, 105; promotions for, 368, 369, 374, 375;

Hill, Clint (*cont.*)
retirement from Secret Service of, 380, 382–83; Rundle as deputy to, 375, 379; *60 Minutes* interview of, 383–90; and theories about JFK assassination, 354, 359; transfer to LBJ detail of, 367–68; and Watergate, 377–78

Hill, Clint, and Jackie Detail: and continuation of protection for Jackie, 311; and Dallas advance, 177, 193, 195; and Dallas motorcade, 196, 200, 201, 202, 203, 204, 205, 206–7, 208, 209, 212, 359, 362–63; and Dallas welcome, 199; and ending of Jackie protection, 345, 367; and Foster-Hill conversation about return of JFK body, 242; and Gwen hopes of meeting Jackie, 103–4, 115; and Hill admiration for Jackie, 191; and Hill assignment to Jackie Detail, 43–44; and Hill family on Cape Cod, 125–26; and Hill report to Behn on JFK assassination, 226, 227, 231; and Hill return home from White House, 270; and Hill viewing of JFK body, 266; and Jackie at Arlington Cemetery, 272, 297, 301–2, 303; and Jackie at Bethesda Naval Hospital, 258, 259–60, 265–66; Jackie concern about, 252, 345, 396; Jackie-Dillon letter praising, 314; and Jackie Fort Worth trip, 174, 175–76, 177, 190, 191; and Jackie in Georgetown, 312, 333; and Jackie Greece and Morocco trip, 132–33; and Jackie at Hammersmith, 131; and Jackie-Hill last conversation, 373; and Jackie-Hill last day together, 367; and Jackie-Hill relationship, 104–5, 114–15, 124–28, 191, 266, 270, 291, 367, 368, 396; and Jackie Houston trip, 170, 171; and Jackie in Hyannis Port, 308; and Jackie India-Pakistan trip, 105, 107–13; and Jackie Italian trip, 193; and Jackie in New York City, 333, 365–66; and Jackie at 1964 Democratic Convention, 364; and Jackie in Palm Beach, 316; and Jackie return to D.C./White House, 242, 249, 252, 262, 267, 268; and Jackie San Antonio trip, 167, 168; and Jackie Texas flight, 158, 160; and Jackie travels after JFK funeral, 333; and Jackie viewing of JFK open casket, 275, 277, 278; and JFK assassination, 2, 5; and JFK casket, 245, 258; and JFK death, 239–40; and JFK funeral events, 275, 291, 293–94, 295; and Kennedy children's burial at Arlington Cemetery, 311; Kennedy (Robert) discussion with, 227–28; and motorcade from Parkland Hospital to Love

Field, 250; and 1968 Democratic National Convention, 374; and Paolella-Jackie horse incident, 106; at Parkland Hospital, 223, 224, 225–26, 227–28, 229, 232, 239–40, 241–42, 245, 247; and Patrick Kennedy birth and death, 127–28; and photos of Jackie and children, 369; and plans for Texas trip, 20, 134; and Radziwill visit, 284; and return of JFK body to D.C., 245, 247, 249, 250; and rumor of shooting of Hill, 5, 6; as SAIC for Jackie, 3–4, 21–22, 113, 170; as saving Jackie's life, 275; and shooting of JFK, 213, 214, 215, 216–17, 218, 219; and transfer of JFK body from White House to Capitol rotunda, 279, 280; and Warren Commission Report, 343; and White-Jackie interview, 304–5; and Zapruder film of JFK assassination, 375

Hill, Corey, 103, 104, 125–26, 308–9, 310, 368, 376

Hill, Gwen: and AFAUSSS meeting, 391–92; Cape Cod vacation of, 125–26; and Clint *60 Minutes* interview, 383, 384, 385, 386, 388, 389; and Clint assignment to Jackie Detail, 43–44; and Clint drinking, 390; and Clint last day on Jackie's Detail, 367; and Clint retirement party, 382; and Clint return from White House, 270; and Clint return visit to Dallas, 392, 393; and Ford attempted assassination, 381–82; and Grant-Brown relationship, 30; Hewitt gift for, 389; home of, 395; and hopes of meeting Jackie, 103–4, 115; illness of, 375; Jackie meeting with, 309–10; jealousy feelings of, 104; moving of family by, 308–9, 368–69; and news of JFK assassination, 3, 5

Hill, Janice, 380–81, 389

Hill, Jennie, 40–41

Hilton Hotel (New York City): and JFK New York City trip, 10, 12, 23, 24, 28–29

Hobbs Motel (Johnson City, Texas), 317

Holt, Harold, 369–70

Homeland Security, U.S. Department of, 399, 400

Honey Fitz (yacht), 130

Hoover, J. Edgar, 12, 233, 244, 318, 321, 323

horse incident, Paolella-Jackie, 106

horses: Jackie's passion for, 113

Hotel Texas (Fort Worth), 163, 164–66, 175, 177–78, 181, 182, 190, 261, 332–33, 335

House Select Committee on Assassinations, U.S. (HSCA), 351–52, 357

Houston, Texas: advance in, 161–63, 288;
   JFK trip to, 159, 168, 169–73, 183, 195;
   motorcade in, 17, 161, 170, 172, 173;
   protests in, 170
Howard, Mike, 166
Hughes, Sarah, 252
Humphrey, Hubert, 366, 373, 374, 383
Hurley, Dan, 320–21
Hyannis Port (Cape Cod), 45, 64, 122–26,
   193, 240–41, 274, 303, 308, 317, 333, 334,
   357

IBM, 334, 336–37, 346–49
inauguration, JFK, 53–56
India: Eisenhower trip to, 111; Jackie trip to,
   105, 107–13
Inter-American Press Association, 150
Ireland: JFK trip to, 100, 139, 184
Italy: Jackie trip to, 193, 395–96; JFK
   motorcades in, 81–84, 139, 184

Jamison, Robert, 74
Japan, 111
Jeffries, Jim, 43, 107, 112, 113, 114
John Birch Society, 62
Johns, Lemuel, 230, 368
Johnsen, Dick, 176, 177, 249, 253, 261, 262
Johnson, Lady Bird: and Dallas advance, 189–
   90; and Dallas motorcade, 200; Hardin as
   SAIC for, 392; Jackie comments about, 305;
   and JFK funeral procession, 292; and JFK
   Houston trip, 172; and JFK San Antonio
   trip, 159, 167; at Kennedy (Robert) funeral,
   373; and motorcade from Parkland
   Hospital to Love Field, 248; at Parkland
   Hospital, 228, 230, 231, 243; return from
   Dallas to D.C. of, 230, 231, 243, 244, 259;
   and transfer of JFK body from White
   House to Capitol rotunda, 279
Johnson, Lucy, 230–31
Johnson, Lynda, 230–31
Johnson, Lyndon B. "LBJ": address to
   Congress by, 338; anxiety of, 322; Behn as
   SAIC for, 271; and Blaine-LBJ gun incident,
   265, 268, 282, 285, 286; challenges facing,
   326; conspiracy theories about, 321; and
   Dallas advance, 97, 189–90, 195; and Dallas
   motorcade, 200; and Dallas welcome, 198;
   and elections of 1964, 327; Elms as home
   of, 256–57, 262, 303; and FBI investigation
   of JFK assassination, 302; gift of pony to
   JFK family from, 114; Hill as SAIC for, 369,
   384; Hill relationship with, 368, 369, 372,
   374; and Holt funeral, 369–70; increased

protection for, 219, 224; Jackie comments
about, 305; and Jackie Secret Service
protection, 311; and JFK body at Capitol
rotunda, 283; and JFK Fort Worth trip,
173, 184, 185; and JFK funeral procession,
273, 290–91, 292, 293; and JFK Houston
trip, 159, 169, 172; and JFK-LBJ security
transition, 256, 282, 303, 315; JFK plans to
stay at ranch of, 18, 181, 182; and JFK San
Antonio trip, 159, 167; JFK travels with,
18–19; Kennedy (Robert) funeral, 372–
73; Kennedy (Robert) relationship with,
371; and King memorial, 371–72; Knight
as SAIC for, 241; at LBJ ranch, 317, 319–
21, 373–74; and mission of White House
Detail, 6; and motorcade from Parkland
Hospital to Love Field, 247–48; and 1964
Democratic National Convention, 366; and
1968 Democratic National Convention,
373–74; at Parkland Hospital, 228–29,
230–31, 243–44, 246; personality/style of,
317–18, 330–31, 332; presidential cars for,
323; return from Dallas to D.C. of, 228–
29, 230–31, 243–44, 246, 247–48, 251, 255,
258–59; round-the-world trip of, 370–71;
and rumors of FBI takeover of presidential
protection, 321; security for, 3, 253, 256–
57, 261, 262, 264–65, 268, 282, 303, 315,
316–17, 322, 344, 372–73; and shooting of
JFK, 218, 219; South Bend trip of, 327–28,
329–31; and State Department reception,
271; swearing-in ceremony of, 248, 252–
53; and Texas politics, 77; threats against,
63, 358; and transfer of JFK body from
White House to Capitol rotunda, 279;
and Vietnam, 371; Warren Commission
appointed by, 305–6; White House Detail
relationship with, 317–18
Jones, Radford "Rad," 124–25
Justice Department, U.S.: investigation of JFK
   assassination by, 302

Keller, Brooks, 23
Kellerman, Roy: as acting SAIC for JFK
   Texas trip, 162; agents' relationship with,
   319; appearance of, 25–26; and Behn
   time off, 19; at Bethesda Naval Hospital,
   258, 259, 265–66; code name for, 24; and
   Dallas advance, 187–88, 195; and Dallas
   motorcade, 196, 199, 201, 202, 205, 206;
   and Dallas welcome, 199, 200; and Jackie-
   Dillon letter praising White House Detail,
   313; and Jackie at Hammersmith, 130, 132;
   and JFK autopsy, 254; and JFK casket at

Kellerman, Roy (*cont.*)
Andrews Air Force Base, 258; and JFK death, 239; and JFK Fort Worth trip, 175–76, 184, 185; and JFK funeral procession, 291, 293; and JFK Houston trip, 170, 171; and JFK Italian motorcades, 82; and JFK New York City trip, 20, 24, 25–26, 31; and JFK Texas flight, 158, 160; JFK views about, 26; and Landis's grief, 252–53; and LBJ swearing-in ceremony, 253; and motorcade from Parkland Hospital to Love Field, 250; at Parkland Hospital, 223, 224, 225, 226, 227, 233, 239, 245, 246, 247, 249; personal and professional background of, 184; personality and character of, 26; and plans for JFK Texas trip, 19, 63; return from Dallas to D.C. of, 252–53, 254; and return of JFK body to D.C., 245, 246, 247, 249, 250; and Rowley-agents meeting, 285; and shooting of JFK, 2, 214–15, 217, 219; tells Behn about assassination, 231; and Texas advance, 101; and theories about JFK assassination, 354, 355; and threats on JFK Texas trip, 164; and Warren Commission Report, 343

Kelly Field (Texas), 168

Kennedy, Caroline: Arlington Cemetery visits of, 296, 303; at Atoka, 57, 71; Berger concern about, 234; on Cape Cod, 124, 125–26, 303; continuation of Secret Service protection for, 311; education of, 324; in Georgetown, 105, 310–12, 333; and Hill assignment to Jackie Detail, 43; and Hill-Foster conversation about JFK return to D.C., 242; impact of JFK death on, 324; and Jackie Greece and Morocco trip, 132; and Jackie in labor with Patrick, 127; Jackie praise for White House Detail for, 314; and Jackie return to D.C., 262–63; and JFK funeral activities, 274, 284, 292, 294, 295, 296; JFK relationship with, 324; Kiddie Detail for, 6, 20, 49, 52–53, 126, 210, 236, 312, 324; kidnapping rumor about, 138–39; and learning about JFK death, 247; love of horses of, 126; in New York City, 333, 365; and news of JFK assassination, 234–37; in Palm Beach, 50, 52–53, 122, 316; personality of, 211; Pozen visit of, 210, 234–37; and snake incident, 52–53; and transfer of JFK body from White House to Capitol rotunda, 279, 280, 281

Kennedy, Edward "Ted," 29, 241, 274, 291, 292, 293, 311, 373, 376–77, 383

Kennedy, Ethel, 373, 383

Kennedy, Jacqueline Bouvier "Jackie": at Arlington Cemetery, 272, 301–2, 311, 396; at Atoka, 57; and Bay of Pigs prisoner return, 70; bereavement letters to, 310; and Berger son's birth, 233; Bethesda trip of, 258, 259, 262, 266; campaigning by, 21, 191; on Cape Cod, 124–25, 303, 333; and Caroline education, 324; and children's burial at Arlington Cemetery, 311; continuation of Secret Service protection for, 311; cuts lock of JFK hair, 278; and Dallas advance, 99, 189, 193, 195; and Dallas flight, 195; and Dallas motorcade, 196, 200, 201, 202, 203, 204, 205, 206–7, 208; and Dallas welcome, 197, 198–99; depression of, 129, 132; Dillon letter about White House Detail of, 313–14; and elections of 1960, 191; and elections of 1964, 134; end of Secret Service Detail for, 345, 367; and eternal flame, 297; filmmaking of, 130–32; Fort Worth trip of, 174, 175, 186, 190–91, 192; in Georgetown, 105, 310–12; and gifts on international trips, 112, 113; at Hammersmith Farm, 129–32; Hill as SAIC for, 3–4, 21–22, 113; Hill as saving life of, 275; Hill assigned to Detail for, 43–44; and Hill gold medal, 309–10; and Hill (Gwen) meeting, 103–4, 115, 309–10; Hill last conversation with, 373; Hill last day with, 367; and Hill papers and photos, 369, 395–96; Hill relationship with, 104–5, 114–15, 124–25, 127–28, 191, 225–26, 252, 266, 270, 291, 345, 367, 368, 396; and Hill retirement party, 383; Hill-Wallace interview about, 385–86; Houston trip of, 159, 169, 170–72, 173; and inauguration, 53, 55; India-Pakistan trip of, 105, 107–13; Italy trip of, 193, 395–96; and JFK autopsy, 253–54; and JFK body at Capitol rotunda, 283, 284; and JFK burial/funeral, 272, 273, 275, 297; and JFK casket at White House, 267, 269; and JFK funeral procession, 285, 291, 292, 293, 296; and JFK funeral service at St. Matthew's, 294–95; and JFK in history, 304; and JFK-LBJ transition, 256; JFK relationship with, 133, 245; John Jr. attachment to, 158, 211; and John Jr. birth, 49, 105, 191, 396; and John Jr. salute, 71; Kennedy (Robert) concern for, 258, 260, 301–2; at Kennedy (Robert) funeral, 373; LBJ concern about, 259; and LBJ swearing-in ceremony, 252, 253; LULAC speech of, 160, 171–72; and motorcade from Parkland Hospital to Love Field, 250; New York move of, 333, 365; at 1964 Democratic Convention, 364; in Palm Beach, 50, 52, 53, 122, 316, 333; and Paolella horse incident, 106; at Parkland Hospital, 223–27, 229, 238–39, 241–42, 244, 245, 246, 249; passion for horses and animals of, 113, 114; and Patrick birth and death, 21, 126–29, 133, 191; and pictures of JFK assassination, 232; and plans for Texas trip, 20, 21, 134, 159–60; popularity of, 21, 111–12, 159–60, 183; pregnancies of, 44, 105, 125; and presidential cars, 186; and public reaction to JFK death, 272–73; and reception following JFK funeral, 301; return from Dallas to D.C./White House of, 231, 244, 245, 246, 249, 250, 252, 253–54, 258, 261, 266–67; and return of JFK body to D.C., 245, 246, 249, 250, 252, 253–54, 258; Rollins photos of children for, 324–25; San Antonio trip of, 166, 167, 168; and shooting of JFK, 2, 213, 214, 216–17, 218, 219; smoking by, 114–15; and Texas campaign trip, 20, 21, 134; Texas flight of, 158; and transfer of JFK body from White House to Capitol rotunda, 279, 280, 281; Tucker loans money to, 49–50; viewing of JFK open casket by, 275, 277–78; and White House Detail mission, 6; White House Detail relationship with, 312; White interview of, 304–5; and Zippo lighter, 267–68

Kennedy, Joan, 274

Kennedy, John F.: Arlington grave of, 297, 302, 311, 325; autopsy of, 246–47, 248–49, 253–54; casket for, 241–42, 245, 250, 258, 260, 266, 350, 354; Catholicism of, 51; code name for, 147; death certificate for, 246; death of, 6, 239–40, 244; Jackie relationship with, 133, 245; and kidnapping of body theory, 353–54; Last Rites for, 230, 239; as legend/idol, 326, 363; look-alikes for, 136–37; papers and personal items of, 311; and Patrick birth and death, 128–29, 133; personality and style of, 47, 159, 398; popularity of, 159, 363; private life of, 350–51, 401; public reaction to assassination of, 251; quotes and sayings by, 1, 9, 32, 57, 75, 93, 119, 135, 152, 157, 181, 197, 220, 243, 251, 264, 283, 301, 346, 365, 379, 395; and return of body to D.C., 243–50; selection of cabinet and advisors to, 50–51; shooting of, 1–6, 213–19; White House Detail relationship with, 123, 398. *See also specific person or topic*

Kennedy, John Jr.: at Arlington Cemetery, 72, 272, 295, 303; at Atoka, 57; attachment to Jackie of, 158, 211; Berger concern about, 234; birth of, 49, 105, 191, 396; birthday of, 211, 295; on Cape Cod, 124, 125–26, 303; continuation of Secret Service protection for, 311; and Foster, 211, 281, 296, 324–25; in Georgetown, 310–12, 333; and helicopters, 20, 71, 126, 157–58, 325; and Hill-Foster conversation about JFK return to D.C., 242; impact of JFK death on, 324–25; Jackie praise for White House Detail for, 314; and Jackie return to D.C., 262–63; and JFK funeral, 274, 292, 294, 295, 296; and JFK New York City trip, 20; JFK relationship with, 211, 324; JFK tells Foster to take care of, 158; and JFK Texas flight, 157, 158; Kiddie Detail for, 6, 20, 49, 126, 236, 312, 314, 324–25; learns about JFK death, 247, 281; in New York City, 333, 365; and news of JFK assassination, 235, 236; in Palm Beach, 50, 122, 316; personality of, 210–11; Rollins photos of, 324–25; salute of, 71–72, 295, 325; and transfer of JFK body from White House to Capitol rotunda, 279, 280, 281

Kennedy, Joseph, 50, 52, 54, 89, 240, 241, 274, 303

Kennedy, Patrick Bouvier, 21, 127–29, 133, 191, 233, 311

Kennedy, Robert "Bobby": Arlington Cemetery grave of, 373; Arlington Cemetery visits of, 272, 301–2; assassination and funeral of, 372–73; Bethesda trip of, 258, 259; concern for Jackie of, 258, 260, 301–2; and elections of 1968, 371; Hill relationship with, 368; Hill reports about JFK assassination to, 227–28; and Jackie return to White House, 266–67; and JFK casket at White House, 267; and JFK casket in Dallas, 260; and JFK death, 239–40; and JFK funeral procession, 291, 292, 293; and LBJ oath of office, 248; LBJ relationship with, 371; and Monroe JFK relationship, 401; at 1964 Democratic Convention, 366; and return of JFK body to D.C., 257–58; and transfer of JFK body from White House to Capitol rotunda, 279, 280; and Vietnam, 62; viewing of JFK open casket by, 277–78; and White-Jackie interview, 304

Kennedy, Rose, 144, 240–41, 274

Kennedy family, 274, 284, 303, 333, 372–73. *See also specific member*

Khan, Ayub, 113, 370
Khrushchev, Nikita, 33, 69, 91, 94, 95, 97, 170
Kiddie Detail, 49, 50, 52–53, 126, 193, 236, 247, 303, 313, 314, 316, 324, 333. *See also specific agent*
kidnapping of JFK body, theory about, 353–54
Kilduff, Mac, 243, 244, 251
King, Coretta Scott, 33
King, Martin Luther Jr., 32–33, 61, 63, 85, 170, 351, 371–72
Kinney, Sam: and Dallas advance, 173, 188, 189, 192, 195; and Dallas motorcade, 196, 202, 203, 204, 205, 207, 212; and Dallas welcome, 197–98, 199; Hickey memories about, 230; and JFK New York City trip, 27; and JFK San Antonio trip, 160; and JFK Tampa trip, 135–36, 147; recollection of shootings by, 218; responsibilities of, 188; and return of presidential cars to Andrews Air Force Base, 254, 261; securing of Dallas motorcade vehicles by, 244–45; and shooting of JFK, 214, 215, 216, 218; and transport of presidential cars, 135–36
Kivett, Ann, 3–4, 5
Kivett, Jerry, 228, 231
Knight, Stuart, 240–41, 318, 378, 380
Knudsen, Robert, 130, 131, 132
Kollar, Bob, 142, 148
Ku Klux Klan, 63
Kunkel, Charlie, 255

Landis, Paul: appearance of, 114; at Arlington National Cemetery, 272; at Bethesda Naval Hospital, 258, 259–60, 265, 266; code name of, 114; and continuation of protection for Jackie, 311; and Dallas advance, 177, 193, 197; and Dallas motorcade, 196, 200, 202, 205, 206, 208; and Dallas welcome, 197–98; eternal flame as reminder of failure for, 325; grief/guilt feelings of, 252–53, 254–55, 303, 353; and Hill retirement party, 383; and Hill *60 Minutes* interview, 389–90; Jackie Detail assignment of, 114; Jackie-Dillon letter praising, 314; and Jackie Fort Worth trip, 174, 176, 177; and Jackie at Hammersmith, 130, 131; and Jackie Houston trip, 170; and Jackie in labor/birth of Patrick, 126–27, 128; and Jackie plans for Texas trip, 20; and Jackie return to D.C., 249, 250; and Jackie San Antonio trip, 167; and Jackie travels after JFK funeral, 333; and Jackie trip to Greece and Morocco, 132–33; and JFK casket, 245, 258; on JFK

Detail, 22; and JFK Fort Worth trip, 184, 185; and Kennedy family in Georgetown, 312; and Kennedy family in Hyannis Port, 303; and Kennedy family in Palm Beach, 316; and LBJ swearing-in ceremony, 253; at Parkland Hospital, 225, 226–27, 229, 242, 245, 249; personal and professional background of, 114; personality of, 197; resignation of, 345, 353; return from Dallas to D.C. of, 252–53, 258; and return of JFK body to D.C., 250; and shooting of JFK, 212–13, 216; and theories about JFK assassination, 352–53, 354; and Warren Commission Report, 343; and Zippo lighter, 267–68
law enforcement: IBM development of technology for, 347–49
Lawford, Christopher, 52–53
Lawford, Patricia Kennedy, 120, 272, 304, 309, 401
Lawford, Peter, 55, 120–21, 401
Lawson, Andrea, 76
Lawson, Barbara, 76, 277, 392
Lawson, Jeff, 76
Lawson, Winston G. "Win": and AFAUSSS, 392; agents' relationship with, 319; and Berlin advance, 91–92; and Blaine-JFK Easter golfing, 88–90; and Dallas advance, 2, 75–77, 85–88, 90–91, 92, 97–102, 152–54, 155, 161, 168–69, 173, 178, 186–90, 192–95, 319, 343; and Dallas motorcade, 196, 201, 202, 204–5, 209–10, 212; and Dallas welcome, 198–99, 200; eternal flame as reminder of failure for, 325; health of, 323; and JFK Italian motorcades, 82; and Oswald, 255, 274, 277; at Parkland Hospital, 223, 225, 226, 229; and return of JFK body to D.C., 245; and shooting of JFK, 215; and theories about JFK assassination, 354; and threats on JFK Texas trip, 164; and Warren Commission, 332, 343
Lawton, Don: and back of the car issue, 361; and Dallas advance, 192, 193; and Dallas motorcade, 200, 202, 359; and JFK Fort Worth trip, 174, 176, 185; and JFK San Antonio, 203; and JFK Tampa trip, 142, 147–49, 150, 203, 286, 287, 288, 361; and JFK Texas flight, 158; and motorcade from Parkland Hospital to Love Field, 248; personality of, 203; and theories about JFK assassination, 359
LBJ Ranch: and AFAUSSS meeting, 392; agents at, 317, 319–21; and Hill on LBJ

Detail, 368; JFK plans to stay at, 18, 181, 182; LBJ at, 317, 373–74; location of, 317; peacock incident at, 320–21

League of United Latin American Citizens (LULAC), 159, 160, 171–72

Life magazine, 304, 305

Lilley, Bob, 56, 257

Lincoln, Abraham: assassination of, 319; JFK visit to tomb of, 94, 95; as model for JFK funeral, 267, 269, 273

Lincoln, Evelyn, 50, 195, 222, 269

local police departments: and White House Detail, 77–78. *See also specific department*

locust story, 108

Loewenwarter, Paul, 383, 384

Love Field (Texas): Air Force One return to D.C. from, 253; arrival of presidential cars at, 173; and Dallas advance, 173, 182, 186, 189, 190, 192, 193, 195; JFK welcome at, 197–202; motorcade from Parkland Hospital to, 247–50; and return of JFK body to D.C., 242, 245–47; and return of presidential cars, 245; Warren Commission report about, 343

MacDill Air Force Base (Tampa), 18, 66, 67, 136, 146

Mack, Gary, 354–55

The Making of the President (White), 304

Mansfield, Mike, 280–81

Manson, Charles, 381

March on Washington (1963), 85

Marine One, 16, 137, 146, 150, 158, 327, 328

Marines, U.S.: and Jackie India-Pakistan trip, 108, 109; and JFK funeral procession, 291, 292; and return of JFK body to White House, 267

Martin, Dean, 120

McCann, Gerard, 307, 312

McCloy, John J., 305–6

McCone, John, 62

McCord, James, 377

McCormick, Harry, 256

McDonnell, Dick, 347, 348

McHugh, Godfrey, 258, 266, 275, 277–78

McIntyre, Tim: agents' relationship with, 319; and Dallas advance, 192, 193; and Dallas motorcade, 196, 200, 202, 205; and JFK Fort Worth trip, 174, 176, 185; and JFK Tampa trip, 142, 148; and motorcade from Parkland Hospital to Love Field, 248; at Parkland Hospital, 228; and Warren Commission Report, 343

McKinley, William, 319

McNamara, Robert, 272

Means, Marianne, 14

media: and Blaine-JFK Easter golfing, 90; and conspiracy theories, 284, 306–8; and Dallas advance, 97, 189, 195; and Dallas motorcade, 204; and Dallas welcome, 198; investigation of JFK assassination by, 302, 321; and Jackie ride on camel, 112–13; and JFK Florida trip, 145; and JFK in Palm Beach, 46; and JFK New York City trip, 14; and JFK Texas campaign trip, 157–58, 159, 167, 169, 173, 174, 176, 177; and John Jr. salute at JFK funeral, 295; and LBJ return from Dallas to D.C., 231, 259; and news of JFK assassination, 234, 235, 238, 247; and Oswald, 255, 256, 276; at Parkland Hospital, 226, 232; public announcement of JFK death by, 251; and return of JFK body to D.C., 257, 258; and Sorrels-McCann report about Secret Service, 312; and transfer of JFK body from White House to Capitol rotunda, 278, 279, 281; Warren Commission report about, 340–41; and White House Detail, 14–15, 176. *See also specific person or organization*

Meredith, Lynn, 50, 52–53, 126, 247, 303, 311, 312, 314, 324, 333

Mexico City: JFK motorcade in, 361

Miami, Florida: JFK trip to, 17, 73–74, 136–37, 141, 149–50

Miami Police Department, 73–74

Mildred's Chowder House (Cape Cod), 122

Milteer, Joseph, 74, 90, 97, 136–37

Monroe, Marilyn, 401

Moore, Sara Jane, 382

Morales, Bernardo, 139

Moro, Aldo, 370

Morocco: Jackie's trip to, 132–33

motorcade(s): agents' signals during, 200; Behn role in, 16; Blaine concerns about, 74; and "confidence factor," 398; and features of presidential cars, 79–80; and Hill-Blaine relationship, 22; for JFK funeral to Arlington Cemetery, 296–97; JFK views about, 398; for LBJ, 327; limousines for, 135–36; for Nixon, 143; publishing routes of, 152–53; Secret Service concerns about, 19; training for, 193. *See also* back-of-the-car issue; Dallas motorcade; motorcycle escorts; *specific motorcade*

motorcycle escorts: for Dallas motorcade, 169, 189, 202, 203–4, 205, 206, 209, 212, 218, 363; and JFK Ireland trip, 100; and JFK Italy trip, 81, 82, 83–84; and JFK Tampa trip, 80–81, 84–85, 147; from Parkland Hospital to Love Field, 245
Mroz, Josef Molt, 63
Mullins, J. P., 70, 73, 77, 78–81, 84–85, 90, 137, 138, 147, 149

Naples, Italy: JFK motorcade in, 81, 82–84, 184
National Crime Information Center (NCIC), 348–49
National Security Council, 94, 96
NBC, and Oswald shooting, 276
new frontier, JFK statement about, 157
New York City: Jackie move to, 333, 365; JFK trip to, 10, 12, 13, 14–15, 16, 20–21, 22–31
New York City Bureau of Special Services and Investigations (BOSSI), 25, 26, 28
New York Police Department: Secret Service relations with, 25
Nixon, Richard M., 32, 33, 37, 143, 169, 374, 376–77, 378
North Dakota: Hill in, 380–82
Norton (special agent), 144
Novak, Kim, 55
nuclear defense code, 248

Obama, Barack, 398
O'Brien, Larry, 50, 158, 246, 249, 258
Ocean's 11 (movie), 120
O'Donnell, Ken: and balance between protection and politics, 19; at Bethesda, 258, 260; and Dallas advance, 91, 153, 188, 189, 192; and Dallas flight, 195; and Dallas motorcade, 196, 202, 207, 212; and JFK autopsy, 246–47, 248–49; and JFK casket, 260; and JFK Dallas comments about assassination, 332–33; and JFK Florida trip, 67, 73, 140, 141; and JFK Fort Worth trip, 183, 192; and JFK Italian motorcades, 82; and JFK Palm Springs trip, 120; and JFK personality, 159; and JFK San Antonio trip, 158, 168; and LBJ return from Dallas to D.C., 229, 230, 231, 243; and LBJ swearing-in ceremony, 252; learns of JFK death, 241; at Parkland Hospital, 229, 245, 246–47, 248–49; return from Dallas to D.C. of, 252; and return of JFK body to D.C., 245, 246–47, 248–49; selection as JFK advisor of, 50; and theories about JFK assassination, 354–55

Ohio University: LBJ trip to, 334
Olsson, Ernie, 176, 177, 253, 261, 262
Onassis, Aristotle, 132–33
Oneal Funeral Home (Dallas), 241, 245, 247
organized crime, 262, 351, 356–57
O'Rourke, Jerry, 163, 164, 165, 166, 175, 237, 269
Oswald, Lee Harvey: arrest and indictment of, 255–56, 274; background of, 284; death of, 281; FBI investigation of, 305, 321; and Hill *60 Minutes* interview, 387; and Hill return visit to Dallas, 393; and HSCA investigation, 351; lack of intelligence about, 316; and LBJ security concerns, 256–57; motives of, 342; Ruby shooting of, 276–77, 281, 282, 284, 302, 341, 363–64; Secret Service investigation of, 262, 276; and theories about JFK assassination, 305, 350, 351, 352–53; and Tippit murder, 340; Warren Commission report about, 340–41, 342, 344
Otis Air Force Base (Massachusetts), 127, 303
Overseas Security Advisory Counsel, 349

Pakistan: Jackie's trip to, 105, 107–13
Palm Beach, Florida: Behn-Blaine discussion about JFK trip to, 17; and Blaine-JFK Easter golfing story, 88–90; Jackie and children in, 50, 52, 53, 122, 193, 316, 333, 365; JFK in, 46–49, 50–53, 64, 141; as JFK retreat, 317; preparation for JFK arrival in, 42, 44–46; termite problem at estate in, 144
Palm Beach Police Department, 45, 51, 52
Palm Springs, California: JFK trip to, 97, 119–22
Pan American Airways, 13, 107
Paolella, Joe, 12, 23, 30, 106, 268, 344–45
Parades, Provie, 267–68, 303
Parkland Hospital (Dallas): Hill memories about, 390; JFK at, 223–31, 232–34, 238–40, 266; and JFK autopsy, 246–47, 248–49; and JFK death certificate, 246; JFK driven to, 4, 219, 220–23; LBJ leaves, 251; motorcade to Love Field from, 247–50; Oswald at, 277, 281–82; removal of JFK body from, 241–42, 248–49; and return of JFK body to D.C., 243–47; and theories about JFK assassination, 353–54
Parks, Gordon, 110
Pashtuns, 113
Paul VI (pope), 370
Paul Young's Restaurant (Washington), 54–55
Pavlick, Richard, 51–52
Payne, Bill, 27, 76, 161

peacock incident, 320–21
Pearson, Drew, 306–8, 312, 313, 316, 321
Peppers, Arnie, 60, 61, 63, 64, 67–68, 70–71, 88
Persian Gulf War, 349
Pierpoint, Bob, 14
Pittsburgh, Pennsylvania: LBJ trip to, 331
politics-protection balance, 19, 146, 147–49, 150–51, 397
Pontius, Barbara, 172–73
Pontius, Ron, 76, 107, 161–63, 170, 172–73, 288, 293
Powell, Barney Grant, 63
Powers, David: at Bethesda, 258, 259, 260; and Dallas advance, 153, 192; and Dallas flight, 195; and Dallas motorcade, 196, 202, 205, 207, 209, 212; grief of, 259; and JFK autopsy, 246, 254; and JFK casket, 260; and JFK Dallas comments about assassination, 332–33; and JFK Florida trip, 73, 140, 141; and JFK Fort Worth trip, 182, 183, 192; and JFK Italian motorcade, 82; and JFK personality, 164; and JFK San Antonio trip, 158, 168; and JFK Texas trip, 159, 160; and LBJ return from Dallas to D.C., 229; and LBJ swearing-in ceremony, 252; at Parkland Hospital, 224, 225, 229, 230, 246, 249; and political advantages of JFK Texas trip, 182; and politics-protection balance, 19; return from Dallas to D.C. of, 252, 253, 254; and return of JFK body to D.C., 246, 249; selection as JFK advisor of, 50; and theories about JFK assassination, 354–55; and White-Jackie interview, 304
Pozen, Agatha, 210
Pozen, Liz, 210, 234, 235–36
Preliminary Survey Report: for Dallas, 154, 192; for State Department reception, 282
presidential candidates: Secret Service protection for, 373
presidential cars: and "confidence factor," 398; and Dallas advance, 173, 186, 188, 195; for Dallas motorcade, 201; in Houston, 170; JFK preference in, 398; and JFK Texas trip, 160, 161–62, 163, 175; for LBJ, 323; leasing of, 161, 163, 175, 195; Paolella responsibility for, 258; return to Andrews Air Force Base of, 254, 261; and securing of Dallas motorcade car, 230, 232, 244–45, 261; Warren Commission report about, 323, 343
Presidential Protective Division. See White House Detail; specific agent
private life, JFK, 350–51, 400–401

Protective Research Section (PRS), Secret Service: and Blaine-IBM development of law enforcement technology, 348, 349; and Dallas advance, 195; and flash card system, 13, 60; function of, 59–60; and LBJ South Bend trip, 329; and staffing concerns for White House Detail, 92; and Tampa advance, 58–64, 93, 358; and Texas advance, 63–64, 76; and threats against JFK, 51–52; Warren Commission report about, 343
protocol: for White House Detail, 15–16
PT 109, JFK on, 129
Puterbaugh, Jack, 76–77, 86–88, 155, 173

race issues, 164, 165–66, 335, 372. See also civil rights
Radziwill, Lee, 107, 112, 132, 284, 303, 304, 309
Radziwill, Stanislaus, 284
Rankin, J. Lee, 360
Ready, Jack: agents' relationship with, 319; and back of the car issue, 360, 362; Blaine thoughts about, 331; and Dallas advance, 177, 192, 193, 195; and Dallas motorcade, 196, 200, 202–3, 205, 206, 208, 212; death in family of, 141, 142; and JFK Fort Worth trip, 174, 176, 177, 185; and JFK Texas flight, 158; and motorcade from Parkland Hospital to Love Field, 248; at Parkland Hospital, 229–30; and shooting of JFK, 212, 213–14, 215–16; and staffing for JFK Florida-Texas trips, 141, 142; and Warren Commission Report, 343
Rice Hotel (Houston), 159, 170–71
Roberts, Emory: agents' relationship with, 319; appearance of, 141; awards and honors for, 143; and back of the car issue, 288, 360, 361; and Blaine-LBJ gun incident, 268; and Dallas advance, 192–94, 195, 197; and Dallas motorcade, 196, 200, 203, 208, 212, 359; and Dallas welcome, 198, 199; grief of, 254–55; and Hickey memories of assassination, 230; and JFK Florida campaign trip, 141–49, 361; and JFK Fort Worth trip, 174, 176, 183, 184, 185; and JFK funeral procession, 291, 293; and JFK Houston trip, 172; and JFK in D.C., 49; and JFK in Palm Beach, 44, 45, 46–47, 141; and JFK New York City trip, 25, 27, 28; and JFK San Antonio trip, 167; and JFK Texas flight, 158; and LBJ return from Dallas to D.C., 228–29, 243–44; and LBJ security, 224, 268; and motorcade from Parkland Hospital

Roberts, Emory (*cont.*)
    to Love Field, 248; and Nixon Venezuela
    motorcade, 143; at Parkland Hospital,
    223–24, 228–29, 231, 242, 248; and
    Pearson Secret Service article, 306;
    personal and professional background
    of, 141; personality and character of, 141;
    return from Dallas to D.C. of, 253; and
    Rowley-agents meeting, 285, 287–88;
    and shooting of JFK, 2, 215, 219; staffing
    concerns of, 141, 143, 183; and theories
    about JFK assassination, 359; and Valenti,
    172; and Warren Commission Report, 343
Rollins, Byron "Beano," 324–25
Rome, Italy: JFK motorcade in, 81–82, 361;
    LBJ trip to, 371
Roosevelt, Franklin D., 32, 33–34, 132, 184
Roosevelt, Katie, 314
Roosevelt, Theodore, 314
Rose, Earl, 246–47, 248, 249
Rosenberg, Tom, 323, 324
Rowles, Tommy, 366
Rowley, James J. "Jim": and AFAUSSS, 391;
    agents' meeting with, 282, 285–89; and
    back of the car issue, 285–89, 360, 363;
    and Blaine at IBM, 346–47; Blaine first
    meets, 39; and Blaine resignation, 337; and
    Bolden allegations, 335; and Eisenhower
    Detail, 33, 40, 41; and Eisenhower-
    JFK transition, 33, 41–42, 47; funding
    requests of, 399; and Hill assignment
    to Jackie Detail, 43; and investigation
    of Secret Service, 262; and JFK funeral,
    273; and JFK Italian motorcades, 82, 83,
    84; and JFK look-alikes, 136–37; learns
    about JFK assassination, 231–32, 255;
    and motto of Secret Service, 15; and
    Pearson Secret Service article, 307; Rankin
    correspondence about back of the car
    issue with, 360–63; retirement of, 378; and
    return of agents to D.C., 261; and return
    of JFK body to D.C., 257; and Roosevelt
    Detail, 34; and Sorrels-McCann report,
    307, 312–13; and staffing for White House
    Detail, 36, 86; and Truman–Blair House
    assassination attempt, 36; as Truman SAIC,
    34, 36
Ruby, Jack, 276–77, 281, 284, 302, 341, 344,
    363–64
Rundle, Paul: and AFAUSSS, 392; Blaine
    relationship with, 39; duck hunting by, 109;
    early career of, 41; and Eisenhower Detail,
    40, 41; and elections of 1972, 375; as Hill
    deputy, 375, 379; Hill relationship with,

375, 389–90; and Hill retirement party, 382;
    and Hill return to White House, 267, 379;
    and Jackie India-Pakistan trip, 107, 108–9,
    111; and Jackie Italian trip, 193; and Jackie
    trip to Greece and Morocco, 132; and LBJ
    security, 257, 262, 318; responsibilities of,
    375; tiger hunting by, 108–9
Rundle, Peggy, 382, 392
Rusk, Dean, 62, 290, 291
Russell, Richard, 305
Rybka, Hank, 82, 135–36, 160, 193, 200, 203,
    248, 359

Sadat, Anwar, 399
Salinger, Pierre, 15, 50
San Antonio *Express-News,* 160
San Antonio, Texas: AFAUSSS meeting in,
    390–91; JFK trip to, 158–60, 166–68, 183,
    195; motorcade in, 17, 159, 160, 167–68
San Francisco Chronicle, 306
Saragat, Giuseppe, 370
Sardar (horse): Khan gift to Jackie of, 113, 114
Saunders, Frank, 240
Schirra, Walter Jr., 140
Scottish Black Watch bagpipes, 103, 292–93
Secret Service, U.S.: accusations against,
    350–51; assassination concerns of, 284,
    319; and Blaine-IBM development of
    law enforcement technology, 348–49;
    code of, 400–401; conference of, 382;
    Congress official recognition of, 397;
    drinking of alcohol by members of,
    307, 312–13; driver agents in, 136, 193;
    funding for, 86, 397, 399; and Homeland
    Security Department, 399; and HSCA,
    351; and investigations about blame for
    JFK assassination, 289, 351; and Kennedy
    (Robert) assassination, 372; and local
    police departments, 77–78; morale of, 373;
    motto of, 15, 359; and Nixon-Kennedy
    (Edward) protection, 376–77; no comment
    policy of, 364; NYPD relations with, 25;
    Office of Investigations of, 376–77; Pearson
    demand for investigation of, 306–8; and
    politics-protection balance, 19, 150–51,
    397; presidential relationship with, 397,
    398, 400; recommendations for changes
    in, 343–44; responsibilities/mission of,
    37, 364, 373, 399–401; and rumors of FBI
    takeover of presidential protection, 318–19,
    321; silence about inner workings of, 335–
    36; and Sorrels investigation of JFK-Texas
    agents, 307; staffing for, 39, 328, 344, 373,
    399; technology development for,

346–48; and theories about JFK assassination, 351, 354, 359–60, 396; and threats against president, 37; and Warren Commission, 323, 342–44, 369; WHCA relations with, 66; wives of agents of, 58. *See also* Protective Research Service; White House Detail; *specific person*

Segni, Antonio, 81, 82, 83

Selassie, Haile, 273, 301

sex parties: Bolden charges about agents and, 334

Shah of Iran: bodyguard for, 347

Shaw, Maud, 20, 53, 210–11, 235, 292, 303

Sheraton Hotel (Dallas), 173, 178, 186

shirt story: JFK-Gibbs, 48–49

Short, Larry, 109

Shoup, David, 72

Shriver, Eunice Kennedy, 267, 274

Shriver, Sargent, 267

Signal Corps, U.S. Army, 66

Silver, Phil, 347, 348

Sinatra, Frank, 55, 120, 121–22, 123

60 Minutes (CBS-TV), 383–90, 391

Skiles, Bill, 40, 41, 42, 44, 45, 46, 47, 49, 107, 257

Smathers, George, 147

Smith, Jean Kennedy, 29, 272, 309, 401

Smith, Merriman "Smitty," 14, 15, 174, 176, 226

snake incident, Palm Beach, 52–53

Sorrels, Forrest: and Dallas advance, 86–88, 97–102, 152, 153, 154, 155, 168–69, 173, 195; and Dallas motorcade, 196, 208; investigation of Secret Service agents by, 307, 312–13; and Oswald, 256, 274; and theories about JFK assassination, 354; and threats on JFK Texas trip, 164; and Warren Commission, 332

South Bend, Indiana: LBJ trip to, 327–28, 329–31

Soviet Union: and challenges facing LBJ, 326; conspiracy theories about, 321; and Cuba, 62, 69, 94–97, 120, 138; and HSCA investigation, 351; and JFK assassination, 262, 342, 351; and JFK inauguration, 54, 284; opinion polls about, 33; and Oswald, 321, 342; space program of, 140

space program, 140–41, 172

Springfield, Illinois: JFK trip to, 94–95

Squaw Island: JFK house on, 124–25, 126, 129

St. Edward's Church (Palm Beach), 51

St. Matthew's Cathedral (Washington, D.C.): and JFK funeral, 272, 273, 285, 290–95

St. Patrick's Cathedral (New York City): Kennedy (Robert) funeral at, 372–73

Stalin, Joseph, 33–34

State Department, U.S.: Blaine advance for reception at, 271, 273, 277, 282, 289, 290, 291, 296; Blaine on loan from IBM to, 349; and Caroline kidnapping rumor, 139; and Jackie India-Pakistan trip, 107, 112

Stemmons, John, 220

Stevenson, Adlai, 18, 85, 99, 156

Stoughton, Cecil, 232, 240, 253, 369

Stout, Stewart "Stu": and back-of-the-car issue, 288; and Dallas advance, 153; Hoover resemblance to, 12; and Jackie San Antonio trip, 167; and JFK Fort Worth trip, 174–75, 176, 182–83; and JFK funeral procession, 291, 293; and JFK Houston trip, 170; and JFK New York City trip, 13, 22; and LBJ security, 253, 261, 262; and motorcade from Parkland Hospital to Love Field, 250; and news of JFK assassination, 221, 222; at Parkland Hospital, 247, 249; and Pearson Secret Service article, 307; and return of JFK body to D.C., 247, 250, 261; and Rowley-agents meeting, 285; and Truman-Blair House assassination attempt, 35, 36; and White House shift work, 12

Strong, Tom, 61, 358

Sulliman, Sam, 176, 253, 261, 262, 296

sunglasses, agents', 13

Swindal, James, 159, 230, 242, 297

Tampa: advance work in, 18, 19, 30, 58–64, 65–71, 72–74, 77–81, 84–85, 88–90, 93–94, 97, 135–42, 151, 357, 358; Behn-Blaine discussion about JFK trip to, 17, 18, 30; Cuban concern in, 94, 138–39, 142, 145, 147; JFK trip to, 145–49, 150, 285–88; motorcade in, 18, 65, 71, 72–73, 77, 79–81, 84–85, 88, 97, 135–49, 162, 193, 285–89, 356, 361, 362; Rowley-agents meeting about JFK request in, 285–89; and theories about JFK assassination, 356, 357

Tampa Police Department, 70, 77–81, 84–85, 137–38, 139

Taylor, Cecil, 60–64, 358

Taylor, Robert H., 374

Taylor, Warren "Woody," 228, 230

Texas: advance work for, 63, 75–76, 151, 288; anti-Kennedy feeling in, 185; civil rights in, 85; elections of 1960 in, 77, 159; JFK and Jackie leave on trip to, 157–58; JFK itinerary for, 182; politics in, 76–77;

Texas (*cont.*)
  reasons for JFK trip to, 159; risks of JFK
  appearances in, 18; and White House
  Detail turnover, 65. *See also specific person
  or location*
Texas School Book Depository: clock at, 219;
  and Dallas advance, 101; Dallas motorcade
  approach to, 209–10; and Hill return visit
  to Dallas, 392, 393–94; museum at, 392,
  393–94; Pearson allegations about, 307;
  rifle found at, 274, 340; and shooting of
  JFK, 213–14, 219; and theories about
  JFK assassination, 350, 352–53; Warren
  Commission report about, 339, 340, 343;
  Zapruder pictures of events at, 256
Thailand: LBJ trip to, 371
Thomas, Albert, 159, 171, 172
Thomas, Helen, 14
threats: categorizing of, 59; against
  Eisenhower, 37; against JFK, 51–52, 58–64,
  68, 73–74, 136–37; against LBJ, 358; and
  role of Secret Service, 37; and Texas/Dallas
  advance, 76, 164, 195. *See also* Protective
  Research Service; *specific person*
tiger hunting, Rundle's, 108–9, 111
Tippit, J. D., 340
Tomb of the Unknown Soldier, 71, 72, 267,
  269, 272
Trade Mart (Dallas): agents at, 176, 197, 253,
  261; and Dallas advance, 87, 91, 98, 101,
  102, 153–54, 169, 174, 176, 177, 178, 182,
  183, 186, 187, 188–89; Dallas motorcade
  to, 202, 209, 210, 212, 215; and news of JFK
  assassination, 220–21; Warren Commission
  report about, 343
Treasury Department, U.S.: Hill award from,
  309–10; and protection for presidential
  candidates, 373; and rumors of FBI
  takeover of presidential protection, 318. *See
  also* Secret Service, U.S.; White House Detail
Truman, Harry S., 32, 34–36, 63, 141, 184,
  397
Tucker, Ed, 49–50, 52–53, 61–62, 257, 345,
  357, 358
Tuckerman, Nancy, 365, 366
Turnure, Pam, 160, 366
turtle story, Jackie-Hill, 114

U-2 spy plane incident, 94
unions: JFK speech to, 18
United Press International, 14
United States Strike Command, 146
University of Texas, 182, 231
USS *Andrew Jackson* (ship), 140

Valenti, Jack, 172
Valera, Eamon de, 273, 291, 301
Vallee, Thomas Arthur, 61–62, 68, 357–58
Vanocur, Sander, 14
Venezuela: Nixon motorcade in, 143, 374
Veterans Day (1963), 71–72
Vietnam, 62, 329, 358, 371, 373
von Braun, Wernher, 140–41
Voss, M. William, 380

Wade, Henry, 249
Walker, Edwin A., 340, 342
Wallace, George, 375–76
Wallace, Mike, 383–89, 390
Walsh, Eileen, 380
War on Poverty, 326, 331
Ward, Theron, 248–49
Warren Commission: agent affidavits and
  reports for, 322–23, 332; and back of the
  car issue, 360–63; and Bolden theory,
  334–36; inconsistencies in findings of, 344;
  investigation by, 322–23, 327–28, 332; LBJ
  appointment of, 305–6; mandate of, 323;
  members of, 305–6; and public belief in
  cover-up of JFK assassination, 351; report
  and recommendations of, 323, 339–44, 348,
  369; and theories about JFK assassination,
  352–53
Warren, Earl, 305
Warrington, John William, 60–61, 62, 63, 68,
  137
Washington National Cathedral: King
  memorial at, 371–72
Watergate, 377–78
Wells, Shirley, 237, 392
Wells, Tom: and AFAUSSS, 392; and Caroline
  visit with Pozens, 210, 234–37; and
  continuation of protection for Kennedy
  children, 311; impact of JFK assassination
  on, 324, 333; Jackie-Dillon letter praising,
  314; and JFK body in Capitol rotunda,
  281; and JFK funeral procession, 292, 294;
  Kennedy children's relationship with, 324;
  and Kennedy family in Georgetown, 312;
  on Kiddie Detail on Cape Cod, 126, 303;
  learns about shooting of JFK, 234–37; and
  motorcade from St. Matthew's to Arlington
  Cemetery, 296
White House: Jackie return to, 266–67; JFK
  casket in East Room of, 267, 269–70,
  277–78; and JFK-LBJ transition, 256;
  LBJ return to, 259; Office of the Chief of
  Protocol at, 273; return of JFK body to,
  266–67; switchboards at, 66

White House Advance Manual, 75–76, 140, 167, 185, 204

White House Communications Agency (WHCA), 66–67, 110, 173, 226

White House Detail: appearance of members of, 13, 14; and Blaine decision to tell about JFK assassination, 364; Bolden charges against, 334–36; characteristics of, 78, 123–24, 177; drinking of alcohol by, 174, 176–77, 307, 312–13, 334; drivers for, 136, 193; and Eisenhower-JFK transition, 33, 41–44, 47, 315; family relationships of members of, 119; firearms proficiency of, 194; funding for, 86, 397; guilt/failure feelings among agents in, 307, 316; illness among agents in, 323; Jackie-Dillon letter praising, 313–14; and JFK-LBJ transition, 282, 303, 315, 317; JFK views about, 123; lack of discussion about JFK assassination among, 316; and local police departments, 77–78; and media, 14–15, 176; overtime for, 12–13; and politics-protection balance, 19, 146, 147–49, 150–51, 397; protocol for, 15–16; race of, 164, 165–66, 335, 372; relationship among members of, 40, 123–24, 315–16, 336, 401; and replacement of agents on JFK Detail, 19–20; responsibilities/mission of, 5–6, 269, 364; and rumors of FBI takeover of presidential protection, 318–19, 321; salary for, 13; shift office of, 11–12; shifts for, 12–13; signals among, 200; staff turnover in, 65; staffing concerns about, 20, 36, 86, 92, 142, 143, 322, 328, 397; supplies and equipment for, 13–14; temporary help for, 92, 123–24; viewing of JFK body at White House by, 269–70; White House duties of, 9–10; workload of, 328. *See also* Presidential Protective Division; Secret Service, U.S.; *specific agent*

White House Police, 136

White House Social Office, 112

White, Theodore H., 304–5

Wiesman, Ken, 257

Wildy, Edgar, 43

Woody's Motel (Palm Beach), 44, 52–53, 141–42

Worthy of Trust and Confidence (motto), 15, 359

Wunderlich (special agent), 144

Yalta Conference (1945), 33–34

Yarborough, Ralph, 77, 184, 200–201

Yeager, Frank: and Austin advance, 151; and Blaine-JFK Easter golfing, 88–90; and JFK Tampa trip, 18, 65–71, 72–73, 78–79, 80, 85, 88, 93–94, 97, 135, 140, 142, 149; personal and professional background, 65; resignation of, 344

Youngblood, Rufus, 219, 228, 229, 230–31, 241, 243, 318, 368, 372, 373

youth vote, 329

Zapruder, Abraham, 175, 256, 375

Zarvos, Nick, 375–76

Zboril, Chuck: appearance of, 11; and back of the car issue, 361; Blaine relationship with, 2, 11; health of, 323; and JFK New York City trip, 25, 27; and JFK Tampa trip, 142, 147–49, 150, 286, 287, 288, 361; and news about JFK assassination, 1–2, 4, 5–6; personal and professional background of, 11; White House duty of, 10–11

Zboril, Jean, 1, 2, 11

Zippo lighter, 115, 225, 267–68